Houghton Mifflin Science
DISCOVERYWORKS

 HOUGHTON MIFFLIN

Boston • Atlanta • Dallas • Denver • Geneva, Illinois • Palo Alto • Princeton

Authors

William Badders
Elementary Science Teacher
Cleveland Public Schools
Cleveland, OH

Lowell J. Bethel
Professor of Science Education
The University of Texas at Austin
Austin, TX

Victoria Fu
Professor of Child Development
and Early Childhood Education
Virginia Polytechnic Institute and
State University
Blacksburg, VA

Donald Peck
Director (retired)
The Center for Elementary Science
Fairleigh Dickinson University
Madison, NJ

Carolyn Sumners
Director of Astronomy and Physical Sciences
Houston Museum of Natural Science
Houston, TX

Catherine Valentino
Author-in-Residence, Houghton Mifflin
West Kingston, RI

Consulting Author

R. Mike Mullane
Astronaut, retired
Albuquerque, NM

Acknowledgements appear on page H46, which
constitutes an extension of this copyright page.

Printed in the U. S. A.

ISBN 0-395-98682-6

1 2 3 4 5 6 7 8 9 10 RRD 08 07 06 05 04 03 02 01 00 99

CONTENTS

UNIT A — Cells and Microbes

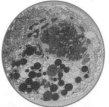

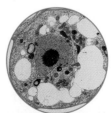

UNIT B — The Changing Earth

UNIT C **The Nature of Matter**

THINK LIKE A SCIENTIST
BERRY, BERRY COLD

CHAPTER 1 **Characteristics of Matter**   **C4**

UNIT D Continuity of Life

THINK LIKE A SCIENTIST
DIG THOSE FOSSILS

UNIT E Oceanography

THINK LIKE A SCIENTIST
SEA OF SERENITY

CHAPTER 1 Ocean Water   **E4**

UNIT F — Forces and Motion

SCIENCE and MATH TOOLBOX

HOW TO THINK LIKE A SCIENTIST

Make Observations

To think like a scientist, learn as much as you can by observing things around you. Everything you hear, smell, taste, touch, and see is a clue about how the world works. As you test your ideas, you'll continue to make careful observations.

Ask a Question

Make Observations

Look for patterns. You'll get ideas. For example, you notice that birds eat a variety of foods. Ask questions such as this.

Do all birds like to eat the same kind of seed?

Make a Hypothesis

If you have an idea about why something happens, make an educated guess, or hypothesis that you can test. For example, suppose that you have a hypothesis, that different kinds of birds eat different types of seeds.

Make Observations

Plan and Do a Test

Plan how to test your hypothesis. Your plan would need to consider some of these problems.

How will you prevent other animals, besides birds, from eating the seeds?

How will you distinguish the different birds?

Then test your hypothesis.

Record and Analyze

When you test your idea, you need to observe carefully and write down, or record, everything that happens. When you finish collecting data, you may need to do some calculations with it. For example, you may need to match the different kinds of seeds eaten with the birds that ate them.

Make Observations

Draw Conclusions

Whatever happens in a test, think about all the reasons for your results. Sometimes this thinking leads to a new hypothesis. If different kinds of birds eat different types of seeds, think about why this might be. Could the size or shape of a bird's beak determine what seeds it could or could not eat?

Make Observations

Now read "Lemon-Aid" to see scientific thinking in action.

S3

Plan and Do a Test • Record and Analyze • Draw Conclusions • Make Observations • Ask a Question • Make a Hypothesis • Plan an

THINK LIKE A SCIENTIST

PRACTICE THINKING LIKE A SCIENTIST

Lemon-Aid

Make Observations

It was a warm summer afternoon. After playing softball outside, Nita and Mark came into the kitchen for something cool to drink. Upon seeing a bowl of fresh lemons on the kitchen counter, Nita had an idea. "Let's make lemonade," she said excitedly.

Nita found a recipe for lemonade. One of the ingredients was one cup of sugar water. The recipe said to "add sugar water to taste." Nita and Mark liked their lemonade sweet. As they added sugar to a cup of cold water, they noticed that not all the sugar dissolved.

To learn about the world, you observe it. Observations can be made with any of the senses—sight, hearing, touch, taste, or smell.

Ask a Question

Nita and Mark wanted to add more sugar to the water. But no matter how much they stirred the water, only a small amount of the sugar dissolved. They tried to think of how they could dissolve more sugar. Mark remembered watching his mother put several spoonfuls of sugar in a cup of hot tea. He wondered if the amount of sugar that could be dissolved in a certain volume of water depended on the temperature of the water. Nita and Mark came up with a question they wanted to investigate.

Does water temperature affect the amount of sugar that will dissolve in a given volume of water?

Together they decided to try to find the answer to their question.

Scientific investigations usually begin with ideas that you're not sure about. Such ideas can help you ask a question that you really want to answer.

Plan and Do a Test • Record and Analyze • Draw Conclusions • Make Observations • Ask a Question • Make a Hypothesis • Plan an

S5

Make a Hypothesis

Nita had often observed her dad making iced tea from a mix. She always noticed that some of the mix did not dissolve in the cool water. She told Mark about her observations. Nita and Mark both thought that more sugar would dissolve in warm water than in cold water. This was their hypothesis.

When you use what you've observed to suggest a possible answer to your question, you're making a hypothesis. Make sure that your hypothesis is an idea that you can test. If you can't test your hypothesis, try changing it.

Plan and Do a Test

Nita and Mark designed an experiment to test their hypothesis. They wanted to find out how much sugar would dissolve in a cup of water at three different temperature — 5°C (near freezing), 70°C (hot), and 100°C (boiling).

Mark and Nita put 250 mL of water into each of three jars and placed a thermometer in each one. When the water in the first jar was chilled to 5°C, Nita began adding teaspoons of sugar to it. After each teaspoon was added, Nita stirred the water gently. She stopped adding sugar as soon as some of the added sugar remained undissolved. The procedure was repeated for the two remaining jars after the water in each was warmed to the desired temperature.

One way to try out your hypothesis is to use a **test** called a **controlled experiment**. The setups in this kind of experiment are identical in all ways except one. The one difference is the **variable**. In Mark and Nita's experiment the variable is the temperature of the water.

Record and Analyze

Mark recorded in a chart the number of teaspoonfuls of sugar that were added to each jar. Nita and Mark made a line graph of their data. When they analyzed the results of their experiment, Nita and Mark were surprised by what they had discovered.

When you do an experiment, you make observations so that you can obtain information called **data**. You need to write down, or **record**, this data and then organize it. Graphs and tables are ways to organize data. **Analyze** the information that you collect by looking for patterns. To see if your results are reliable, **repeat the experiment** several times.

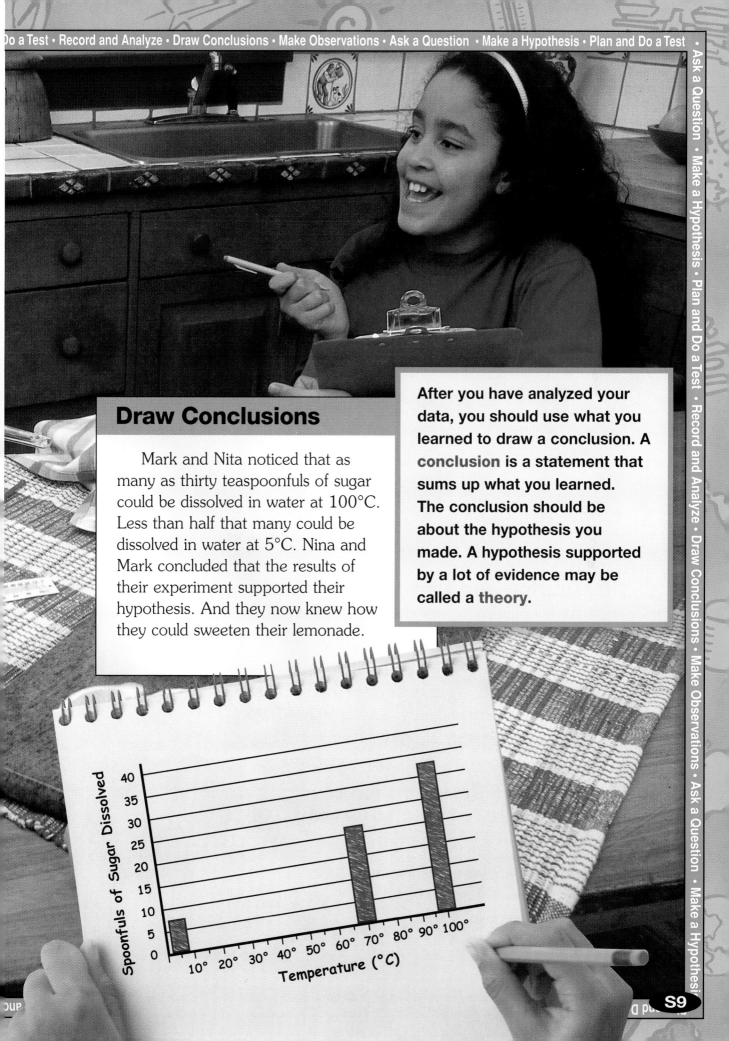

Draw Conclusions

Mark and Nita noticed that as many as thirty teaspoonfuls of sugar could be dissolved in water at 100°C. Less than half that many could be dissolved in water at 5°C. Nina and Mark concluded that the results of their experiment supported their hypothesis. And they now knew how they could sweeten their lemonade.

After you have analyzed your data, you should use what you learned to draw a conclusion. A **conclusion** is a statement that sums up what you learned. The conclusion should be about the hypothesis you made. A hypothesis supported by a lot of evidence may be called a **theory**.

USING SCIENCE PROCESS SKILLS

Observing involves gathering information about the environment through your five senses—seeing, hearing, smelling, touching, and tasting.

Classifying is grouping objects or events according to common properties or characteristics. Often you can classify in more than one way.

Measuring and using numbers involves the ability to make measurements, including time measurements, and to make estimates, and record data.

Communicating involves using words, both speaking and writing, and using actions, graphs, tables, diagrams, and other ways of presenting information.

Inferring means coming to a conclusion based on facts and observations you've made.

Predicting involves stating in advance what you think will happen based on observations and experiences.

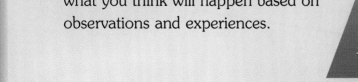

Collecting, recording, and interpreting data

all involve gathering and understanding information. This skill includes organizing data in tables, graphs, and in other ways. Interpretation includes finding patterns and relationships that lead to new questions and new ideas.

Identifying and controlling variables

involves determining the effect of a changing factor, called the variable, in an experiment. To do this, you keep all other factors constant, or unchanging.

Defining operationally

means to describe an object, an event, or an idea based on personal observations. An operational definition of a plant might be that it is a green living thing that is attached to soil and that does not move around.

Making a hypothesis

is suggesting a possible answer to a question or making an educated guess about why something happens. Your hypothesis should be based on observations and experiences.

Experimenting

is testing your hypothesis to collect evidence that supports the hypothesis or shows that it is false.

Making and using models

includes designing and making physical models of processes and objects, or making mental models to represent objects and ideas.

READING TO LEARN

Radioactive Elements

Reading Focus What is a radioactive element?

On March 1, 1896, French scientist Henri Becquerel wrapped a sheet of photographic film in paper that light couldn't penetrate. He placed the package in a desk drawer, together with a few small rocks, and closed the drawer.

A few days later, Becquerel developed the film, expecting to see an unexposed white negative. Instead he was shocked to see darkened areas on the film. Something had changed the chemicals on the film—but what?

▲ Becquerel discovers radioactivity.

Nuclear Radiation

Becquerel's film had been exposed to nuclear radiation (rā dē ā′shən), invisible energy that came from the rocks. The rocks contained the radioactive element uranium (yo͞o rā′nē əm). A **radioactive element** is made up of atoms whose nuclei (*nuclei* is the plural of *nucleus*)

break down, or decay, into nuclei of other atoms. When a radioactive element decays, it changes into a different element. This happens because some of the radiation released by the decaying nucleus is in the form of protons and neutrons. And when an atom loses protons from its nucleus, its atomic number changes.

Recall that an element is identified by its atomic number. The drawing shows how a uranium nucleus decays to form a thorium (thôr′ē əm) nucleus. Notice how the atomic number changes from 92 to 90.

When a nucleus decays, large amounts of energy are released. The particles released from the nucleus will have lots of energy. Sometimes high-energy rays called gamma rays are produced as well.

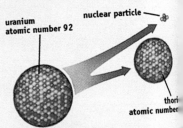

uranium atomic number 92

nuclear particle

thori
atomic number

▲ When a uranium nucleus decays, it loses 2 protons and 2 neutrons, leaving a nucleus with 90 protons. The element with atomic number 90 is thorium.

C76

Before You Read

1. **Scan** each page.
   - titles
   - photos and illustrations
   - captions
   - subheads
   - highlighted words

2. **Identify** the main topic.

3. **Ask** yourself what you know about the topic.

4. **Predict** what you will learn by turning subheads into questions.

Scientists use scientific methods when they do experiments. They also use special methods when they read to learn. You can read like a scientist, too. Just follow the steps below.

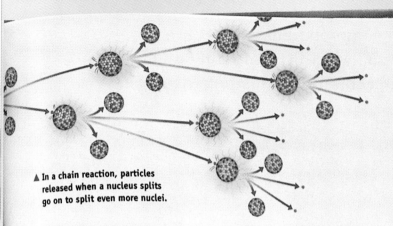

▲ In a chain reaction, particles released when a nucleus splits go on to split even more nuclei.

Using Energy From Atoms

Radioactive elements occur naturally. Scientists have also learned how to split the nuclei of some atoms by bombarding them with neutrons. This reaction is called **nuclear fission** (nōō′klē ər fish′ən). *Fission* means "splitting."

The drawing above shows how neutrons are used to split nuclei of uranium atoms. Two new atoms are produced each time a nucleus splits. Also, some single neutrons and energy are released. Some of these neutrons collide with and split other nuclei, producing a chain reaction.

An uncontrolled nuclear chain reaction releases energy so fast that an explosion takes place. A nuclear reactor is a device in which a nuclear chain reaction is controlled. In a controlled chain reaction, energy is released slowly.

Radiation—Helpful and Harmful

Nuclear reactors provide energy that is used to generate electricity. Reactors are also used to make radioactive forms of many elements. These elements are used in medical research and in the treatment of certain illnesses.

Clearly, nuclear energy has many uses that are beneficial. But nuclear radiation can also damage human tissues. Thus, radioactive materials must be handled safely and must not be allowed to get into the environment by accident. ■

─── INVESTIGATION 1 WRAP-UP ───

THINK IT WRITE IT

REVIEW

1. How does heating sugar in a spoon differ from dissolving it in a cup of hot water?

2. Write the following chemical equation in words.

$$2H_2O \rightarrow 2H_2 + O_2$$

CRITICAL THINKING

3. When might a Bohr model of an atom be more helpful than an electron cloud model?

4. If two neutrons escaped the nucleus of an atom, what would be the effect on the atom's atomic number and its total electric charge?

C77

While You Read

1. **Look** for words that signal cause and effect and sequence.

2. **Make** inferences and draw conclusions.

3. **Ask** questions when you don't understand and then reread.

After You Read

1. **Say** or **write** what you've learned.

2. **Draw, chart,** or **map** what you've learned.

3. **Share** what you've learned.

THINK LIKE A SCIENTIST

SAFETY

The best way to be safe in the classroom and outdoors is to use common sense. Prepare for each activity before you start it. Get help from your teacher when there is a problem. Always pay attention.

Stay Safe From Stains

- Wear protective clothing or an old shirt when you work with messy materials.
- If anything spills, wipe it up or ask your teacher to help you clean it up.

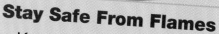

Stay Safe From Flames

- Keep your clothes away from open flames. If you have long or baggy sleeves, roll them up.
- Don't let your hair get close to a flame. If you have long hair, tie it back.

Make Wise Choices About Materials

- Use only the amount of material you need.
- Recycle materials so they can be reused.
- Take care when using valuable tools so they can be used again.

Stay Safe From Injuries

- Protect your eyes by wearing safety goggles when you are told that you need them.
- Keep your hands dry around electricity. Water is a good conductor of electricity, so you can get a shock more easily if your hands are wet.
- Be careful with sharp objects. If you have to press on them, keep the sharp side away from you.
- Cover any cuts you have that are exposed. If you spill something on a cut, be sure to wash it off immediately.
- Don't eat or drink anything unless your teacher tells you that it's okay.

Stay Safe During Cleanup

- Wash up after you finish working.
- Dispose of things in the way that your teachers tells you to.

HAIR Keep it out of the way of a flame.

EYES Wear safety goggles when you are told to.

HANDS Keep your hands dry around electricity. Cover any cuts. Wear gloves when told to. Wash up after you finish.

MOUTH Don't eat or drink ANYTHING unless your teacher tells you it's okay.

CLOTHES Keep long sleeves rolled up. Protect yourself from stains. Stay away from open flames.

DON'T MAKE A MESS If you spill something, clean it up right away. When finished with an activity, clean up your work area. Dispose of things in the way your teacher tells you to.

MOST IMPORTANTLY

If you ever hurt yourself, or one of your group members gets hurt, tell your teacher right away.

UNIT A

Cells and Microbes

Theme: Models

THINK LIKE A SCIENTIST

BOLD MOLD

What are these objects? No, they're not trees in a land-scape out of a science-fiction movie. They're actually parts of a greatly magnified section of bread mold, a type of fungus! When moisture and warmth are present, molds can spread rapidly over the surface of breads and other foods. As they grow, molds digest and absorb the nutrients in the food. Molds can be harmful, so moldy food should not be eaten. Some molds, however, produce useful substances, such as penicillin. Penicillin is an antibiotic that can help save lives.

THINK LIKE A SCIENTIST

Questioning In this unit you'll study cells, their structure and function, and several different types of microscopic organisms. You'll investigate questions such as these.

- What Are Some Life Processes of Cells?
- How Do Bacteria and Viruses Affect Other Living Things?

Observing, Testing, Hypothesizing
In the Activity "Lifestyles of Fungi," you'll attempt to grow bread mold under various conditions. You'll observe the best growing conditions for this fungus.

Researching In the Resource "Fungi—Good and Bad," you'll learn about fungi that are beneficial, and even fungi that taste good. You'll also find out about some of the ways fungi are harmful.

Drawing Conclusions After you've completed your investigations, you'll draw conclusions about what you've learned—and get new ideas.

CHAPTER 1

CELLS

The brain and liver are very important organs. But then, so are the body's muscles. All these body parts do very different and vital jobs. Yet they all are similar in one way—they are all made up of cells.
Cells are the basic units of life.

PEOPLE USING SCIENCE

Phlebotomist Have you ever had a sample of blood taken from your arm? How can your blood show whether or not you are healthy? Carlton Donovan could tell you. Mr. Donovan is a phlebotomist (flē bät'ə mist). His job involves obtaining and testing the blood of patients such as Meghan Delaney. To get a sample of Meghan's blood, Mr. Donovan inserts a needle into a blood vessel in her arm. He draws blood up the needle into a test tube.

Next, Mr. Donovan must place the blood in a machine that will count the red and white blood cells in the sample. Too many white blood cells could mean that Meghan's body is fighting off an infection.

There are many types of cells besides blood cells. In this chapter you'll learn what cells are, what they do, and how cells make more cells.

Coming Up

◄ Phlebotomist Carlton Donovan
prepares to take blood from
patient Meghan Delaney.

INVESTIGATION 1

WHAT ARE CELLS?

Look at the skin on the back of one of your hands. What do you think you would see if you could look at a layer of your skin under a microscope? You would see cells—the tiny basic units that make up all living organisms. But what are cells made of? Are all cells alike? These are some of the questions you'll find answers to in Investigation 1.

Activity

Observing Plant Cells

In this activity you'll use a microscope to examine plant cells. You might be surprised at what you see.

Procedure

1. Place a drop of aquarium water on a clean microscope slide. Add a small piece of *Elodea* leaf to the drop. Hold a cover slip by two corners and gently lower it onto the microscope slide.

2. Use a microscope to **observe** the slide under low power. In your *Science Notebook*, **draw** what you see.

See **SCIENCE** and **MATH TOOLBOX** page H2 if you need to review **Using a Microscope.**

3. Focus the microscope to **observe** the slide under high power. **Make a drawing** of one cell, including any structures you see.

4. Locate the outer border, or **cell wall**, of one *Elodea* cell. Next look for small round green structures in the cell. These are **chloroplasts** (klôr′ə plasts). **Label** these structures.

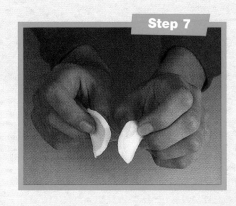

5. Now locate the light-colored material, called **cyto-plasm** (sīt′ō plaz əm), that fills much of the cell. In the cytoplasm, look for spaces that appear empty. These spaces are called **vacuoles** (vak′yo͞o ōlz). In your drawing, show and **label** a vacuole. Also **label** the cytoplasm.

6. Repeat step 1, using a salt solution instead of aquarium water. Then repeat steps 2 through 4. **Describe** any differences you observe between the *Elodea* in salt water and the *Elodea* in aquarium water.

7. Have your teacher place one drop of iodine solution on a microscope slide. Bend an onion section against its curve until it breaks. Use tweezers to pull off a layer of onion skin and place it in the drop of iodine solution. Add a cover slip to the slide.

8. Use the microscope to **observe** the onion cell under low power and then under high power. Locate the **nucleus** (no͞o′klē əs)—the large dark structure. **Make a drawing** of the onion cell and **label** the nucleus and any other structures you can identify.

Analyze and Conclude

1. Each cell you observed was surrounded by a cell wall. **Infer** the function of this structure.

2. The **cell theory** states that all organisms are made of cells. How did your observations support or not support this theory?

3. Salt water changes the appearance of *Elodea* cells. **Infer** the effect of salt on *Elodea* cells.

INVESTIGATE FURTHER!

EXPERIMENT

Make a slide of tomato skin in a drop of water. Observe the skin under a microscope, using low power and high power. Draw what you see. What cell parts are similar to those in the onion skin? What cell parts are different from the onion cells? How can you account for these differences?

▼ *Elodea* cells in aquarium water

Activity
Observing Animal Cells

You've seen that plants are made up of cells.
Animals are also made up of cells. How do animal
and plant cells compare? Find out in this activity.

Procedure

1. **Observe** a prepared slide of human cheek cells under the low power of a microscope. **Describe** what you see and **record** your observations in your *Science Notebook*.

2. **Observe** the cheek cells under high power. **Make a drawing** of one cell. **Label** any structures you can identify.

3. Repeat steps 1 and 2, using a prepared slide of frog blood.

4. The outer border of an animal cell is the **cell membrane**. **Label** the cell membrane in each of your drawings.

Step 1

Analyze and Conclude

1. **Infer** the function of the cell membrane. All cells have a cell membrane. Where do you think the cell membrane of a plant cell is located?

2. **Compare** the drawings you made in this activity with those you made of the plant cells in the activity on pages A6 and A7. In what ways are animal cells similar to plant cells? In what ways are animal cells different from plant cells?

3. Do your observations in this activity support the theory that all organisms are made up of cells? Explain your answer.

INVESTIGATE FURTHER!

RESEARCH

You observed the red blood cells of a frog. Observe prepared slides of human red blood cells. What difference do you observe between the two types of red blood cells? Use a reference book to find out more about this difference.

Plant and Animal Cells

Reading Focus How are all cells alike?

From a distance the surface of a brick wall looks smooth. However, as you get closer, you can see the individual bricks. If you get close enough to examine one of the bricks, you can see the texture and maybe even some large particles of the brick.

What if you get close to a plant or an animal? Can you see any of the "building blocks" that make up each organism? How close do you have to get to an organism to see its building blocks?

The Cell Theory

What do you see if you look through a microscope at material from plants and animals? If you look closely, you see the building blocks that make up plants and animals. These building blocks are called cells. Just as bricks are the basic units of a brick wall, **cells** are the basic units of all living things. A microscope is used to observe plant cells in the activity on pages A6 and A7. Animal cells are observed in the activity on page A8.

The cells of an organism are, in some ways, like the bricks in this building. From a distance all you see is the solid wall (*above*). But up close you can see the characteristics of each brick (*inset*).

The discovery that all living things are made of cells led to the development of the cell theory. This theory resulted from the work of many scientists. The main points of the **cell theory** are listed here.

- All living things are made up of cells.
- Cells are the basic units of structure and function of all living things.
- All new cells are produced from existing cells.

Cells Are Alike

Cells differ in the various structures, or organelles (or′gə nelz), that they contain. The activities on pages A6 and A7 and on page A8 show that all cells are not identical. For example, organelles called chloroplasts are found in *Elodea* cells, but not in human cheek cells. In fact, cells from different parts of the same organism can differ. However, as the drawings on these pages show, cells are similar.

CELL PARTS

①CELL MEMBRANE The **cell membrane** holds the cell together and lets substances pass in and out of the cell.

②CELL WALL The **cell wall** is found in plant cells and some protists but not in animal cells. It is stiff and gives a rigid shape to the cell.

③CHLOROPLASTS The **chloroplasts** (klôr′ə plasts) are organelles in some plant and protist cells. They contain chlorophyll, a chemical that enables plants to store solar energy.

④CHROMOSOMES The **chromosomes** (krō′mə sōmz) are structures inside the nucleus that are made up of genes. Genes carry the code for all the cell's traits and its activities.

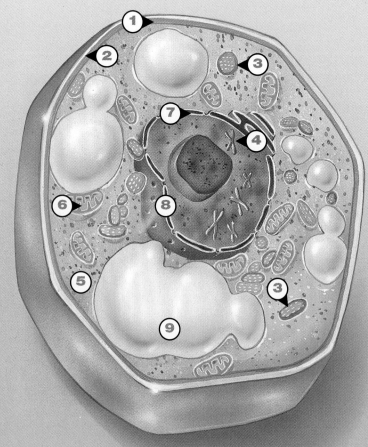

PLANT CELL

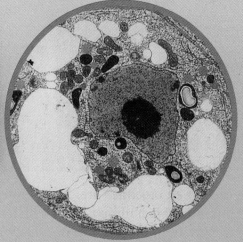

All cells are surrounded by a cell membrane and contain cytoplasm. Within the cytoplasm of most cells can be found mitochondria, vacuoles, and a nucleus that is surrounded by a nuclear membrane and contains chromosomes. Although there are differences between the cells of different organisms, all living things must carry out similar life processes. Therefore, it should not be surprising that all cells are somewhat similar. ■

UNIT PROJECT LINK

For this Unit Project you will make models for a "micromenagerie." With your group, choose a specific kind of plant or animal cell. Build a model of your cell to display in your micromenagerie. Work with your group to select the materials you will need.

TechnologyLink

For more help with your Unit Project, go to **www.eduplace.com**.

5 **CYTOPLASM** The **cytoplasm** (sīt'ō plaz-əm) is the watery gel inside the cell. Many materials are dissolved or suspended in the cytoplasm. Various organelles are found in the cytoplasm.

6 **MITOCHONDRIA** The **mitochondria** (mīt ō kän'drē ə) are organelles in which energy is released from food.

7 **NUCLEAR MEMBRANE** The **nuclear** (noo'klē ər) **membrane** allows substances to pass in and out of the nucleus.

8 **NUCLEUS** The **nucleus** (noo'klē əs) controls cell activities.

9 **VACUOLES** The **vacuoles** (vak'yoo ōlz) are spaces in the cytoplasm where food and chemicals are stored.

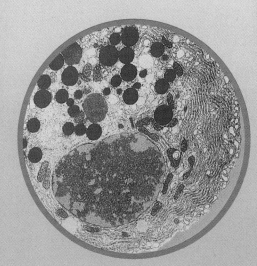

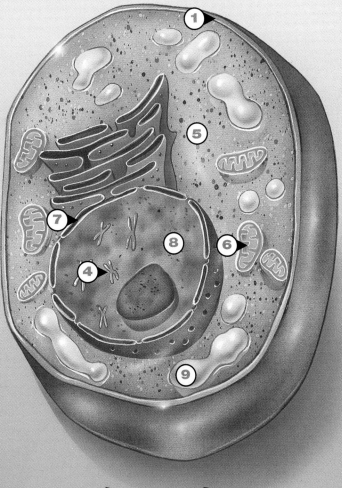

ANIMAL CELL

A Closer Look at Cells

Reading Focus How have improvements in the microscope helped scientists better study cells?

When the first microscopes were made, a new world opened up for scientists. For the first time, scientists could see single cells and single-celled organisms—things invisible to the eye alone. How does a microscope make these cells visible? The magnifying power comes from its lenses. A lens is a thin piece of glass with at least one curved surface. In a microscope, lenses create an enlarged image of a tiny specimen.

Matthias Schleiden, Germany
Schleiden states that all plants are made up of cells. In 1839, German physiologist Theodor Schwann concludes that all animals are made up of cells.

1838

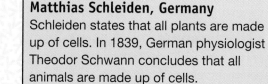

Robert Hooke, England
Hooke coins the term *cells* to describe the boxlike structures that make up cork. In 1665 he publishes drawings of his compound microscope (a microscope with two lenses) and of his observations in *Micrographia*.

1665

1674

Anton van Leeuwenhoek, Netherlands
Leeuwenhoek builds a simple microscope (a microscope with only one lens). The microscope magnifies objects 270 times. Van Leeuwenhoek is the first to see one-celled organisms, which he calls "wee beasties."

The scanning electron microscope (SEM) is developed. The SEM allows scientists to create three-dimensional (3-D) images of the surfaces of specimens.

1969

Rudolf Virchow, Germany

Virchow states that cells can come only from other living cells. This idea, along with the hypotheses of Schleiden and Schwann, becomes part of the cell theory.

1855

1980
Heinrich Roher, Germany
Roher and Gerd Binning develop the scanning tunneling microscope (STM). Using the STM, scientists can see the smallest units of matter—individual atoms!

1931
Ernst Ruska, Germany
Ruska builds the first transmission electron microscope (TEM). In 1933, Ruska builds a second TEM with magnification so great that scientists can use it to study the insides of cells.

INVESTIGATION 1 WRAP-UP

REVIEW

1. What are the three main points of the cell theory?

2. Name five ways in which most cells are alike.

CRITICAL THINKING

3. You are observing two unlabeled cells. One is a plant cell, and the other is an animal cell. What cell parts can you look for to determine which is the plant cell and which is the animal cell?

4. Why do scientists infer from the cell theory that all living things are related?

INVESTIGATION 2

WHAT ARE SOME LIFE PROCESSES OF CELLS?

In order to survive, your body must use oxygen from the air you breathe to get energy from the food you eat. Processes that occur within your cells make these activities possible. In this investigation you'll discover what these cell processes are and how they occur.

Activity

Moving In and Out of Cells

When you breathe, air moves in and out of your body. Inside your body, materials move in and out of cells. These materials move from areas where they are concentrated (present in great amounts) to areas where they are less concentrated. This movement of materials is called diffusion. Make a model of a cell membrane to see how diffusion works.

MATERIALS

- goggles
- spoon
- starch
- 2 beakers
- water
- sealable plastic bag
- container of iodine solution
- timer
- *Science Notebook*

SAFETY /////

Wear goggles. Iodine will stain clothing and is poisonous if swallowed. Clean up spills immediately.

Procedure

1. Put a spoonful of starch into a beaker of water. Stir until well mixed.

2. Pour the starch mixture into a plastic bag. Seal the bag.

 Step 1

A14

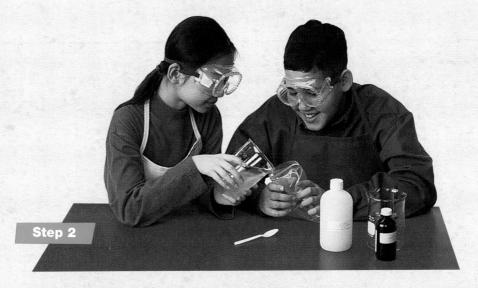

Step 2

3. When iodine mixes with starch, the mixture changes in color to a dark blue-black. **Talk with your group** and together **predict** what will happen if you place the bag containing the starch mixture in contact with the iodine solution. **Record** your prediction in your *Science Notebook*.

4. Place the bag into a beaker containing iodine solution.

5. **Observe** the setup every 15 minutes for the next 2 hours. **Record** your observations.

Analyze and Conclude

1. You have made a model that shows how substances move into or out of a cell. What cell part does the plastic bag represent?

2. Infer which substance moved through the plastic bag. How can you tell? How did your prediction compare with your observations?

3. Having **observed** this model, what conclusions can you make about how materials enter and leave cells?

4. Hypothesize as to why only one substance seemed to move through the bag. **Explain** your hypothesis.

INVESTIGATE FURTHER!

EXPERIMENT

Can food coloring diffuse through the plastic bag? Make a plan and show it to your teacher. Then carry out your plan. Share your results with your classmates.

Coming and Going With Cells

Reading Focus How does diffusion help materials move in and out of cells?

In the activity on pages A14 and A15, a substance, iodine, passes through a thin layer of plastic. The iodine moves from the fluid in a beaker to a starch-water mixture in a plastic bag. When the iodine moves from one side of the plastic to the other, it causes the starch-water mixture to turn blue-black in color.

Like the plastic, a cell membrane is also a thin layer. However, a cell membrane is made of living material. It controls, or regulates, the movement of materials into and out of the cell. The process of moving materials through the cell membrane is called cell transport. This process ensures that needed materials are able to pass into and out of a cell.

Some substances, such as oxygen, pass freely through the cell membrane by diffusion (di fyōō′zhən). **Diffusion** is the tendency of a substance to move from an area of greater concentration to an area of lesser concentration. Diffusion continues until the two areas have equal concentrations of a substance.

The diffusion of water through a membrane is called **osmosis**, (äs mō′sis). During osmosis, water moves from regions with lesser concentrations of dissolved substances (greater concentrations of water) to regions with greater concentrations of dissolved substances (lesser

▲ *Elodea* cells in fresh water (*top*); when these cells are placed in salt water (*bottom*), water leaves the cells and the cell membranes shrink.

concentrations of water). Water moves into or out of a cell depending upon the concentrations of other substances inside and outside that cell.

The movement of materials through the cell membrane by diffusion or by osmosis occurs without the cell using energy. However, most materials, such as sugars, salts, and chemicals used to make proteins, do not enter the cell by diffusion. These materials are moved through the cell membrane into the cell by a type of cell transport called active transport. In **active transport** the cell uses energy to move materials through the cell membrane. Food molecules are moved into a cell by active transport and some molecules of waste materials that build up inside a cell are also moved out of the cell through active transport. ■

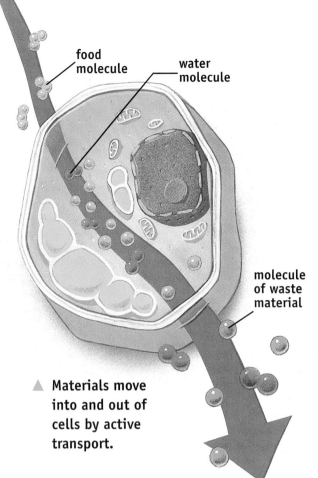

food molecule

water molecule

molecule of waste material

▲ Materials move into and out of cells by active transport.

 # Science in Literature

Under the Microscope

"Even the single-celled plants you can find in a drop of water come in many shapes and varieties. Larger plants, though, are built up of thousands of cells having many different functions. Under the microscope you can see the cells that make up the roots, stems, leaves, and reproductive parts of a plant."

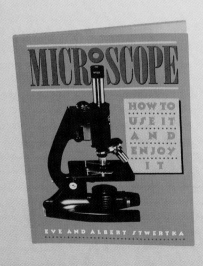

Microscope: How to Use It and Enjoy It
by Eve and Albert Stwertka
Julian Messner, 1988

Looking at cells through a microscope takes a little practice. *Microscope: How to Use It and Enjoy It* by Eve and Albert Stwertka can help you develop your skills. You'll soon be able to prepare your own slides for viewing.

A17

Cells and Energy

Reading Focus How do photosynthesis and cell respiration help a cell get energy?

Cells grow, reproduce, produce wastes, and carry out other life processes. All of these life processes require energy. Cells obtain energy from food. But plant cells and animal cells differ in the ways that they obtain food.

Photosynthesis

In the activity on pages A6 and A7, structures called chloroplasts are observed in an *Elodea* leaf. These structures do not occur in animal cells. Chloroplasts contain a green chemical, called chlorophyll, that is able to capture, or absorb, the light energy in sunlight. Plant cells are able to use this energy to build sugar from carbon dioxide and water. So, plant cells make their own food. Animal cells, however, must obtain food from their environment.

Photosynthesis (fōt ō sin'thə sis) is the process by which light energy is used to make food. The equation for photosynthesis is shown on the photograph below. Note that oxygen is a waste product of this process.

Where do plants get the carbon dioxide and water to carry out photosynthesis? Carbon dioxide is a gas found in air. Most plants absorb this gas through their leaves, and in most plants, photosynthesis takes place in the leaves. Water, found in the soil, is absorbed by the roots and carried to the leaves.

In the next chapter you'll learn about some other organisms that also contain chlorophyll and carry out photosynthesis. All organisms that can carry out photosynthesis are called producers.

Through photosynthesis the rain forests of the world provide much of the oxygen needed by other organisms. ▼

CARBON DIOXIDE + WATER → Light → SUGAR + OXYGEN

SUGAR + OXYGEN ➤ CARBON DIOXIDE + WATER + ENERGY

Cell Respiration

What happens inside cells when energy is needed? The reverse of photosynthesis takes place! Look above to see what happens when the photosynthesis equation is turned around.

The process of using oxygen to release stored energy by breaking down sugar molecules is called **cell respiration** (res pə rā′shən). This process occurs in the mitochondria of both plant and animal cells. Plants use the energy they have stored as a result of photosynthesis. Animals use energy they receive when they eat plants or eat animals that have eaten plants.

The equation at the top of this page summarizes cell respiration. Notice that cell respiration produces the same materials that are used for photosynthesis.

When oxygen isn't available in sufficient amounts, some cells obtain energy

▲ Cell respiration—the reverse process of photosynthesis—provides energy needed for physical activity.

from sugar in a different way. In the process called **fermentation** (fur mən-tā′shən), the sugar is only partly broken down. This occurs, for example, when you exercise very hard. Your heart cannot pump blood fast enough to keep your muscle cells supplied with oxygen, so the sugar cannot be broken down into carbon dioxide and water. Fermentation causes your cells to produce a waste product called lactic acid. Fermentation and cell respiration are both life processes that release the energy stored in food. ■

INVESTIGATION 2 WRAP-UP

REVIEW

1. How is osmosis related to diffusion?

2. What materials are needed for a cell to go through the process of cell respiration? What materials are produced as a result of cell respiration?

CRITICAL THINKING

3. How is diffusion important to cell processes such as photosynthesis?

4. How might your life be affected if your cells contained chloroplasts?

HOW DO CELLS MAKE MORE CELLS?

You've grown a lot since you were very young. Your cells have been busy making new cells to add to your body. Investigation 3 will give you some clues as to how cells reproduce and specialize to do specific jobs.

Activity

Multiplying by Dividing

When an organism grows, it adds new cells. Cells also wear out and are continually replaced by new cells, even after the organism is fully grown. In this activity you will learn how cells multiply by dividing.

MATERIALS

- microscope
- prepared slide of onion root tip
- *Science Notebook*

Procedure

1. Observe an onion root tip under low and high power of a microscope. Try to locate cells that look like the photographs on page A21. Study each cell and each photograph and **record** your observations in your *Science Notebook*.

Step 1

Can you put these stages in order?

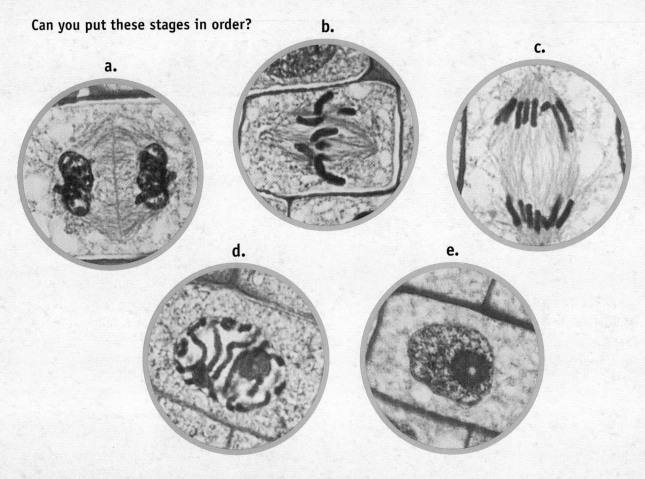

a.

b.

c.

d.

e.

 See **SCIENCE** and **MATH TOOLBOX** page H2 if you need to review *Using a Microscope.*

2. The photographs shown above are not in the proper order to show the process of cell division. Look for evidence that one cell is dividing into two and **hypothesize** about the correct sequence of the photos. **Compare** your sequence with that of another student. **Work together** to order the pictures. Then **draw a diagram** to **record** your suggested sequence.

Analyze and Conclude

1. What evidence did you **observe** that suggests that one cell is dividing into two?

2. **Infer** why the tip of an onion root is a good place to look for dividing cells.

3. **Infer** where you might find dividing cells in a human being.

INVESTIGATE FURTHER!

RESEARCH

What is cloning? Consult library sources to find out about the cloning of plant and animal cells.

Cell Division

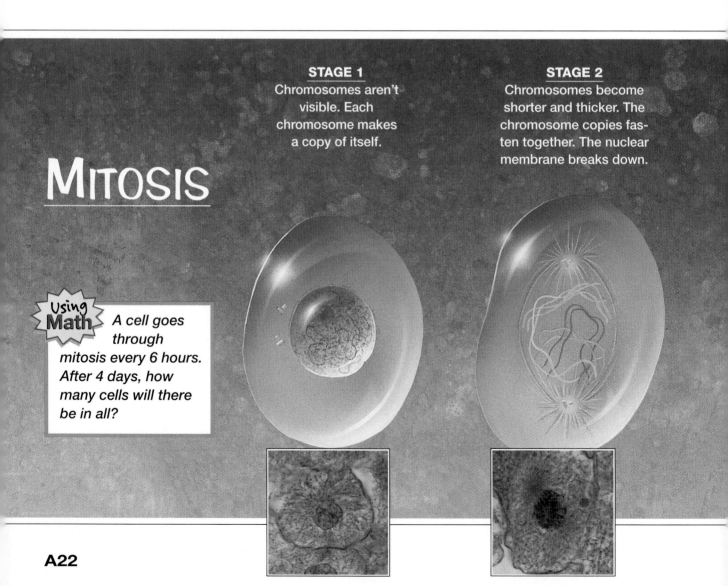

Reading Focus What happens in a cell during each stage of cell division?

A meteorite flashes out of the night sky and into a small lake. Deep in the water, a single-celled amoeba absorbs radiation given off by the space rock. The amoeba begins to grow rapidly. Within hours, it's the size of a car. Slowly, the amoeba oozes out of the lake. Feeding on everything in its path, the amoeba continues to grow and move. Could something like this really happen?

Is Bigger Better?

Recall how cells get the oxygen and food they need. These substances must move into the cell by passing through the cell membrane. Cell wastes must also move out through the cell membrane by the process of active transport.

As a cell grows larger, it requires more and more energy and thus needs greater amounts of sugar. Additional oxygen is

MITOSIS

STAGE 1
Chromosomes aren't visible. Each chromosome makes a copy of itself.

STAGE 2
Chromosomes become shorter and thicker. The chromosome copies fasten together. The nuclear membrane breaks down.

Using Math *A cell goes through mitosis every 6 hours. After 4 days, how many cells will there be in all?*

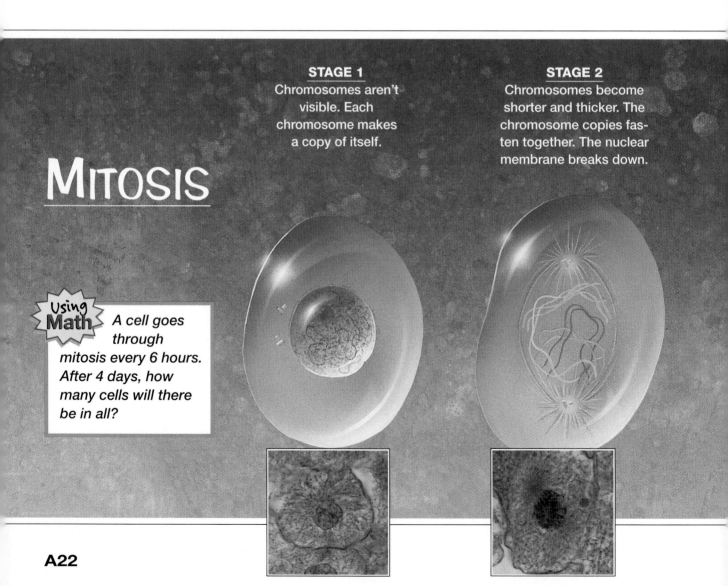

needed to react with the sugar and release the energy. The growing cell also produces more waste products.

As a cell gets bigger, both its cell membrane and its volume get bigger. But the volume actually increases faster than the cell membrane. At some point, the cell membrane wouldn't be large enough to let enough materials in (or out) quickly enough to keep the cell's life processes going. But before reaching this point, another life process begins in the cell.

Splitting in Two

Instead of continuing to grow, cells divide once they reach a certain size. (For this reason, the giant amoeba described could never exist.)

When a cell divides, two new cells are formed. Most of the cells in living organisms divide by a process called mitosis (mī tō'sis). In **mitosis**, a cell divides into two exact copies of itself.

Before mitosis begins, the cell's chromosomes make copies of themselves. During mitosis the copies are pulled to opposite ends of the cell, and the cell splits in half. The two new daughter cells, each with a complete set of chromosomes, now begin to grow. Follow the stages of mitosis in the diagram below. ■

Internet Field Trip

Visit **www.eduplace.com** to learn more about the different stages of mitosis.

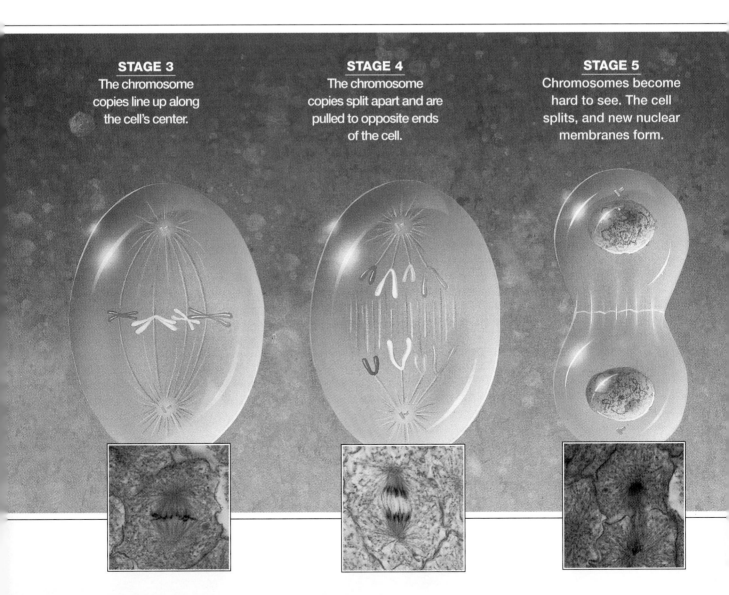

STAGE 3
The chromosome copies line up along the cell's center.

STAGE 4
The chromosome copies split apart and are pulled to opposite ends of the cell.

STAGE 5
Chromosomes become hard to see. The cell splits, and new nuclear membranes form.

Artificial Blood

Reading Focus What is one way that artificial blood is made?

 SCIENCE TECHNOLOGY & SOCIETY

Have you ever heard a radio or television announcement asking people to donate blood? People need to receive blood for a variety of reasons. Some have been in major accidents and have suffered a loss of blood. Others require blood during surgery.

Not Enough Blood

The transfer of blood from one person to another is called a transfusion. The person donating the blood is the donor. The person receiving the blood is the recipient. Although many recipients receive whole blood, blood banks routinely separate blood into its parts, because some patients need only certain types of blood cells.

Unfortunately the need for blood is so great that the demand often exceeds the supply. What can be done when there are not enough blood donors?

A Possible Answer

One answer is to use artificial blood. Whereas real blood is a complex tissue that performs many functions, artificial blood is much simpler. It's designed and used for only one of the jobs that blood does—carrying oxygen, for example. Oxygen is carried by a protein in red blood cells. The protein captures oxygen when blood passes through the lungs and releases the oxygen as blood flows through the body.

In one process for making artificial blood, red blood cells are separated out and broken down to obtain the oxygen-carrying protein. The oxygen-carrying protein is processed to kill any viruses. Then the protein is enveloped in an artificial membrane, bottled, and packaged in transfusion bags for shipment. Since only the oxygen-carrying protein from real blood is used, there is no need to match blood types. ■

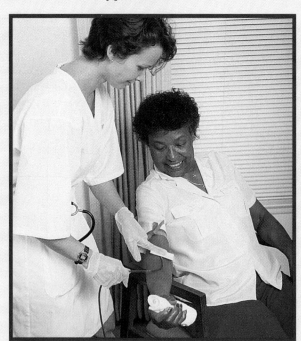

Using Math *The creation of artificial blood depends upon blood donations. The human body contains about 5 L of blood. A donation is usually about $\frac{1}{2}$ L. What percent of the total volume of blood does the donation represent?*

Tissues, Organs, and Systems

Reading Focus How do specialized cells work together?

As organisms grow, their cells continue to divide. The cells develop into different and specialized cell types, such as blood cells or skin cells. Each type of cell has certain structures and characteristics that make the specialized cell better at its job than a cell that must carry out many tasks.

The specialization of cells is called **cell differentiation** (dif ər en shē-ā'shən). It begins early in development, when organisms still consist of only a few cells. In humans, once a cell differentiates, it never becomes anything different.

But in some other organisms, cells can change their specialties throughout the organism's life. Salamanders can grow a new leg or tail if they lose one. One piece of a planarian, a type of flatworm, can grow into a whole new planarian. Some plants can even grow a whole new plant from just a leaf or stem.

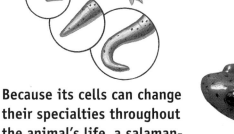

Because its cells can change their specialties throughout the animal's life, a salamander can replace body parts that are lost. ▶

Groups of specialized cells that work together to do a specific job form **tissues**. For example, muscle tissue contains cells that contract. These contracting cells make it possible for you to move. Another example is the nerve tissue that carries information between different parts of your body. Messages from your muscle tissue are carried to your spinal cord and brain by nerve tissue. Other nerve tissue carries messages back to tell your muscle tissue when to contract.

Tissues Make Up Organs

The heart and liver are examples of organs. An **organ** is a group of tissues that function together to do a specific job. Organs are usually made of several different kinds of tissues.

The heart, for example, has muscle tissue which contracts, squeezing the blood out of the heart's chambers and into the arteries. The heart also has tissue that forms membranes that cover and protect the heart. There is also nerve tissue present in the heart. This nerve tissue carries signals to the heart from the brain.

A25

Organ Systems

Specialized cells combine to form tissues. Tissues connect to form organs, each with its own task. But in many living things, groups of organs work together. An **organ system** is a group of organs that work together to do a job.

An example of an organ system is your digestive system. This system is made up of the group of organs that work together to digest food. These include the esophagus, the stomach, and the intestines. Each organ has its specific job in the process of digestion.

Plants also have organs and organ systems. Leaves, stems, and roots are all plant organs. They work together to transport water throughout the plant. ■

Technology Link
CD-ROM

INVESTIGATE FURTHER!

Use the **Best of the Net—Science CD-ROM**, Human Body, *The Human Heart* to learn how the different kinds of muscle tissue that make up the heart work together to pump blood to all parts of the body. You'll also find out how electricity helps keep the heart pumping.

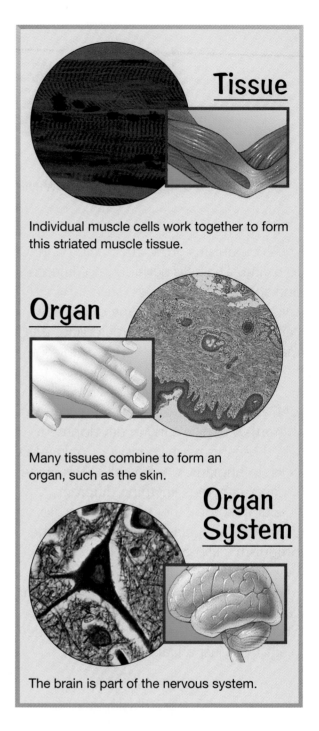

Tissue

Individual muscle cells work together to form this striated muscle tissue.

Organ

Many tissues combine to form an organ, such as the skin.

Organ System

The brain is part of the nervous system.

INVESTIGATION 3 WRAP-UP

REVIEW

1. Describe the five stages of mitosis.

2. Explain how the heart is made of different tissues.

CRITICAL THINKING

3. Why is the duplication of chromosomes necessary for mitosis?

4. Explain how cell differentiation in salamanders differs from that in humans.

REFLECT & EVALUATE

Word Power

Write the letter of the term that best matches the definition. *Not all terms will be used.*

1. Cell part that controls the cell's activities
2. Group of tissues that function together to do a specific job
3. Organelles in which energy is released from food
4. Tendency of a substance to move from an area of greater concentration to an area of lesser concentration
5. Cell division
6. Specialization of cells
7. Structure found only in plant cells that gives a rigid shape to the cell

a. cell differentiation
b. cell membrane
c. cell wall
d. diffusion
e. fermentation
f. mitochondria
g. mitosis
h. nucleus
i. organ

Check What You Know

Write the term in each pair that best completes each sentence.

1. The diffusion of water through a membrane is called (fermentation, osmosis).
2. All life processes are carried out by (vacuoles, cells).
3. The process of using oxygen to release stored energy by breaking down sugar molecules is called (cell respiration, photosynthesis).

Problem Solving

1. What are some life processes of cells? How do cells carry out these processes? Do animal cells carry out any of these processes in different ways from plant cells? Explain.

2. Based on your knowledge of cells, how is it possible for a one-celled organism to survive? What advantages or disadvantages do you think a many-celled organism possesses?

BUILD YOUR PORTFOLIO

Study the photograph of the cell. Then identify as many cell structures as you can. Do you think this is a plant cell or an animal cell? Why?

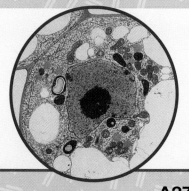

CHAPTER 2

PROTISTS AND FUNGI

Green scum floats like a water plant on a pond. Amoebas grow and move like animals in a bowl of pond water. Yet scum isn't a plant, and an amoeba isn't an animal. These living things are microbes, tiny one-celled organisms.

Connecting to Science
CULTURE

Bread You know that different cultures have different kinds of foods. You may have eaten in restaurants that specialize in food from Italy, France, or Mexico. One type of food that many cultures share is bread. Throughout history, bread has been used not just as a food source but also as a part of ceremonies and rituals. For example, ancient Egyptians placed bread in tombs to be buried with their pharaohs. In ancient Rome, ovens for baking bread were built in temples.

The basic recipe for baking bread usually includes a type of flour, a liquid, and yeast, which makes the bread rise. Yeast, a type of fungus, is a one-celled organism. In this chapter you'll learn how the action of yeasts helps to produce bread. You'll also learn about other types of fungi and about organisms called protists.

Coming Up

◄ Sourdough bread, popular in San Francisco today, gets its sour taste from the action of yeasts in the air.

INVESTIGATION 1

WHAT ARE PROTISTS?

You've just entered a world of tiny, unusual organisms. Some act like plants, while others act like animals. A few of these organisms seem to be both plants and animals! Welcome to the kingdom of protists. Find out about the characteristics of these organisms in this investigation.

Activity

Microorganisms

Protists are mostly single-celled, microscopic organisms. In this activity you'll examine some of these fascinating creatures.

Procedure

Place a drop of pond water on a clean microscope slide. Then place a cover slip on the drop. Look at the slide under the low power and then the high power of a microscope. **Observe** any tiny organisms you see and **sketch** them in your *Science Notebook*.

See **SCIENCE** *and* **MATH TOOLBOX** *page H2 if you need to review* ***Using a Microscope.***

Analyze and Conclude

1. **Describe** how the organisms move.

2. **Infer** how the organisms obtain food.

▼*Paramecium*

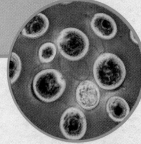

▲ *Euglena*   ▲ *Chlamydomonas*

A30

Activity
Observing Protists

Some protists are animal-like and some are plant-like. Some are one celled, and some are many celled. In this activity you'll compare an animal-like protist and a plantlike protist.

Procedure

1. **Predict** how an animal-like protist may be different from a plantlike protist. **Record** your prediction in your *Science Notebook*.

2. Place a drop of an amoeba culture on a clean microscope slide. Then place a cover slip on the drop. Look at the slide under the low power of the microscope and then under high power. **Record** your observations.

3. **Observe** an amoeba and **make a drawing** of it.

4. Place a prepared slide of *Spirogyra* on the microscope. Focus the slide under low power and then under high power. **Record** your observations.

5. **Make a drawing** of several *Spirogyra* cells that show the shape of the cells and how they are arranged.

Analyze and Conclude

1. Based on your observations, which protist is animal-like and which protist is plantlike? **Describe** how both types of protists are similar. **Describe** how they are different. How does your prediction compare with your observations?

2. Protists live in wet environments. **Infer** how an amoeba moves around in its environment. What can you **infer** about the movement of *Spirogyra*?

Step 3

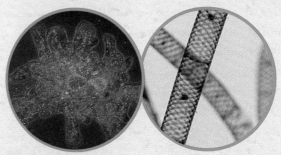

▲ *Amoeba*   ▲ *Spirogyra*

The World of Protists

Reading Focus What are the differences between animal-like protists and plantlike protists?

Swarming in the murky water of a lake, strange-looking creatures dart here and there in search of prey or bright rays of sunlight. This is the world of **protists**, a kingdom of microbes—mostly single-celled, microscopic organisms that have traits of animals, plants, or both.

In the activity on page A30, pond water is observed through a microscope. Pond water teems with a variety of protists. However, protists also live in lakes, rivers, oceans, and damp soil. Some protists even live inside other organisms. Scientists have found many thousands of protist species in all parts of the environment.

Most protists are single-celled and contain a nucleus and other cell structures needed to carry out all basic life functions. Some protists are **multicellular** (mul ti sel'yōō lər), which means they are made up of more than one cell. Multicellular protists may not be microscopic. In fact, some grow to be many meters in length. But all the cells of multicellular protists are very similar, and each carries out its own life functions.

Most protists reproduce by **fission** (fish'ən), the dividing of a cell to produce two new cells. In this form of reproduction, there is only one parent, and the new cells are identical to the parent. In some protists, cells from two parents join. This joining produces new cells that are not identical to either parent.

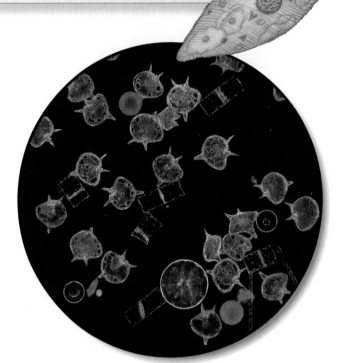

▲ **A single drop of pond water may contain a world of life—much of it protist.**

Animal-like Protists

Many protists have traits that are like those of animals. Such protists are called **protozoans**. Like animals, these protists get their energy by feeding on other organisms. Most protozoans have some method of locomotion, or movement, that helps them obtain food.

An amoeba moves by pushing out its cytoplasm and forming pseudopods (sōō'dō pädz). These pseudopods, or false feet, also help the amoeba capture food. The amoeba completely surrounds the food and ingests it, or takes it in.

How an Amoeba Captures Food

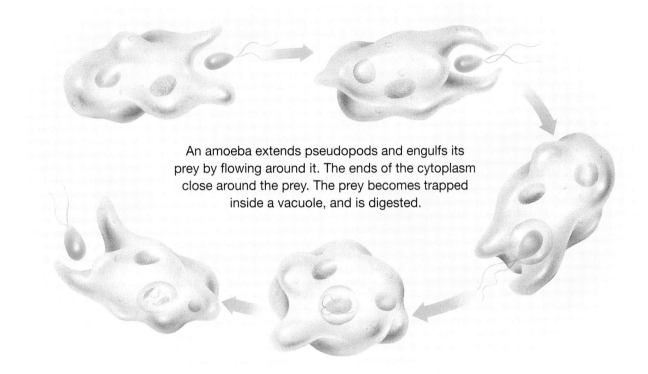

An amoeba extends pseudopods and engulfs its prey by flowing around it. The ends of the cytoplasm close around the prey. The prey becomes trapped inside a vacuole, and is digested.

Once inside the amoeba, the food is digested and used for energy. Amoebas are observed in the activity on page A31.

Other kinds of protozoans have different methods of locomotion. Parameciums (par ə mē′sē əmz) have hairlike structures called cilia (sil′ē ə). The beating of the cilia propels a paramecium. Cilia also draw water and food into the paramecium's mouthlike opening. Some protozoans have threadlike tails, called flagella (flə jel′ə), that cause movement when they whip around.

There are also protozoans that do not move on their own. Most of these protozoans are parasites. A parasite is an organism that lives in or on another organism. The organism on which it lives is the host. While some parasitic (par ə sit′ik) protozoans are harmless to their hosts, others are extremely harmful and may even be deadly.

Plantlike Protists

Plantlike protists are capable of producing their own food. Like plants, these protists contain chlorophyll. You learned that chlorophyll is the green chemical that helps plants capture energy from the Sun to make food.

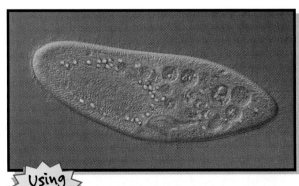

Using Math *The tiny cilia on a paramecium enable it to move and gather food. Its rate of movement is about 7 cm per minute. How far can a paramecium move in one hour?*

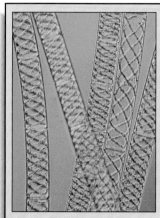
Spirogyra is a common freshwater alga.

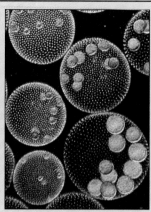
Volvox is a freshwater alga that lives in colonies.

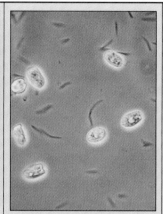
Chlorella is a freshwater alga with one large chloroplast.

Sargassum is an algal seaweed. It can cover miles of ocean surface.

Chlorophyll helps these plantlike protists make their own food and are also contained in chloroplasts.

Some plantlike protists are able to move on their own. The *Euglena*, for example, has a flagellum. The whiplike movement of the flagellum helps it to move around in its watery environment. It also has a light-sensitive eyespot that helps it locate the brightest areas in its surroundings. The *Euglena* is also animal-like because it can feed on other organisms when there is not enough light for it to make food.

Many plantlike protists are called **algae** (al'jē). If you've ever been to the beach, you've probably seen seaweed. But those plantlike strips aren't weeds at all—they're algae.

Most kinds of algae, such as the **diatoms** (dī'ə tämz) shown on this page, are single-celled. The most plentiful of all algae, diatoms are found in both fresh water and sea water. Like other algae, diatoms contain chlorophyll. In some diatoms the green color is hidden by yellow and brown chemicals. The cell walls of diatoms are tiny glasslike shells, resembling little boxes with lids. These

jewel-like organisms come in a variety of shapes and colors.

In addition to their beauty, diatoms are important to other organisms. A large part of ocean plankton is made of diatoms. **Plankton** includes all the tiny organisms that float freely near the surface of the ocean. It is plantlike plankton that forms the base of the ocean food chain. Tiny animals that live in the plankton feed on diatoms. Small fish also feed on them. In turn, larger fish feed on the small fish. Even some very large marine animals, such as baleen whales, have a diet that consists mainly of plankton!

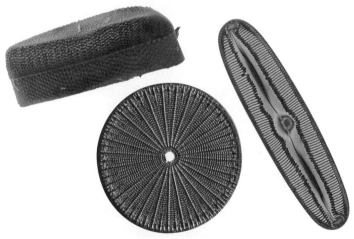

▲ **Diatoms are single-celled algae containing chlorophyll and rigid cell walls.**

Multicellular Protists

The most familiar kinds of multicellular protists are the algae commonly called seaweed. *Spirogyra*, which is observed in the activity on page A31, is a microscopic multicellular alga found in fresh water. Kelp, a multicellular saltwater alga, grows to be many meters long and is made up of millions of cells. If you've ever eaten food in a Japanese restaurant, you may have tasted kelp. Some kinds of algae are used to make products such as cosmetics, dog food, and ice cream.

Like plants, all algae contain chlorophyll. Some algae contain other chemicals in addition to chlorophyll. These chemicals may cause the algae to be a color other than green, such as brown, gold, or red. Algae are also like plants in another way—they have cell walls.

Multicellular algae play an important role in the life cycles of organisms on Earth. Freshwater and saltwater animals depend on them for food and shelter. And all animals depend on them for the oxygen they give off as they use the Sun's energy to make food. ■

Using Math

Kelp is a multicellular alga that can grow to more than 16 m in length. Is 16 m longer or shorter than the length of your classroom?

Science in Literature

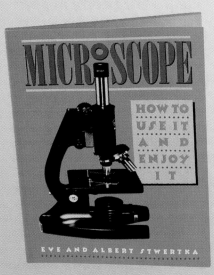

**Microscope:
How to Use It and Enjoy It**
by Eve and Albert Stwertka
Julian Messner, 1998

RECIPE FOR PROTOZOANS

"*Proto* means first and *zoa* means animals. . . . Nature has given their jellylike bodies many variations. With a bit of luck, you will see protozoa that are bullet-shaped, pointed, round as a ball, eel-shaped, slipper-shaped, or even trumpet-shaped."

Grow your own specimens! The book *Microscope: How to Use It and Enjoy It* by Eve and Albert Stwertka will give you the recipe. You'll be amazed to see all the different protozoans.

A35

Protozoan Diseases

Reading Focus How is the disease malaria caused by a protozoan?

Unlike the creature in the science-fiction movie *The Blob*, protozoans are not giant creatures that eat people. However, tiny protozoans can still be quite dangerous to people.

Some kinds of protozoans are parasites. They cause disease by invading the body of another living thing. When a disease-causing parasite settles in a host, the host is said to have an infectious disease. Some diseases caused by protozoans include amoebic dysentery (ə mē′bik dis′ən ter ē) and sleeping sickness.

A common and dangerous disease—malaria (mə ler′ē ə)—is caused by the protozoan *Plasmodium* (plaz mō′dē əm). The protozoan is carried by the *Anopheles* mosquito. When an infected mosquito bites someone, that person is infected with the parasite and will become ill with malaria. Refer to page A37 to learn about the life cycle of *Plasmodium* and how it causes malaria.

Controlling Malaria

Malaria is a widespread disease in parts of Africa, Asia, India, and South America. Every year millions of people in these areas are infected by the parasite.

Different methods are used to prevent the spread of the disease. The *Anopheles* mosquito is usually active at night. To avoid being bitten, some people in affected areas drape mosquito nets around their beds. Other people try to control the spread of malaria by draining swamps where the mosquitoes breed. Insecticides are also used to kill the mosquitoes. But none of these methods has wiped out the mosquitoes or the protozoan.

People with malaria can be treated with a variety of medicines. Though there are a number of different medicines to treat malaria, research is being done to find new ways to stop the disease's spread. Roll Back Malaria (RBM), a global project of the World Health Organization, is spearheading this research.

INVESTIGATE FURTHER!

RESEARCH

Consult library sources to read about sleeping sickness and amoebic dysentery, two diseases caused by protozoans. How are people infected? Where are these diseases most common? How can the diseases be prevented and treated?

Life Cycle of Plasmodium

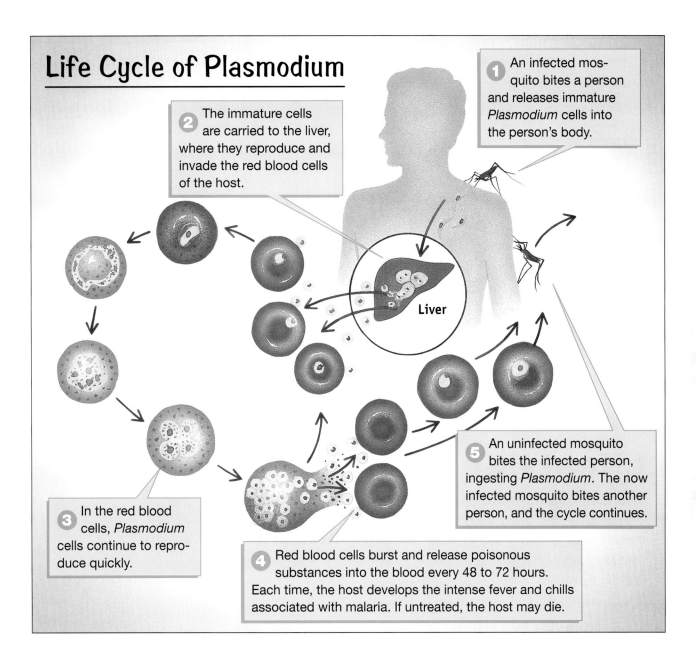

1 An infected mosquito bites a person and releases immature *Plasmodium* cells into the person's body.

2 The immature cells are carried to the liver, where they reproduce and invade the red blood cells of the host.

3 In the red blood cells, *Plasmodium* cells continue to reproduce quickly.

4 Red blood cells burst and release poisonous substances into the blood every 48 to 72 hours. Each time, the host develops the intense fever and chills associated with malaria. If untreated, the host may die.

5 An uninfected mosquito bites the infected person, ingesting *Plasmodium*. The now infected mosquito bites another person, and the cycle continues.

Liver

INVESTIGATION 1 WRAP-UP

THINK IT WRITE IT

REVIEW

1. Compare the structures of locomotion for an amoeba and a paramecium.

2. Explain how plantlike protists are similar to plants.

CRITICAL THINKING

3. Explain how algae play an important role in an underwater food chain.

4. The *Anopheles* mosquito usually bites after dark, from dusk to dawn. Discuss three preventive measures you would use to protect yourself from getting the disease.

INVESTIGATION 2

WHAT ARE FUNGI?

If somebody told you that you ate a fungus for lunch, you might make a face and say, "No way!" But if you ate a pizza with mushrooms on it, you did eat a fungus—a mushroom is a type of fungus. Find out more about fungi in this investigation.

Activity

Lifestyles of Fungi

You may have gobbled down the mushrooms on a pizza, but you had better stay away from molds on bread and fruit. These fungi can be extremely dangerous if eaten. In this activity you'll investigate bread molds.

Procedure

1. Use a spray bottle to moisten three pieces of bread. Expose the bread to the air for about half an hour. Put each piece of bread into a separate plastic bag that has been labeled *1*, *2*, or *3*. Seal the bag.

2. Predict what conditions are best for growing mold. **Test your prediction** by leaving the bags of bread in three different places for several days. Use a thermometer and a series of measurements over time to determine the average temperature at each location.

See **SCIENCE** *and* **MATH TOOLBOX** page H5 if you need to review *Finding an Average.*

MATERIALS

- goggles
- plastic gloves
- spray bottle filled with water
- 3 pieces of bread
- 3 sealable plastic bags
- marker
- thermometer
- hand lens
- tweezers
- microscope slide
- cover slip
- microscope
- *Science Notebook*

SAFETY

Wear goggles and gloves. To prevent allergic reactions, keep bags that may contain mold sealed when not in use. Wash your hands in warm soapy water after handling the bags.

Step 5

▲ Mold on bread

3. Use a hand lens to **observe** the slices of bread through the plastic bags. **Make a drawing** of your observations in your *Science Notebook*.

4. **Compare** your results with those of your classmates.

5. Use tweezers to remove a small piece of mold from the bread. Reseal the bag. Place a small piece of mold on a slide. Place a cover slip over the mold. **Observe** the mold under low power with the microscope and then under high power. **Make drawings** of your observations. Follow your teacher's instructions to properly dispose of the moldy bread.

Analyze and Conclude

1. **Describe** what happened to the bread in each sealed bag after a few days. From your observations of the bags, what do you **conclude** about the growing conditions needed by bread mold?

2. **Infer** where mold comes from and how mold obtains its food. **Tell what evidence** in the bags and under the microscope supports your inferences.

UNIT PROJECT LINK

With your group, choose a specific fungus or protist that you learned about earlier and build a model for your micromenagerie. Use a variety of materials to model the fungus or protist. Brainstorm with your group how your model can be displayed. Then decide how many times larger your model is than the actual fungus or protist.

TechnologyLink

For more help with your Unit Project, go to **www.eduplace.com**.

Yeasts, Bread, and Fuels

STS
SCIENCE TECHNOLOGY & SOCIETY

The bread you see in the picture has something in common with what may be the car of the future. Each uses a product made from yeast.

Yeasts are single-celled fungi. During the process of fermentation, yeasts feed on sugars and break them down, producing carbon dioxide and a kind of alcohol called **ethanol** (eth'ə nôl).

Ethanol is used in many different products, from drugs and industrial materials to food. The food industry uses ethanol to make products such as olives, pickles, dairy products, and flavorings. It is also used in antifreeze, colognes, mouthwashes, detergents, and as a raw material for certain manufacturing processes. In addition, the alcohol in wine and beer is produced when sugars found in fruits and grains are fermented.

Scientists are currently working with different plant products that can be fermented to produce ethanol. Corn, wheat, wood chips, and grass clippings can be treated with chemicals and placed in fermentation vats. The yeast ferments the sugars in the plant products, producing ethanol. The ethanol is then mixed with other chemicals to produce a fuel that can be used in motor vehicles.

Why make fuel from ethanol? Unlike other fuel sources, ethanol is made from products that are renewable or have been discarded as wastes. Wood chips created when hardwood is cut for lumber are used in ethanol production. Corn plants left in the field after harvesting are also used to make ethanol. In both cases, new plants can be grown to replace the old.

Ethanol, like other fuels, releases carbon dioxide during combustion. Some of this carbon dioxide is used by growing plants. These plants can be used to produce more ethanol fuel. ■

◄ **The gas that is produced as a byproduct of yeast fermentation causes bread dough to rise.**

Fungi— Good and Bad

Reading Focus How are fungi both harmful and helpful?

▲ Mold may be seen on old bread or vegetables. The mold digests the bread or vegetable by releasing a chemical that breaks down organic matter.

A quick trip through your refrigerator and kitchen cupboard would probably lead to the discovery of several members of the fungi kingdom. Canned mushrooms, mold growing on old bread and vegetables, and packets of yeast used for baking are all types of fungi.

A mushroom may look like a plant, but mushrooms and other fungi are not plants. **Fungi** are organisms that live on the remains of dead organisms. Fungi do not have chlorophyll and cannot make their own food by photosynthesis. Although most are multicellular, some fungi, such as yeasts, are single-celled organisms.

Making More Fungi

One way that most fungi reproduce is by releasing spores. **Spores** are reproductive cells that develop into new organisms. The spores of fungi are carried in special sacs called spore cases.

One common type of mold, *Rhizopus* (rī′zō pəs), grows on bread. Spores in the air fall on the bread. The mold grows by spreading out over the surface of the bread. As the mold spreads, short extensions called rhizoids (rī′zoidz) grow from it and penetrate the bread. The rhizoids anchor the mold to the bread. They also produce digestive fluids and absorb nutrients. The activity on pages A38 and A39 investigates bread molds.

The Roles of Fungi

Most fungi attach to and grow on organic matter. As they feed, fungi break

down this matter and return some nutrients to the soil. Without this process, Earth would soon become buried under mountains of dead waste material! Organisms that live on dead or decaying matter, such as molds, mildews, yeasts, and mushrooms, are called **saprophytes** (sap′rə fīts).

Fungi can also be parasitic. Rusts, smuts, and powdery mildews, for example, are fungi that cause great damage to crops. Cereal and vegetable crops can

▲ *Penicillium*, which can grow on fruit, is the source of the antibiotic penicillin.

be easily infected by rusts and smuts. Apples, roses, and grapes are likely to be infected by powdery mildew. Often, the only way to control the fungus is to destroy the infected plants.

Some fungi, like certain molds, produce important substances. For example, the medicine penicillin is made from a group of molds called *Penicillium* (pen i-sil′ē əm). Discovered in 1928 by Sir Alexander Fleming, penicillin has been used to save millions of lives. Other fungi, like yeasts, are used to make foods such as bread. What other uses for fungi can you think of? ■

▲ Some fungi, like the corn smut shown, are parasites that get food from other living organisms.

Internet Field Trip

Visit **www.eduplace.com** to find out what types of fungi are edible.

INVESTIGATION 2 WRAP-UP

REVIEW

1. How does fermentation produce ethanol?

2. How are fungi both harmful and helpful?

CRITICAL THINKING

3. Why don't fungi require light in order to survive?

4. What is the best way to store food to prevent fungi from growing?

REFLECT & EVALUATE

Word Power

Write the letter of the term that best completes each sentence. *Not all terms will be used*.

a. algae
b. diatom
c. ethanol
d. fermentation
e. fungi
f. multicellular
g. protist
h. protozoan
i. saprophyte

1. A single-celled type of alga with a glasslike shell is a ____.
2. A plantlike or an animal-like organism that belongs to the large group of mostly single-celled microscopic organisms is called a ____.
3. Mushrooms, molds, and yeasts are types of ____.
4. Organisms that are made up of more than one cell are referred to as ____.
5. The process of breaking down sugars to produce carbon dioxide and a kind of alcohol is called ____.
6. An animal-like protist, such as an amoeba, is a ____.

Check What You Know

Write the term in each pair that best completes each sentence.

1. Fermentation of plant products produces (sugar, ethanol).
2. The tiny organisms that float near the surface of the ocean are called (plankton, fungi).
3. An amoeba moves and captures food by using (cilia, pseudopods).
4. Like plants, plantlike protists have (rhizoids, chlorophyll).

Problem Solving

1. You notice the growth of mold and mildew along some wood paneling in your basement. How are the fungi getting energy? What steps could you take to get rid of them?

2. Some members of a camping trip have developed stomachaches. These same people drank water from a nearby pond. How might microscopic pond life have caused their illness?

Study the photo. Then explain if the protist is more like an animal or a plant. Give reasons for your choice.

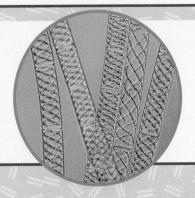

CHAPTER 3

BACTERIA AND VIRUSES

"Have you gotten your flu shot?" That's something you hear at the beginning of the flu season. How does a flu shot protect you against this disease? You'll learn the answer to this question as you explore bacteria and viruses.

● ●

PEOPLE USING SCIENCE

Research Biologist Dr. Flossie Wong-Staal is on a mission to stop the spread of the deadly AIDS disease and to successfully treat those who have already contracted it. In 1983 she was a codiscoverer of HIV, the virus that causes the disease. In 1985 she cloned the virus so that its structure could be further studied. Her research led to the development of tests that are used to screen blood for HIV.

Dr. Wong-Staal grew up in China but came to the United States to study biology. Her work as a research biologist has earned her recognition as a leader in AIDS research. In 1990 she was selected as the top woman scientist by the Institute for Scientific Information.

In this chapter you will learn how viruses and bacteria cause disease. You'll also find out how some microbes can be helpful.

Coming Up

◀ Dr. Flossie Wong-Staal is a leading AIDS researcher.

A45

INVESTIGATION 1

WHAT ARE BACTERIA AND VIRUSES?

You may not realize it, but you are surrounded by millions of organisms that you cannot see. In fact, these one-celled organisms, called bacteria, live just about everywhere—even in and on you. You'll find out about bacteria in this investigation.

Activity

Classifying Bacteria

Bacteria may be everywhere, but they are too small to see with the unaided eye. In this activity you'll examine several different types of bacteria in photographs taken through a microscope.

MATERIALS
• Science Notebook

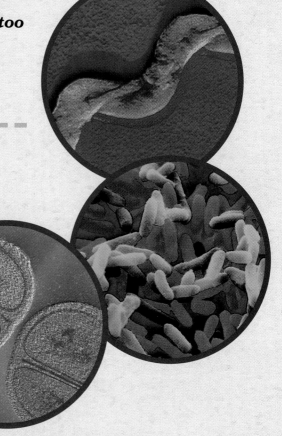

Procedure

1. The photographs on these two pages show some different kinds of bacteria. **Study** each photo and **record** your observations in your *Science Notebook*.

2. Working with your group, use your observations to classify the types of bacteria that you see. Give reasons for your system of classification.

How would you classify the bacteria on these pages?

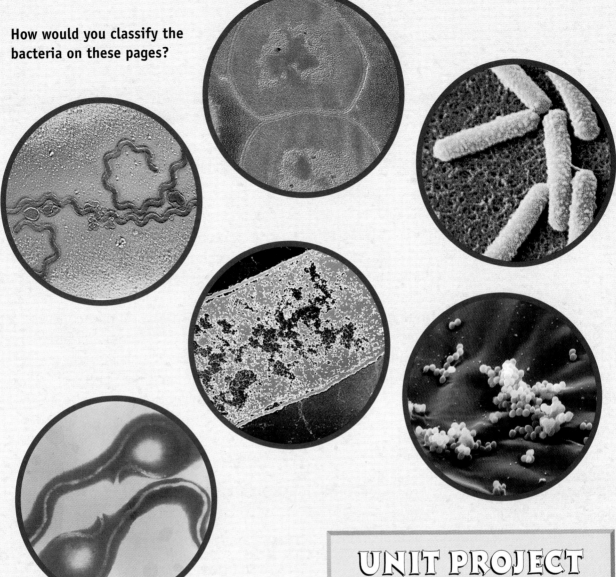

Analyze and Conclude

1. Compare your system of classification with that of another group. How do the two systems compare? **Discuss** any changes you may want to make in your classification system with the members of your group.

2. Biologists classify bacteria according to shape. Generally, bacteria have one of these shapes: rod-shaped (bacillus), spherical (coccus), and spiral (spirillum). How does your classification system compare with that of biologists?

UNIT PROJECT LINK

Rod-shaped and spherical bacteria can form clumps or chains. Research one of these types of bacteria in a biology text. Work with classmates to create a model of a bacterium for your micromenagerie. Use a variety of materials, such as modeling clay, construction paper, plastic foam, toothpicks, beads, wire, and tape.

TechnologyLink

For more help with your Unit Project, go to **www.eduplace.com**.

Bacteria and Viruses

Reading Focus What are some characteristics of monerans and viruses?

There are millions of kinds of organisms living on Earth. Most of those familiar to you are classified into the plant kingdom or the animal kingdom. You've also learned about organisms in two other kingdoms, the protists and the fungi. But Earth is home to another kingdom of creatures—the kingdom Monera.

The Moneran Kingdom

A **moneran** (mə nir'ən) is a one-celled organism that lacks a nucleus. Monerans are among the smallest and simplest organisms in the world. They exist everywhere that life can be found, from the ocean depths to the tops of mountains.

A moneran cell has features similar to the plant and animal cells you studied in Chapter 1. These features include cytoplasm, a cell wall, a cell membrane, and chromosomes. A major difference is that a moneran cell lacks a nucleus. It also differs because its cell wall is made of a material different from that of a cell wall found in plant cells. Some monerans have a covering that helps protect the cell.

Most monerans thrive in moist, dark, and warm conditions. The ideal temperature range for many monerans is between 25°C and 40°C. But some monerans are able to grow in very high temperatures and others in very low temperatures.

Bacteria are classified by shape: rod-shaped, spherical, and spiral. Identify each shape below. ▼

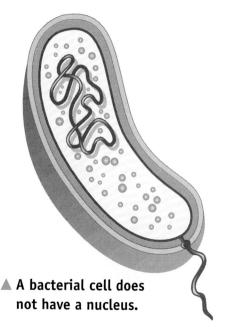

▲ A bacterial cell does not have a nucleus.

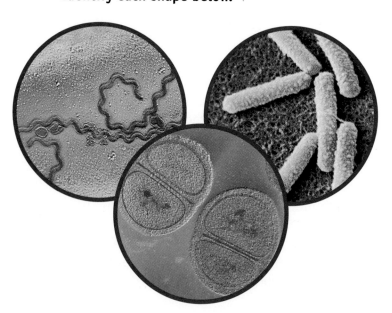

A microscope might reveal the pond scum (*above*) to be *Oscillatoria* (*inset*), a blue-green bacteria.

Many types of monerans cannot move on their own. These cells get transported through the air, on clothing, and in water currents. Other types of monerans have flagella, the threadlike tail that some protozoans use for movement.

Kinds of Monerans

There are more than 10,000 kinds of monerans. Scientists divide monerans into two large groups, the bacteria and the blue-green bacteria.

Bacteria are monerans that feed on dead organic matter and on living things. They occur in water, soil, and air, as well as on and in the bodies of other organisms. Most live as single cells, but they may join into pairs, chains, or clusters.

Scientists classify bacteria into three groups according to shape. These groups are bacillus (rod-shaped), coccus (spherical), and spirillum (spiral). Bacteria are classified on the basis of shape in the activity on pages A46 and A47.

Blue-green bacteria are monerans that contain chlorophyll. Like plants, they carry out photosynthesis and make their own food. Blue-green bacteria live in a variety of places—in salt water, in fresh water, and on land. Some live in the very hot water of natural springs. Others grow on snow in the Arctic and Antarctic.

Reproduction in Monerans

Monerans reproduce through fission. Recall that fission produces two identical cells from the parent cell. First, the genetic material in the cytoplasm of the cell duplicates itself. Then the cell wall pinches inward and divides the cell, forming two new cells. Each new bacterial cell has received its own copy of the genetic material of the parent cell.

Under ideal conditions, bacteria can reproduce every 20 minutes. At that rate, in 24 hours a single bacterium could produce a mass of cells equal to 2 million kg (4.4 million lb). Fortunately, this could never happen because the environment would not be able to provide enough nutrients for this great a mass of bacteria.

Viruses: Alive or Not Alive?

Smaller even than monerans are viruses. If you were to use a very powerful microscope to examine these microbes, you wouldn't see anything that you could recognize as an organism. What you would find is that some viruses are shaped like a cube, some are round, some are tube-shaped, and still others appear to have geometric shapes.

Not only do viruses have unusual shapes, they also have some unusual characteristics. Unlike bacteria, a virus doesn't have a cell wall, a cell membrane, or cytoplasm. In fact, a virus isn't a cell at all! A **virus** is a tiny fragment of genetic material wrapped inside a capsule, or coating, of protein.

For years, scientists have debated whether viruses are alive or not. A virus can reproduce itself, but only within a cell

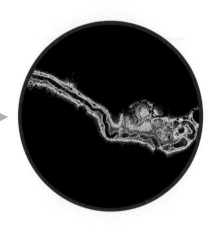

This virus causes one kind of flu! ▶

of a host organism. Although a virus contains genes, it cannot obtain or use energy on its own. So viruses seem to fall between the living world and the nonliving world. They are not organisms, but they have some characteristics of organisms.

Viruses are active only within the cells of living things. It is this ability to reproduce within cells that makes them dangerous. Many diseases, including the flu, polio, and AIDS, are caused by viruses.

Science in Literature

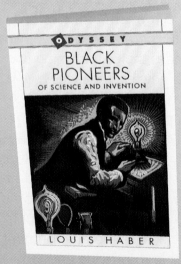

Black Pioneers of Science and Invention
by Louis Haber
Harcourt Brace, 1970

HE DARED TO OPERATE

"Dr. Dan worked swiftly. He opened the chest cavity. . . . He decided that the heart muscle did not need any suturing (sewing up), but he did suture the pericardium. . . . It was a daring operation. . . . Would the dread infection set in and kill the patient?"

During a time when antibiotics were unheard of and patients died of infection, Dr. Daniel Hale Williams dared to perform open heart surgery. Read about the incredible career of Dr. Williams and other African American scientists in *Black Pioneers of Science and Invention* by Louis Haber.

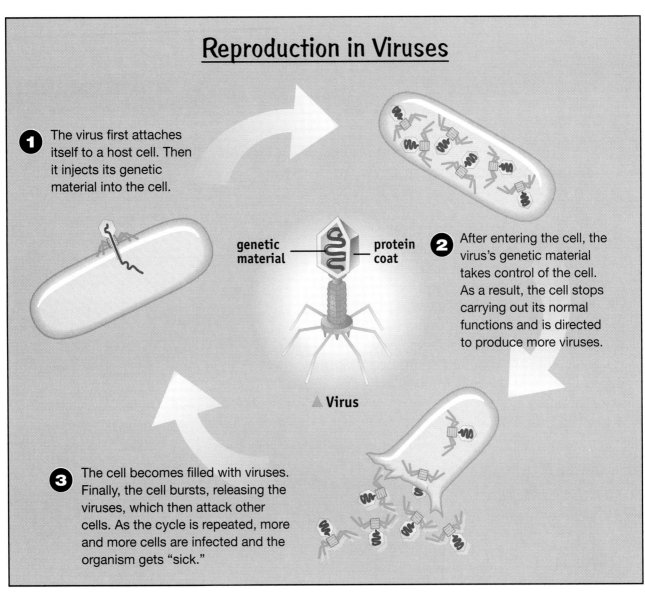

Reproduction in Viruses

1 The virus first attaches itself to a host cell. Then it injects its genetic material into the cell.

genetic material — protein coat

▲ **Virus**

2 After entering the cell, the virus's genetic material takes control of the cell. As a result, the cell stops carrying out its normal functions and is directed to produce more viruses.

3 The cell becomes filled with viruses. Finally, the cell bursts, releasing the viruses, which then attack other cells. As the cycle is repeated, more and more cells are infected and the organism gets "sick."

A virus takes control of the normal functions of the cell it infects, damaging and even destroying the cell. The diagram above explains this process.

A virus attacks only a specific type of cell. For example, the virus that causes the disease rabies infects only the nerve cells of mammals. If a turtle comes in contact with the rabies virus, the turtle will not be affected by the virus. If a dog comes in contact with the virus, the dog will not be infected unless the virus finds a way to the dog's nerve cells. Then the dog will become ill with rabies. ■

This virus infects alfalfa plants. ▶

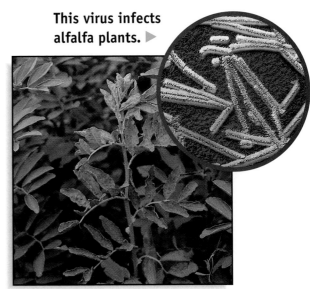

Microbe Discoverers

Reading Focus What advances have been made in the fight against diseases caused by microbes?

Some kinds of bacteria and viruses are harmful to humans and other animals. For this reason, scientists often focus on these kinds of microbes when looking for causes of diseases. When trying to find cures for diseases, scientists also study how these microbes react to different substances. Here are just a few of the important discoveries scientists have made over time.

Carlos Finlay, Cuba
Finlay correctly hypothesizes that the virus that causes yellow fever is transmitted by mosquitoes.

1881

Louis Pasteur, France
Pasteur suggests that bacteria can cause disease. He invents pasteurization, a process that uses heat to kill bacteria in milk.

1867

Edward Jenner, England
Jenner discovers that injecting people with the cowpox virus prevents them from getting the disease smallpox.

1796

1880s
Daniel Hale Williams, United States
Williams, using the discoveries of Pasteur and Lister, performs the first surgeries under sterile conditions. His methods result in fewer bacterial infections and a high survival rate.

1857
Joseph Lister, England
Lister shows that infections in open wounds come from bacteria. He develops sterilization techniques.

**Robert Gallo,
United States, and
Luc Montagnier,
France**
Gallo and Montagnier
identify the virus HIV,
which causes AIDS.

1983

**Jane Wright,
United States**
Wright becomes
a pioneer in cancer
research. She supports
the theory that some
cancers are caused by
a virus or viruses.

1945

**1997
Julia Hurwitz and
Karen Slobod,
United States**
Hurwitz and Slobod
begin extensive testing of
a possible AIDS vaccine.

1954

Jonas Salk, United States
Salk develops a vaccine for
polio, a viral disease that can
cause paralysis.

1928

**Sir Alexander
Fleming, England**
Fleming shows that
penicillin, an antibiotic,
can be used to treat
bacterial diseases.

INVESTIGATION 1 WRAP-UP

REVIEW

1. Name and compare the two groups of monerans.

2. Describe how viruses affect living things.

**CRITICAL
THINKING**

3. A person looks at a cell through a microscope and
thinks it's a plant cell. You identify it as a bacterial
cell. Explain the features of the cell that allow you to
draw your conclusion.

4. Explain how the reproduction of a bacterium
differs from the reproduction of a virus.

INVESTIGATION 2

HOW DO BACTERIA AND VIRUSES AFFECT OTHER LIVING THINGS?

You've probably had a cold. But have you ever had chickenpox or pneumonia? These and other illnesses are caused by viruses or bacteria. In this investigation you'll find out how bacteria and viruses affect people and other living things.

Activity

Warm Milk

Young people are advised to drink milk for good health. But the sugars and other nutrients in milk can also help bacteria to grow and reproduce. What evidence can you find that bacteria are numerous in a sample of milk?

MATERIALS
- goggles
- measuring cup
- milk
- 2 plastic soda bottles (1 L) with caps
- *Science Notebook*

SAFETY //////
Wear goggles. Do not drink the milk.

Procedure

1. Pour 250 mL of milk into each of two soda bottles. Tightly seal each bottle with its bottle cap.

See **SCIENCE** *and* **MATH TOOLBOX** page H7 if you need to review *Measuring Volume.*

2. **Predict** what will happen to the milk in each bottle if one is kept in the refrigerator and the other is kept at room temperature for two days. **Record** your prediction in your *Science Notebook.*

Step 1

3. Place one bottle in a refrigerator and keep the other bottle at room temperature.

4. After two days, **observe** the milk in each bottle. **Record** any difference you see between the milk in the two bottles.

5. Follow your teacher's instructions for observing the smell of the milk in each bottle. **Compare** the smell of the milk in each bottle. **Record** your observations.

Analyze and Conclude

1. Describe any differences that you observed between the two samples of milk. **Compare** your prediction with your observations.

2. Hypothesize the causes of any changes you observed in either sample of milk.

3. What do you think prevented the milk in the other bottle from undergoing the same changes?

4. Infer what might happen if an animal consumed the milk that was kept at room temperature.

INVESTIGATE FURTHER!

EXPERIMENT

Make yogurt. Slowly heat one quart of milk but do not let it boil. Stir in a packet of freeze-dried bacteria culture. Pour the mixture into a wide-mouthed thermos that has just been warmed and cover it. Let the mixture sit in the thermos, without disturbing it, for 5 to 10 hours. Then chill the thickened yogurt in the refrigerator for at least 12 hours. How do you think the bacteria you added to the milk caused the changes you observed?

AIDS—
Searching for a Cure

Reading Focus What are two ways scientists are trying to fight AIDS?

SCIENCE
TECHNOLOGY
& SOCIETY

The letters in AIDS stand for **A**cquired **I**mmune **D**eficiency **S**yndrome. Everyone has an immune system to protect the body from disease. Most of the time the body's immune system works so well that invading bacteria and viruses are destroyed before they can make a person sick.

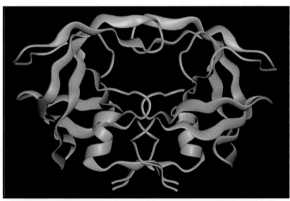

▲ This image shows a protein, called protease, that HIV uses to reproduce.

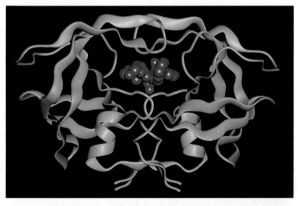

▲ A protease inhibitor (the colored spheres) is a medicine that doctors use to prevent the virus from reproducing.

However, if a person has a weak immune system, he or she can get sick very easily. Infections and diseases that the immune system normally would fight can be very harmful and even deadly.

HIV, human immunodeficiency virus, is the virus that causes AIDS. If it infects a person, it may attack the immune system by destroying the disease-fighting white blood cells. This action weakens the body's defenses against infection. As a result, the person can easily get sick from many infections.

HIV can sometimes live in someone's cells for years before it begins to destroy the immune system. It also tends to evolve, or change, very quickly. This makes it difficult to find a cure or a vaccine for AIDS.

Currently, HIV is treated with a combination of medicines. These medicines help prevent the virus from reproducing in body cells. However, this treatment does not help every HIV-infected person. Another approach being investigated is to insert HIV genetic material into another virus. The altered virus would then be injected into a host who is not HIV-infected. The host would develop an immunity to both the virus in which HIV genetic material was placed and to HIV itself. These are some of the ways scientists are working to find a cure for AIDS or a vaccine against the disease. ■

Helpful Bacteria

Reading Focus In what ways are bacteria helpful?

The activity on pages A54 and A55 demonstrates how bacteria can multiply in milk and cause it to spoil. You've learned about the harm some bacteria can do by causing diseases. However, most kinds of bacteria are harmless.

Bacteria on the Job

Some kinds of bacteria are even helpful. For example, bacteria are used in the production of some foods. Examples include cheese, pickles, butter, yogurt, sour cream, and chocolate. Think about it. Without bacteria, pizza would not be possible! Some bacteria are beneficial when they are in the human body. They help digest food, and they help the body produce certain vitamins.

Humans obtain many health benefits from the action of bacteria. Some bacteria are used to fight diseases. For example, bacteria are used to produce antibiotics. Bacteria are also used to produce insulin (in'se lin). Insulin is a protein that is usually produced by the body. Insulin helps control the rate at which the body breaks down sugar. People who do not produce enough insulin have a disease called diabetes (dī'ə bētēz). People with this disease can be treated with insulin that is produced by bacteria.

Helping Other Organisms

A close relationship between two organisms that helps at least one of them to survive is called symbiosis (sim bī-ō'sis). Many grazing animals, such as cows and sheep, have a symbiotic relationship with certain kinds of bacteria. These animals depend on bacteria in their intestines so that they can digest

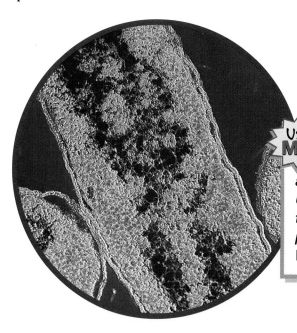

Using Math E. coli *bacteria (left) can cause severe food poisoning and death. There are* about 20,400 cases of E. coli *infections in the United States annually. If the population in the United States is 270 million, what percentage of the population is infected by* E. coli *each year?*

A59

plant materials that they eat. The bacteria also benefit because they obtain energy as they break down the plant matter.

Nature's Cleanup Crew

Every autumn, millions of leaves fall from trees. Over a ton of leaves may fall in just a small portion of a forest. Some kinds of bacteria help break down these dead leaves as well as other dead plant and animal materials. In the process these bacteria are returning nutrients to the soil. They are making nutrients available to plants growing in that soil.

Imagine what the world would be like if bacteria did not break down dead plants and animals. Land and water would quickly become polluted with these materials. And the nutrients in these once-living materials would not be available for reuse.

Because bacteria break down materials, they are sometimes used in sewage treatment plants to break down wastes. Bacteria may even be used to break down the oil in oil spills. You can see that bacteria can be helpful in many different ways. ■

Trees are constantly absorbing nutrients from the soil. When a tree dies and falls to the ground, bacteria in the soil help to break down the wood, returning nutrients to the soil for use by other plants. ▼

INVESTIGATION 2 WRAP-UP

REVIEW

1. How does a person's body fight bacterial and viral attacks? What type of medicine can be used to treat bacterial infections if the body's immune system is not successful?

2. Give two examples of ways in which bacteria are helpful.

CRITICAL THINKING

3. You visit the doctor because you have a bad cold. The doctor prescribes medicine for your symptoms but does not prescribe antibiotics. Why not?

4. Explain how a vaccine that contains the cowpox virus can prevent smallpox.

REFLECT & EVALUATE

Word Power

Write the letter of the term that best matches the definition. *Not all terms will be used.*

1. The body system that defends against disease
2. A tiny fragment of genetic material wrapped inside a capsule of protein
3. Chemical poison that is harmful to the body
4. Medicine that stops the growth and reproduction of bacteria
5. Monerans that feed on dead organic matter or on living things
6. Protein that can attach to bacterial cells or viruses to destroy them

a. antibiotic
b. antibody
c. bacteria
d. communicable disease
e. fission
f. immune system
g. toxin
h. vaccine
i. virus

Check What You Know

Write the word in each pair that correctly completes each sentence.

1. Monerans reproduce through a process called (mitosis, fission).
2. Monerans that contain chlorophyll are called (blue-green bacteria, viruses).
3. A cell wall but no nucleus are characteristics of (viruses, bacteria).
4. A vaccine can cause the body to produce (antibodies, antibiotics).

Problem Solving

1. Scientists have debated whether viruses should be considered a form of life. Compare viruses to other forms of matter. How do viruses resemble forms of life? How do they differ from most forms of life?

2. Describe several ways that bacteria help people because of their ability to break down substances.

BUILD YOUR PORTFOLIO

Copy the diagram. It shows a virus reproducing. Label the diagram. Then write a brief description of each step.

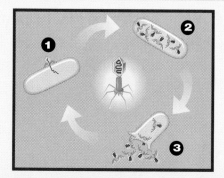

Using Reading Skills

Detecting the Sequence

Sequence is the order in which things happen. To keep track of the sequence, look for signal words such as *before, during, next,* and *later.* When a passage doesn't contain signal words, look for other clues, such as numbers in the text or numbered steps in a diagram.

Look for these clues to detect the sequence.

• Signal words: *before, during, next, later*

• Numbers in the text

• Numbered steps in a diagram

Read the following paragraphs. Then complete the exercises that follow.

Splitting in Two

When a cell divides, two new cells are formed. Most of the cells in living organisms divide by a process called mitosis. In **mitosis,** a cell divides into two exact copies of itself.

Before mitosis begins, the cell's chromosomes make copies of themselves. During mitosis the copies are pulled to opposite ends of the cell, and the cell splits in half. The two daughter cells, each with a complete set of chromosomes, now begin to grow.

1. **Which statement tells what happens first in the process of mitosis? Which tells what happens last? Write the letters of those statements.**

    a. Chromosomes are pulled to opposite ends of the cell.

    b. The cell's chromosomes make copies of themselves.

    c. The cell splits in half.

    d. Two daughter cells begin to grow.

2. **Write each clue that helped you keep track of the sequence.**

Using Math Analyze Data

Viruses exist in a variety of shapes and sizes. The lengths of common viruses, in nanometers, are shown in the chart. One nanometer (nm) is equal to one billionth of a meter.

Lengths of Viruses	
Virus	**Length (nm)**
Foot–and–mouth	10
Poliomyelitis	20
Yellow–fever	22
Bacteriophage	95
Influenza	100
Mumps	100
Smallpox	250

Use the data in the table to complete these exercises.

1. Which virus measures $\frac{1}{25}$ the length of a smallpox virus?

2. Which virus is 2.5 times the length of the influenza virus?

3. Find the range for the lengths of the viruses that are shown in the chart.

4. A mumps virus is about how many times as long as a yellow-fever virus? Explain.

5. How many foot-and-mouth viruses, laid end to end, equal the length of a mumps virus?

6. The ratio of which two virus lengths is 1:1?

7. Explain how you could estimate the number of bacteriophages, laid end to end, that can fit across the diameter of a coin.

WRAP-UP!

On your own, use scientific methods to investigate a question about cells and microbes.

THINK LIKE A SCIENTIST

Ask a Question

Pose a question about fungi, such as yeast, that you would like to investigate. For example, ask, "How does temperature affect the rate at which yeast carries out fermentation?"

Make a Hypothesis

Suggest a hypothesis that is a possible answer to the question. One hypothesis is that the rate of fermentation of yeast increases as temperature increases.

Plan and Do a Test

Plan a controlled experiment to test the effect of different temperatures on the rate of fermentation of yeast. You could start with a package of yeast, containers of water at different temperatures, thermometers, sugar, and a spoon. Read the directions on the yeast package. Then develop a procedure that uses the materials to test the hypothesis. With permission, carry out your experiment. Follow the safety guidelines on pages S14–S15.

Record and Analyze

Observe carefully and record your data accurately. Make repeated observations.

Draw Conclusions

Look for evidence to support the hypothesis or to show that it is false. Draw conclusions about the hypothesis. Repeat the experiment to verify the results.

WRITING IN SCIENCE
Outline

A useful way to record information is to make an outline. Outline the information in Chapter 3, "Bacteria and Viruses." Use these guidelines to write your outline.

- Decide on a title and the main heads for your outline.
- Use Roman numerals (I, II, III) for the main heads.
- Use capital letters (A, B) for the details under each main head.
- Include at least two subheads for each main head.

UNIT B

The Changing Earth

Theme: Models

THINK LIKE A SCIENTIST

GIANT PUZZLE PIECES

The colorful world map shown on these pages was produced by a computer. And although the bright colors are a bit unusual, you can easily tell that the illustration is a map of the world. That's because you're familiar with the shapes and relative sizes and positions of the continents and other land areas. But do you think you'd recognize the world if the continents were all grouped together as a single, giant landmass? Probably not. But that's how most earth scientists think the world looked hundreds of millions of years ago. To these scientists, the continents are pieces of a giant jigsaw puzzle.

THINK LIKE A SCIENTIST

Questioning In this unit you'll learn about why scientists think the continents are moving and where the energy comes from to make them move. You'll investigate questions such as these.

- Do Continents Really Drift About?
- What Do the Locations of Earthquakes and Volcanoes Tell Us?

Observing, Testing, Hypothesizing In the Activity "The Great Puzzle," you'll observe outlines of the present-day continents in a random arrangement. Then you'll use the outlines to reconstruct an ancient landmass.

Researching In the Resource "Volcanoes and Plate Tectonics," you'll learn several ways to classify a volcano, including by the shape of its cone.

Drawing Conclusions After you've completed your investigations, you'll draw conclusions about what you've learned—and get new ideas.

CHAPTER 1

CRACKED CRUST

Beneath the oceans are the highest mountains and the deepest trenches on Earth. Here molten rock erupts along underwater mountain ranges. The eruptions are part of the constant change taking place on the ocean floor.

PEOPLE USING SCIENCE

Cartographer Imagine a world without maps. We use maps to find our way around a shopping mall, around town, or around the country. Anna M-M Hamann knows about maps. She is a cartographer (kär täg′rə fər), or mapmaker, for the National Imagery and Mapping Agency of the United States government.

Anna M-M Hamann was trained as a nautical cartographer. She specialized in creating contour maps of the sea floor. Today, Hamann prepares international agreements for the production of topographic maps of Central and South America.

Anna Hamann's first love was animals. Growing up in Puerto Rico, she wanted to be a veterinarian. Today her love of animals is as strong as ever. She is a volunteer guide at the National Zoological Park in Washington, D.C.

Coming Up

◀ Computers are a vital tool in Anna M-M Hamann's work as a cartographer.

DO CONTINENTS REALLY DRIFT ABOUT?

About 80 years ago, Alfred Wegener suggested that at one time all the continents were joined together in one large "supercontinent." Further, he suggested that the continents split apart and drifted to their current locations. Other scientists laughed at him. Could he have been right?

Activity

The Great Puzzle

Take a look at a map of the world. Notice that the continents seem to fit together like the pieces of a jigsaw puzzle. Can you reconstruct Wegener's supercontinent from today's continents?

MATERIALS
- scissors
- outline map of the continents
- sheet of paper
- glue
- map of the world
- *Science Notebook*

SAFETY
Handle scissors with care.

Procedure

1. Your teacher will give you an outline map of Earth's continents. Using scissors, cut out each of the continents along the dark outlines.

2. Arrange the continents on a sheet of paper so that they all fit together, forming one supercontinent.

3. After you have obtained your best fit, **make a map** by gluing the pieces onto the sheet of paper in the pattern that you obtained. Keep your map in your *Science Notebook*.

4. Using a map of the world, locate the name of each continent for your map. **Label** the continents.

Step 1

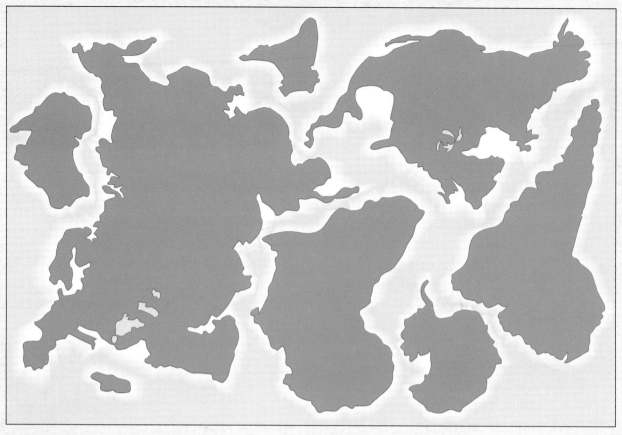

▲ Outline map of the continents

Analyze and Conclude

1. How well did the continents fit together to make a single supercontinent?

2. **Compare** the map that you made with one showing the present locations of the continents. What can you **infer** about Earth's continents if both maps are accurate?

3. In your reconstruction, what continents border the continent of North America?

4. What evidence, besides the shapes of the continents, might scientists look for to confirm Alfred Wegener's idea that continents were once joined in a supercontinent?

INVESTIGATE FURTHER!

RESEARCH

Look in a world atlas, such as *Goode's World Atlas*, to find a map that shows Earth's landforms. Use this information to explain why Wegener thought Earth's landmasses were once joined as a supercontinent.

Alfred Wegener and the Drifting Continents

Reading Focus What was Wegener's hypothesis about the movement of the continents?

The year was 1911. Nabisco introduced the Oreo cookie. Marie Curie won a Nobel Prize for isolating pure radium. The National Urban League was founded.

That same year, Alfred L. Wegener read a scientific paper that changed his life. The paper presented evidence that millions of years ago a land bridge may have connected South America with Africa. To Wegener the evidence suggested that the two continents were once a continuous landmass. From this he hypothesized that *all* of Earth's continents might once have been joined.

In 1912, Wegener gave a talk about his ideas on moving continents. He suggested that Earth's landmasses had once been joined and had since drifted apart. Most people in the scientific community thought Wegener's idea was ridiculous. Wegener still held on to his hypothesis.

In 1915, Wegener published a book explaining how Earth's continents and oceans might have formed and changed over time. His evidence came from many fields of science. Wegener noted that the continental shelves fit together like the pieces of a puzzle. A **continental shelf** is the part of a continent that extends under shallow water from the ocean's edge down to a steeper slope. He noted that the fossil remains of certain species

of plants and animals were found on widely separated continents. The plants and animals that left these fossil remains could not have crossed the oceans.

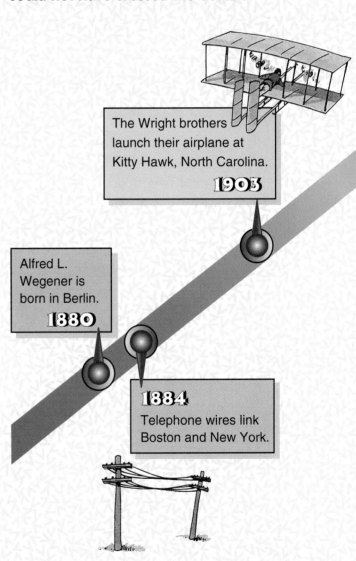

The Wright brothers launch their airplane at Kitty Hawk, North Carolina. **1903**

Alfred L. Wegener is born in Berlin. **1880**

1884 Telephone wires link Boston and New York.

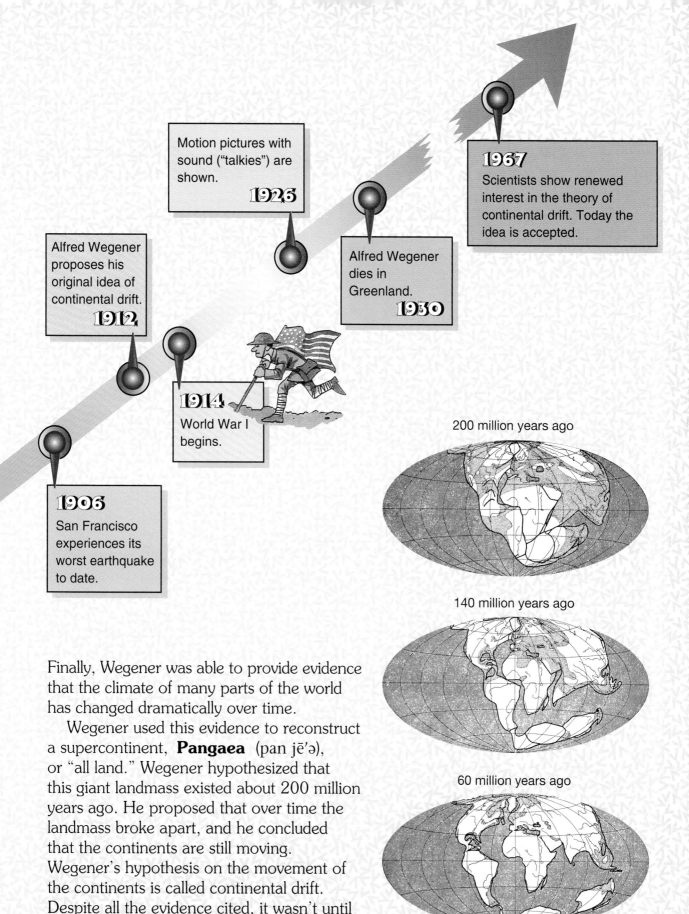

Motion pictures with sound ("talkies") are shown. **1926**

Alfred Wegener proposes his original idea of continental drift. **1912**

Alfred Wegener dies in Greenland. **1930**

1967 Scientists show renewed interest in the theory of continental drift. Today the idea is accepted.

1914 World War I begins.

1906 San Francisco experiences its worst earthquake to date.

200 million years ago

140 million years ago

60 million years ago

Finally, Wegener was able to provide evidence that the climate of many parts of the world has changed dramatically over time.

Wegener used this evidence to reconstruct a supercontinent, **Pangaea** (pan jē′ə), or "all land." Wegener hypothesized that this giant landmass existed about 200 million years ago. He proposed that over time the landmass broke apart, and he concluded that the continents are still moving. Wegener's hypothesis on the movement of the continents is called continental drift. Despite all the evidence cited, it wasn't until the 1960s that scientists took Wegener's hypothesis seriously. ■

▲ **Wegener's maps of drifting continents**

Evidence for Continental Drift

Reading Focus What evidence led Wegener to believe that Earth's continents used to be one landmass?

Alfred Wegener was a meteorologist— a scientist who studies weather. But he was interested in many fields of science. His **theory of continental drift** stated that the continents were once one landmass that had broken apart and moved to their present positions. This theory was supported by many pieces of evidence.

The Rock Record

In the activity on pages B6 and B7, the outlines of the continents seem to fit together like pieces of a jigsaw puzzle. This apparent fit was an important piece of evidence for Wegener's theory. He found that the continental shelves of Africa and South America fit together almost perfectly. In addition, many of the rocks that make up mountains in Argentina were identical to those found in South Africa. It seemed unlikely to Wegener that these identical rock layers were formed in such widely separated places at the same time.

By the time Wegener published the third edition of his book, he had discovered diamond-rich rocks in South Africa that were similar to rocks in Brazil. He also found that many of the coal beds in North America, Britain, and Belgium had been deposited in the same geological period. And a thick red sandstone layer crossed continental boundaries from North America to Greenland, Britain, and Norway. Look at the map shown below. What pieces of evidence can you name that support the theory of continental drift?

Using Math *Scientists think that South America and Africa were once joined. They estimate that the Atlantic Ocean formed at a rate of 2 cm to 4 cm a year for 200 million years. Estimate the width of the Atlantic Ocean today.*

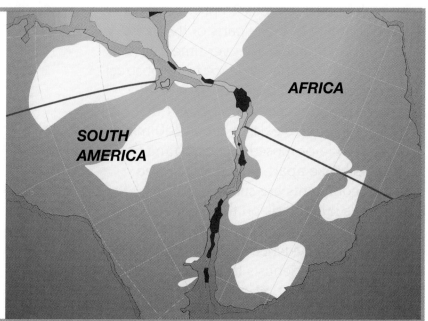

Areas of overlap

Continental shelf

Similar geologic formations

SOUTH AMERICA

AFRICA

The Fossil Record

Wegener also noted that certain fossils were preserved in rocks of the same age on different continents. He argued that the remains of these once-living organisms were so similar that they must have been left by the same kinds of organisms. One of these creatures was a small reptile called *Mesosaurus*, which had lived in fresh water. Other fossils found in rocks that were very far apart were those of the plant *Glossopteris*. Remains of the plant had been discovered in South America, Australia, Asia, and Africa. How, Wegener asked, could this plant have survived the different climates of these four landmasses?

Because of his training as a meteorologist, much of Wegener's evidence included information about climate. You probably already know that Earth can be divided into three major climate zones. The tropics are located near the equator and extend to about $23\frac{1}{2}°$ north and south of the equator. The temperate zones lie between the tropics and the polar zones. The polar climatic zones extend from about $66\frac{1}{2}°$ north and south to the poles.

Wegener noted that fossils of beech, maple, oak, poplar, ash, chestnut, and elm trees had been found on a small island named

◀ A variety of *Glossopteris*, a plant with fossil remains found in widely separated continents

Spitsbergen, near the North Pole. These trees generally grow only in temperate areas. Today, however, the island is covered for much of the year with snow and ice because it has a very cold climate —a polar climate.

Coal forms in swampy marshes that receive a lot of rain each year. Today coal beds are forming near the equator and in some temperate regions. Wegener proposed that coal beds in the eastern United States, Europe, and Siberia formed when the continents were joined and were located closer to the equator.

Another variety of *Glossopteris* ▽

Wegener used all of these different lines of evidence to reconstruct the supercontinent Pangaea. He hypothesized that this single landmass existed about 200 million years ago. Over time, he proposed, the landmass broke apart and the continents drifted to their present positions on Earth's surface. ■

◀ Fossil remains of this reptile, *Mesosaurus*, were found on widely separated continents.

Continents on the Move

Reading Focus How did Pangaea break apart, and in what direction did its pieces move?

Wegener's hypothesis stated that Pangaea began to break apart about 180 million years ago. The smaller pieces of land drifted to their present position as Earth's continents. Although Wegener's idea was at first criticized, today it is accepted by scientists.

The maps on the next four pages show how landmasses—later Earth's continents—moved over time. Arrows on the continents show the direction in which they moved. Compare the location of the continents millions of years ago with their present location.

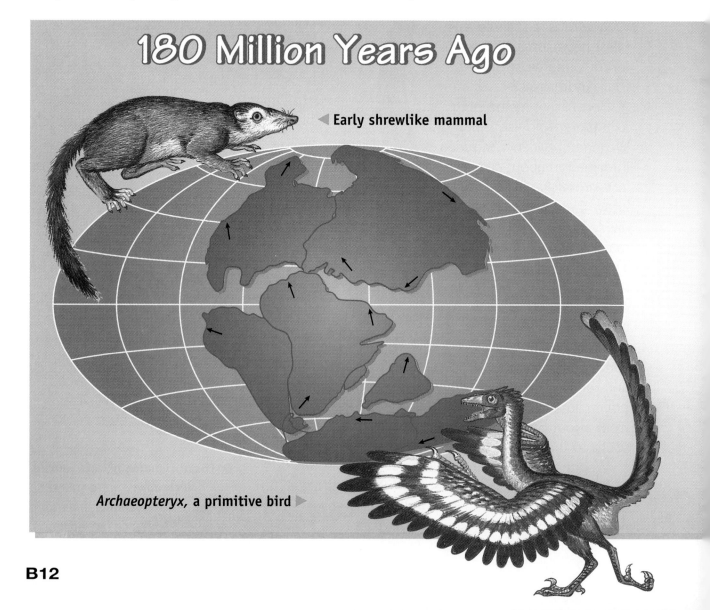

180 Million Years Ago

◀ Early shrewlike mammal

Archaeopteryx, a primitive bird ▶

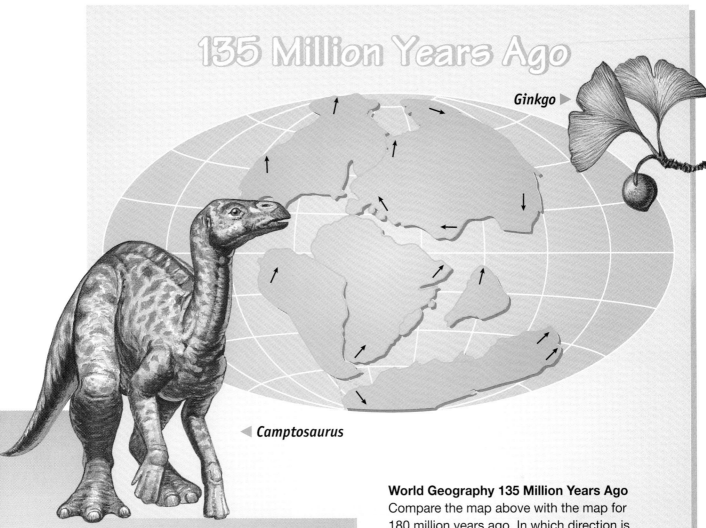

Ginkgo ▶

◀ *Camptosaurus*

World Geography 180 Million Years Ago
About 180 million years ago, North America, Europe, and much of Asia began to split from South America and Africa. India separated from the landmass around the South Pole and started moving northward. Australia and Antarctica drifted to the south and west. The Atlantic and Indian oceans began to form.

Life About 180 Million Years Ago
Green algae, corals, and sponges lived in the warm waters that covered much of Earth. Ammonites, which looked like giant snails, also inhabited Earth's oceans. Many amphibians, including ancestors of modern frogs, roamed the land. The first dinosaurs appeared on Earth. Somewhat later, *Archaeopteryx*, a birdlike animal, also lived on Earth. Conifers were the dominant plants.

World Geography 135 Million Years Ago
Compare the map above with the map for 180 million years ago. In which direction is North America moving? How does the location of India compare with that on the map for 180 million years ago? In which direction is Australia moving? What has happened to South America and Africa?

Life About 135 Million Years Ago
Sea urchins, sand dollars, and green algae populated the seas. Dinosaurs such as *Camptosaurus*, *Stegosaurus*, *Allosaurus*, and *Apatosaurus* roamed the land. Birds soared through the sky. Conifers, ferns, and ginkgoes made up the plant life on the planet.

65 Million Years Ago

World Geography 65 Million Years Ago

Although the map below shows Earth's landmasses 65 million years ago, it probably looks much more familiar to you than do the two maps on the previous pages. Describe how the locations of South America and Africa differ from their locations 135 million years ago. Describe the direction in which North America is moving. How far north has India moved as compared with its position 135 million years ago? Which two southern present-day continents are shown here still joined?

Life About 65 Million Years Ago

Fish, plankton, corals, and sponges were major forms of marine life. Insects were very abundant on land. These creatures pollinated the new flowering plants. *Ankylosaurus*, *Triceratops*, and *Tyrannosaurus* were some of the kinds of dinosaurs that lived at this time.

Ankylosaurus, a heavily plated dinosaur ▶

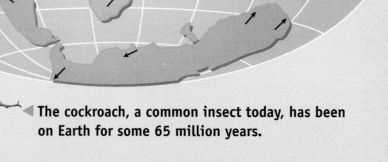

◀ The cockroach, a common insect today, has been on Earth for some 65 million years.

Today

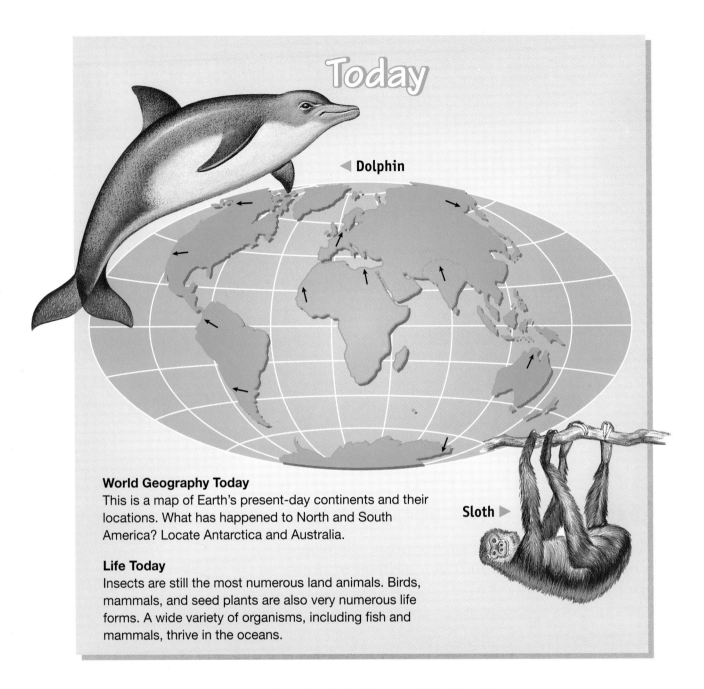

◄ **Dolphin**

Sloth ►

World Geography Today
This is a map of Earth's present-day continents and their locations. What has happened to North and South America? Locate Antarctica and Australia.

Life Today
Insects are still the most numerous land animals. Birds, mammals, and seed plants are also very numerous life forms. A wide variety of organisms, including fish and mammals, thrive in the oceans.

INVESTIGATION 1 WRAP-UP

REVIEW

1. What is Pangaea?

2. Describe some of the evidence Alfred Wegener used to show that the continents are moving.

CRITICAL THINKING

3. Evidence of glaciers has been found in southern Africa. What can you infer about where this continent may have been located in the past?

4. It is 1912 and you are Alfred Wegener. Write a short outline for your speech defining your ideas about moving continents.

INVESTIGATION 2

WHAT DO THE LOCATIONS OF VOLCANOES AND EARTHQUAKES TELL US?

Earthquakes and volcanoes make our world a bit shaky! Think of all the stories you have heard about earthquakes and volcanic eruptions. Can the locations of these events give us clues about continental drift?

Activity

Earth—Always Rockin' and Rollin'!

Did you ever wonder why earthquakes occur where they do? See if you can find any pattern in the locations of earthquakes.

How is Earth's crust like a cracked eggshell? ▼

Procedure

1. Study the earthquake map. Every dot on the map represents a place where a strong earthquake has occurred. Look for a pattern that the dots form. **Describe** this pattern in your *Science Notebook*. **Discuss** your observations with your team members.

2. On tracing paper, use your pencil to trace and then darken the pattern formed by the earthquake dots. Work with your team members to decide how to draw the pattern.

3. Think about the way a cracked eggshell looks. Earth's **crust**, which is its outermost, solid layer, is a lot like a cracked eggshell, broken up into large pieces. Look again at the pattern of the earthquake dots. How is the pattern of the dots like the cracks of an eggshell? **Record** your answer.

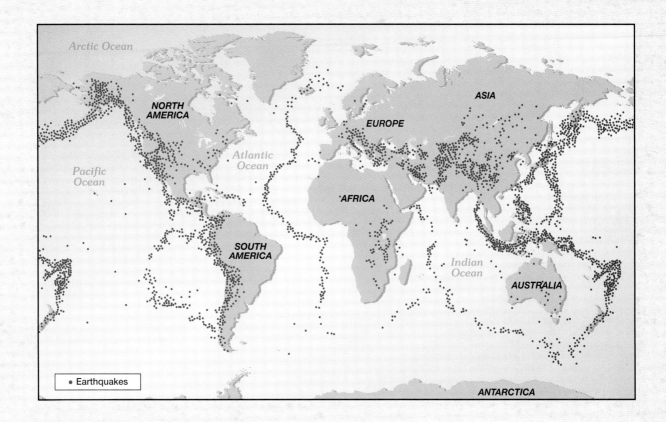

• Earthquakes

Analyze and Conclude

1. Earth's crust is broken into large pieces called **tectonic plates**. Use your tracing and the map to locate some of these tectonic plates.

2. Earthquakes occur mostly along cracks in Earth's crust. **Predict** some locations where earthquakes are likely to occur. **Record** your predictions.

UNIT PROJECT LINK

For this Unit Project you will collect data about earthquakes and volcanic activity around the world. Then you will place map pins on a classroom map to show where this activity is taking place. Start by creating a map that shows the tectonic plate on which your town is located and the surrounding tectonic plate(s). Place a map pin to show the location of your town. If possible, determine how far your town is from the edge of a plate. Predict how likely your town is to have an earthquake.

Technology Link

For more help with your Unit Project, go to **www.eduplace.com**.

Activity

Volcanoes and Earth's Plates

MATERIALS
- map of Earth's volcanoes
- map of Earth's earthquakes (page B17)
- *Science Notebook*

Earthquakes occur at the edges of huge slabs of crust and upper mantle called tectonic plates. Do volcanoes and earthquakes occur in the same places?

Arctic Ocean — Arctic Ocean

NORTH AMERICA

EUROPE

ASIA

Pacific Ocean

Atlantic Ocean

AFRICA

Pacific Ocean

SOUTH AMERICA

Indian Ocean

AUSTRALIA

▲ Volcanic Activity

ANTARCTICA

Procedure

Study the map of Earth's volcanoes and **compare** it with your map of Earth's earthquakes. In your *Science Notebook*, list the places where volcanoes occur.

Form a hypothesis about the locations of volcanoes, earthquakes, and the edges of Earth's tectonic plates. **Record** your hypothesis. **Discuss** your observations with your group.

Analyze and Conclude

1. Using the maps on pages B17 and B18, **describe** where both earthquakes and volcanoes occur.

2. How do the locations of earthquakes and volcanoes help identify Earth's tectonic plates?

Technology Link
CD-ROM

INVESTIGATE FURTHER!

Use the **Science Processor CD-ROM**, *The Changing Earth* (Investigation 1, Map It!) to map earthquakes and volcanoes. Predict where future earthquakes and volcanoes will occur.

The Cracked Crust: Tectonic Plates

> **Reading Focus** What are tectonic plates, and how do they help explain the drifting continents?

Sometimes you'll hear the expression "It's as solid as a rock." This expression means that whatever is referred to is permanent and dependable. We may like to think that rock is solid and permanent, but even large slabs of rock move. Actually, nothing on the surface of Earth is permanent. Even the continent of North America is moving very slowly. The slow movement of Earth's continents can be explained by the theory of plate tectonics.

Floating Plates

In the late 1960s, scientists expanded Alfred Wegener's idea of drifting continents and proposed the theory of plate tectonics. The word *tectonics* refers to the forces that cause the movement of Earth's rock formations and plates.

The **theory of plate tectonics** states that Earth's crust and upper mantle are broken into enormous slabs called plates or **tectonic plates**. (The **crust** is Earth's outermost, solid layer. The **mantle** is the layer of Earth between the crust and the core.) The plates are like enormous ships, and the continents are like their cargo. Scientists believe that currents in the plasticlike mantle cause the plates to move across Earth's surface. The currents are caused by differences in temperature in Earth's interior regions.

This theory has guided scientists in trying to figure out how Earth might have looked millions of years ago. Plate tectonics has helped them reconstruct the ways the continents might have moved over millions of years.

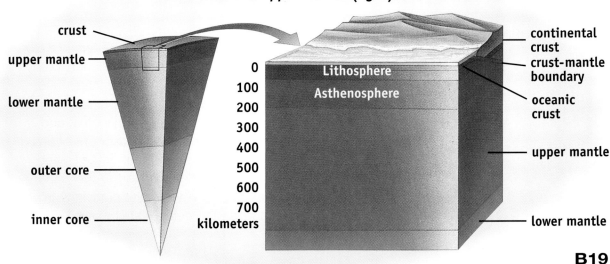

A wedge showing Earth's layers (*left*); a section of the crust and upper mantle (*right*).

B19

Makeup of the Plates

What do tectonic plates consist of? Each plate is formed of a thin layer of crust, which overlies a region called the upper mantle. In a plate that carries a continent, the crust can be 40 to 48 km (25 to 30 mi) thick. In a plate that is under an ocean, the crust may be only 5 to 8 km (3 to 5 mi) thick. The drawing below shows the makeup of part of two different tectonic plates.

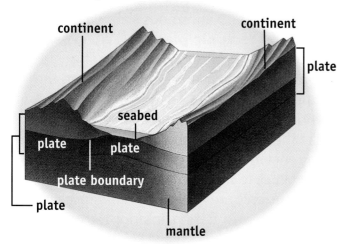

▲ Tectonic plates can carry a continent, an ocean, or both.

Interacting Plates

Plates can interact in three ways: (1) They can come together, (2) they can move apart, and (3) they can slide past one another. Places where plates interact are called **plate boundaries**. As you probably know by now, earthquakes and volcanoes occur along plate boundaries. In Chapter 2 you will find out much more about what happens along these boundaries. ■

Internet Field Trip

Visit **www.eduplace.com** to see an illustration of Earth's crust, mantle, and core.

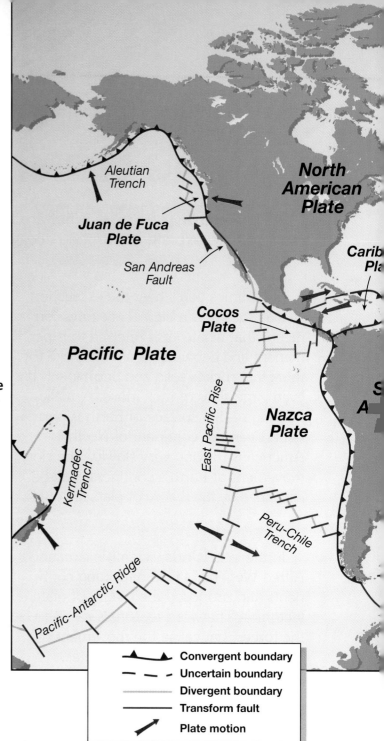

	Convergent boundary
	Uncertain boundary
	Divergent boundary
	Transform fault
	Plate motion

EARTH'S TECTONIC PLATES There are seven major plates and several minor ones. Many of the plates are named after the major land-masses that are parts of the plates. The plates act like ships that carry Earth's crust and upper mantle around on a layer of semisolid material. Observe that most of the United States is located on the North American Plate. In what direction is this plate moving? In what direction is the Pacific Plate moving?

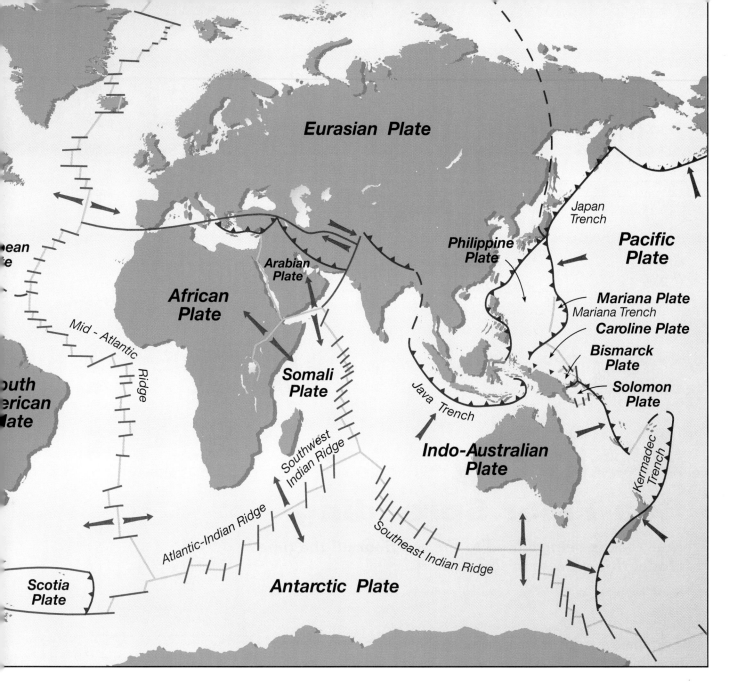

Eurasian Plate

Japan Trench

Pacific Plate

Philippine Plate

Mariana Plate
Mariana Trench
Caroline Plate
Bismarck Plate
Solomon Plate

Arabian Plate

African Plate

Somali Plate

Mid - Atlantic Ridge

ean te

uth erican late

Java Trench

Kermadec Trench

Indo-Australian Plate

Southwest Indian Ridge

Atlantic-Indian Ridge

Southeast Indian Ridge

Scotia Plate

Antarctic Plate

INVESTIGATION 2 WRAP-UP

REVIEW

1. Use the maps in this investigation to infer the connection between earthquakes, volcanoes, and plates.

2. What are the three ways that tectonic plates can interact?

CRITICAL THINKING

3. Suppose the Pacific Plate and the North American Plate continue moving in the directions they are now traveling. What might eventually happen to California's coastline?

4. Why is it unlikely that some of the tectonic plates will stop moving?

B21

INVESTIGATION 3

WHAT DOES THE SEA FLOOR TELL US ABOUT PLATE TECTONICS?

How do scientists know what the sea floor looks like? Is there evidence for plate tectonics hidden beneath the waters? Find out in this investigation.

Activity

Sea-Floor Spreading

New rock is being added to the sea floor all the time. Model this process in this activity.

MATERIALS
- sheet of paper with 3 slits, each 10 cm long
- 2 strips of notebook paper, each 9.5 × 27 cm long
- metric ruler
- scissors
- pencil
- *Science Notebook*

Procedure

Prepare a sheet of white paper as shown in the top drawing. Draw mountains along the sides. The middle slit represents a mid-ocean ridge, which is a very long crack in the ocean floor, with mountain ranges on either side.

Pull two strips of notebook paper up through the middle slit and down through the side slits, as shown. These strips represent magma that is flowing up through the ocean ridge and then hardening. As you pull the strips, you **model** a process called sea-floor spreading.

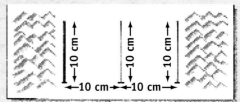

Analyze and Conclude

Consider that the magma coming up through the ridge is hardening into rock. What can you **infer** about the age of the rock along each side of the ridge? **Record** your ideas in your *Science Notebook*. Where on the sea floor do you think you would find the oldest rock?

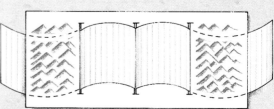

Activity
Mapping the Ocean Floor

MATERIALS
- clay
- shoebox
- pencil
- metric ruler
- tape
- plastic straw
- graph paper
- *Science Notebook*

As on dry land, mountains, valleys, and plains exist on the ocean floor. You can model these structures and then model a way to map the sea floor.

Procedure

1. Use clay to **model** some sea-floor structures on the bottom of a shoebox. Use a pencil to punch a line of holes about 3 cm apart down the center of the lid. Number the holes in sequence and tape the lid onto the box. Exchange boxes with another team.

2. Insert a straw into a hole until it hits the "ocean floor." Remove the straw and **measure** the part of the straw that was beneath the lid. This measurement represents the depth of the "ocean" at that hole. Repeat for each hole. **Record** the depths in your *Science Notebook*.

3. **Make a line graph** of your results. The vertical axis should be *below* the horizontal axis. Show depth on the vertical axis and distance on the horizontal axis.

See **SCIENCE** *and* **MATH TOOLBOX** page H6 if you need to review **Making a Line Graph.**

Step 2

Analyze and Conclude

1. What does the lid of the shoebox represent?

2. Remove the lid and **compare** your graph to the "ocean floor." Does your graph resemble the clay model?

B23

Sonar: Mapping the Sea Floor

Reading Focus How do scientists use sound to make a map of the ocean floor?

In the activity on page B23, a shoebox, clay, and straws are used as a crude model of sonar—a method for finding the shape and depth of the ocean floor. *Sonar* stands for "**so**und **na**vigation and **r**anging."

Listening for Echoes

British naval scientists first developed sonar in 1921. During World War II (1939–1945), sonar was used to detect enemy submarines. Scientists realized that sound could be used to measure the distance from a ship on the surface of the water to the bottom of the ocean.

A sonar device sends out a sound and then listens for an echo to return. By using sonar, scientists can measure the time between sending out a sound and receiving the echo of that sound. Then, by knowing this time and the speed at

which sound travels through sea water, they can compute the depth of the ocean at that point. In the activity "Mapping the Ocean Floor," a straw pushed through the holes in a shoebox lid represent sound impulses sent out from a sonar device.

Mapping by Sound

As a ship with sonar moves along the surface of the ocean, it sends out sound impulses. The impulses travel down through the sea water, strike the ocean

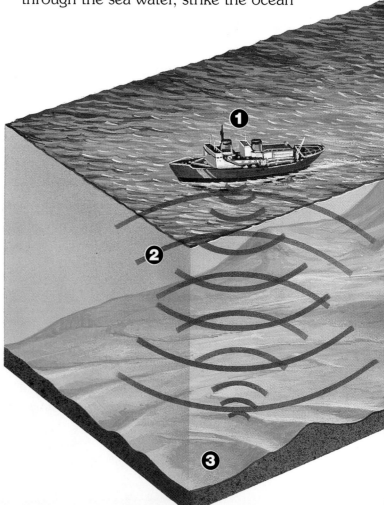

Mapping With Sonar

 1 Ship sends out sound impulses from sonar device. Impulses travel at a rate of 5,130 m/s.

 2 Returning echo of sound impulses

 3 Sea floor

 B24

floor, and then bounce back as an echo. Each echo arrives at a receiver back at the ship and is recorded on a recording chart. The sonar device records the length of time required for the impulse to travel to the ocean floor and for the echo to return to the ship. It then computes the depth of the ocean floor at that point, which is registered on a scale.

Suppose the total time for a sound to travel from the ship to the ocean floor and back is 6.60 s. Since sound travels through sea water at 1,530 m/s, the sound has traveled a total of 10,098 m. The distance from the ship to the ocean floor is half the total, or 5,049 m. By assembling all the measurements taken as the ship moves through the water,

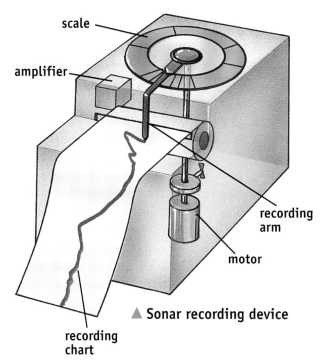

▲ **Sonar recording device**

scientists can produce a map of a section of the ocean floor. The more readings they take, the more accurate their map will be.

Sonar has allowed scientists to discover many new features of the ocean floor. For example, they have found some places that are over 10,600 m (6.3 mi) deep. That's over 10 km! They also have found undersea mountains higher than the highest mountain on the surface, Mount Everest, which is 8,848 m (29,198 ft) high!

Sonar can also be used on land. Sound pulses can be sent through the ground, and the returning echoes can be used to identify different layers of soil and rock as well as to locate deposits of natural gas and oil. ■

Using Math *The* Titanic *lies about 4,000 m (13,200 ft) below the ocean's surface. About how long would it take a sound impulse to travel from a ship at the ocean's surface to the* Titanic *and back to the ship?*

Magnetism Tells a Story

Reading Focus How is Earth like a magnet?

You have probably used magnets many times. Perhaps you used one to pick up a string of paper clips or to hold notes on the refrigerator door.

A magnet is an object that attracts certain metals, including iron, steel, and nickel. A magnet has two ends, or poles. When a magnet is suspended from a

inclined, or tilted, about 11° from the geographic poles. The magnetic field around Earth is thought to be due to movements within Earth's fluid outer core, which is composed mainly of iron and nickel. For reasons unknown, Earth's magnetic field sometimes reverses itself. This is called a **magnetic reversal**.

▲ Iron filings show the magnetic field around a magnet.

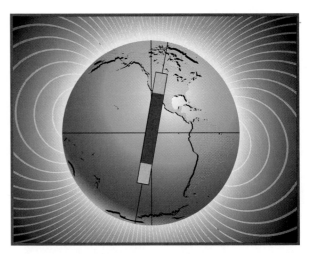

▲ Earth is like a giant magnet surrounded by a magnetic field.

string, the pole that turns toward north is called the *north pole* of the magnet. The pole that points south is the *south pole* of the magnet. A **magnetic field** is the area around a magnet where the effects of magnetism are felt.

Earth as a Magnet

Earth is like a giant magnet, and it has two magnetic poles. These poles are

At present, the magnetic field is said to be normal. This means that the north-seeking needle of a compass will point toward Earth's north magnetic pole. What do you think happens when the field is reversed?

You probably know that some of Earth's rocks contain iron. When these rocks formed from magma, the iron atoms lined up with the magnetic field of

the time, much as a compass needle lines up with Earth's magnetic field. Scientists can use this lining-up of iron atoms to find the direction of Earth's magnetic field at the time the rock formed.

Scientists use a device called a magnetometer (mag nə täm′ət ər) to detect how iron atoms line up within rock. These devices have been used by oceanographers to study the magnetic fields of rock on the ocean floor.

Sea-Floor Magnetism

A **mid-ocean ridge** is a continuous chain of mountains on the ocean floor. When scientists studied the ocean floor along these ridges and on either side of the ridges, they found a magnetic pattern in the rock. There were long stretches of rock in which iron atoms were lined up in one direction. Then there were other stretches of rock, parallel to the first, in which the iron particles lined up in the reverse direction. This pattern of reversals continued from the mid-ocean ridge outward, away from the ridge. A further

finding was that the pattern on one side of the ridge was exactly the same as the pattern on the other side of the ridge.

The drawing below helps explain the magnetic patterns on the ocean floor. As tectonic plates on either side of the ridge move apart, magma flows up from below the ridge and hardens into rock on the sea floor. Only when iron-containing rock is fluid can the iron atoms line up in a magnetic field. Once the rock hardens, the iron atoms do not change direction. The arrows show the magnetic directions of the iron atoms in the rock at the mid-ocean ridge and on either side of the ridge. Note the repeating pattern.

Scientists have found that rocks closer to a mid-ocean ridge are younger than rocks farther from the ridge. The magnetic patterns in the sea-floor rocks and the different ages of the rocks led scientists to a startling conclusion. New sea floor is continually being formed along underwater mountain chains, or mid-ocean ridges! As two plates separate along a ridge, magma fills the separation.

SEA-FLOOR SPREADING Magma bubbles up and flows out along the ridge. When it hardens, it forms rock. On either side of a mid-ocean ridge are layers of magnetized rock. Each arrow represents a magnetic reversal. ▼

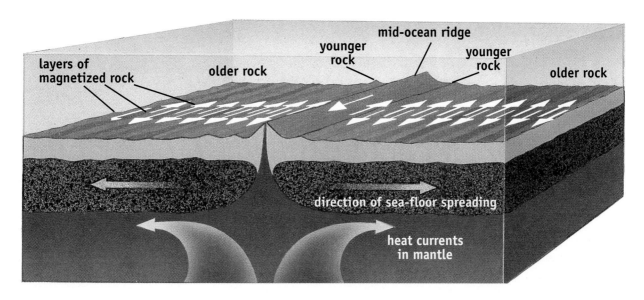

mid-ocean ridge

younger rock

younger rock

older rock

older rock

layers of magnetized rock

direction of sea-floor spreading

heat currents in mantle

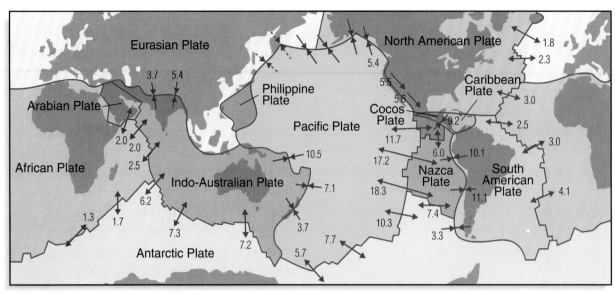

Using Math

This map shows rates at which plates separate and move together. The rates are in centimeters per year. Where is sea-floor spreading taking place the fastest? Where is it occuring the slowest?

As the magma cools, the iron atoms in the magma line up with Earth's magnetic field. This process by which new ocean floor is continually being added is called **sea-floor spreading**. The activity on page B22 involves a model of sea-floor spreading. Sea-floor spreading is strong evidence for the plate tectonics theory. ■

Science in Literature

THE LONGEST FOUR MINUTES

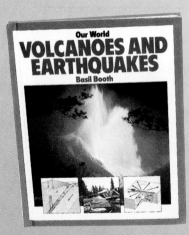

Volcanoes and Earthquakes
by Basil Booth
Silver Burdett Press, 1991

"The earthquake lasted for four minutes, during which time the shocks set off avalanches and landslides . . . buildings rocked back and forth, while large cracks opened in the ground and swallowed objects as large as cars. On Turn Again Heights, the whole area slid more than 1,640 ft (500 m) . . . ."

In *Volcanoes and Earthquakes* by Basil Booth, you can read more about the 1964 earthquake that struck Prince William Sound in Alaska. You can also read about volcanoes and other famous earthquakes.

Heating Up Iceland

Reading Focus How can the movement of Earth's plates help produce energy, and what can that energy be used for?

GLOBAL Views

In Iceland, some families don't need ovens to bake their bread; they simply place the dough inside a hole in the ground. Do they have underground ovens? Yes, but these ovens are created by natural processes taking place inside Earth. Rocks just below the surface are heated by magma that rises from deep inside Earth. Icelanders use these heated rocks as underground ovens.

Why It Is Hot

Iceland lies on the Mid-Atlantic Ridge, which marks the boundaries of two tectonic plates—the North American Plate and the Eurasian Plate. As these plates move apart, the heat produced by rising magma creates giant geysers. The drawing below shows how this happens.

Helpful Shifting Plates

The movement of Earth's plates can cause trouble. Earthquakes and volcanic eruptions often occur along the edges of moving plates. But there are regions where plate movement can be helpful. In Iceland, for example, moving plates provide an inexpensive source of energy—geothermal ("hot earth") energy.

A geothermal plant in Iceland ▼

GEYSERS Hot magma rises from inside Earth, heating the underground rock. The heated rock in turn heats any nearby ground water, changing it to steam. Some of this steam and heated water spurts out of the ground in the form of huge geysers. ▼

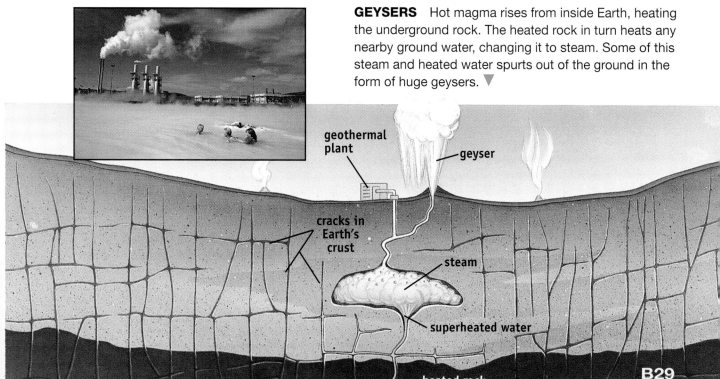

geothermal plant

geyser

cracks in Earth's crust

steam

superheated water

heated rock

B29

Energy From Earth

Icelanders use this heated underground water as geothermal energy. This energy, which comes from heat produced inside Earth, is used by Icelanders to heat their homes, businesses, swimming pools, and greenhouses. The steam produced by the heated water runs generators that produce electrical energy.

Value of Geothermal Energy

Compared to other forms of energy, geothermal energy has many advantages, as you can see in the table below. Which form of energy is used where you live?

Geothermal energy is used in several parts of the world besides Iceland, such as in Italy, Japan, Australia, New Zealand, Russia, and the United States. Some of the same processes that can lead to a volcanic eruption can also be turned to useful purposes. The use of geothermal energy in Iceland shows that processes inside Earth can provide people with the heat and electricity they need every day. ■

Comparison of Forms of Energy

Energy	Advantages	Disadvantages
Fossil fuels	fairly plentiful	nonrenewable, polluting
Geothermal	less polluting than fossil fuels or nuclear energy	produces sulfur, boron, and ammonia wastes
Hydroelectric	cheap form of energy; renewable, nonpolluting	dams cause flooding of valuable land
Nuclear	cheap, powerful	toxic waste; risk of radiation leaks
Solar	renewable, nonpolluting	expensive development and maintenance

INVESTIGATION 3 WRAP-UP

THINK IT WRITE IT

REVIEW

1. What features might be found along the sea floor that could help us understand plate tectonics?

2. Explain how scientists use sonar to map the sea floor.

CRITICAL THINKING

3. You are planning a documentary film about the mysteries of the sea. How would you explain sea-floor spreading to your viewers?

4. You have just invented something that will make mapping the sea floor easier. Draw a diagram or write a paragraph explaining how your invention works.

REFLECT & EVALUATE

Word Power

Write the letter of the term that best matches the definition. *Not all terms will be used*.

1. Part of a continent that extends under shallow water from the edge of the land down to a steeper slope
2. Process by which new ocean floor is continually added
3. Supercontinent that existed 200 million years ago
4. Places where plates interact
5. Earth's outermost solid layer
6. Area around a magnet where effects of magnetism are felt

a. continental shelf
b. crust
c. magnetic field
d. magnetic reversal
e. mantle
f. Pangaea
g. plate boundaries
h. sea-floor spreading

Check What You Know

Write the word in each pair that correctly completes each sentence.

1. Wegener hypothesized that Pangaea existed about 200 (thousand, million) years ago.
2. Rocks close to a mid-ocean ridge are (younger, older) than rocks farther from the ridge.
3. The movement of Earth's continents can be explained by (magnetic reversal, the theory of plate tectonics).

Problem Solving

1. Careful measurements along the Mid-Atlantic Ridge show that South America is moving away from Africa at about 3 to 5 cm each year. How would you explain this?
2. Explain how the same kinds of rock could be found in Norway, Scotland, and parts of eastern Canada and the eastern United States.

The map shows the location of earthquakes and volcanoes worldwide. Explain in your own words why there are so many earthquakes and volcanoes located in coastal areas that border the Pacific Ocean.

2

TECTONIC PLATES AND MOUNTAINS

The Himalayas, the Andes, and other great mountain ranges have existed for millions of years. The largest of all mountain ranges is actually beneath an ocean. How do mountains form? Do mountains on land and beneath the ocean form in the same way?

Connecting to Science
CULTURE

The High Life The type of culture that develops in a region is greatly influenced by the geography of the region. No place on Earth is this fact more evident than in the Andes Mountains, which stretch along much of the west coast of South America. For people in the Andean highlands, life is much the same as it was for their Inca ancestors more than 500 years ago. The homes and clothing are designed to withstand the rugged conditions of the region. The main industry is farming. The chief crop is potatoes, which grow well in the thin soils and cool climate. Sheep, llamas, and alpacas are raised for their wool. Plant dyes are used to create beautifully bright patterns on blankets and other wool products. And as the picture shows, the goods are displayed and sold in colorful outdoor markets.

Coming Up

▲ Marketplace in Pisac, Peru.

WHY DO TECTONIC PLATES MOVE?

Wegener's hypothesis on continental drift helped to explain why the continents appear to be just so many pieces of a jigsaw puzzle. However, his hypothesis didn't explain why the continents moved. What force can move such huge plates of rock?

Activity

The Conveyor

Heat is a form of energy. Energy can do work. How can heat energy from Earth's interior move tectonic plates? In this activity you'll construct a model that shows what moves tectonic plates.

MATERIALS

- aquarium
- cold water
- milk carton (0.24 L)
- 2 lengths of string (30 cm each)
- duct tape
- measuring cup
- hot water
- food coloring
- scissors
- metric ruler
- paper towels
- *Science Notebook*

Procedure

1. Fill an aquarium with cold water.

2. Punch a 5-mm hole in the side of a milk carton, near the bottom. Punch another hole near the top of the carton.

3. Place a length of string over the hole near the bottom so that it extends down 2.5 cm below the hole. Cover the string and hole securely with a strip of duct tape, as shown.

4. Repeat step 3, this time covering the hole near the top of the carton.

Step 3

B34

5. Using a measuring cup, fill the milk carton with hot water colored with food coloring. Seal the carton with duct tape.

6. Place the carton in the middle of the aquarium. **Predict** what will happen when the holes in the carton are opened. **Record** your predictions in your *Science Notebook*.

7. Have one group member hold down the milk carton while another member gently pulls the strings to peel the tape off the holes. Be careful not to stir up the water as you work. Watch what happens. **Record** your observations.

8. Form a **hypothesis** on how the movement in the aquarium is a model of the movement of material in Earth's crust and upper mantle. **Discuss** your hypothesis with your group.

Step 5

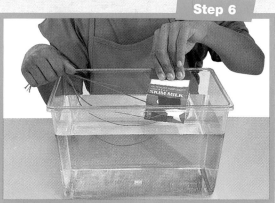
Step 6

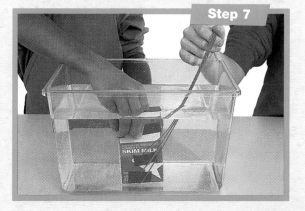
Step 7

Analyze and Conclude

1. What happened in step 7 when you removed the tape from the holes?

2. Did the hot water do what you predicted it would do? **Compare** your predictions with what actually happened.

3. If the hot and cold water represent the layer of Earth known as the mantle, which is just below the crust, how might material in the mantle move tectonic plates?

Technology Link
CD-ROM

INVESTIGATE FURTHER!

Use the **Science Processor CD-ROM**, *The Changing Earth* (Unit Opener Investigation, On the Edge) to observe several earthquakes and volcanic eruptions. Find out about how tectonic plates interact and what makes plate boundaries so important.

Moving Plates

Reading Focus What force makes the tectonic plates move and how does this force work?

Recall from Chapter 1 that Earth's crust and upper mantle are broken into seven large slabs and several small ones. The slabs are called tectonic plates. These plates move over Earth's surface an average of several centimeters a year. Just what keeps these enormous slabs in motion?

Earth's Lithosphere

Tectonic plates make up a part of Earth called the lithosphere. The word part *litho-* means "rock." You probably know that *sphere* means "ball."

The **lithosphere** (lith′ō sfir), then, is the solid, rocky layer of Earth. It is about 100 km (62 mi) thick. This part of Earth includes the crust, with the oceans and continents, and the rigid upper mantle.

The layer of Earth below the lithosphere is the **asthenosphere** (as then′ə sfir). Unlike the lithosphere, the asthenosphere is not rigid. In fact, the part of the asthenosphere just below the lithosphere behaves something like silicon putty.

Silicon putty has properties of both a liquid and a solid. When a slow, steady force is applied to the putty, it flows like a thick liquid. However, when a quick, sharp force is applied to the putty, it snaps like a solid.

Pulling slowly on silicon putty (*left*)
Giving silicon putty a sharp tug (*right*)

Layers of Earth's crust and upper mantle ▼

continental crust

oceanic crust

ASTHENOSPHERE
The layer just below the lithosphere, in the upper mantle, is the asthenosphere. It is made up of rock that is hot, soft, and slightly fluid.

LITHOSPHERE
Earth's rigid outer layer is the lithosphere. It includes the crust and solid upper part of the mantle.

Temperature increases steadily as you move deeper into the asthenosphere. In the lower part of the asthenosphere, temperatures are so high that the rock is partially melted. This mixture of molten and solid rock material behaves something like a very thick, very slow-moving syrup.

Convection currents in a pot of boiling pasta ▼

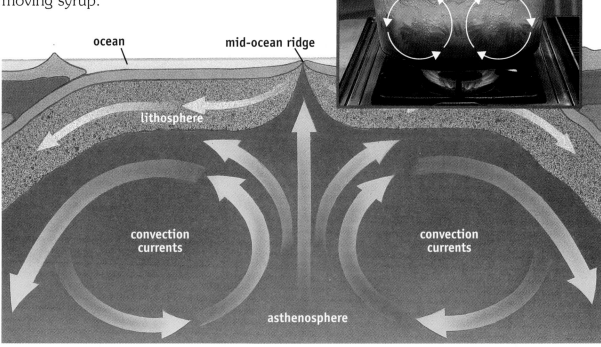

▲ Convection currents in the asthenosphere are thought to drive the movement of the tectonic plates.

Heating and Cooling Rock

Scientists think that Earth's plates move over its surface because of convection in the asthenosphere. **Convection** (kən vek′shən) is a process by which heat energy is transferred through a fluid. Convection occurs when a fluid is placed between a hot surface below and a cold surface above. A **convection current** is the path along which the energy is transferred.

You are probably familiar with several kinds of convection currents. Have you ever watched rice or pasta whirl around in a pot of boiling water? Convection currents are set in motion when water or air is heated. The heated fluid then rises because it is less dense than the surrounding fluid. In a pot of rice or pasta, when the heated water reaches the top of the pot, it cools and flows back down to begin another journey around the pot. In the activity on pages B34 and B35, when the hot water in the milk carton is released into the colder water in the aquarium, convection currents are set into motion.

Convection in the Mantle

How does convection occur in Earth's mantle? The partly melted hot rock in the asthenosphere rises because it is less

dense than the surrounding materials. It slowly makes its way toward the lithosphere. When the melted rock reaches the cooler lithosphere, the melted rock begins to cool and harden. The cooler rock then moves horizontally along the bottom of the lithosphere. When the rock reaches the edge of a plate, it sinks down under the plate into the mantle. As the rock moves down into the asthenosphere, it begins to melt, and the cycle starts again.

Moving Tectonic Plates

Today scientists generally agree that convection currents in the asthenosphere are the force that moves tectonic plates. Recall from Chapter 1 that Alfred Wegener, despite all his evidence, could

How Plates Interact

Places where plates interact are called plate boundaries Examples of three kinds of interacting plates are shown on this page and the next. The map on pages B20–B21 shows the location of these boundaries.

COLLIDING PLATES Plates collide, or come together, at **convergent boundaries**. What do you think might happen when two enormous slabs of rock collide? What kinds of features do you think you'll find along convergent boundaries?

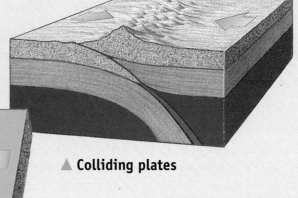

▲ **Colliding plates**

SEPARATING PLATES Plates move away from one another at **divergent boundaries**. Most divergent boundaries are found on the ocean floor. These boundaries are places where new oceanic crust forms through the process of sea-floor spreading. The photograph shows a divergent boundary.

▲ **The walls of this riverbank in Iceland are on plates that separated.**

not explain what caused the continents to move over Earth's surface. Thus, his idea of continental drift was really a hypothesis, or a guess based on observations. In the 1960s the theory of plate tectonics was proposed. A theory is an idea that is supported by evidence. And a theory can be used to make accurate predictions about future events. Recall that the theory of plate tectonics states that Earth's crust and upper mantle are made up of a series of rigid or nearly rigid plates that are in motion. ■

Internet Field Trip

Visit **www.eduplace.com** to see animations of the three types of movement between plates.

SLIDING PLATES Plates move past one another at **transform-fault boundaries**. A fault is a very large crack in Earth's rocks, along which movement has taken place. The photograph shows the San Andreas Fault, found in the western United States. This fault, one of the longest and most famous in the world, is the site of many earthquakes.

▲ **San Andreas Fault, California, as seen from an airplane**

INVESTIGATION 1 WRAP-UP

REVIEW

1. What might cause tectonic plates to move?

2. Explain the convection currents in a pot of boiling pasta.

CRITICAL THINKING

3. Can convergent and divergent plate boundaries be considered opposites? Explain.

4. What do you suppose would happen if Earth's tectonic plates began moving at a much faster rate, such as several meters per year instead of centimeters per year?

HOW DOES THE MOTION OF TECTONIC PLATES BUILD MOUNTAINS?

The tectonic plates that make up Earth's surface are large, thick, and massive. When they move, something has to give! Find out what "gives" in Investigation 2.

Activity

Take a Dive

Some plates are thicker than others and some bend easier than others. What do you think happens when an ocean plate collides with a continental plate?

MATERIALS

- shoebox lid
- scissors
- paper strip
- metric ruler
- rice
- *Science Notebook*

SAFETY

Be careful when using scissors.

Procedure

1. Turn a shoebox lid upside down. Make a slit from one side of the lid to the other about 1 cm from one end of the lid.

2. Cut a sheet of paper to form a strip several cm longer than the box lid and about 2 cm narrower. Lay it inside the lid. Then sprinkle a thin layer of rice on the paper.

3. The paper represents the plate that is the ocean floor. The end of the box near the slit is a continent. The slit is an ocean trench next to the continent. The rice is a layer of sediment on the ocean floor. **Predict** what will happen when you pull the paper through the slit.

Step 2

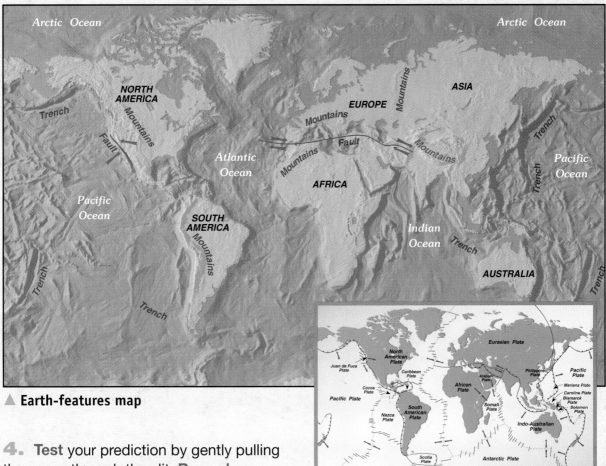

▲ Earth-features map

▲ Tectonic-plates map. For the full-size map, see pages B20 and B21.

4. **Test** your prediction by gently pulling the paper through the slit. **Record** your observations in your *Science Notebook*.

5. Form a **hypothesis** about what happens when two plates meet at a convergent boundary.

Analyze and Conclude

1. How does the model show what happens as ocean plates collide with continental plates?

2. What happens to sediment on an ocean plate when the plate descends beneath a continent? Infer what all this sediment might build.

UNIT PROJECT LINK

After several earthquakes shook California in the 1990s, the Sierra Nevada range became more than 0.3 m (1 ft) taller. Use newspapers and magazines to find out about earthquakes and volcanoes that have recently lifted other mountains. Use a map to identify the locations of the growing mountains.

Technology Link

For more help with your Unit Project, go to **www.eduplace.com**.

Activity

A Big Fender Bender

Think about what happens to the metal when two cars collide. What do you think happens when two continents collide? You'll use a simple model to find out.

MATERIALS

- shoebox lid
- paper strip
- block of wood
- rice
- colored beans or peas
- *Science Notebook*

Procedure

1. Use the shoebox lid and paper strip from the last activity. Tape a block of wood to the end of the paper strip farthest from the slit in the lid. The block represents a continent.

2. Build a second model continent on the paper strip in front of the wood block. Use rice and colored beans or peas to represent layers of rock.

3. **Predict** what will happen when you pull the model ocean floor down into the "trench" so that the continents collide. **Test** your prediction. **Record** your observations in your *Science Notebook*.

Step 2

Analyze and Conclude

1. What happened to the "layers of rock" on the continent?

2. **Infer** what happens to actual rock when continents collide. **Hypothesize** about the relationship between Earth's tectonic plates and mountains.

Technology Link
CD-ROM

INVESTIGATE FURTHER!

Use the **Science Processor CD-ROM**, *The Changing Earth* (Investigation 2, On the Move) to learn how plate movements affect the way that mountains form.

Mountain Building

> **Reading Focus** What are the four different ways that mountains are formed?

Have you ever gone mountain climbing? A mountain is any feature that rises above the surrounding landscape. So even if you've only hiked a local hill, you've gone mountain climbing.

Mountains form as the result of four basic processes: folding, faulting, doming, and volcanic activity—so mountains can be classified as folded mountains, fault-block mountains, dome mountains, or volcanoes. Three of these—folded, fault-block, and volcanic—result from plate movements.

Folded Mountains

Look at the picture of the paper fan at the bottom of this page. Notice that the folds form a series of crests, or high points, and troughs, or low points. Folded mountains form when masses of rock are squeezed from opposite sides. The activities on pages B40 to B42 show that folded mountains form when two plates collide. The Appalachians, the Alps, the Urals, and the Himalayas are classified as folded mountains.

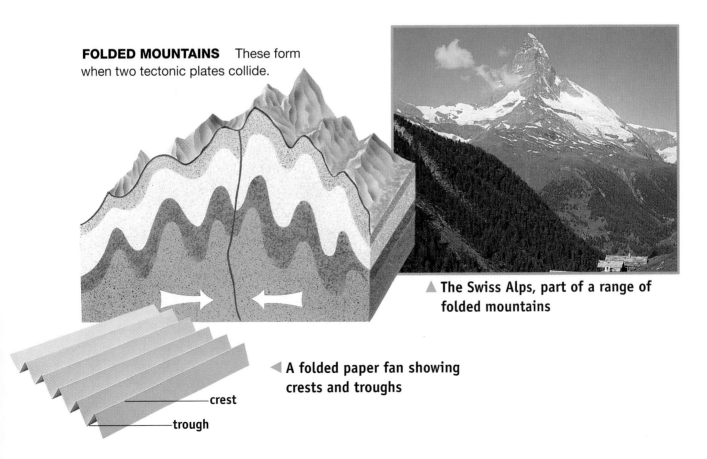

FOLDED MOUNTAINS These form when two tectonic plates collide.

▲ The Swiss Alps, part of a range of folded mountains

◀ A folded paper fan showing crests and troughs

crest

trough

Fault-Block Mountains

Recall that a fault is a large crack in Earth's rocks, along which movement has taken place. Forces produced by moving plates can move rock along faults. When blocks of rock move up or down along a fault, a mountain can form.

Examples of fault-block mountains include those in the Dead Sea area, the Grand Tetons in Wyoming, and those in the Great Rift Valley of Africa. In the mountains of the Great Rift Valley, scientists have unearthed some of the oldest known human fossils.

Dome Mountains

Have you ever heard of Pikes Peak? This granite summit in the Colorado Rockies is 4,341 m (14,110 ft) tall. It was explored in 1806 by Zebulon Pike. Although the peak was eventually named after him, Pike never even reached its summit! Pikes Peak is a dome mountain that formed millions of years ago when forces deep within Earth pushed magma toward the surface, where it cooled and hardened. Although dome mountains have an igneous core, sedimentary rocks can border such mountains. But erosion often strips away the sedimentary rocks to reveal the harder igneous core.

Other dome mountains in the United States include the Sangre de Cristo Mountains, the Bighorn Mountains, the Black Hills, and Longs Peak. Find these dome mountains on a map of the United States. Are any of them in your state or in nearby states?

Science in Literature

THE BIG SQUEEZE

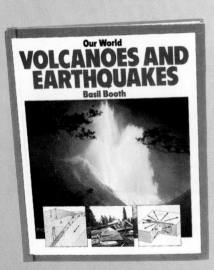

Volcanoes and Earthquakes
by Basil Booth
Silver Burdett Press, 1991

"Mountain chains are formed when two continents collide. . . . Rock debris eroded from these colliding continents pours into the trenches where the oceanic plate is being destroyed. This adds to the ocean floor material to form thick sediments. When the two continents eventually meet, the sediments are folded and squeezed up, like putty in a vice. This creates mountains, such as the Alps and the Himalayas."

Read more about the formation of mountains in *Volcanoes and Earthquakes* by Basil Booth.

FAULT-BLOCK MOUNTAINS These mountains form when masses of rock move up or down along a fault.

▲ Wasatch Range, Utah, fault-block mountains

DOME MOUNTAINS These mountains form when the surface is lifted up by magma, forming a broad dome, or bulge. Wind and rain erode the dome, stripping away layers of sedimentary rock and exposing the igneous rock below.

▲ Pikes Peak, Colorado, a dome mountain

INVESTIGATE FURTHER!

EXPERIMENT

Use a few different colors of modeling clay to demonstrate how folded mountains form. Then use the clay and a plastic knife to show how fault-block mountains form. USE CARE IN HANDLING THE KNIFE. Make sketches of your models in your *Science Notebook*.

Volcanoes

Have you ever opened a bottle of warm soda and had it spray all over you? The spraying of the soda is a bit like the eruption of magma when a volcano forms. Volcanoes, a fourth type of mountain, are most common along convergent and divergent plate boundaries. They form when magma, or molten rock, erupts from an opening in Earth's surface. Sometimes the eruption is quiet; at other times it is quite forceful.

Mount St. Helens is a volcano in the Cascade Range. This mountain chain extends from northern California to British Columbia, in Canada. On May 18, 1980, Mount St. Helens blew its top and threw dust, ash, and volcanic rocks more than 18,000 m (60,000 ft) into the air! As the ash rained back down to Earth, it blanketed some places with as much as 2 m (6.6 ft) of fine material. In some places the air was so thick with ash that it looked like midnight when it was actually noon! You will learn much more about different kinds of volcanoes and volcanic cones in Chapter 4. ■

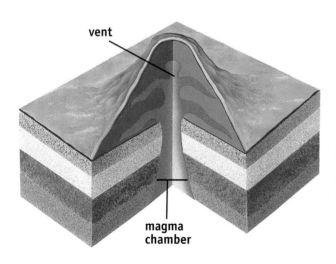

vent

magma
chamber

▲ A typical volcano

Mount St. Helens, Washington, before the 1980 eruption (*top*); during the eruption (*middle*); and after the eruption (*bottom*).

B46

Life at the Top

Reading Focus Why is living at high altitudes a problem, and what adaptation helps people deal with the problem?

You now know that folded mountains are formed by the interactions of tectonic plates. The Himalaya Mountains, for example, were formed millions of years ago when the plate carrying India, then a separate continent, rammed into the plate carrying Asia. This enormous collision of plates crumpled the crust and lifted up sediment from the ocean floor, forming the Himalayas. In some places the sediment was raised up thousands of meters, forming folded mountains.

Climbers of very high mountains can experience many difficulties. The lower air pressure at higher altitudes means that less oxygen is taken in with each breath. A lack of oxygen can affect vision and make walking dangerous. Heart rate quickens sharply, and the heart tries to supply more oxygen to the body.

People in Nepal, a country in the Himalayas, have adapted to living high

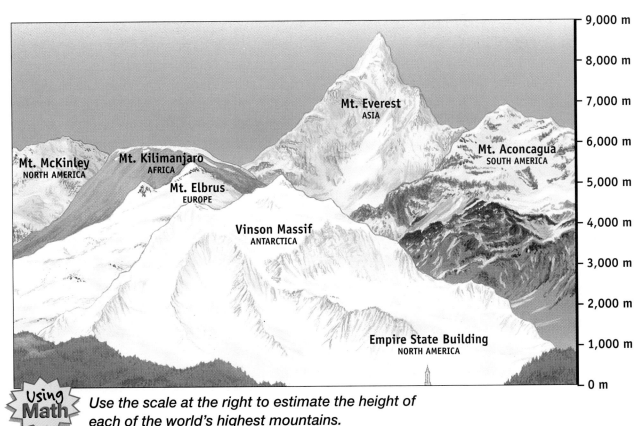

Use the scale at the right to estimate the height of each of the world's highest mountains.

B47

▲ Tenzing Norgay climbed Mount Everest.

▲ Sherpa women in their mountain village

up in the mountains. Nepal is the home of the highest mountain peak in the world—Mount Everest, which towers 8,848 m (29,028 ft) above sea level.

The Sherpas, a people of Tibetan ancestry who live mainly in Nepal, are known for their ability to live and work in the high terrain of their country.

Because the Sherpas have lived all their lives in the mountains, their blood contains more oxygen-carrying red blood cells than that of most other people. So, with each breath the Sherpas take, they can absorb more available oxygen and pump it throughout their bodies. The ability to move enough oxygen through-out the body prevents many problems. In fact, Tenzing Norgay, a Sherpa, was one of the first two men to climb to the top of Mount Everest!

Visitors to the high mountains adapt to the lower air pressure after several weeks. What happens? Like the bodies of the native peoples, their bodies produce more of the oxygen-carrying red blood cells. In time, newcomers to the high mountains can also pump more oxygen throughout their bodies. ■

INVESTIGATION 2 WRAP-UP

REVIEW

1. Describe how plate movements contribute to the formation of mountains.

2. Why do people who are used to living at or near sea level have difficulty at higher altitudes?

CRITICAL THINKING

3. Compare and contrast folded mountains and fault-block mountains.

4. Suppose a Sherpa moved to a lower altitude. How might his or her blood cells adapt to conditions at the lower altitude?

REFLECT & EVALUATE

Word Power

Write the letter of the term that best completes each sentence. *Not all terms will be used*.

1. The solid, rocky layer of Earth about 100 km thick is the ___.
2. When a fluid has a hot surface below and a cold surface above, this condition produces ___.
3. Pikes Peak is a ___.
4. Tectonic plates interact at ___.
5. Tectonic plates move apart at ___.

a. asthenosphere
b. convection
c. divergent boundaries
d. dome mountain
e. folded mountains
f. lithosphere
g. plate boundaries

Check What You Know

Write the word in each pair that correctly completes each sentence.

1. Volcanoes form when (magma, lava) erupts onto Earth's surface.
2. Pikes Peak in Colorado is an example of a (dome, folded) mountain.
3. The (lower, higher) air pressure at higher altitudes means that less oxygen is taken in with each breath.
4. The hot rock in the asthenosphere rises to the lithosphere because it is (less, more) dense than the surrounding materials.

Problem Solving

1. You are in a research vehicle riding along a convection current in Earth's upper mantle. Describe the journey.

2. You skid on a small rug into a wall. How is what happens to the rug like tectonic plates building mountains?

3. The San Andreas Fault in California is a transform-fault boundary between the North American Plate and the Pacific Plate. Describe and model how the plates are moving along this boundary.

Look at the map. Describe what features you might see along the convergent boundary.

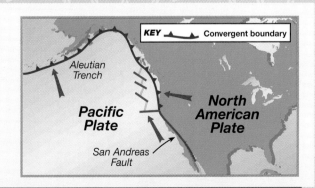

3

SHAKE, RATTLE, AND ROLL

Many men and women in science try to solve problems that affect people's daily lives. Earthquakes have terrified people throughout history, and they continue to threaten loss of life and property today. How can science help?

• •

PEOPLE USING SCIENCE

Seismologist Among the first people to investigate an earthquake are seismologists (sīz mäl'ə jists). These scientists study how and why earthquakes happen. Waverly Person is the chief of the National Earthquake Information Service in Denver, Colorado. He and his staff monitor movements in Earth's crust, using seismographs and other technology.

Seismologists examine the strength of each earthquake, how long it lasts, and where it is located. They exchange ideas about why an earthquake has happened. Over the years, seismologists have developed hypotheses about where future earthquakes will happen. How might such predictions be useful?

Coming Up

◀ Waverly Person checking a seismograph

WHAT CAUSES EARTH-QUAKES, AND HOW CAN THEY BE COMPARED?

Picture two railroad cars rolling past each other on side-by-side tracks. Could they get by each other if their sides were touching? Some tectonic plates are a little like these trains. This investigation is about the sudden changes that can occur when plates that touch move past one another.

Activity

A Model of Sliding Plates

Did you ever try to slide a heavy box over a rough sidewalk and have the box get stuck? Tectonic plates have rough surfaces, too. What happens when the plates keep pushing but the rocks don't slide?

MATERIALS
- 2 blocks of wood
- coarse sandpaper
- 4 rubber bands
- tectonic-plates map
- Earth-features map
- *Science Notebook*

Procedure

1. Cover two blocks of wood with coarse sandpaper. Use rubber bands, as shown, to hold the sandpaper on the blocks of wood.

2. Predict what will happen if you hold the sandpaper surfaces tightly against each other and then try to slide the blocks past each other. **Record** your prediction in your *Science Notebook*.

Step 1

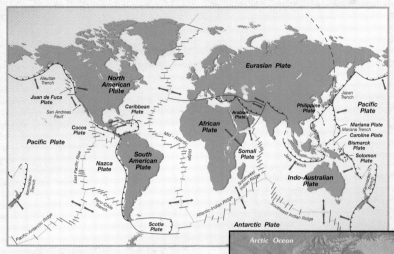

▲ Tectonic-plates map. For a larger map, see pages B20 and B21.

3. Try sliding the blocks past each other. (Hold together the surfaces on which there are no rubber bands.) **Observe** what happens and **record** your observations.

4. Explain how this action might be like two tectonic plates passing each other.

▲ Earth-features map. For a larger map, see page B41.

5. Now list the places shown on your tectonic-plates map where plates are sliding past each other. For example, note that the Pacific Plate and the North American Plate are sliding past each other near the west coast of the United States.

6. Find the same places on the Earth-features map. List any features you find in those places that seem to be related to the motion of the plates.

Analyze and Conclude

1. Think about places you identified in steps 5 and 6. Have you read or heard anything about any of these locations that might involve changes in Earth's crust? What do you conclude might happen when two tectonic plates slide past each other?

2. Did you find anything that looks as if it might be caused by the sliding of two plates? If so, what did you find?

INVESTIGATE FURTHER!

EXPERIMENT

Find two bricks. Slide one over the other. Do they slide easily? What do you hear? What do you feel? What happens when two smooth rock surfaces slide past each other?

Sliding Plates

Reading Focus What are earthquakes, and where are they most likely to occur?

VOL. LV...NO. 17,617.   • • • • •   NEW YORK, THURS

OVER 500 DEAD, $200,000,000 LOST IN SAN FRANCISCO EARTHQUAKE

Nearly Half the City Is in Ruins and 50,000 Are Homeless.

firemen and United States soldiers, who
assisted them, blew down building af
ter building. Their efforts, however
were useless, so far as checking the
headway of the flames was concerned
    The shortage of water was due t
the breaking of the mains of the Sprin
Valley Water Company at San Mateo
The water needed so badly in the cit,
rad in a flood over San Mateo.

    Burning of the Opera House.

▲ City Hall after the 1906 San Francisco earthquake; a 1906 newspaper headline

TIME Capsule It was a few minutes after 5:00 A.M. on April 18, 1906. Many San Franciscans were awakened by a deep rumbling of the ground beneath them. Homes, stores, offices, hotels, churches, and bridges collapsed. Sergeant Jesse Cook, a police officer, observed, "The whole street was undulating [waving]. It was as if the waves of the ocean were coming toward me."

The "Big One" of 1906

Scientists estimate that the earthquake that struck San Francisco in 1906 would have had a reading of about 8.3 on the Richter scale. (You'll read more about the Richter scale in "Our Active Earth" on pages B56 and B57.) The earthquake

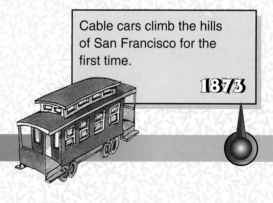

Cable cars climb the hills of San Francisco for the first time.

1873

1848
Gold is discovered at Sutter's Mill.

lasted for only a little over a minute. But its effects were enormous. About 500 people died, and nearly 250,000 were left homeless. Water mains were destroyed. Fires due to broken gas lines raged throughout the city for days. More than 28,000 buildings were destroyed by the fires.

Shortly after the earthquake, San Franciscans began to rebuild their destroyed city and their disrupted lives. By December 1906 many new buildings stood where others had collapsed. Within about three years, 20,000 buildings had been constructed to replace those lost to fire and to the quake itself.

Today, just as in 1906, people ask "What are earthquakes? Why do these tremors happen in some places and not in others?" An earthquake is a vibration of Earth, caused by a sudden release of energy stored along a fault. Most earthquakes occur along tectonic plate boundaries, places on Earth where vast slabs of rock separate, collide, or slide past one another.

Faults

The 1906 earthquake occurred when blocks of rock deep within Earth's surface began to move along a crack called the San Andreas Fault. A fault is a large crack in layers of rock along which movement has occurred. The San Andreas Fault runs through much of California and separates the North American Plate from the Pacific Plate. The 1906 San Francisco earthquake wasn't the first "earthshaking" event to occur along the San Andreas Fault, and it wasn't the last. Many large earthquakes have struck that region since 1906. A major earthquake struck the San Francisco Bay area in October 1989. That quake, measuring 7.1 on the Richter scale, caused 63 deaths and $7 billion in damage. Scientists predict that a much larger earthquake—the "Big One"—is yet to come. ■

Internet Field Trip

Visit **www.eduplace.com** to learn more about plate movement along the San Andreas Fault.

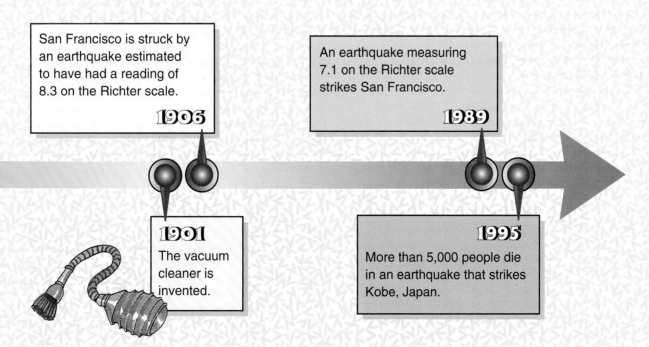

San Francisco is struck by an earthquake estimated to have had a reading of 8.3 on the Richter scale.
1906

An earthquake measuring 7.1 on the Richter scale strikes San Francisco.
1989

1901
The vacuum cleaner is invented.

1995
More than 5,000 people die in an earthquake that strikes Kobe, Japan.

Our Active Earth

Reading Focus How do scientists measure the strength of an earthquake, and how can they predict future earthquakes?

Earth is an ever-changing planet. Some changes happen in a matter of seconds. Other changes occur over months or years. Soils are eroded by water, wind, and gravity. Mountains take hundreds, thousands, or even millions of years to form and just as long to be worn away. And some changes, such as those caused by earthquakes, occur suddenly and violently.

Earthquakes

Earthquakes usually last for only a few minutes. But it takes many years to build up the energy that is released during an earthquake. As blocks of rocks move past one another along faults, friction prevents some sections of rock from slipping very much. Instead, the rocks bend and change shape, until the force becomes too great. It is only when the rocks suddenly slide past each other that an earthquake occurs.

An **earthquake** is a vibration of Earth, caused by the release of energy that has been stored along a fault. Most earthquakes occur along tectonic plate boundaries. California is one area where earthquakes are likely to occur. Part of southern California is on the edge of the Pacific Plate, which is moving slowly toward the northwest.

The San Andreas Fault

During the 30-million-year history of the San Andreas Fault in California, hundreds of earthquakes and many thousands of aftershocks have occurred along its length of 1,200 km (720 mi). An **aftershock** is a shock that occurs after the principal shock of an earthquake.

In October 1989 an earthquake centered in Loma Prieta, California, was felt as far away as Oregon and Nevada. This earthquake caused more than 60 deaths and registered 7.1 on the Richter scale.

The Richter Scale

If you've ever listened to or read a news report about an earthquake, you've heard the term *Richter scale*. The **Richter scale**, with numbers ranging from 1 to 10, describes the magnitude,

Damage caused by the Loma Prieta, California, earthquake in October 1989 ▼

or strength, of an earthquake. The **magnitude** of an earthquake is the amount of energy released by the quake. The Richter scale is named after the American seismologist Charles Richter. Minor earthquakes have magnitudes of 4 or less. The largest recorded earthquakes have magnitudes of about 8.5.

Each increase of 1.0 on the Richter scale represents a difference of about 30 times more energy than the previous number. For example, an earthquake measuring 5.0 on the Richter scale releases about 30 times more energy than a quake measuring 4.0. Likewise, an earthquake measuring 5.7 on the Richter scale releases about 30 times less energy than an earthquake measuring 6.7 on the scale.

Major Earthquakes of the San Andreas Fault	
Richter Scale Magnitude	Earthquake
8.25	San Francisco April 18, 1906
8.25	Fort Tejon Jan. 9, 1857
7.4	Yucca Valley June 28, 1992
7.1	Imperial Valley May 9, 1940
7.1	Loma Prieta Oct. 17–18, 1989
6.6	Superstition Hills Nov. 24, 1987
6.5	Coalinga May 2, 1983

Using Math The Pacific and the North American plates border the San Andreas Fault. About how many times more energy was released during the 1992 Yucca Valley earthquake than in the 1983 Coalinga earthquake?

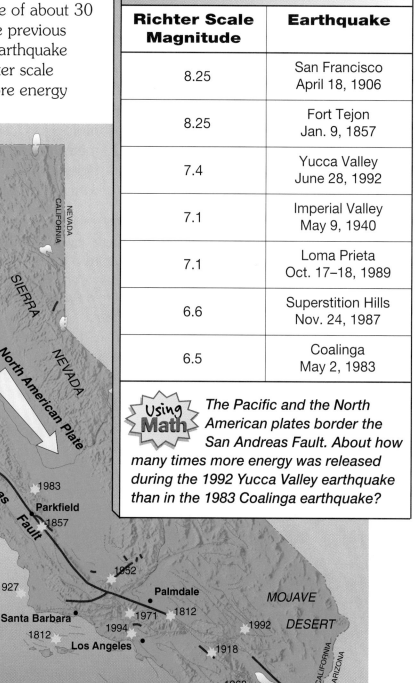

Now study the table and map on page B57, showing some of the earthquakes that occurred along the San Andreas Fault over the past century. Where along the San Andreas did most of the quakes occur? Where did the strongest earthquakes occur? Then look at the map below. Where is the strongest earthquake likely to occur in the future?

Predicting Earthquakes

Scientists know that earthquakes are more common in some parts of the world than in others. Yet the actual timing of these Earth movements is difficult to predict. Seismologists, scientists who study earthquakes, have no sure way of knowing when or where an earthquake will strike or how strong it will be. They can only give estimates of the probability that an earthquake will strike in a certain place within a certain span of years.

Once in a while, seismologists are lucky in predicting earthquakes. In 1988, seismologists with the United States Geological Survey predicted that Loma Prieta, California, was likely to have an earthquake. Loma Prieta is along the San Andreas Fault. On October 17, 1989, a severe earthquake struck Loma Prieta and nearby San Francisco and Oakland.

Seismologists have found that there are changes in Earth that come before most earthquakes. Knowing this, the seismologists closely watch instruments that measure and record these changes. Seismologists are especially careful to watch the instruments in regions where

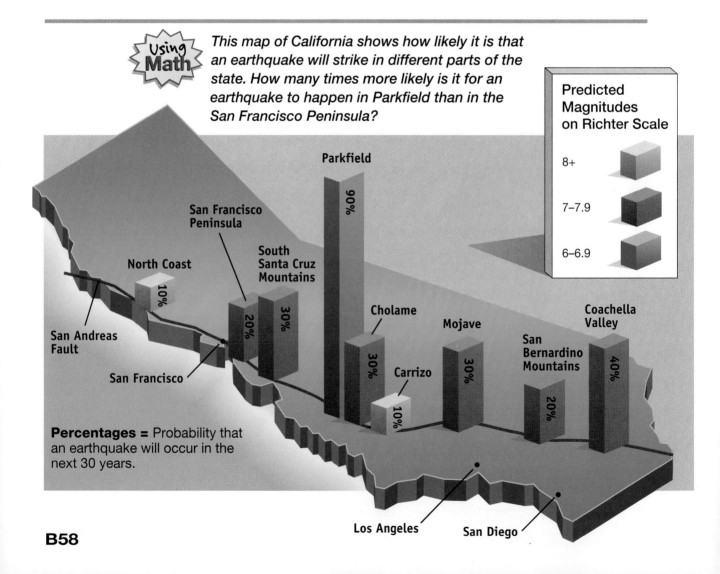

Using Math

This map of California shows how likely it is that an earthquake will strike in different parts of the state. How many times more likely is it for an earthquake to happen in Parkfield than in the San Francisco Peninsula?

Predicted Magnitudes on Richter Scale

8+

7–7.9

6–6.9

Parkfield 90%

San Francisco Peninsula

North Coast 10%

South Santa Cruz Mountains

San Andreas Fault

San Francisco

20%

30%

Cholame 30%

Carrizo 10%

Mojave 30%

San Bernardino Mountains 20%

Coachella Valley 40%

Percentages = Probability that an earthquake will occur in the next 30 years.

Los Angeles

San Diego

earthquakes are likely to occur. For example, changes in the tilt of slabs of rock below ground can indicate that an earthquake is brewing. Studies have shown that rock formations will swell before an earthquake. Changes in Earth's magnetic and gravitational fields can mean an earthquake is soon to strike. Increases in the amount of a radioactive gas called radon from within Earth often come before an earthquake. Micro-earthquakes, or minor tremors, can also indicate that a more intense earthquake will strike an area.

Just how accurate are these warnings? Some scientists argue that watching changes in various instruments can lead to the prediction of earthquakes. Eleven days before the 1989 Loma Prieta earthquake, an instrument in the area recorded natural radio waves from Earth that were nearly 30 times stronger than usual. Just a few hours before the earthquake struck, these radio signals became so strong that they shot off the scale of the instrument.

A study by scientists at the Southern California Earthquake Center suggests that in the next 30 years there will be a severe earthquake in southern California. Exactly when and where it will strike is anyone's guess. ■

▲ **Laser beams are being used to monitor Earth's movements and to predict quakes.**

INVESTIGATE FURTHER!

RESEARCH

Some people believe that animals are very sensitive to the changes that occur before events such as storms and earthquakes. Find out about this hypothesis concerning animal behavior before an earthquake as a possible warning sign for people. What do you think about this idea?

INVESTIGATION 1 WRAP-UP

REVIEW

1. How is the movement of tectonic plates related to the occurrence of earthquakes?

2. What is the Richter scale, and what does each increase of 1.0 represent?

CRITICAL THINKING

3. Is the likelihood of an earthquake greater in California or New York? Explain.

4. Should scientists alert the public about an increase in the strength of natural radio waves? Why or why not?

WHAT HAPPENS TO EARTH'S CRUST DURING AN EARTHQUAKE?

Have you ever pushed a desk across a floor? Sometimes the desk starts to vibrate, and you can feel the vibrations in your hands and arms. In this investigation you'll find out how this experience is similar to what happens during an earthquake.

Activity

Shake It!

In this activity you'll make a model for observing what can happen to buildings during an earthquake. In your model you'll make the vibrations.

MATERIALS

- small block of wood
- clear plastic bowl, filled with sand
- water
- measuring cup
- clear plastic bowl, filled with gelatin
- *Science Notebook*

Procedure

1. Think of a block of wood as a building and a bowl filled with sand as the surface of Earth. Stand a block of wood in a bowl full of sand.

2. **Predict** what will happen if you shake the bowl. **Record** your prediction in your *Science Notebook*.

3. Shake the bowl rapidly by sliding it back and forth. **Observe** what happens to the block and the surface of the sand. **Record** your observations.

A highway toppled during the 1995 earthquake in Kobe, Japan. ▶

4. Pour water over the sand until the water is at the same level as the sand. Again stand the wooden block on the sand. **Predict** what will happen to the block if you shake the bowl with the wet sand. Repeat the shaking, **observe** what happens, and **record** your observations.

5. Now **predict** what will happen when you set the block in a bowl of gelatin and shake the bowl. Try it; then **record** your observations.

Step 4

Analyze and Conclude

1. During the "earthquake," what happened to the dry sand? the wet sand? the gelatin? What, do you think, did the dry sand, the wet sand, and the gelatin represent?

2. What happened to the "building" as it stood on the different surfaces?

3. Which model showed the most damage to the "building"? What evidence supports your conclusions?

UNIT PROJECT LINK

At 5:30 P.M. on March 27, 1964, the most powerful earthquake to hit North America struck Anchorage, Alaska. More than 130 people in Alaska and 12 people in Crescent City, California, were killed by the tsunami that followed the quake. (You'll find out about tsunamis on pages B74–75.)

Use a map to trace how far the tsunami traveled. Then compute the distance that the tsunami traveled. Look at an earthquake map of the world. Outline in red those North American coastlines that might experience tsunamis.

TechnologyLink

For more help with your Unit Project, go to **www.eduplace.com**.

Bend Till It Breaks

Reading Focus What are faults, and how do tectonic plates move along them?

Imagine that you are holding a flexible wooden stick that is about 2 cm wide and 1 m long. You are holding one end in each hand and are gently bending the stick. If you stop bending the stick, it will return to its original shape. What will happen if you keep on bending it? Eventually it will snap!

Forces and Faults

Although Earth's rocks are hard and brittle, in some ways they can behave like the bending wooden stick. You probably know that a force is a push or a pull. If a pulling force is applied slowly to rocks, they will stretch. But like the wooden stick, the rocks will break or snap if the

Movement Along Faults

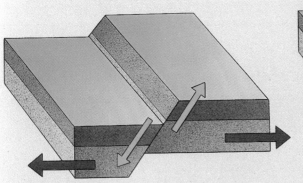

NORMAL FAULT The rock slabs are pulling apart, and one slab has moved up, while the other has moved down along the fault.

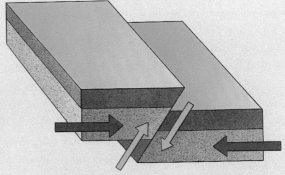

REVERSE FAULT The rock slabs are pushing together, and one rock slab has pushed under the other along the fault.

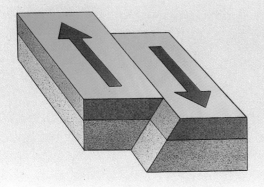

STRIKE-SLIP FAULT Slabs of rock are moving horizontally past each other along a fault. This type of fault is produced by twisting and tearing of layers of rock. The San Andreas Fault is an example of a strike-slip fault.

force on them is too great. A break in rocks along which the rocks have moved is called a **fault**.

What do you think happens when rocks are squeezed together from opposite sides? If pushing forces are applied to rocks, they bend, or fold. But, just as with pulling forces, pushing forces will eventually cause rocks to break. So, pushing forces also create faults in rocks. You can see the effect of these pushing forces in the drawing of the reverse fault on page B62.

Movement Along Faults

Forces may continue to be applied to slabs of rock that contain faults. The forces, which may be either up-and-down or sideways, may continue for many years. The three drawings on page B62 show examples of the main kinds of movement along faults. In time the forces on the rocks become so great that the slabs overcome the friction that has kept them from moving. Then the rock slabs move violently along the fault.

Earthquakes and Faults

Imagine that your hands are the two rock walls on either side of a fault. Picture rubbing your hands together when they are in soapy water. Then picture rubbing them together when they are dry. Sometimes the movement of rocks along a fault is quick and smooth, like the rubbing together of soap-covered hands. But at other times the movement can be slow and rough. As the movement causes rocks to lock and bend, energy builds up in the rocks, much as energy builds up in a flexed wooden stick. When the energy in the rocks is released, an earthquake occurs.

You know that an earthquake is a vibration of the Earth produced by the quick release of this stored energy. The point at which an earthquake begins is the **focus** of the earthquake. Most earthquakes begin below the surface. The point on Earth's surface directly above the focus is called the **epicenter** (ep'i sent ər) of the earthquake.

Earthquakes can begin anywhere from about 5 km (3 mi) to 700 km (420 mi) below Earth's surface. Scientists have found that most earthquakes are shallow—they occur within 60 km (about 35 mi) of the surface. The most destructive earthquakes seem to be the shallow ones. The focus of the 1906 San Francisco earthquake was no deeper than about 15 km (9 mi).

Earthquake Focus and Epicenter

Waves are sent out in all directions from the focus of the earthquake. Notice that the epicenter is the spot on the surface of Earth that lies directly above the focus. ▼

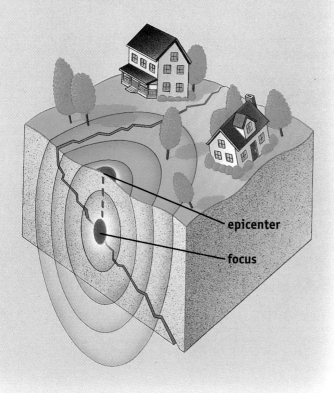

epicenter

focus

Earthquakes Around the World

When earthquake locations are plotted on a world map, patterns emerge. From the map on page B17, you can see that earthquakes occur along certain belts, or zones. Do these zones look familiar? They should! Most earthquakes occur along tectonic plate boundaries. Many occur near the edges of the Pacific Ocean.

Japan, the western United States, Chile, and parts of Central America are just a few of the areas around the edges of the Pacific Ocean that experience earthquakes.

Where do most earthquakes occur in the United States? Even without looking at a map, you probably could have guessed that most earthquakes in the United States happen in California. Now look closely at the map on page B17. Some earthquakes have occurred in the eastern part of the country—far from the San Andreas Fault. Is your area at risk for an earthquake? Although most earthquakes in the United States occur in California, earthquakes can happen anywhere in this country. What is the risk that your state or surrounding states will experience an earthquake?

Earthquake Waves

Have you ever stood in a pool, lake, or ocean and felt water waves break against your body? Have you ever "done the wave" at a sports event? What do all waves have in common? A wave is a rhythmic disturbance that carries energy. The energy released by an earthquake

Science in Literature

A Rude Awakening

"The moment I felt the house tremble and the plaster and bric-a-brac begin to fall, I leaped out of bed and rushed out to the front door, which I had a time unbolting on account of shifting of the house, and while trying to get it opened I was bumped back and forth against it until I was sure the house would fall. . . ."

Each chapter begins with a quotation from a letter written by Edith Irvine—a photographer who experienced the 1906 earthquake. Read about the impact of the earthquake on people's everyday lives, view photographs, and read more of Irvine's letter in *Earthquake at Dawn* by Kristiana Gregory.

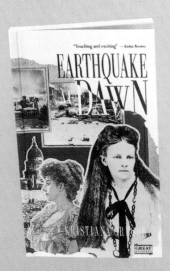

Earthquake at Dawn
by Kristiana Gregory
Harcourt Brace, 1992

travels outward from the earthquake's focus in all directions. The energy is carried by waves. Much of what is known about Earth's structure has been learned from studying the effects of earthquake waves.

There are three different kinds of earthquake waves: P waves, S waves, and L waves. The drawings and captions below show how the three kinds of waves differ. ■

Earthquakes can severely damage property. ▶

P WAVES P waves, or primary waves, move out in all directions from the earthquake focus. These waves push and pull the rocks, causing them to vibrate in the same direction in which the wave is traveling.

S WAVES S waves, or secondary waves, move out in all directions from the earthquake focus. These waves cause the rocks to move at right angles to the direction in which the wave is traveling.

L WAVES L waves, or surface waves, are caused by P and S waves. L waves move along the surface, causing rock material to move up and down. These are the most destructive earthquake waves.

INVESTIGATION 2 WRAP-UP

REVIEW

1. Describe the changes taking place in Earth's crust during an earthquake. What forces cause these changes?

2. Explain the difference between the focus and the epicenter of an earthquake.

CRITICAL THINKING

3. What is the connection between a fault and the production of an earthquake?

4. Why, do you think, are L waves the most destructive of the three types of waves?

HOW ARE EARTHQUAKES LOCATED AND MEASURED?

The newscaster read, "The earthquake last night in Prince William Sound, Alaska, measured 8.4 on the Richter scale. It was a BIG one!" What tools and methods do scientists use to measure how strong an earthquake is or determine where it began?

Activity

Shake It Harder!

The energy of an earthquake is measured with a device called a seismograph. In this activity you'll build a working model of a seismograph and then test how it works as you create your own small "earthquake."

MATERIALS

- string
- chair
- metric ruler
- 2 heavy books
- masking tape
- fine-point marker
- table
- shelf paper (2 m long)
- *Science Notebook*

SAFETY

Be careful not to push or shake the chair off the tabletop while doing this activity.

Procedure

1. Tightly wrap several lengths of string around the seat of a chair in two places (about 10 cm apart), as shown on page B67.

See **SCIENCE** and **MATH TOOLBOX** page H6 if you need to review *Using a Tape Measure or Ruler*.

2. Tightly wrap string around two heavy books in two places (about 6 cm from each end of the books).

3. Tape a fine-point marker to one end of the books. The tip of the marker should hang about 3–4 cm below the edges of the books.

4. Place a length of shelf paper on the top of a table. Place the chair with the string wrapped around the seat on the table, above the shelf paper. Make sure the legs of the chair don't touch the shelf paper.

5. Using string, suspend the books from the chair so that the tip of the marker just touches the surface of the shelf paper. Make sure that the books are parallel to the paper.

Steps 1–5

6. You have just built a model seismograph. You'll use it to measure an "earthquake" that you'll create by gently shaking the table from side to side. The shelf paper will become the seismogram, or record of the earthquake.

7. Predict what will be shown on the seismogram if you shake the table gently. **Record** your predictions in your *Science Notebook*.

8. Place your hands against the side of the table and gently shake it as another member of your group slowly pulls the paper under the pen.

9. Repeat step 8. This time, shake the table a little harder (move the table farther but not faster).

Analyze and Conclude

1. How did your prediction in step 7 compare with what actually happened?

2. How did changing the energy with which you shook the table change the seismogram? How did the record on the seismogram for the first "earthquake" differ from that for the second "earthquake"?

3. How do you think a real seismograph is like the one you built? How might it be different?

INVESTIGATE FURTHER!

EXPERIMENT

Does the seismograph work as well if you shake the table in the same direction in which the paper is being pulled? What would this mean with a real seismograph?
Is there any connection between the length of the strings and the working of the seismograph?

Activity

Locating Earthquakes

The point on Earth's surface above the origin of an earthquake is called the epicenter. The location of the epicenter can be found by comparing the travel times of P waves and S waves at different locations.

MATERIALS
- metric ruler
- Earthquake Travel Time graph
- map of the United States
- drawing compass
- *Science Notebook*

Data

The table below shows the times at which shock waves reached three cities in the United States after the earthquake in California on October 17–18, 1989. Use this information to find the epicenter of that earthquake.

Procedure

1. In your *Science Notebook*, copy the table below. For each city, **calculate** the difference in arrival time between the P wave and the S wave. **Record** your results.

Math Hint *When you subtract, remember to rename 1 minute as 60 seconds.*

Arrival Times of P Waves and S Waves (hr: min: sec)			
City	P Wave	S Wave	Difference
Tucson, AZ	5:06:35	5:08:50	
Billings, MT	5:07:10	5:10:00	
Houston, TX	5:09:10	5:13:35	

2. Place a sheet of paper along the *y*-axis of the Earthquake Travel Time graph provided by your teacher. On the sheet of paper, mark the time interval between the arrival of the P wave and the S wave in Tucson. For example, if the time difference is 4 minutes, you would make marks next to "0" and "4."

3. Keep the edge of the paper parallel to the *y*-axis. Move the paper to the right and up until the space between the marks matches the space between the S-wave curve and the P-wave curve.

4. The point on the *x*-axis directly below (or along) the edge of the paper is the distance from Tucson to the epicenter of the quake. **Record** this distance.

5. Repeat steps 2 through 4 for Billings and Houston.

6. On a United States map, use a drawing compass to draw a circle around each city in the chart. Use the calculated distance from the quake as the radius of each circle. The point at which the circles intersect is the epicenter of the October 1989 earthquake.

Step 6

Analyze and Conclude

1. What is the distance from each of the cities to the epicenter?

2. Where was the epicenter of the October 1989 earthquake?

3. What are the fewest reporting locations necessary to locate an epicenter? Explain your answer.

4. **Compare** your results with those of other members of your class. Account for any differences you find.

INVESTIGATE FURTHER!

TAKE ACTION

Contact or visit an office of the U.S. Geological Survey for more information about locating earthquakes. You may write to the U.S. Geological Survey at Distribution Branch, Box 25286, Federal Center, Denver, CO 80225.

Activity

Be an Architect

The competition is stiff! You and your teammates will build an "earthquake-proof" building. Then you will create a mini-earthquake and test your building. Will it remain standing? Which team will have the most earthquake-proof building?

MATERIALS

- several small cardboard boxes
- masking tape
- large aluminum pan
- clay
- sand
- soil
- wooden dowels
- timer with a second hand
- *Science Notebook*

Procedure

1. With other members of your team, **design** a high-rise "building" that will not tip over in an earthquake. The building must be made of cardboard boxes and any other materials, such as clay, sand, soil, and wooden dowels, that your teacher provides for you. You will subject this building to an "earthquake" that you create by shaking your desk or table. **Draw** your design in your *Science Notebook*.

2. With the rest of your class, **design** a standard that describes when a building is considered earthquake-proof. Make sure the standard will clearly separate good designs from poor designs following an earthquake.

3. **Construct** your building on top of your desk or table.

4. **Predict** how well your building will withstand an earthquake. **Discuss** your prediction with other members of your group.

Step 1

5. With the rest of your class, determine how long the earthquake will last and how strongly you'll shake the table. Note the length of time the building remains standing during the earthquake. Note whether the building undergoes any kind of damage during the earthquake. Use the standard to determine if your building is earthquake-proof. **Record** all observations.

6. **Compare** your results with those of other groups of students in your class.

Analyze and Conclude

1. How closely did your results agree with your prediction of how well your building could withstand an earthquake?

2. How did your design compare with those of other teams of students?

3. Which design best stood up to the earthquake? What was important about that design?

Technology Link
CD-ROM

INVESTIGATE FURTHER!

Use the **Science Processor CD-ROM**, *The Changing Earth* (Investigation 3, Feel the Quake!) to learn about S waves, P waves, and seismographs. Then find the epicenter of an earthquake.

The Seismograph

Reading Focus What does a seismograph do, and how does it work?

Energy from an earthquake travels outward from its focus in all directions, in much the same way that energy is released when a pebble is dropped into a pond. Seismic waves travel at different speeds through Earth's crust and upper mantle. P waves are the fastest; L waves are the slowest. These waves are recorded by an instrument called a **seismograph** (sīz′mə graf).

One of the earliest seismographs used bronze balls to detect earthquake waves. The dragons on this Chinese earthquake detector clenched the bronze balls in their mouths. When the ground vibrated, one or more balls fell from the dragons' mouths. The balls landed in the mouths of waiting metal toads around the base of the instrument. The noise the balls made when they reached the toads' mouths alerted people to the fact that the ground had shaken. People could then determine the direction from which the waves came by observing the direction in which the dragons' empty mouths pointed.

A modern seismograph is a device that generally includes a frame (mounted to bedrock), a weight, a pen, and a rotating drum. In the activity on pages B66 and B67, most of these parts are included in the model seismograph.

A pendulum seismograph consists of a support frame, a heavy weight to which a pen is attached, and a rotating drum. This type of seismograph measures side-to-side Earth movements. A spring seismograph measures up-and-down Earth movements. The drawings on page B73 show all the parts of these earthquake-recording devices.

This Chinese earthquake detector is known as Chang Heng's seismoscope. Chang Heng invented this seismoscope in A.D. 132. How many years ago was that?

Parts of the Seismograph

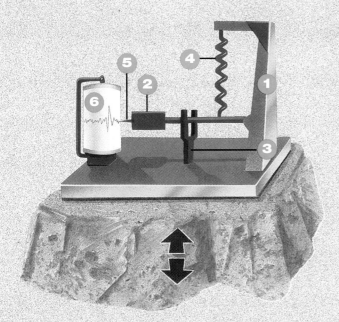

Spring Seismograph

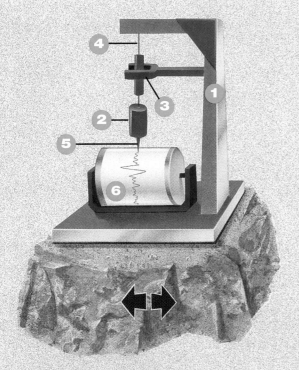

Pendulum Seismograph

1 SUPPORT FRAME
The frame is anchored to solid rock, deep beneath the soil.

2 WEIGHT
The weight of a seismograph keeps the pen steady.

3 MAGNET
The magnet reduces the motion of the weight.

4 WIRE OR SPRING
In the spring seismograph, the spring supports the weight. In the pendulum seismograph, the wire keeps the weight suspended above the rotating drum.

5 PEN
The pen, which touches the rotating drum, records movements caused by seismic waves.

6 ROTATING DRUM
The drum rotates, or turns, all the time. When seismic movements of Earth occur, the pen touching the drum records these movements.

INVESTIGATE FURTHER!

RESEARCH

Find out about early seismographs. How are they like modern ones? How are they different from modern ones?

Earthquakes on the Sea Floor

Reading Focus What happens when an earthquake occurs on the ocean floor?

Tsunamis—What Are They?

You have probably heard the term *tsunami* (tsoo̅ nä′me̅). This Japanese word means "harbor wave." You may have heard such waves incorrectly called tidal waves. A **tsunami** has nothing to do with ocean tides. Rather, this seismic sea wave forms when an earthquake occurs on the ocean floor. The earthquake's energy causes the sea floor to move up and down. This movement can produce destructive waves of water. Why are these waves so dangerous?

Most tsunamis are related to the earthquakes that occur around the edges of the Pacific Plate. In these areas, massive slabs of rock are being forced down into the mantle. Plates often lock when they collide, allowing energy to build up. Eventually this energy is released as

1 **TSUNAMI FORMING**
When an earthquake triggers a tsunami in deep water, the wave's height is only about a meter (3 ft).

2 **TSUNAMI TRAVELING**
In the open ocean, the distance between two crests or troughs can be about 100 km (60 mi). A tsunami is often unnoticed in the open ocean, even though it can be traveling close to 800 km/h (500 mph)!

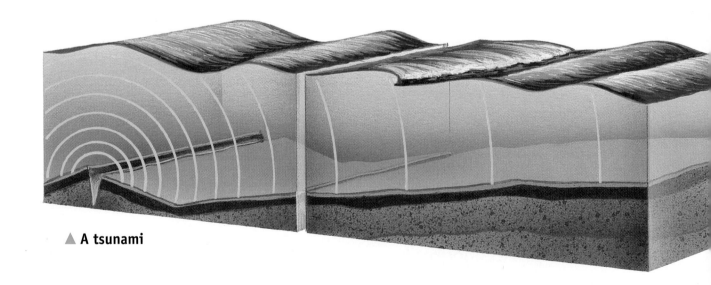

▲ A tsunami

an earthquake, which raises and lowers the nearby ocean floor. This movement sets a tsunami in motion.

Destructive Walls of Water

Most tsunamis are caused by earthquakes. But landslides on the ocean floor and volcanic eruptions can also cause tsunamis. Fortunately, tsunamis only occur about once a year. Study the table on page B76. What was the cause of the 1993 tsunami that began off the coast of Japan?

As with earthquakes, tsunamis cause destruction where they begin as well as along their paths. The tsunami that began with the 1964 Alaskan earthquake, for example, struck the Alaskan coastline and then Vancouver Island in Canada. Waves also struck California

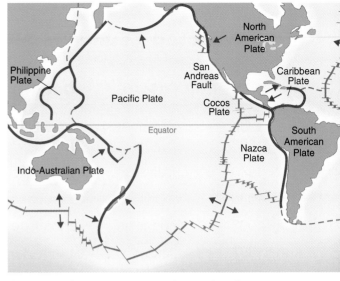

▲ **Tsunamis are common along the shores close to the edges of the Pacific Plate.**

and the Hawaiian Islands. The seismic sea waves finally lost their energy at the Japanese coast—over 6,400 km (about 4,000 mi) from their point of origin!

③ **TSUNAMI NEARING SHORE**
As the wave makes its way toward shore, it slows down because of friction between the advancing water and the ocean floor. But as the water becomes shallower, the height of the wave increases.

④ **TSUNAMI STRIKING SHORE**
Close to shore a tsunami can reach a height of tens of meters! On March 2, 1933, a tsunami that struck the Japanese island of Honshu reached a height of 14 m (46 ft).

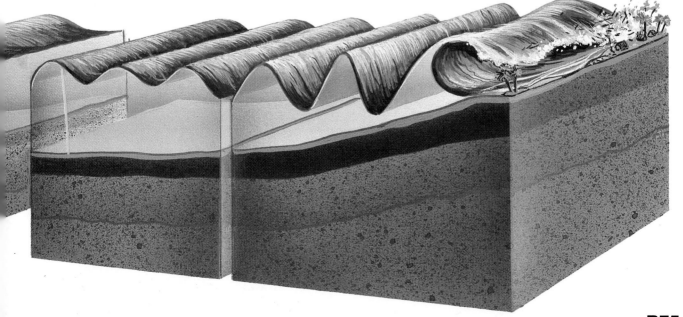

Selected Tsunamis and Their Effects

Year	Place of Origin	Cause	Height of Water (m)	Deaths
1883	East Indies	volcano	>40 m	>36,000
1896	Japan	earthquake	38 m	26,000
1946	Alaska	earthquake	>30 m	164
1960	Chile	earthquake	6 m	144
1992	Indonesia	earthquake	10 m	71,000
1993	Japan	earthquake	32 m	120

Predicting Tsunamis

Unlike earthquakes and volcanic eruptions, some tsunamis can be predicted. In 1946 the Tsunami Warning System was established to forewarn people in the areas surrounding the Pacific Ocean of these destructive events.

There are two tsunami warning centers in the United States. One center is near Honolulu, Hawaii; the other is just north of Anchorage, in Palmer, Alaska. Scientists at these centers use satellites to gather seismic data from more than 20 countries that border the Pacific Ocean. If earthquakes registering more than about 6.5 on the Richter scale are found, warnings are sent to other centers.

Recall that in the open ocean, tsunamis are hardly detectable at the surface of the water. So in addition to setting up warning centers, scientists with the National Oceanic and Atmospheric Administration are studying the usefulness of tsunami sensors that rest on the ocean floor. These devices look promising. In water 4,000 to 5,000 m (13,200 to 16,500 ft) deep, the sensors can detect a change in sea level of less than a millimeter!

Tsunami sensors are flexible metal tubes that are weighted down on the ocean floor. Each tube measures the mass of the water column above it. When a wave passes over the tube, the mass of the water column increases, causing the tube to straighten. After the wave has passed, the tube coils up again. The straightening and coiling of the tubes record changes in water pressure—and the presence of large waves. Such changes can show the presence of tsunamis. ■

Huge waves from a tsunami strike the shore. ▶

Designing for Survival

Reading Focus How are buildings constructed to withstand the force of an earthquake?

Much of the damage done during an earthquake is caused by the earthquake's L waves. Recall that as L waves move, they cause surface rocks to move up and down. These destructive waves cause the foundations of most buildings to move with the passing waves. The buildings themselves, however, tend to resist the movements.

Because of the damage earthquakes can do, building codes in the western United States and in other earthquake-prone areas of the world have been

CONVENTIONAL FOUNDATION With this foundation, the ground movement is exaggerated on upper floors. The building "drifts," and a lot of damage occurs. Upper floors can collapse onto lower floors.

EARTHQUAKE-RESISTANT FOUNDATION This foundation is built of steel and rubber around concrete columns with lead cores. Since the frame is flexible, the floors can move from side to side, and the building isn't badly damaged.

Pillars such as this one support the building and flex during an earthquake. ▶

changed. The new codes deal with the design of new buildings that will help to withstand earthquakes. The building codes also suggest ways to prevent damage in older buildings. Drawings in this resource show some ways that structures are strengthened against earthquakes. ■

Damage to the Golden Gate Freeway following an earthquake in California in 1989 ▼

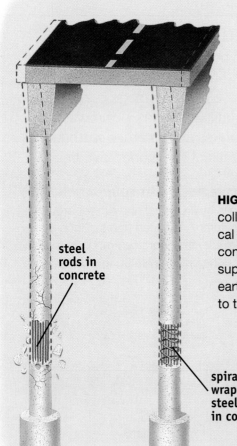

steel rods in concrete

spiral-wrapped steel rods in concrete

HIGHWAY SUPPORT The column at the left will probably collapse in an earthquake. The column at the right has vertical steel rods that are spiral-wrapped in steel. This kind of construction could prevent collapse during a quake. Blocks supporting the columns should be able to move with the earthquake. At the same time, they must be firmly anchored to the columns.

━━━━━━━━━━ **INVESTIGATION 3 WRAP-UP** ━━━━━━━━━━

REVIEW

1. How does a seismograph measure an earthquake?

2. Explain how to locate the epicenter of an earthquake.

CRITICAL THINKING

3. Compare the effects of an earthquake in which the focus is under the ocean with an earthquake in which the focus is under land.

4. Why is it easier to design warning systems for tsunamis than it is for earthquakes?

REFLECT & EVALUATE

Word Power

Write the letter of the term that best completes each sentence. *Not all terms will be used*.

a. aftershock
b. earthquake
c. epicenter
d. fault
e. focus
f. Richter scale
g. seismograph

1. A vibration of Earth caused by a sudden release of energy stored in the crust is a (an) ——.
2. The main shock of an earthquake may be followed by a (an) ——.
3. The point at which an earthquake begins is the ——.
4. Rocks move along a break called a ——.
5. Earthquake waves are recorded by a (an) ——.

Check What You Know

Write the word in each pair that correctly completes each sentence.

1. The most destructive seismic waves are (L waves, S waves).
2. The strength of an earthquake is called its (epicenter, magnitude).
3. In a (reverse, normal) fault, the rock slabs push together.
4. Most tsunamis are caused by (earthquakes, volcanoes) on the ocean floor.
5. The Richter scale measures the (epicenter, magnitude) of an earthquake.

Problem Solving

1. Why are earthquakes in the United States more common on the West Coast than on the East Coast?

2. The 1993 earthquake near Los Angeles registered about 7.5 on the Richter scale. The 1964 earthquake near Anchorage, Alaska, registered 8.4. Compare the energy released in the two earthquakes.

3. Assume that you live in an area that experiences strong earthquakes. What could you do to prepare for an earthquake?

What is shown in the drawing? Describe what might occur at such a location.

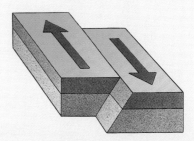

4

VOLCANOES

Never trust a volcano! Millions of people live near active volcanoes. And over the past 20 years, sudden volcanic eruptions have killed over 28,000 people. Volcanoes have always been unpredictable and dangerous.

PEOPLE USING SCIENCE

Geophysicist The West Antarctic ice sheet stretches for hundreds of kilometers across the continent of Antarctica. This seemingly unchanging land with its thick cover of ice holds a secret that reminds us of how highly active Earth is.

Donald Blankenship and Robin Bell are both geophysicists (jē ō fiz′i sists), scientists who deal with Earth's weather, wind, earthquakes, and so forth. Blankenship and Bell were flying over the West Antarctic ice sheet when they noticed a caved-in area that measured 48 m deep and 6.4 km across. What could cause such a strange hole in the thick ice?

Using radar to see through the ice, the researchers discovered a 630-m mountain—a volcano. Imagine finding a volcano under a thick sheet of ice!

◀ Map showing presence of volcanic rock under the ice sheet

INVESTIGATION 1

WHERE DO VOLCANOES OCCUR, AND HOW ARE THEY CLASSIFIED?

Volcanoes form when magma erupts from an opening in Earth's surface. Where are most volcanoes found in relation to tectonic plates? In this investigation you'll locate volcanoes and find out how they are compared and classified.

Activity

Worldwide Eruptions

You can plot volcanic eruptions from news articles to figure out how the eruptions relate to tectonic plates.

MATERIALS
- wall map of the world
- table of eruptions
- world almanac
- red map pins
- yellow map pins
- map of tectonic plates
- *Science Notebook*

Procedure

1. Break up into teams of researchers. Each team will research the location of active volcanoes during a different six-month period in the last two years. Collect news articles about active volcanoes throughout the world.

2. In your *Science Notebook,* **record** the date of each eruption, the name of the volcano, and its location. Also **list** whether each volcano is on a spreading ridge, on a plate margin near a descending plate, on a transform fault, or in the middle of a plate. **Record** how each volcano erupted: Was it a quiet lava flow, did it explode, or did it belch heavy clouds of ash?

See **SCIENCE** *and* **MATH TOOLBOX** page H11 if you need to review **Making a Chart to Organize Data.**

Step 3

Selected Major Volcanic Eruptions			
Date	Volcano	Area	Death Toll
79	Vesuvius	Pompeii, Italy	3,000
1169	Etna	Sicily, Italy	15,000
1669	Etna	Sicily, Italy	20,000
1793	Unzen	Japan	50,000
1883	Krakatau	Java, Indonesia	36,000
1902	Pelée	St. Pierre, Martinique	28,000
1919	Kelut	Java, Indonesia	5,500
1980	Mount St. Helens	Washington State	62
1985	Nevado del Ruiz	Armero, Colombia	22,000
1991	Pinatubo	Luzon, Philippines	200
1993	Mayon	Legazpi, Philippines	67

3. Use a world almanac to find the sites of major volcanic activity over the last 500 years.

4. Tack a large world map to your bulletin board. Using the data gathered by the teams, the data from the almanac, and the data in the table, mark the locations of volcanoes. Stick a red map pin on the map at the site of any volcanic eruption; stick a yellow map pin at the site of any active volcano.

5. Throughout the school year, keep adding to your records and to the world map. **Record** new volcanic activity and new eruptions as they occur. Note how the location of volcanoes is related to Earth's tectonic plates.

Analyze and Conclude

1. How many volcanic eruptions did you find in the news during the six months your team researched? What was the total number of eruptions found by your class during the two-year period?

2. Where on tectonic plates were the volcanoes located?

3. Were any of the volcanic eruptions on a mid-ocean ridge? What kind of an eruption did they have?

4. **Hypothesize** about the relationship between volcanic eruptions and Earth's tectonic plates.

Technology Link
CD-ROM

INVESTIGATE FURTHER!

Use the **Science Processor CD-ROM**, *The Changing Earth* (Investigation 4, Thar She Blows) to learn about the different types of volcanoes and how they form. Plot volcanoes on a map and predict locations of other volcanoes.

Volcanoes and Plate Tectonics

Reading Focus What are volcanoes, and how are they classified?

Volcanoes

What comes to mind when you hear the word *volcano*? Probably you think of a large mountain spewing red-hot lava and other material high into Earth's atmosphere. Some volcanoes are like that. But a **volcano** is *any* opening in Earth's crust through which hot gases, rocks, and melted material erupt.

Have you ever opened a can of cold soda that has been dropped on the floor? Soda probably squirted into the air above the can. More soda bubbled out and flowed down the side of the can. Now, what do you think would happen if you opened a can of warm soda that had been dropped? The release of the warm soda from the can would be *even more* violent. Volcanoes are like cans of soda. Some erupt violently; others have more gentle eruptions.

The high temperatures and pressures deep within Earth can cause rock to melt. This melted rock is called **magma**. Because it's less dense than surrounding material, magma slowly makes its way toward Earth's surface. As it travels toward the surface, the magma melts surrounding material to form a central pipe, which is connected to the magma chamber. Eventually this hot molten material escapes through an opening in the crust

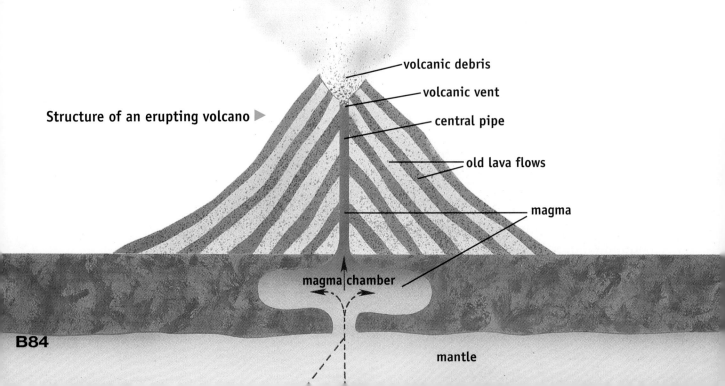

Structure of an erupting volcano ▶

- volcanic debris
- volcanic vent
- central pipe
- old lava flows
- magma
- magma chamber
- mantle

▲ Mount Tolbackik erupts in former U.S.S.R.

▲ Mount Kilauea erupts in Hawaii.

called a volcanic vent. When magma reaches Earth's surface, it is called **lava**.

When lava flows from a volcano, its temperature can be higher than 1,100°C (2,012°F)! Lava is not the only kind of material that can be spewed from an erupting volcano. Solid volcanic debris includes bombs, cinders, ash, and dust. Bombs are volcanic rocks the size of a baseball or bigger. Large bombs can weigh nearly 100 metric tons (1,100 short tons). Volcanic dust and ash, on the other hand, range from about 0.25 mm to 0.5 mm (0.009 in. to 0.02 in.) in diameter and can be carried hundreds or thousands of kilometers from a volcano.

Volcanism and Plate Tectonics

Like earthquakes, volcanoes occur along certain plate boundaries. Many volcanoes occur around the edges of the Pacific Plate in an area that scientists have named the Ring of Fire (see map at right).

Between 500 and 600 active volcanoes make up the region called the Ring of Fire. ▶

Volcanoes in the Ring of Fire were formed in subduction zones. In a subduction zone, plates collide and one plate descends below the other. The descending plate melts as it sinks slowly into the mantle. The magma then rises to the surface, forming a chain of volcanoes near the boundaries of the two plates.

Lava also erupts at divergent plate boundaries. Find the purple faults on the map. These indicate divergent plate

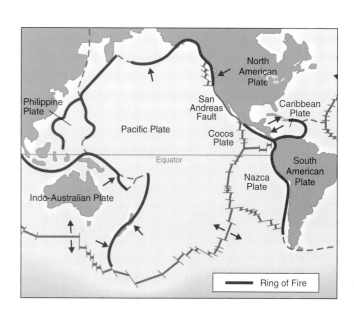

CINDER CONE Paricutín, in Mexico (*left*); drawing of a cinder cone (*below*). Notice the very steep slopes.

vent

magma

layers of cinders

boundaries, where new ocean floor is formed as magma wells up between the separating plates.

Classifying Volcanoes

Volcanoes can be classified in different ways. One classification system is based on how often eruptions occur. An *active* volcano is one that erupts constantly. Some volcanoes that make up the Hawaiian Islands are active volcanoes. *Intermittent* volcanoes are those that erupt on a fairly regular basis. Mount Vesuvius, in Italy, is an intermittent volcano. Volcanoes that haven't erupted in a while but could erupt in the near future are called *dormant* volcanoes. Mount Lassen, in the California Cascade Range, is a dormant volcano. Volcanoes that have not erupted in recorded history are classified as *extinct* volcanoes. Mount Kenya, in Africa, is an extinct volcano.

Volcanoes can also be classified by the way they erupt. The way a volcano erupts depends on the type of lava that is ejected by the volcano. One type of lava

is a very hot fluid, which erupts quietly. Another kind of lava is thick and sticky. This sticky lava erupts violently.

The way a volcano erupts determines the shape of the mountain, or cone, that is produced. This shape can also be used to classify volcanoes. The three main types of volcanic cones—cinder, shield, and composite—are shown on these pages.

Cinder Cones

Cinders are sticky pea-sized bits of hardened lava. A **cinder cone** is made up of layers of cinders. The cinder cone forms around a central vent from which the cinders erupt.

These volcanic cones are produced by explosive eruptions. Generally, cinder cones are relatively small, less than 300 m (984 ft) tall, with very steep slopes. There is usually a bowl-shaped crater. Cinder cones often form in groups. Paricutín, a dormant volcano just west of Mexico City, and Stromboli, a very active volcano off the coast of Italy, are cinder-cone volcanoes.

Shield Cones

Shield cones form from lava that flows quietly from a crack in Earth's crust. What kind of lava do you think makes up a shield cone? Because of the composition of the lava, shield cones are large mountains that have very gentle slopes. Mauna Loa, the largest volcano on Earth, is a shield cone. Mauna Loa, which is a part of the island of Hawaii, towers over 4,100 m (13,448 ft) above sea level. The rest of this vast cone—about 5,000 m (16,400 ft)— is below the waters of the Pacific Ocean.

COMPOSITE CONE Mount Fuji, in Japan (*top*); a drawing of a composite cone (*bottom*). This type of cone has steep slopes near its top and gentle slopes near its base.

Composite Cones

Composite cones form when explosive eruptions of sticky lava alternate with quieter eruptions of volcanic rock bits. Composite cones are also called stratovolcanoes. A composite cone has very steep slopes near its top but the slopes become gentler as you get closer to its base.

Composite cones are formed by the most explosive volcanoes. Their eruptions often occur without warning and can be very destructive. Mount Vesuvius, a once-dormant volcano in Italy, erupted in A.D. 79 and killed thousands of residents in Pompeii and nearby cities. This same volcano still erupts from time to time. You will learn more about Mount Vesuvius on pages B90–B91. ■

SHIELD CONE Mauna Loa (*top*); a drawing of a shield cone (*bottom*). Notice the very gentle slopes.

B87

Surtsey

Reading Focus Where is Earth's youngest volcano, and what can we learn from it?

▲ Surtsey, a young volcanic island, begins to form.

▲ Living things begin to populate the new island of Surtsey.

In 1963, off the southern coast of Iceland, a sailor on a fishing boat observed a pillar of smoke in the distance. He ran to alert his captain that he had spotted a ship that was on fire. Soon the odor of sulfur filled the salty air. The crew of the fishing vessel measured the water's temperature. It was much warmer than usual. The captain soon informed his crew that the smoke in the distance wasn't a burning ship at all. The smoke and fire signaled that one of the youngest volcanic islands on Earth was beginning to rise from the icy waters. Named after the Norse god Surtur, a giant who bore fire from the sea, Surtsey started to form as lava spewed from a long, narrow rift on the ocean floor.

Within a couple of weeks, an island nearly half a kilometer wide rose about 160 m (530 ft) above the water's surface. And after spewing lava, gases, and bits of rock debris from its vent for almost four years, Surtsey became inactive—geologically, that is. Scientists then had Surtsey designated as a nature preserve in order

to study how living things inhabit a newly formed area. Today Surtsey is home to 27 species of plants and animals. Among the first organisms to inhabit the island were plants called sea rockets. Seeds from faraway places were carried to the island by birds and the wind. A few varieties of grasses and mosses painted colorful splotches against the black rock of the island. In the spring, seals now crawl up the black beaches to have their young.

Few people are allowed to visit this volcanic island. The Surtsey Research Council allows only a few scientists to visit the island to study the living things growing there. The impact of the few human beings that visit the island is very small. Only natural forces, such as wind and rain, have acted upon the land and its inhabitants. Erosion has shrunk the island to about three fourths of its original size. Unless it erupts again, the effects of wind and water will eventually make Surtsey disappear. ■

INVESTIGATE FURTHER!

RESEARCH

In 1973 a volcanic eruption occurred on Heimaey, an island off the southern coast of Iceland. Find out how much destruction occurred as a result of this eruption. Look also for ways that the eruption benefited the island. Compare the eruption on Heimaey with the eruption on Surtsey.

Science in Literature

ISLAND WITHOUT A PAST

Surtsey: The Newest Place on Earth
by Kathryn Lasky
Photographs by Christopher G. Knight
Hyperion Books for Children, 1992

"This is the place where the animals have come one kind at a time—a bird, a seal, a fly. And often they have come alone, without a mate, at intervals over the years. This is the place where once upon a time was just twenty-nine years ago. This is the newest place on earth. This is Surtsey island."

Surtsey: The Newest Place on Earth by Kathryn Lasky combines the story of Surtsey with selections from ancient Icelandic mythology. As you read, you can also examine more than 40 photographs recording the formation of this island.

RESOURCE

Mount Vesuvius

ITALY

MOUNT VESUVIUS

Reading Focus What is the impact of Mount Vesuvius on the people living nearby?

TIME Capsule

Over the past 2,000 years or so, Mount Vesuvius, a cinder-cone volcano in southern Italy, has erupted about 50 times. Before its eruption in A.D. 79, Vesuvius was a picturesque cone-shaped mountain, towering over 1,000 m (3,300 ft) above the Bay of Naples. Vineyards and orchards crept nearly halfway up the mountain's slopes. Most historians think that very few people knew that Vesuvius was a volcano—until the fateful morning of August 24 in the year A.D. 79.

During the early-morning hours of that day, an earthquake rumbled through the area. By early afternoon loud thunder ripped through the air, and red-hot ash rained from the skies. Within 24 hours the twin Roman cities of Pompeii and Herculaneum were destroyed.

In the city of Pompeii, about 3,000 people were buried beneath about 5 to 8 m (16 to 26 ft) of volcanic ash. Because the ash was so hot and fell so quickly, it preserved many of the city's residents doing what they normally did in their day-to-day lives. By studying the remains of people, animals, utensils, and decorations found in Pompeii, archaeologists have learned a lot about the people who lived at that time. Archaeologists are scientists who study ancient cultures by digging up the evidence of human life from the past.

The city of Herculaneum, which was several kilometers from Pompeii, met its fate not from volcanic ash, such as that which buried Pompeii, but from a mudflow. A mudflow is a mixture of wet materials that rushes down a mountainside and destroys everything in its path. Volcanologists, or scientists who study volcanoes, think that flowing hot volcanic debris swept over the city and covered it to depths of over 20 m (66 ft)!

The eruption of Mount Vesuvius in A.D. 79 is probably most famous because

◀ **Cast of man buried by the eruption of Mount Vesuvius** (*far left*); **nuts buried and preserved by the eruption** (*left*).

it perfectly preserved the people and customs of ancient Rome. However, it was not the last or the worst eruption in the area. In the summer of 1631, earthquakes once again shook the area. By winter, molten rock filled the volcano. On December 16, 1631, ash was spewing from the mountain. By the next day, red-hot lava raced down the volcano's slopes. The destructive toll of this eruption included 15 villages. At least 4,000 people and 6,000 animals died.

Since the 1631 eruption of Mount Vesuvius, the volcano has erupted every 15 to 40 years. The ash and rock fragments have made the soil very fertile. Farmers successfully grow grapes, citrus fruits, carnations, beans, and peas in this region. But the threat of losing it all to the volcano is always there. ■

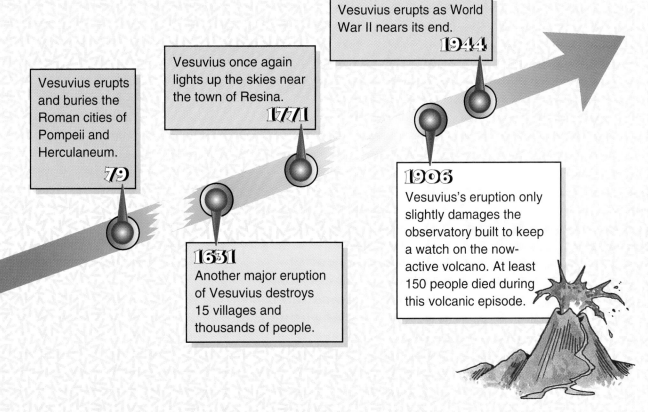

Vesuvius erupts and buries the Roman cities of Pompeii and Herculaneum.
79

Vesuvius once again lights up the skies near the town of Resina.
1771

Vesuvius erupts as World War II nears its end.
1944

1631
Another major eruption of Vesuvius destroys 15 villages and thousands of people.

1906
Vesuvius's eruption only slightly damages the observatory built to keep a watch on the now-active volcano. At least 150 people died during this volcanic episode.

INVESTIGATION 1 WRAP-UP

REVIEW

1. Describe how most volcanoes form.

2. Make a chart that compares and contrasts cinder cones, shield cones, and composite cones. Include a sketch of each type of volcano.

CRITICAL THINKING

3. Imagine you are visiting Surtsey with a group of scientists. Write a diary entry describing what you see.

4. How might Surtsey have developed differently if tourism had been allowed?

HOW DO VOLCANIC ERUPTIONS AFFECT EARTH?

In March 1980, a strong earthquake rocked Mount St. Helens, in the state of Washington. For the next two months, steam and ash blew out. Then in May the volcano exploded with great violence. In this investigation you'll find out what you can expect before, during, and after a volcanic eruption.

Activity

Volcanoes You Can Eat!

How is an erupting volcano like a pot of cooking oatmeal? Volcanoes erupt because materials are forced out of a hole, called a vent. Can you see a vent in a pot of oatmeal?

- - - - - - - - - - - - - - - - -

Procedure

1. Use a measuring cup to **measure** the amounts of quick oats and water shown in the picture.

See **SCIENCE** and **MATH TOOLBOX** page H7 if you need to review *Measuring Volume.*

2. Pour the oats and water into a saucepan and mix together.

MATERIALS
- goggles
- measuring cup
- quick oats
- saucepan
- water
- hot plate
- mixing spoon
- oven mitt
- *Science Notebook*

SAFETY

Do this activity only under the direct supervision of your teacher. Wear goggles.

Step 4

3. Using an oven mitt, place the saucepan on a hot plate and set the hot plate on *Medium High*.

4. After the hot plate has warmed up, stir the oats and water constantly for one minute.

5. Carefully **observe** the top surface of the oatmeal as it cooks. **Record** your observations in your *Science Notebook*.

6. After one minute, turn off the hot plate. Remove the oatmeal from the heat.

Analyze and Conclude

1. What did you observe on the surface of the oatmeal as it cooked?

2. How is cooking oatmeal like an erupting volcano? How is it different?

3. What, do you think, would happen if you covered the pot and continued to heat the mixture? What kind of volcano would be modeled?

UNIT PROJECT LINK

Have you ever dreamed of living on your own island paradise? Locate the Ring of Fire on a map and identify those islands created by volcanic activity. Predict where future volcanic islands might rise out of the ocean; indicate these areas on your map. Draw a small picture of your island paradise and describe where you think your island will emerge.

Technology Link

For more help with your Unit Project, go to **www.eduplace.com**.

Mount Pinatubo

THE PHILIPPINES

MOUNT PINATUBO

Reading Focus What are some of the long-term effects of the eruption of Mount Pinatubo?

Mount Pinatubo, which towers more than 1,900 m (6,200 ft) above sea level, is only one of about 13 active volcanoes in the Philippines. This volcano, which is located on the island of Luzon, is a composite cone. At times when it erupts, there is a sticky lava flow. At other times a combination of ash, dust, and other volcanic rock bits erupt.

Mount Pinatubo and the other volcanoes in the Philippines formed as a result of tectonic activity. The Philippine Islands are a part of the Ring of Fire.

You already know that at some convergent plate boundaries, one oceanic plate collides with another oceanic plate. At such boundaries, one plate goes down deep into Earth's mantle. As the plate is dragged down, it bends, and a deep canyon, or ocean trench, forms. As this oceanic plate descends into the asthenosphere, parts of the plate melt, forming magma. The magma then rises and forms a chain of volcanoes called **island arcs**. The islands that make up the Philippines are a mature island arc system that formed long ago when two oceanic plates collided.

There She Blows!

After being dormant for over six centuries, Mount Pinatubo began to erupt in mid-June of 1991. As the eruption began, brilliant lightning bolts colored the skies above the volcano. Within minutes, these same skies were black because of the enormous amounts of ash, dust, and gases that spurted from the mountain. Scientists estimate that the mountain's violent eruption had a force equal to that of 2,000 to 3,000 exploding atomic bombs! The ash clouds produced by the eruption polluted the air so much that astronauts in space aboard the space shuttle could not get a clear view of Earth's surface!

This period of volcanic activity lasted for several months and stopped in early September 1991. The first eruption destroyed about 42,000 houses and

Two oceanic plates colliding ▼

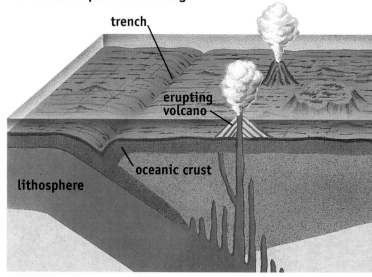

trench

erupting volcano

oceanic crust

lithosphere

nearly 100,000 acres of farmland. Over 900 people died. Much of the damage and many of the deaths were caused by flowing mud and hot volcanic material. Also, masses of gas, ash, and igneous rock called pumice covered many villages at and near the base of Mount Pinatubo.

The cause of the 1991 eruption of Mount Pinatubo is not completely understood. It is likely that many months prior to the eruption, magma began forcing its way up through the lithosphere. Slowly the magma made its way toward the surface. As it snaked along its path, the magma increased temperatures and pressures beneath the mountain. In some places the magma crept into cracks in the bedrock, causing the bedrock to swell. On June 15, 1991, the mountain erupted, sending clouds of gases and tons of lava to Earth's surface.

Mount Pinatubo's Warning Signs

Earthquakes and volcanoes are more common in some parts of the world than in others. Both are closely related to the

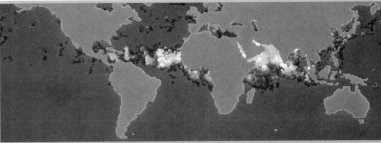

JUNE 19–27, 1991

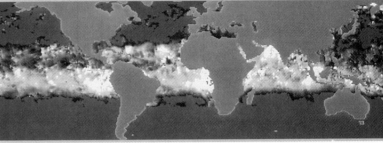

AUGUST 8–14, 1991

Using Math

Effect of the eruption of Mount Pinatubo. The yellow band shows how volcanic debris travels around the globe and extends over time. About how many weeks have elapsed from one image to the next?

movements of tectonic plates. Scientists monitor earthquake- and volcano-prone areas for changes. But the exact time of volcanic eruptions can be difficult to predict accurately. However, in the case of Mount Pinatubo, the volcanic mountain "cooperated." There were many warnings of its explosive 1991 eruption.

First, there was an earthquake that shook the area in July 1990. There is

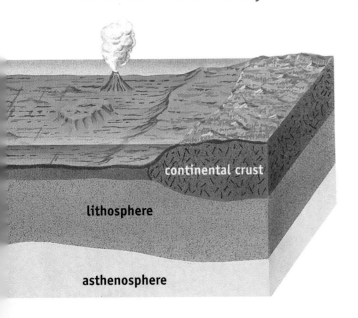

continental crust

lithosphere

asthenosphere

INVESTIGATE FURTHER!

RESEARCH

Find out about another famous volcano in the Philippines called Mount Mayon. Where is it located? How do you think this volcano formed? When did it last erupt? What kind of volcano is it?

◀ **Clouds and gases rise from Mount Pinatubo.**

is produced when sticky lava is slowly squeezed from a volcano's vent, had doubled in size in a little over two months!

Because the volcano gave these warning signs, many lives were saved. For several months before the explosion, scientists explained what the mountain was doing and urged people to leave the area. Over 200,000 people had been safely evacuated from the area before the explosion occurred.

What Goes Up Must Come Down— But When?

Before the eruption, instruments aboard weather satellites monitored the atmosphere above the volcano. These instruments were looking for increases in the amount of sulfur dioxide in the air around the composite cone. About two weeks before the explosion, the amount of sulfur dioxide was ten times what it had been the month before. This increase

often a relationship between earthquake activity and later volcanic activity. In April 1991, small clouds of smoke and ash were forced from cracks along the mountain's slopes. These clouds prompted earth scientists from the Philippines and the United States to more closely monitor the majestic Pinatubo.

Watching Pinatubo

Two kinds of measuring devices—seismometers and tiltmeters—were put into place near the mountain and then connected to computers. A **seismometer** is an instrument that detects Earth's movements. These movements can indicate that a volcano is preparing to blow its top! A **tiltmeter** measures any change in the slope of an area. Installing these devices allowed scientists to note any bulges that formed in the mountain's slopes. Such bulges indicate the presence of magma and gases welling up into the volcano. In fact, Mount Pinatubo did bulge before the 1991 eruption. Its lava dome, a bulge that

Evacuation of people before the eruption of Mount Pinatubo ▶

was another warning that Mount Pinatubo might be ready to erupt.

These same instruments measured the amount of sulfur dioxide that had been spewed out into the air during the eruption. About 15 to 20 million tons of this gas blew nearly 40 km (25 mi) into the air! This volcanic gas combined with other gases in the air and formed a thin layer of sulfuric acid droplets that circled the globe within about three weeks.

Mount Pinatubo, like other active volcanoes, is a source of pollution. The dust, gases, and ash spewed out in 1991 have effected Earth and its atmosphere. First, soon after the eruption, vivid sunsets colored the skies in many places far removed from the Philippines.

Second, the sulfuric acid droplets remained above the planet for a few years after the eruption. The droplets reflected back into space about 2 percent of the Sun's energy that normally reached Earth's surface. This in turn led to a global cooling of about 1°C (1.8°F). This short period of cooling reversed a global warming trend for a short time. The warming trend is caused by the collection of gases

▲ **Sunset after the 1991 eruption of Mount Pinatubo**

that trap the Sun's heat. Called the greenhouse effect, it is the result of natural climatic changes and human activities, such as burning fossil fuels and cutting down forests.

Another effect of the 1991 eruption of Mount Pinatubo is that the 30 to 40 million tons of sulfuric acid added to the air may speed up the breakdown of Earth's ozone layer. The ozone layer in the upper atmosphere protects you and Earth's other inhabitants from harmful solar rays. ■

INVESTIGATION 2 WRAP-UP

REVIEW

1. What are some long-term effects of volcanic eruptions? Use Mount Pinatubo as an example.

2. What events may occur before a volcanic eruption?

CRITICAL THINKING

3. Explain the process that creates island arcs.

4. You have just invented a tool that can accurately predict a volcano. Write a short paragraph to convince scientists to use it.

IN WHAT OTHER PLACES CAN VOLCANOES OCCUR?

So far, you have learned that volcanoes can occur along mid-ocean ridges and where one tectonic plate is descending under another. In this investigation you'll explore two other kinds of places where volcanoes can occur.

Activity

How Hawaii Formed

Geologists have a hypothesis that magma rising from a large chamber of molten rock—called a hot spot—deep below the Pacific Plate has built the volcanic islands that make up the state of Hawaii. In this activity you'll examine some of their evidence.

MATERIALS

- metric ruler
- map of the Hawaiian Islands, showing volcanoes
- calculator
- *Science Notebook*

Procedure

1. **Measure** the distance between the center of the island of Hawaii and the center of each of the other islands. **Record** this information in your *Science Notebook*. Use the scale on the map to find out how far apart the centers are.

Math Hint *To determine the youngest and oldest islands, compare the same place values.*

2. The table on this page tells you the estimated age of the rock on each island. **Record** the youngest island and the oldest island.

| The Hawaiian Islands ||
Island	Estimated Age of Rock
Maui	1.63 million years
Molokai	1.84 million years
Oahu	2.9 million years
Kauai	5.1 million years
Hawaii	375,000 years
Lanai	1.28 million years
Niihau	5.5 million years
Kahoolawe	1.03 million years

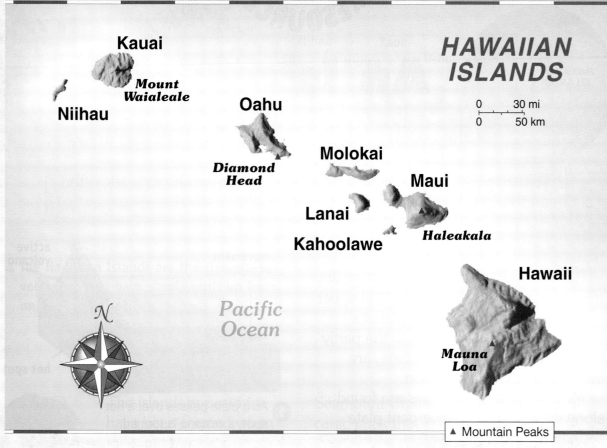

Kauai

Mount
Waialeale

Niihau

Oahu

Diamond
Head

Molokai

Maui

Lanai

Kahoolawe

Haleakala

Hawaii

Pacific
Ocean

N

Mauna
Loa

HAWAIIAN
ISLANDS

0   30 mi
0   50 km

▲ Mountain Peaks

▲ The Hawaiian Islands

3. **Make a chart** that shows the age difference between Hawaii and each of the other islands.

See **SCIENCE** and **MATH TOOLBOX** page H4 if you need to review **Using a Calculator.**

Analyze and Conclude

1. Based on your measurements, what is the distance between Hawaii and Kauai?

2. Which island is the youngest? Which is the oldest?

3. If the hot spot stays in the same place and the Pacific Plate moves over it, the hot spot may have created one island after another. Based on the ages of the islands, in which direction is the Pacific Plate moving?

4. Based on the ages of Hawaii and Kauai, what was the speed of the plate's movement?

5. What can you **infer** about the speed at which the Pacific Plate moves—does it move at a constant speed or does its speed change from time to time?

INVESTIGATE FURTHER!

RESEARCH

Look at a map of Earth's surface features. Observe the northwestward underwater extension of the Hawaiian Islands. Notice that there is an abrupt northward bend where the Hawaiian chain meets the Emperor Seamount chain. What do you think this bend means?

Great Rift Valley of Africa

> **Reading Focus** Where in Africa is the Great Rift Valley, and what makes it special to scientists?

Rifting

What happens if you slowly pull on some silicon putty? At first the putty stretches and sags. Eventually the putty breaks. The process of rifting is similar to the stretching and breaking of the putty.

Rifting is a process that occurs at divergent plate boundaries. As two plates separate, hot magma in the asthenosphere oozes upward to fill the newly formed gap. In general, rifting occurs along mid-ocean ridges deep beneath the oceans. Rifting along mid-ocean ridges leads to the process of sea-floor spreading. Some rifting, however, occurs where two continental plates are moving apart. When rifting occurs on land, the continental crust breaks up, or splits. Study the drawings on these two pages. What eventually forms when rifting occurs in continental crust?

The Great African Rift System

Over the past 25 million to 30 million years, continental rifting has been pulling eastern Africa apart—at the rate of several centimeters per decade. Jokes a Djibouti geologist, "[We are] Africa's fastest-growing nation!" Three rifts—the East African Rift, one in the Gulf of Aden, and a third in the Red Sea—form a system 5,600 km (3,472 mi) long known as the Great Rift Valley. The place where the three rift systems meet is called the Afar Triangle, named after the people who live in the region.

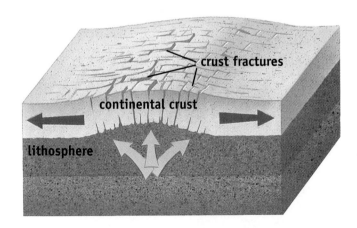

1 Magma produced by Earth's mantle rises through the crust, lifts it up, and causes fractures in the crust.

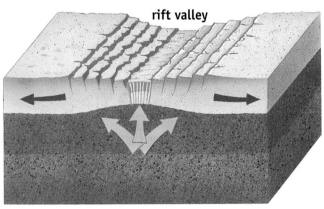

2 The crust pulls apart, faults open, and blocks of crust fall inward. Volcanoes begin to erupt. A rift valley forms.

The Great Rift Valley runs through Mozambique, Zambia, Zaire, Tanzania, Uganda, Kenya, and Sudan, up into the Ethiopian highlands and down into the Djibouti coastal plains. It is the place where humans had their first encounters with volcanoes. In fact, it is because of volcanic eruptions that anthropologists today are finding very old human remains. Some human ancestors living in the Afar region of Africa were buried under the volcanic debris of an eruption that occurred millions of years ago! Their fossil remains continue to be unearthed, and they provide important information about where early humans lived.

Found along the Great Rift Valley are some of the world's oldest volcanoes—including Mount Kenya and Mount Kilimanjaro. Mount Kilimanjaro, a volcano that towers nearly 5,900 m (19,500 ft) above the surrounding land, is Africa's highest peak.

Rifting along the Great Rift Valley has produced some of Earth's deepest lakes as well as some of the highest volcanic mountains. Lake Tanganyika, the longest freshwater lake on Earth, is the second

Mount Kilimanjaro compared to Lake Tanganyika

Height/Depth (in meters)

6000
5000
4000 — Mount Kilimanjaro
3000
2000
1000
Sea Level
-1000 — Lake Tanganyika
-2000

Using Math *About how many times higher is Mount Kilimanjaro than Lake Tanganyika is deep?*

deepest lake in the world. It formed millions of years ago when two tectonic plates shifted horizontally.

All along the Great Rift Valley, as with any rift zone, earthquakes and volcanoes are common. Study the map on page B108. Notice that along the East African

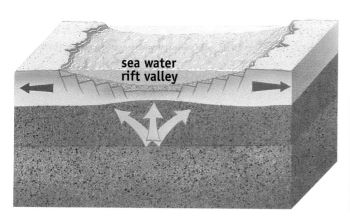

3 The rift valley widens, allowing sea water to fill the basin that has formed.

sea water
rift valley

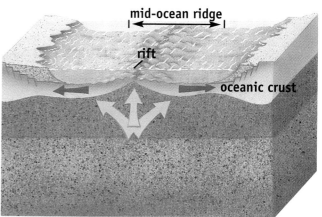

mid-ocean ridge

rift

oceanic crust

4 A new rift begins in the middle of the ocean basin that was formed. This rift is known as a mid-ocean ridge.

Main Idea and Details

When you read science, it's important to recognize which facts and details support or explain the main idea. First identify the main idea by looking for clues such as a title or a topic sentence that states the main idea. Then look for statements that support that idea.

Look for clues to find the main idea.

Look for statements, facts, and details that support the main idea.

Read the paragraphs below. Then complete the exercises that follow.

Earth as a Magnet

Earth is like a giant magnet, and it has two magnetic poles. These poles are inclined, or tilted, about 11° from the geographic poles. The magnetic field around Earth is thought to be due to movements within Earth's fluid outer core, which is composed mainly of iron and nickel. For reasons unknown, Earth's magnetic field sometimes reverses itself. This is called a **magnetic reversal**.

At present, the magnetic field is said to be normal. This means that the north-seeking needle of a compass will point toward Earth's north magnetic pole.

1. Write the letter of the sentence that states the main idea of the paragraphs.

   a. Earth's outer core is fluid.

   b. Earth is like a giant magnet with two magnetic poles.

   c. Earth's magnetic field is normal at present.

   d. Scientists don't know why Earth's magnetic field sometimes reverses itself.

2. What clues helped you find the main idea?

3. List the most important facts and details that support the main idea.

Bar Graph

This bar graph shows the heights of various volcanoes. Each height has been rounded to the nearest 50 meters.

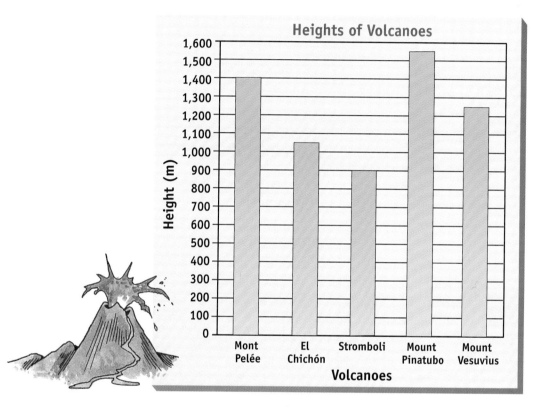

Heights of Volcanoes

Use the data in the bar graph to complete the exercises.

1. Which volcano's height is the median?

2. What is the estimated range of heights?

3. How does the range of the volcano heights compare to the median height?

4. The height of which volcano is 500 m less than the height of Mont Pelée?

5. Do the data have a mode? Tell why or why not.

6. About how many kilometers tall is Stromboli?

7. Suppose a volcano that is not shown on the graph has a height of 1,060 m. Which volcano on the graph has the same height?

WRAP-UP!

On your own, use scientific methods to investigate a question about the changing Earth.

THINK LIKE A SCIENTIST

Ask a Question

Pose a question about Earth changes and their effects. For example, ask, "How can columns that support buildings and roadways be made more resistant to earthquakes?"

Make a Hypothesis

Suggest a hypothesis that is a possible answer to the question. One hypothesis is that the columns could be made stronger or more flexible in some way.

Plan and Do a Test

Plan a controlled experiment to find out what type of materials would make support columns more resistant to earthquakes. You could start with plaster of Paris, cardboard or plastic tubes to use as column molds, and different materials to make your model columns stronger—or stronger and more flexible. Develop a procedure that uses these materials to test the hypothesis. With permission, carry out your experiment. Follow the safety guidelines on pages S14–S15.

Record and Analyze

Observe carefully and record your data accurately. Make repeated observations.

Draw Conclusions

Look for evidence to support the hypothesis or to show that it is false. Draw conclusions about the hypothesis. Repeat the experiment to verify the results.

WRITING IN SCIENCE
Research Report

Research information about earthquakes and what scientists have learned about where they occur. Present your findings in a research report. Use these guidelines to prepare your report.

- Gather information from several sources, including the Internet.

- Keep track of each source, page reference, and Web site.

- Organize the information into main categories.

- Draw a conclusion from your research.

UNIT C

The Nature of Matter

Theme: Scale

THINK LIKE A SCIENTIST

BERRY, BERRY COLD

Have you ever seen a tree or a bush after an ice storm? If so, it may have looked something like the tree in the photo. The day before the photo was taken, the branches and berries were dry. During the night, rain covered the tree with water. Then a drop in the air temperature caused the water to lose heat. The result is ice-encrusted berries. Scientists study such changes in water and in other kinds of matter. They also study how energy is related to these changes.

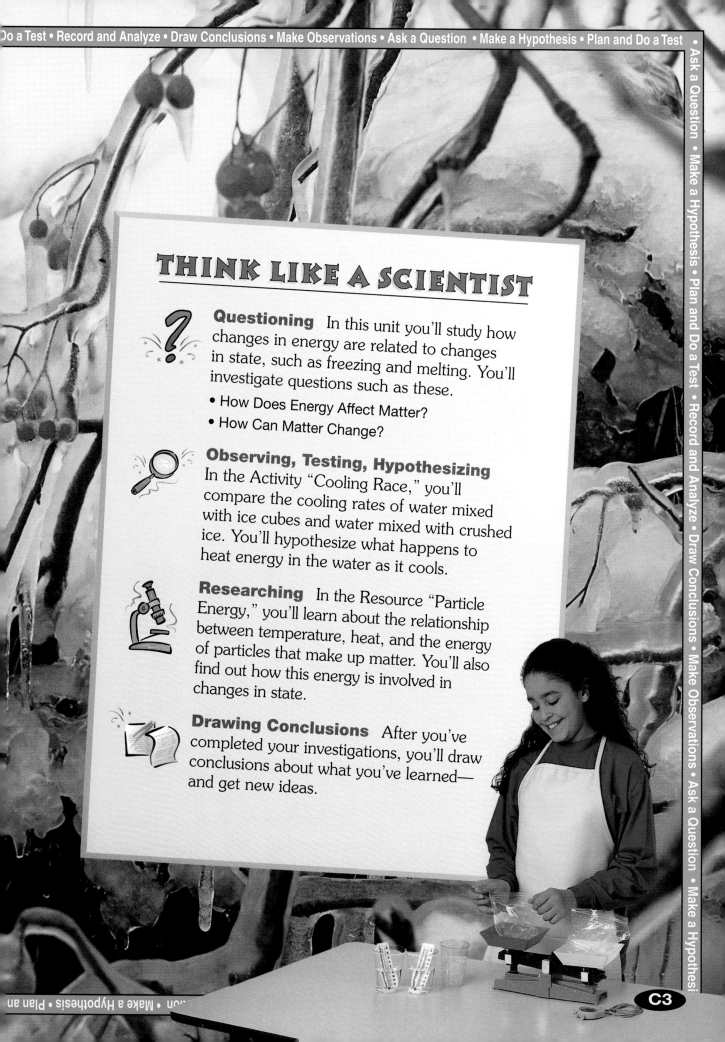

THINK LIKE A SCIENTIST

Questioning In this unit you'll study how changes in energy are related to changes in state, such as freezing and melting. You'll investigate questions such as these.

- How Does Energy Affect Matter?
- How Can Matter Change?

Observing, Testing, Hypothesizing In the Activity "Cooling Race," you'll compare the cooling rates of water mixed with ice cubes and water mixed with crushed ice. You'll hypothesize what happens to heat energy in the water as it cools.

Researching In the Resource "Particle Energy," you'll learn about the relationship between temperature, heat, and the energy of particles that make up matter. You'll also find out how this energy is involved in changes in state.

Drawing Conclusions After you've completed your investigations, you'll draw conclusions about what you've learned— and get new ideas.

1

CHARACTERISTICS OF MATTER

When you take ice cubes from the freezer of your refrigerator, you are removing solid chunks of water. Yesterday, you put liquid water in the ice-cube trays. Besides becoming cold and solid, how else has the water changed? Have the mass, density, and volume of the water been affected?

PEOPLE USING SCIENCE

Glaciologist   Erik Blake surveys the bleak, white landscape around him. As a glaciologist (glā shē äl' ə-jist), or scientist who studies glaciers, he is exploring Hubbard Glacier in Canada's rugged Yukon Territory. A glacier is a giant mass of ice that moves slowly over land. The Hubbard Glacier, which is 140 km (87 mi) long, is among the largest in North America. The glacier is a natural laboratory for Blake. He seeks to understand how it moves and the kinds of wildlife found in this harsh environment. By studying ice cores taken from deep in the glacier, he can learn what conditions were like thousands of years ago, when the ice formed.
Where a glacier meets the ocean, great mountains of ice break off and fall into the sea. Yet these massive ice mountains float! What questions would you like to ask about how glacial ice differs from liquid water?

Coming Up

◀ Erik Blake, glaciologist

C5

HOW CAN YOU DESCRIBE MATTER?

Suppose you were asked to compare a brick and a basketball. List the characteristics you would use to describe each object. Could another person identify both objects based on your lists?

Activity

A Matter of Mass

A golf ball and a table-tennis ball are about the same size. Which contains more matter? How can you measure the amount of matter in an object?

MATERIALS

- 3 sealed containers, labeled *A*, *B*, and *C*
- balance and masses
- *Science Notebook*

Procedure

1. Look at the three containers your teacher will provide. Without picking them up, **compare** their sizes and shapes. **Record** your observations in your *Science Notebook*.

2. Now pick up each container, but don't shake it. Based on the way the containers feel, arrange them in order from heaviest to lightest.

3. **Make a chart** like the one shown.

4. Using a balance, **measure** in grams the **mass**—the amount of matter—of each container. **Record** the results in your chart.

Container	Mass (g)	Contents
A		
B		
C		

Step 2

See **SCIENCE** and **MATH TOOLBOX** page H9 if you need to review **Using a Balance.**

Step 4

5. One container is filled with sand, one with water, and one with cotton. Based on your observations, **infer** which material is in each container. In the *Contents* column of your chart, **record** your inferences. Then open each container and check your inferences.

Analyze and Conclude

1. By studying and handling the containers, what can you **infer** about the amount of space taken up by each of the materials?

2. What did you learn about the amount of matter in each container? How did you learn this?

3. **Describe** what you learned about mass and matter by doing this activity.

Science in Literature

CAN ICE SINK?

"Place an ice cube in a glass of water. Why do you think it floats? . . . Now add an ice cube to half a glass of alcohol. Why do you think the ice sinks?

An ice cube will float in cooking oil, but just barely. It's beautiful to see because the melting ice forms giant drops of water that flow ever so slowly through the clear, thick oil. It's like watching rain drops falling in slow motion."

Read *Kitchen Chemistry* by Robert Gardner to find out how to complete this experiment and for other experiments that will help you explore the nature of matter on your own.

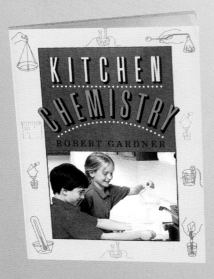

Kitchen Chemistry
by Robert Gardner
Julian Messner, 1988

Activity

A Matter of Space

Does a softball take up more space than a shoe? Try to describe the amount of space each of these objects takes up. Does the amount of matter an object contains affect how much space it takes up?

Procedure

1. If you place some cotton in one container and an equal mass of sand in another container, **predict** which material will take up more space.

2. Fill a plastic bag with cotton balls. Put as much cotton as you can in the bag without squashing it down.

3. Use a balance to **measure** the mass of the cotton. **Record** this measurement in your *Science Notebook*.

4. Remove the bag of cotton from the balance. Place another plastic bag on the empty balance pan. Add sand to the bag until it has the same mass as the bag of cotton.

5. Pour the sand from the plastic bag into a measuring cup. **Measure** and **record** how many milliliters of sand were in the bag. Then pour the sand back into its original container.

See **SCIENCE** *and* **MATH TOOLBOX** page H7 *if you need to review* **Measuring Volume.**

Step 5

6. Take the cotton balls from the bag and push them down into the measuring cup. **Record** how many milliliters of cotton you have. You may have to fill the measuring cup more than once.

Analyze and Conclude

1. Which bag contained more mass, the bag of cotton or the bag of sand?

2. Which material took up more space, the cotton or the sand?

3. Can an object's volume be determined just from its mass? Explain your answer.

Activity
Checking for Purity

The sphere and cube are about the same size. One is made of clay; the other is a mixture of clay and some lighter material. How can you tell which is which?

MATERIALS
- clay cube
- clay ball
- balance and masses
- metric measuring cup
- water
- *Science Notebook*

Procedure

1. Study a clay ball and a clay cube carefully. You may handle them, but do not change either object's shape or size. **Make inferences** about the mass and volume of each object and **record** your inferences in your *Science Notebook*.

Step 1

Math Hint *Record your inferences using the >, <, or = symbols.*

2. **Measure** and **record** the mass of each object.

3. Half fill a measuring cup with water. **Record** the volume of the water in milliliters.

4. Carefully place the ball in the measuring cup. **Observe** what happens to the water level. **Record** the new volume reading. **Calculate** the volume of the ball. Then remove the ball, shaking any excess water into the measuring cup.

5. Repeat step 4 with the cube.

Analyze and Conclude

1. What did you **infer** about the mass and volume of the two objects in step 1?

2. How did the masses of the ball and cube compare?

3. What did the changing water level in the measuring cup tell you about each object?

4. **Hypothesize** which object is made of pure clay and which is made of clay and some lighter material. Give evidence to support your hypothesis.

Measuring Mass and Volume

Reading Focus How can you find the mass and volume of an object?

▲ **Which package would you rather be holding?**

It's a cold day, and you and a friend are standing at a bus stop. You've been shopping, and you each have a package to hold. One package is quite heavy; the other is lighter but is larger and more bulky. Which package would you choose to hold?

Like everything around you, the packages are made up of matter. **Matter** is anything that has mass and volume. In fact, the problem of which package is easier to hold involves these two physical properties—mass and volume. As seen in the activities on pages C6 to C8, these properties can be measured. To review and practice your skills for measuring these and other properties, read pages H6 to H9 in the Science and Math Toolbox.

Mass

The heaviness of each package is directly related to its mass. **Mass** is a measure of how much matter something contains. Weight is a measure of the force of gravity acting on a mass. So the more matter an object contains—the greater its mass—the more it will weigh.

When you weigh yourself on a bathroom scale, the scale measures the effect of Earth's gravitational force on the mass of your body. So how could you find the mass of your body? You would have to compare the unknown mass of your body to some known mass. For example, you could sit on one end of a seesaw and have someone add objects of known mass to the other end. When the seesaw

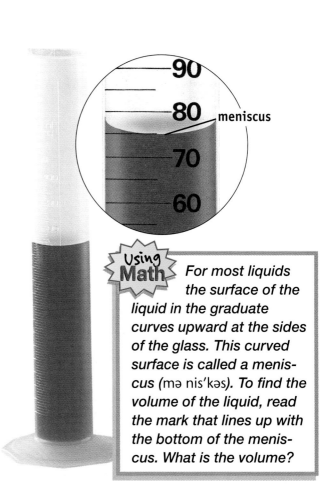

Finding the Mass of an Object
The mass of an object is found by placing the object in one pan of a balance and objects of known masses in the other.

balanced, you'd know that your mass was the same as the total mass of the objects. Now you can see why the instrument used to measure the mass of an object is called a balance.

The most common metric units used to measure mass are grams (g) and kilograms (kg). A penny has a mass of about 2 g. A kilogram is one thousand times the mass of a gram. A large cantaloupe has a mass of about 1 kg.

Other units are also used for measuring mass in the metric system. For example, the mass of a very light object could be measured in milligrams (mg). One milligram is equal to one thousandth ($\frac{1}{1000}$) of a gram.

Volume

The **volume** of an object is the amount of space it takes up. For example, an inflated balloon takes up more space—has greater volume—than an empty balloon. Volume can also be used to express *capacity*—that is, how much material something can hold. A swimming pool can hold a lot more water than a teacup can.

The basic unit of volume in the metric system is the cubic meter (m³). But because 1 m³ is such a large amount, the liter (L) is more commonly used. A liter (lēt′ər) is slightly larger than a quart. Many

soft drinks are sold in 2-L containers. Units used to measure smaller volumes include the centiliter (cL), which is one hundredth of a liter, and the milliliter (mL), which is one thousandth of a liter.

An instrument called a graduated cylinder, or graduate, is used to measure liquid volumes. Using a graduate is similar to using a measuring cup.

90
80 meniscus
70
60

Using Math *For most liquids the surface of the liquid in the graduate curves upward at the sides of the glass. This curved surface is called a meniscus (mə nis′kəs). To find the volume of the liquid, read the mark that lines up with the bottom of the meniscus. What is the volume?*

Suppose you want to know how much water or some other liquid is in a container of some kind. First you pour the liquid from the container into a graduate. Then you measure the level of the liquid against the scale marked on the side of the graduate. Graduates come in many sizes. This makes it possible for you to measure small volumes, large volumes, and all volumes in between.

There are two methods for finding the volume of a solid. One method is used for finding volumes of solids that have regular geometric shapes, such as cubes, spheres, and rectangular blocks. For any solid with a regular shape, you can measure such dimensions as length, width, height, and diameter. Then you can calculate the volume of the solid by substituting the measurements into a mathematical formula. For example, the volume of a rectangular block can be found by multiplying its length times its width times its height. The formula for this calculation is below.

$$V = l \times w \times h$$

Many solids do not have a regular shape. A rock, for example, is likely to have an irregular shape. The volume of these kinds of solids can be found by using the water displacement method.

Suppose you want to use the water displacement method to find the volume of a rock, such as the one shown in the picture. The first step is to find a graduate large enough to hold the rock. Next, you fill the graduate about one-third full with water. Then you lower the rock into the graduate, as shown. ■

Internet Field Trip

Visit **www.eduplace.com** to find out more about measurement.

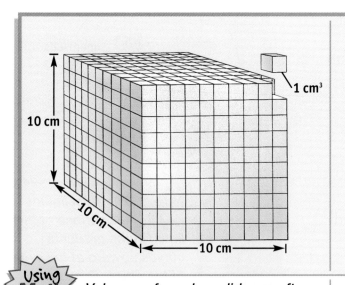

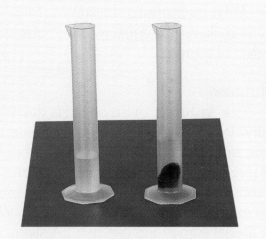

Using Math *Volumes of regular solids are often expressed in cubic centimeters (cm³). A cubic centimeter is the volume of a cube 1 cm long on each edge. One cm³ is equal to 1 mL. What is the volume of this regular solid?*

The volume of water in the graduate is 30 mL. When the object being measured is lowered into the water, the water level rises to 45 mL. What is the volume of the object?

Density

Imagine yourself in this situation. You have just packed and sealed two identical boxes. One box contains a down pillow and the other box contains books. The problem is, you have forgotten which box contains which item. Since the two boxes look exactly alike, how can you solve this problem without opening one of the boxes?

You can probably think of an easy solution. All you have to do is pick up each box. The box containing books will be much heavier than the one containing the pillow.

Density

You solved your problem by comparing the masses of two objects (cartons) having equal volumes. You may not have realized it, but you used a very important property of matter—density—to solve your problem.

Density refers to the amount of matter packed into a given space. In other words, **density** is the amount of mass in a certain volume of matter. To get an

idea of what density is, look at the objects on the balance shown in the photograph below.

What will happen if the block on the left is replaced with another block made of the same stuff, but equal in size (volume) to the block on the right? The balance will tilt to the left. The block on the left has the greater density.

You can calculate the density of any sample of matter if you know two things—its mass and its volume. You can find the density of the sample by dividing its mass by its volume. The formula for finding density is below.

$$D = m/v$$

For example, suppose you are working with a piece of metal that has a volume of 2.0 mL and a mass of 9.0 g. By using the formula, you can determine the density of that metal. Notice that density measurements always include mass and volume units.

$$D = 9.0 \text{ g}/2.0 \text{ mL} = 4.5 \text{ g/mL}$$

Understanding Density
Since the two blocks balance each other, they must have the same mass. But the block on the left is obviously smaller than the one on the right—its volume is less. Thus the block on the left has a greater density than the block on the right. ▶

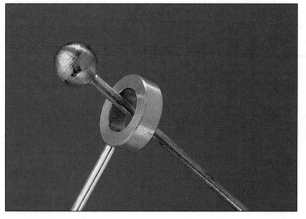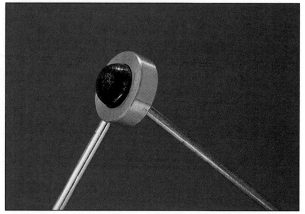

The ball and ring are both made of brass. When they are at the same temperature (*left*), the ball fits easily through the ring. How does heating the ball affect its volume (*right*)?

Using Density to Identify Materials

Density is a characteristic property of all matter. This means that a particular kind of matter always has the same density, regardless of where the matter comes from or where it is measured. For example, the density of pure water is 1.0 g/mL. This means that a milliliter of water has a mass of 1 g. The table below gives the densities of some common materials.

Since every substance has a definite density, this property can be used to identify materials. For example, suppose you measure the mass and volume of an object and find its density is 7.9 g/mL. Could you make a reasonable guess as to what material the object is made of? You could if you had a table of densities like the one on this page. Use the table to find what the object is most likely made of.

Density and Temperature

Notice that the table lists the densities of the materials at a particular temperature—in this case, 20°C. This is done because temperature affects density. As a general rule, matter expands when it gains heat and contracts when it loses heat. In other words, the volume of a material increases as its temperature goes up and decreases as its temperature goes down.

How does a change in volume affect density? Look again at the formula for density: $D = m/v$. If the mass of a material doesn't change and the volume of the material increases, its density

Densities of Some Common Materials at 20°C			
Material	**Density (g/mL)**	**Material**	**Density (g/mL)**
gold	19.3	water	1.0
lead	11.3	oil	0.90
silver	10.5	wood (oak)	0.7
copper	8.9	wood (pine)	0.4
iron	7.9	oxygen	0.0014
aluminum	2.7	helium	0.0002

decreases. On the other hand, if the volume of a material decreases and its mass stays the same, its density increases. How does heating the ball shown on page C14 change its density?

Float or Sink?

Density can be useful in predicting whether an object will sink or float in water. The density of water is 1.0 g/mL. Any material with a density less than 1.0 g/mL will float in water. Anything with a density greater than 1.0 g/mL will sink. How might such information be useful?

Imagine you're going to boil some eggs for breakfast. You want to make sure the eggs aren't spoiled. The density of a fresh egg is about 1.2 g/mL. The density of a spoiled egg is about 0.9 g/mL. If you

place an egg in water and it floats, what does this tell you about the egg?

Density in Calculations

Density can also be used to answer questions about the purity of a material. Suppose you have a chunk of metal with a volume of 10 mL. You're told that the metal is pure silver. How could you find out for sure?

You could start by looking up the density of silver, which is 10.5 g/mL. This tells you that 1 mL of silver has a mass of 10.5 g. So 10 mL of pure silver will have a mass of 10 × 10.5 g, or 105 g. Now all you have to do is measure the mass of your chunk of metal. ∎

CD-ROM

INVESTIGATE FURTHER!

Use the **Science Processor CD-ROM**, *The Nature of Matter* (Investigation 1, Good as Gold) to travel to San Francisco during the 1849 gold rush. While there, decide whether a miner is trying to sell you real gold or fool's gold.

INVESTIGATION 1 WRAP-UP

THINK IT WRITE IT

REVIEW

1. Define *mass*, *volume*, and *density*.

2. How can you find the volume of a cube and of an irregularly shaped object?

CRITICAL THINKING

3. When might you want to find the density of an object?

4. Suppose you have a 10-g cube that floats in water and a 10-g sphere that does not. What can you infer about the volume of each object? Why?

WHAT MAKES UP MATTER?

Think about what happens when water is spilled on a kitchen countertop. If you wipe the countertop with a dry sponge, where does the water go? How is the sponge different from the countertop? In this investigation you'll find out how the particles that make up matter give matter its properties.

Activity

Always Room for More

When you add sugar to a glass of iced tea, where does the sugar go? How does the sugar "fit" into the full glass?

MATERIALS

- goggles
- 2 plastic cups
- marbles
- spoon
- sand
- water
- sugar
- *Science Notebook*

SAFETY

Wear goggles during this activity.

Procedure

1. Fill a cup to the brim with marbles. **Infer** whether the cup is full or whether there is room for more matter. **Record** your inference in your *Science Notebook*.

2. Using a spoon, carefully add sand to the cup. Gently tap the sides of the cup as you add the sand. Continue until no more sand will fit in the cup. **Make an inference** about the space in the cup now.

3. Slowly and carefully pour water into the cup until no more water can be added.

4. Fill a second cup with water. Carefully add a spoonful of sugar and stir. **Record** your observations.

Step 1

C16

Step 3

Step 4

Analyze and Conclude

1. Was any matter in the cup before you added the marbles? If so, what happened to it?

2. Why could the cup full of marbles still hold sand and water?

3. How would this activity have been different if you had started by filling the cup with water?

4. Use your observations of the first cup to **infer** what happened to the sugar that was added to the second cup. How does the sugar "fit" in the water?

5. **Make a sketch** of what you think the mixture of sugar and water would look like if you could see how the two materials fit together.

Technology Link
CD-ROM

INVESTIGATE FURTHER!

Use the **Science Processor CD-ROM**, *The Nature of Matter* (Unit Opening Investigation, What's the Matter?) to compare the characteristics of liquids, solids, and gases.

Activity

Racing Liquids

A paper towel soaks up water. Do other types of paper do the same? Paper strips can help you model how particles are packed in different materials.

Procedure

1. Cut a strip 2.5 cm wide and 15 cm long from each kind of paper in the Materials list. Cut one end of each strip to form a point.

 See **SCIENCE** *and* **MATH TOOLBOX** page H6 if you need to review *Using a Tape Measure or Ruler.*

2. Study dry samples of each kind of paper with a hand lens. In your *Science Notebook*, **describe** how they are different. **Predict** which paper strip water will move through most quickly.

3. Tape the strips to the bottom of a coat hanger so that the points of the tips hang the same distance below the hanger.

4. Pour water into a pan and add a few drops of food coloring to the water. Hold the coat hanger above the pan so that the tips of the paper strips touch the water.

5. **Observe** as the water "races" up the strips. When the water reaches the top of one strip, remove the hanger. Then lay all five strips of paper on a flat surface.

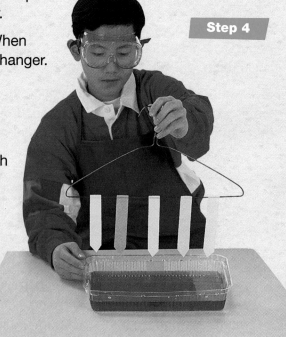

Step 4

Analyze and Conclude

1. Using the distances that water traveled through the strips, **list** the types of paper in order from fastest to slowest.

2. Imagine that you could observe the water and paper through an extremely high powered microscope. **Make a sketch** showing how you think the water moves through the paper.

3. Do samples of matter contain "empty" spaces? **Give evidence** to support your conclusion.

Structure of Matter

Reading Focus What are some effects of the motion of particles of matter?

▲ **Even in still air, specks of dust dance and dart about.**

Picture yourself sitting in your room on a quiet summer afternoon. You're home alone, there's nothing to do, and you're *bored*! You're so bored that you begin staring at the specks of dust dancing in a sparkling beam of sunlight. Even with all the doors and windows closed and no hint of a breeze, you notice that the tiny specks dart about as if they were being stirred by an invisible hand. What could be moving the dust around?

Particles in Motion

The moving specks of dust offer evidence of the structure and nature of matter. Matter is composed of very tiny particles that are constantly in motion. The particles that make up matter are much smaller than the tiniest speck of dust. These particles are so small, in fact, that they can't be seen, even with the best microscope your school owns.

Air is made up of such particles, moving through space. As the particles of air move about, they collide with each other and with everything in your room, including the specks of dust. The movements of dust specks are caused by particles of air bouncing the specks of dust around!

It's easy to see the effects of moving air particles. Inflated objects, such as balloons and basketballs, provide evidence that air is made up of particles. When you put air into a container, the moving air particles continuously bang against the sides of the container. It's these collisions that keep objects inflated.

Air, of course, is a gas. Actually it's a mixture of several different gases. Because gases are invisible, it's easy to think of them as being made up of tiny

Evidence for Particle Motion

▲ A colored liquid being added to water

▲ The mixture 5 minutes later

▲ The mixture after an additional 10 minutes

moving particles. But what about other forms of matter? What evidence do we have that liquids and solids are made up of moving particles? Look at the pictures on this page.

❶ Like still air in a room, the water in the jar seems calm. Yet the water and the colored liquid mix together on their own. This mixing indicates that liquids, like gases, are made up of moving particles.

❷ As the particles of water and colored liquid bump into each other, the particles spread out and mixing occurs.

❸ If left to stand, the particles of colored liquid and water continue to move until they are evenly mixed together.

So evidence indicates that gases and liquids are made up of tiny moving particles. What about solids? It's hard to visualize something as hard and unchanging as a rock or your desk being made up of moving particles. But it's true! You'll find out about evidence that supports this idea as you read on.

States of Matter

Think about some kinds of matter that you see every day, such as air, water, ice, iron, wood, syrup, sugar, and cloth. As different as these materials are, they can all be classified into one of three major categories, or states. The three common **states of matter** are solid, liquid, and gas. Study the drawings and descriptions of these states on page C21.

As you have just read, solids, liquids, and gases are all made up of tiny particles in constant motion. The particles that make up a substance are attracted to each other to some degree. The state in which a substance is found depends on two things: how fast the particles are moving and how strongly the particles are attracted to each other.

The forces of attraction among particles are different for different substances. For example, particles of helium gas barely attract each other at all. These particles fly around even when they are moving at fairly slow speeds.

Particles of water have slightly stronger attractions to each other. These particles have to be moving at a pretty good speed before they actually separate and fly around. The chemical forces between particles of iron are very strong. These particles have to be moving at very high speeds before they overcome the forces of attraction and fly around.

The state in which a substance is found depends on the nature of its particles and the speed at which they are moving. As you will discover, the motion of the particles can be changed. ■

States of Matter

SOLIDS
In a solid, chemical forces hold the particles in place. The particles vibrate back and forth but don't leave their positions. This is why a solid keeps its shape.

LIQUIDS
In a liquid, particles move faster and farther apart than particles in a solid. The particles in a liquid can slip and slide past each other. This is why a liquid has no definite shape.

GASES
In a gas, particles move so fast that chemical forces can't hold them together. This is why particles in a gas spread out to fill their container and why gas has no definite shape or volume.

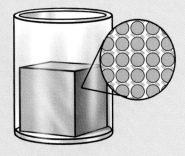
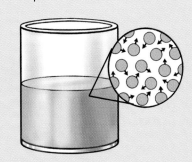
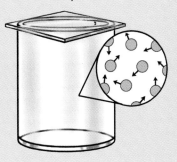

INVESTIGATION 2 WRAP-UP

REVIEW

1. What is matter made of?

2. Why do solids have a definite shape but liquids and gases do not?

CRITICAL THINKING

3. Iron expands when it is heated. Draw a sketch of how the particles of a piece of iron might look at 10°C and at 50°C.

4. If you add 2 mL sugar to 100 mL of water, the volume of the water does not change. What do you think will happen if you keep adding more and more sugar? Why?

HOW DOES ENERGY AFFECT MATTER?

What happens when you put some hard kernels of corn in a pan, hold the pan over a fire, and shake it? A few minutes later you have popcorn! In this investigation you'll find out how energy changes matter in different ways.

Activity

Cooling Race

Suppose you are enjoying a glass of lemonade on a hot day. What happens to your drink when you add ice cubes? How do the ice cubes change? Can these changes be described in terms of energy?

MATERIALS
- 2 plastic cups
- 2 thermometers
- water
- 2 different colored markers
- ice cubes
- 2 small plastic bags
- balance and masses
- spoon
- crushed ice
- timer
- graph paper
- *Science Notebook*

Procedure

1. **Make a chart** in your *Science Notebook* like the one below.

2. Half fill two plastic cups with water. Put a thermometer in each cup. **Record** the water temperature under *Start* in your chart.

	Water Temperature					
	Start	**3 min**	**6 min**	**9 min**	**12 min**	**15 min**
Water + Ice Cubes						
Water + Crushed Ice						

Step 3

3. Put two ice cubes in a plastic bag and set them on one pan of a balance. Place a second bag on the other pan. Use a spoon to add crushed ice to this bag until the pans balance.

4. Add the ice cubes to one cup and the crushed ice to the other cup.

5. At three-minute intervals, **measure** the temperature of the water in each cup. **Record** each measurement in your chart. Continue for 15 minutes.

6. **Make a line graph** that shows how the temperature of the ice-water mixtures changed over time. Use a different color for each line on your graph.

 See **SCIENCE** *and* **MATH TOOLBOX** *page H13 if you need to review* **Making a Line Graph.**

Analyze and Conclude

1. **Describe** how the ice in each cup changed.

2. In which cup did the ice change faster?

3. In which cup did the water cool more quickly? What difference between the ice cubes and the crushed ice might explain why the water in one cup cooled faster?

4. Heat energy is needed to melt ice. **Suggest a hypothesis** to explain where the heat energy came from. **Give evidence** to support your hypothesis.

5. The water contained more heat energy at the start of the activity than it did at the end. **Hypothesize** what happened to this heat energy. Support your hypothesis.

INVESTIGATE FURTHER!

EXPERIMENT

Predict the changes that would occur if you added an equal number of ice cubes to both a glass of cold water and a glass of warm water. Try the experiment and check your predictions.

C23

Activity

Speeding Up Change

Wet your finger and hold it up in the air. How does it feel? Does the feeling change when you blow on the finger? What does energy have to do with these changes?

Procedure

1. Use a dropper to place a small drop of water in a dish. Place a drop of the same size in a second dish. Set one dish in direct sunlight and the other in a cool, shaded spot. **Predict** what will happen to the two drops of water.

2. Allow the dishes to stand undisturbed, checking on the water drops every few minutes. Each time you check, **record** your observations and the time in your *Science Notebook*.

3. Between observations, **brainstorm** with members of your group. Try to think of ways to make a drop of water evaporate faster. **Record** your suggestions.

4. Put identical drops of water in two dry dishes. Leave one drop alone. **Experiment** with the other drop to see if you can make it evaporate.

5. Repeat step 4 for each technique you try. **Record** each technique and **describe** your results.

Step 4

Analyze and Conclude

1. Which drop of water from step 1 evaporated more quickly? **Suggest a hypothesis** to explain your results.

2. What techniques were successful in causing a drop of water to evaporate faster? Explain why you think each technique was successful.

3. **Make a general statement** about what causes water to evaporate.

Particle Energy

Reading Focus How is the motion of particles involved in changes of state?

Using Math

Water is the only common substance that can be found in all three states of matter at the same time and place. Earth's atmosphere contains only 0.001 percent of all the fresh water on Earth. What fraction is equivalent to 0.001 percent?

Picture in your mind a sample of iron. What do you see? You probably see a hard, grayish solid. This is the state in which iron is usually found. But under the proper conditions, iron can also exist as a liquid. It can even exist as a gas!

Most forms of matter can exist in all three states—solid, liquid, and gas. Perhaps the best example of a substance in all three states is water. You are familiar with water as a solid (ice), a liquid, and a gas (water vapor).

You have also seen water change from one state to another. You have seen ice melt, puddles "dry up," and water vapor change to a liquid and fog up a mirror. In the activities on pages C22 to C24, water

changes from the solid state to the liquid state, and it also changes from the liquid state to the gas state.

Materials change state when energy is added to them or taken away from them. These changes can be understood by thinking about the motion of the particles that make up all matter.

Energy and Temperature

You know from experience that a thrown ball or a falling rock has energy. These objects have energy because of their motion. This energy of motion is called **kinetic energy**. Even the particles that make up matter have kinetic energy because they're moving.

Look back at the drawings on page C21, which show the relative motion of particles in the three states of matter. Would you like to know how fast the particles of a material are moving? Take the material's temperature! **Temperature** is a measure of the average kinetic energy of the particles in a material.

The term *average* indicates that not all particles in a material are moving at the same rate of speed. Some are traveling (or vibrating) a little bit faster or slower than most of the particles.

Temperature and Heat

Many people think that temperature and heat are exactly the same. Although temperature is related to heat, the two are quite different. To help you understand the difference, study the two wasp nests in the drawing.

Now think of a glass of water and a bathtub full of warm water at the same temperature. Just like the wasps, the particles of water in each container have the same average speed. But because there are more particles in the tub, that water would have more heat energy.

Heat energy includes the total kinetic energy of the particles in a material. So a large sample of matter will have more heat energy than a smaller sample of the same matter, even though both samples have the same temperature.

What would happen if you added five or six ice cubes to the warm water in the glass and in the bathtub? The ice cubes in the bathtub would melt more quickly than those in the glass because the water in the tub has more energy to give them.

This example helps to define heat. **Heat** is energy that flows from warmer to cooler regions of matter. In both the glass and the bathtub, energy travels from warm water to cool ice.

Energy and Change of State

Energy is always involved in a change of state. When heat energy is added to a solid at its melting point or a liquid about to evaporate, the temperature does not increase. However, the energy does overcome the forces holding the molecules in solid or liquid form. In the reverse processes, energy is released, allowing a liquid or a solid to form.

Water is the best substance to study in order to learn about changes in state. Study the pictures on page C27 as you read about energy and changes of state.

▲ **Average Versus Total Energy**
The wasps in both of these hives have energy—they are buzzing around. The average speed of the wasps in each hive is the same. But the wasps in the larger hive have more total energy because there are more wasps.

Water Changes State

◀ Ice Changes to a Liquid
The ice absorbs energy from the Sun. This causes the particles to vibrate more. When enough energy has been added, the force holding particles together in the solid is overcome, and the ice changes state, or **melts,** to become liquid water.

◀ Water Changes to a Gas
As more energy is added, particles of liquid water escape and enter the air as a gas. The change of state from liquid to gas is called **evaporation**.

▲ Water as a Gas
Evaporation will continue until all the liquid water has changed into the gas state.

UNIT PROJECT LINK

For this Unit Project, you will put on a magic show, using your knowledge of matter. Choose one of the following magic tricks to master.

1. The Disappearing Liquid What happens when you mix two different liquids and some liquid disappears?

2. The Great Tissue Bust How can a tissue be stronger than you are? Find out, and then use what you learn in this unit to explain how your trick works.

TechnologyLink
For more help with your Unit Project, go to **www.eduplace.com**.

Evaporation occurs over a wide range of temperatures and takes place only at the surface of liquid water. If enough heat is added to liquid water, the water will eventually boil. When this happens, bubbles of water vapor form throughout the liquid, as you can see in the picture below. These bubbles will rise through the liquid and escape into the air.

A Change in Direction

Changes in state also take place when heat is removed from water. If enough heat is removed from a gas, it will change to a liquid. This process is called **condensation**. If enough heat is then removed from the liquid, it will change to a solid. This change from a liquid to a solid is called **freezing**. ■

▲ Boiling is rapid evaporation that takes place throughout a liquid at high temperatures.

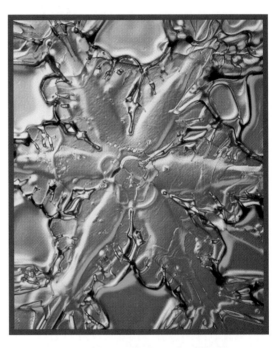

▲ When liquid water freezes, forces between water particles hold them in definite fixed patterns called crystals.

INVESTIGATION 3 WRAP-UP

REVIEW

1. How are temperature and heat different?

2. What happens during condensation?

CRITICAL THINKING

3. Bubbles of gas often form in tap water left at room temperature. Do you think this gas is water vapor, or is it something else? Explain your reasoning.

4. If you put one hand in cold water and the other in hot water, one hand feels cold and the other feels hot. Explain these feelings in terms of the movement of heat.

REFLECT & EVALUATE

Word Power

Write the letter of the term that best matches the definition. *Not all terms will be used*.

1. The change of state from a gas to a liquid
2. The amount of mass in a given volume of matter
3. Anything that has mass and volume
4. The amount of space an object takes up
5. Energy that flows from warmer to cooler regions of matter
6. A measure of the amount of matter in an object

  a. condensation
  b. density
  c. evaporation
  d. heat
  e. mass
  f. matter
  g. temperature
  h. volume

Check What You Know

Write the word in each pair that correctly completes each sentence.

1. To calculate the density of an object, you need to know its volume and its (mass, height).
2. In a liquid, the particles move faster than in a (solid, gas).
3. Energy that flows from warmer to cooler regions of matter is known as (heat, temperature).

Problem Solving

1. A 20-mL sample of grayish metal has a mass of 54 g. What is the density of the metal? After you've found its density, use the table of densities on page C14 to identify the metal.

2. Water is an unusual substance in that it expands when it freezes. Use this information to explain why ice cubes float in liquid water.

Study the drawings of the empty box and the football. Then, in your own words, describe how you would determine the volume of each object.

CHAPTER 2

KINDS OF MATTER

Solids, liquids, and gases of countless different kinds make up Earth's lands, waters, and the air. Since prehistoric times, people have used Earth's materials to make things. For example, artists use clay, a kind of matter that comes from the land, to create works of art that are both beautiful and useful.

Connecting to Science
ARTS

Pueblo Pottery   Pueblo artist Nancy Youngblood Lugo creates pottery that is known for its bold, fluid designs, which are modern, yet traditional. Youngblood Lugo is a descendant of the Native American Tafoya family, whose name has stood for creativity and excellence in Pueblo pottery through many generations.

The matter in moist clay has the property of being easily shaped. To make one of her pots, Youngblood Lugo first shapes clay into a form. As shown in the photo, she then carves a design on the clay. Another property of clay is its ability to hold its shape after drying and firing. Many artists fire pots in ovens called kilns. But in the traditional way of the Tafoyas, Youngblood Lugo fires her pots in an open flame. At the end of the firing, the flame is put out in a way that changes the matter of the clay to another kind that is hard, shiny, and dark. The finished pots in the lower picture have these properties.

Coming Up

Nancy Youngblood Lugo carving a design on a clay pot called a melon bowl *(top)*, four more clay pieces by the artist *(bottom)*.

HOW CAN MATTER BE CLASSIFIED?

If you were asked to organize all the matter in the world into groups, how many groups do you think you'd need? What characteristics would you choose to identify each group? In this investigation you'll classify matter into two groups: kinds of matter that cannot be broken down and kinds that can.

Activity

Testing Your Metal

Aluminum and copper are kinds of matter. This activity will help you decide which group they belong in.

MATERIALS
- goggles
- samples of aluminum
- samples of copper
- *Science Notebook*

SAFETY
Wear goggles during this activity.

Procedure

Obtain samples of aluminum and copper. In your *Science Notebook,* **list** some properties of each of these metals. **Brainstorm** with members of your group about things you can do to change these samples. **Make a list** of your ideas and, after getting your teacher's approval, carry out your plans. **Describe** your actions and **record** all changes in the samples.

Analyze and Conclude

1. Based on your observations, what properties do copper and aluminum have in common? How are the two metals different?

2. Did any of the changes you caused produce any new materials? Explain your answer.

Activity

A Change for the Wetter

Sugar is a kind of matter. Can sugar be broken down into other materials? Heat some sugar and find out.

Procedure

1. Sprinkle a small amount of sugar on a sheet of black paper. Examine the grains of sugar with a hand lens. **Make a sketch** of a sugar grain in your *Science Notebook*.

2. Obtain about a half spoonful of sugar. Place a candle in the center of a shallow dish and ask your teacher to light the candle. Using a potholder, hold the spoon over the candle so that the flame just touches the bowl of the spoon.

3. While you heat the sugar, have your partner use tongs to hold a glass square 2–3 centimeters above the sugar.

4. **Observe** the sugar and the glass square carefully. Continue heating the sugar until all the white crystals have disappeared. **Record** your observations of the sugar and the glass.

Analyze and Conclude

1. What was the first sign that a change was taking place?

2. **Compare** the appearance of the material in the spoon at the end of the activity with the sugar you started with. What evidence is there that you've produced different kinds of matter from the sugar?

3. What appeared on the glass square? **Infer** where this material came from.

Step 2

Elements

Reading Focus What are elements, and how are they organized?

Look at the familiar materials in the photographs on this page and the next. These materials are all different, yet they have at least one thing in common—they are all matter.

Matter can be identified by its properties, or characteristics. **Physical properties** are characteristics that can be measured or detected by the senses. Color, size, odor, and density are examples of physical properties. **Chemical properties** describe how matter changes when it reacts with other matter. The fact that paper burns is a chemical property of paper.

Given time, you could probably list hundreds or even thousands of kinds of matter. Yet scientists are able to classify all matter into two large groups—substances and mixtures. These two groups can be divided into smaller groups, as shown in the graphic organizer on page C35.

A **substance** is a material that always has the same makeup and properties, wherever it may be found. Of the materials shown in the photographs below, gold, aluminum, sugar, and water are all substances. Milk is a mixture. A **mixture** is a combination of two or more substances. You will learn about mixtures later in this chapter.

There are two kinds of substances—elements and compounds. An **element** is a substance that cannot be broken down by simple means into any other substance. The activity on page C32 shows that aluminum and copper cannot be changed into simpler kinds of matter. Aluminum and copper are elements.

A **compound** is a substance made up of two or more elements that are chemically combined. Water and sugar are examples of compounds. In the activity on page C33, sugar is changed

What properties can be used to identify these different materials? ▼

milk
water
gold
aluminum
sugar

Classifying Matter

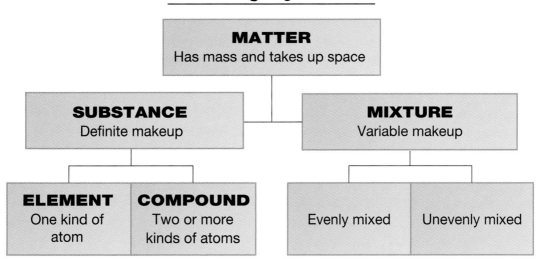

into simpler substances. One is water. The black material remaining in the spoon is an element, carbon.

Identifying Elements

Elements have been described as the building blocks of matter. All matter, regardless of its form, is made up of one or more elements. What, then, are elements made of?

Recall that all matter is made up of very tiny particles. Think about cutting a small piece of aluminum in half and then cutting one of the halves in half. Now imagine continuing to divide the aluminum into smaller and smaller pieces. Eventually you would have a particle so small that it could not be divided anymore and still be aluminum.

The tiny particle would be a building block of aluminum—an aluminum atom. An **atom** is the smallest particle of an element that has the chemical properties of the element.

All the atoms that make up a particular element are the same. Gold, for example, is made up only of gold atoms. Aluminum atoms make up the element aluminum. Gold atoms differ from aluminum atoms,

and both gold atoms and aluminum atoms differ from the atoms of all other elements.

Today scientists know of 112 elements. Each element is made up of only one kind of atom. This means that there are 112 different kinds of atoms.

Ninety elements are found in nature. These elements include many familiar substances, such as iron, copper, iodine, aluminum, and tin. But many unfamiliar elements exist too, such as ruthenium (roo thē′nē əm), francium (fran′sē əm), and xenon (zē′nän). From just these 90 elements are built the many kinds of matter that make up the whole universe!

Technology Link CD-ROM

INVESTIGATE FURTHER!

Use the **Science Processor CD-ROM**, *Nature of Matter* (Investigation 2, Sorting Space Stuff) to explore a new planet and test the materials you discover. Decide which ones are compounds, which ones are mixtures, and which ones are elements.

Twenty-two of the known elements are not found in nature. These elements are known only because scientists have produced them artificially in the laboratory.

Chemical Symbols

When writing about elements, scientists use a kind of shorthand in which each element has its own chemical symbol. A **chemical symbol** is one or two letters that stand for the name of an element. Chemical symbols are like abbreviations for the names of elements.

For many elements, the symbols come from the elements' names in English or other modern languages. Some examples of such symbols include O for oxygen, H for hydrogen, and Ca for calcium.

Sometimes the connection between an element's name and its symbol is not so obvious. For example, the symbol for iron is Fe and the symbol for gold is Au. These symbols come from the Latin names for the elements, which are *ferrum* (fer'əm) for iron and *aurum* (ô'rəm) for gold.

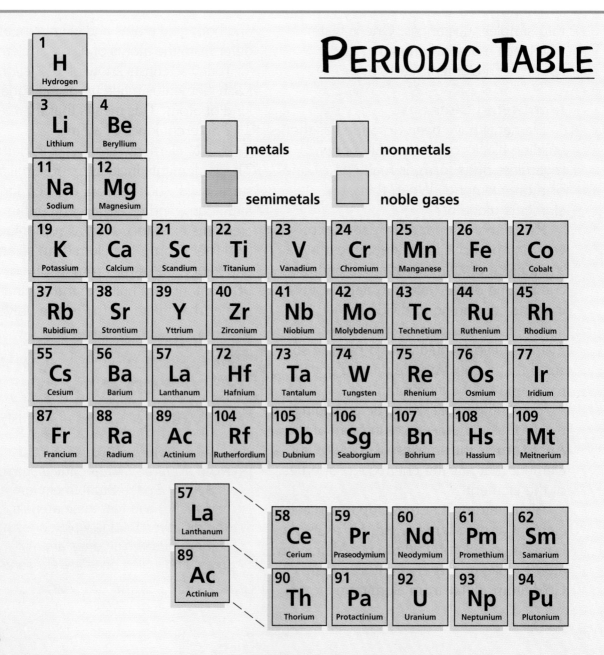

PERIODIC TABLE

metals   nonmetals

semimetals   noble gases

| 1 H Hydrogen |
| 3 Li Lithium | 4 Be Beryllium |
| 11 Na Sodium | 12 Mg Magnesium |

19 K Potassium	20 Ca Calcium	21 Sc Scandium	22 Ti Titanium	23 V Vanadium	24 Cr Chromium	25 Mn Manganese	26 Fe Iron	27 Co Cobalt
37 Rb Rubidium	38 Sr Strontium	39 Y Yttrium	40 Zr Zirconium	41 Nb Niobium	42 Mo Molybdenum	43 Tc Technetium	44 Ru Ruthenium	45 Rh Rhodium
55 Cs Cesium	56 Ba Barium	57 La Lanthanum	72 Hf Hafnium	73 Ta Tantalum	74 W Tungsten	75 Re Rhenium	76 Os Osmium	77 Ir Iridium
87 Fr Francium	88 Ra Radium	89 Ac Actinium	104 Rf Rutherfordium	105 Db Dubnium	106 Sg Seaborgium	107 Bn Bohrium	108 Hs Hassium	109 Mt Meitnerium

| 57 La Lanthanum |
| 89 Ac Actinium |

| 58 Ce Cerium | 59 Pr Praseodymium | 60 Nd Neodymium | 61 Pm Promethium | 62 Sm Samarium |
| 90 Th Thorium | 91 Pa Protactinium | 92 U Uranium | 93 Np Neptunium | 94 Pu Plutonium |

The Periodic Table

The idea that there are certain basic kinds of matter—elements—is an old one. Some early scientists thought there were four elements—fire, earth, air, and water. However, by the seventeenth century, scientists had identified a number of elements. By the nineteenth century, more than 50 elements were known.

In 1869 a Russian chemist, Dmitri Mendeleev, published a table of the 63 elements known at that time. Mendeleev organized the elements into a table according to the weights of their atoms and their properties. The elements in each column of the table had similar properties. The table below is a modern version of Mendeleev's table. It is called the Periodic Table of Elements.

Each block of this periodic table includes information about a particular element. For example, hydrogen is the simplest element. That is, hydrogen atoms have the simplest structure. For this reason, hydrogen is listed first and it is given the atomic number 1.

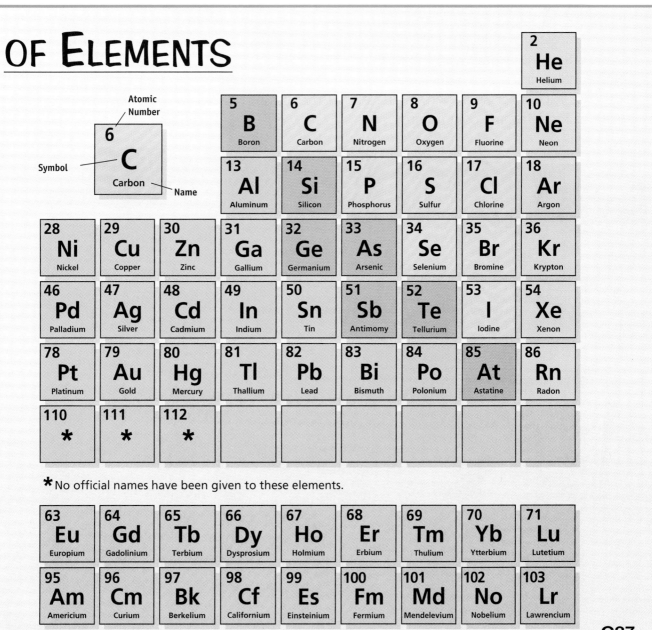

*No official names have been given to these elements.

Classifying Elements		
Group	**Examples**	**Properties**
Metals	iron, copper, aluminum	Usually shiny; can be formed into sheets and wire; good conductors of heat and electricity
Nonmetals	sulfur, carbon, chlorine	Dull; cannot be easily shaped; poor conductors of heat and electricity; some are gases
Semimetals	silicon, boron	Have some properties of both metals and nonmetals
Noble Gases	helium, neon, radon	Do not combine readily with other elements

Using the Periodic Table

In addition to information about each element, the periodic table tells you something about groups of elements. Like Mendoleev's table, this table is organized so that the elements in the same column have similar properties. For example, except for hydrogen, all the elements in the left-hand column are chemically active metals. All the elements in the right-hand column are inactive gases. Use the table on pages C36 and C37 to find out which elements have properties similar to those of chlorine.

Elements can also be classified into four groups—metals, nonmetals, semimetals, and noble (nō′bəl) gases as shown in the table above. ■

Science in Literature

A UNIVERSE OF ELEMENTS

"Hydrogen is the simplest element. Over 90 percent of the Universe is made up of hydrogen created at the time of the Big Bang—the explosion that produced the Universe. All other heavier elements have been formed from hydrogen by nuclear reactions. . . . The elements in a meteorite, such as iron and nickel, are identical to those found on Earth. . . ."

Read *Eyewitness Science: Chemistry* by Dr. Ann Newmark to find out more about elements. For example, which do you think contains more oxygen, air or Earth's crust? The answer may surprise you.

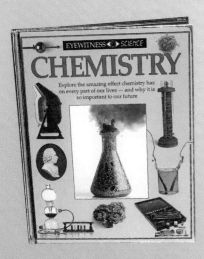

Eyewitness Science: Chemistry
by Dr. Ann Newmark
Dorling Kindersley, 1993

Compounds

One of the most beautiful materials found in the laboratory is a reddish-orange powder sometimes known as red precipitate (prē sip'ə tit). The photographs show what happens to this powder if you heat a small amount of it in a test tube.

In the photographs you can see the contents of the test tube change from a reddish-orange solid to a dark powder and then to a shiny liquid on the sides of the test tube. What you can't see is the gas escaping from the mouth of the test tube. How can you tell that red precipitate is *not* an element?

The Composition of Compounds

Red precipitate is a compound of mercury and oxygen. Its scientific name is mercuric (mər kyoor'ik) oxide, and it forms when the elements mercury and oxygen combine. When elements combine to form a compound, their atoms become chemically linked, or joined. In most compounds, such as water, the linked atoms form **molecules** (mäl'i kyoolz). In some compounds, such as salt, or sodium chloride, the atoms are held together in hundreds or thousands of units, forming crystal-like structures.

When elements join to form compounds, the joined elements lose their original properties and take on new ones. For example, mercury is a shiny liquid metal. Oxygen is a colorless, invisible gas. But as you have seen, the compound made up of these elements, mercuric oxide, is a reddish-orange powdery solid.

▼ **As it is heated, mercuric oxide separates into mercury and oxygen.**

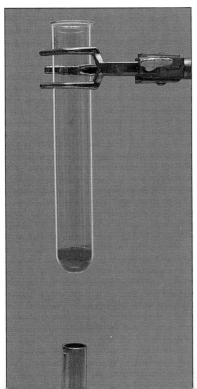
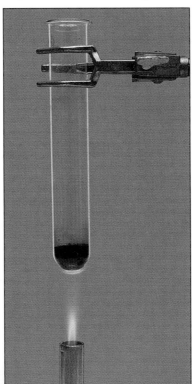
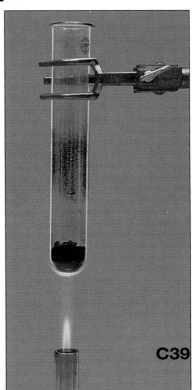

▲ Sodium is a soft metal that reacts explosively with water.

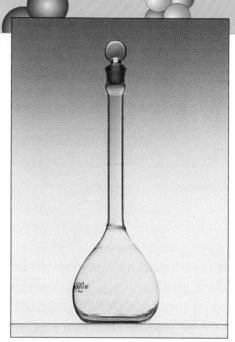

▲ Chlorine is a poisonous, greenish-yellow gas.

Water and salt are two common substances that show how much elements can change when they combine to form compounds. Water is a compound made up of the elements hydrogen and oxygen, which are both colorless gases. Hydrogen burns with a very hot blue flame. Oxygen helps other substances to burn but does not burn itself.

So what are the properties of the compound that is made when these two gases combine with each other? Water is a liquid that does not burn. In fact, it can be used to put out fires!

Sodium chloride (commonly known as table salt) is made up of sodium and chlorine. The photographs above show what these elements are like. It's hard to believe that the white crystals you sprinkle on your popcorn are made up of such dangerous elements!

Chemical Formulas

Just as chemical symbols are used to represent elements, chemical formulas are used to represent compounds. A **chemical formula** is a group of

symbols that shows the elements in a compound. For example, the chemical formula for water is H_2O. This formula shows that a single molecule of water is made up of 2 hydrogen atoms and 1 oxygen atom.

In the formula for water, look at the number 2 after the symbol for hydrogen. A number written to the right of and below a symbol in a chemical formula is called a subscript (sub'skript). A subscript shows how many atoms of an element are present in a single molecule or the simplest unit of a compound.

No subscript is written to show a single atom. So if you don't see a subscript in a formula (as with the O in H_2O), you can assume that there is one atom of that element. The formula for sulfuric acid, for example, is H_2SO_4. This formula shows that each unit of sulfuric acid contains 2 atoms of hydrogen, 1 atom of sulfur, and 4 atoms of oxygen.

Compounds of Carbon

Many compounds found in nature are very complex. This is especially true of

compounds of carbon. Carbon is an element that is found in all living things. An entire field of chemistry, called organic chemistry, is devoted to the study of carbon compounds.

The table sugar you put on your cereal in the morning has the chemical formula $C_{12}H_{22}O_{11}$. How many atoms make up a single molecule of this compound? Does this sound like a giant, complex molecule? Not when it's compared with a particle of cholesterol (kə les'tər ôl).

Cholesterol is a compound found in the cells of many living things. Although cholesterol plays some important roles in living organisms, an excess of the compound can cause serious health problems, such as heart disease, in humans. The chemical formula for cholesterol is $C_{27}H_{45}OH$.

How many atoms are present in a single molecule of cholesterol? You would probably agree that this molecule is, indeed, complex. But carbon is a very "linkable" atom. The number of different carbon compounds is seemingly endless. And many of these compounds are more complex than cholesterol. ∎

Eggs and fried foods are sources ▶ of cholesterol.

UNIT PROJECT LINK

Here are some more magic tricks. Choose one to work on with your group.

1. What Color Is Blue Ink? Is ink a mixture or a compound?

2. The Invisible Force Can an index card be used as a cap to keep a glass full of water from spilling?

3. The Leakproof Strainer How can one liquid keep another liquid from passing through the holes in a strainer?

Technology Link

For more help with your Unit Project, go to **www.eduplace.com**.

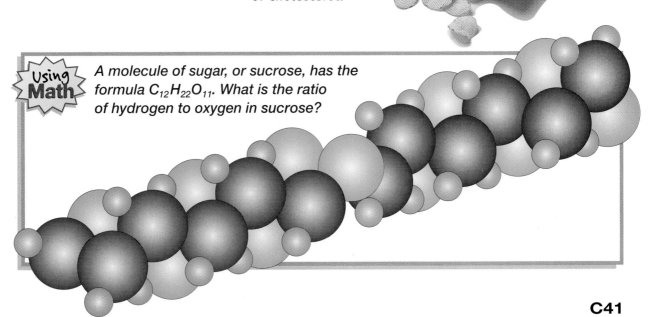

Using Math
A molecule of sugar, or sucrose, has the formula $C_{12}H_{22}O_{11}$. What is the ratio of hydrogen to oxygen in sucrose?

Ancient Elements

Reading Focus How has our understanding of elements changed over time?

Chemistry got its start as an experimental science in the Middle Ages with the alchemists (al′kə mists). The goal of the alchemists was not scientific knowledge. Alchemists were mainly interested in wealth and long life. Much effort was spent trying to change iron and lead into gold and searching for a substance that could give everlasting life.

Though many of the ideas of the alchemists were wrong, much good came from their efforts. At least five elements and many chemicals were discovered or identified by alchemists. The time line shows that alchemists helped pave the way for modern chemistry. ■

The term *element* is coined by Plato, a famous Greek philosopher. The Greeks consider the four basic kinds of matter, or elements, to be fire, water, air, and earth.

400–300 B.C.

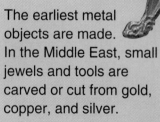

The earliest metal objects are made. In the Middle East, small jewels and tools are carved or cut from gold, copper, and silver.

10,000 B.C.

1550 B.C. Plows made of bronze are used in what is now Vietnam.

3200 B.C. Copper is mined on a large scale in Egypt. Copper is used in the making of bronze during the Bronze Age.

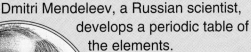

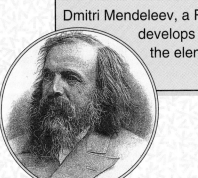

Dmitri Mendeleev, a Russian scientist, develops a periodic table of the elements.

1869

1803

English chemist John Dalton proposes his atomic theory.

1661

English chemist Robert Boyle re-introduces the idea of basic types of matter called elements.

A.D. 700–1300

Science declines in Europe and thrives in the Arab world. Chemistry develops into an experimental science through the efforts of the alchemists. They learn many things about how elements behave and combine with each other.

INVESTIGATION 1 WRAP-UP

REVIEW

1. What do elements and compounds have in common? How do they differ?

2. What is the meaning of the formula H_2O?

CRITICAL THINKING

3. The formula for carbon dioxide is CO_2. The formula for sulfur trioxide is SO_3. The formula for carbon tetrachloride is CCl_4. Infer the meanings of the prefixes *di-, tri-,* and *tetra-*.

4. A certain element has the atomic number of 53. What is its name and symbol? Is it more similar to oxygen or to chlorine? Explain.

WHAT IS A MIXTURE?

Perhaps the two most common kinds of matter at Earth's surface are rocks and ocean water. Neither is a substance. Both kinds of matter are made up of different elements and compounds mixed together. Find out about mixtures in this investigation.

Activity

Working With Mixtures

How can you tell if something is a mixture? With some things, such as chocolate chip ice cream or vegetable soup, it's easy to tell. With others, such as vanilla ice cream or salt water, it's more difficult.

MATERIALS

- goggles
- scissors
- aluminum foil
- copper foil
- sugar
- 2 clear jars with lids
- spoon
- hand lens
- aquarium gravel
- sand
- *Science Notebook*

SAFETY

Wear goggles. Be careful working with scissors.

Procedure

1. Cut a piece of aluminum foil and a piece of copper foil into small pieces. Add the pieces to a clear jar.

2. Add 2 or 3 spoonfuls of sugar to the jar. **Predict** whether the properties of any of the materials in the jar will be changed by being mixed together. Place the lid on the jar and shake the jar vigorously.

Step 2

3. Use a hand lens to examine the contents of the jar carefully. In your *Science Notebook*, **describe** the contents of the jar and tell how you would separate the parts of this mixture.

4. Add 2 spoonfuls each of aquarium gravel and sand to another jar. Cover the jar and shake it vigorously.

5. Brainstorm with your partner to **plan an experiment** for separating the parts of the sand-gravel mixture. After showing the plan to your teacher, obtain the necessary materials and carry out your plan.

6. Return the sand and gravel to the jar. Add 2 spoonfuls of sugar to the jar and repeat step 5 for this mixture.

Analyze and Conclude

1. Were any properties of the aluminum, copper, or sugar changed by being mixed together? How do you know?

2. What can you **infer** about the differences between a mixture and an element? a mixture and a compound?

3. **Describe** your method for separating the mixture of sand and gravel. Were you able to use the same method to separate the mixture of sand, gravel, and sugar? Why or why not? If not, **describe** the method you used to separate this mixture.

INVESTIGATE FURTHER!

EXPERIMENT

Wearing disposable gloves and goggles, mix a spoonful of sand and a spoonful of iron filings. Think of a property of iron that you could use to help separate this mixture. Write up a plan for separating the mixture. Show the plan to your teacher. If the plan is approved, carry it out.

Activity
Racing Colors

Is black ink a substance or a mixture? Find out if you can separate it into parts.

MATERIALS
- water
- wide-mouth jar
- scissors
- filter paper
- water-based marker
- rubber band
- *Science Notebook*

SAFETY

Handle scissors with care.

Procedure

1. Fill a jar with water to within a few millimeters of its rim.

2. Cut a small hole in the center of a piece of filter paper. Use a water-based marker to make a circle of round dots near the hole in the filter paper, as shown.

3. Stretch the filter paper over the mouth of the jar and hold it in place with a rubber band.

4. Cut a second piece of filter paper in fourths. Roll up one of the fourths to make a cone. Insert the tip of the cone through the hole in the filter paper until it touches the water.

5. Predict what will happen as water moves up the cone and past the marker spots. **Record** your prediction in your *Science Notebook*.

6. Observe the setup until the water has reached the edge of the jar. **Record** your observations.

Step 2

marker dot

hole

Step 4

Analyze and Conclude

1. Describe what happens to each marker spot.

2. Is ink a substance or a mixture? What evidence can you give to support your answer?

Activity

A Mixed-Up State

Some mixtures behave like a liquid. Some behave like a solid. The behavior of some mixtures, as you will discover, is not easy to describe.

MATERIALS

- goggles
- cornstarch
- spoon
- shallow dish
- dropper
- food coloring
- water
- plastic cup
- tongue depressor
- plastic knife
- marbles
- *Science Notebook*

SAFETY

Wear goggles during this activity.

Procedure

1. Place four or five spoonfuls of cornstarch in a dish. **Predict** how the cornstarch will change if you add water to it.

2. Add several drops of food coloring to some water in a plastic cup. Add this colored water, a few drops at a time, to the cornstarch. Stir with a tongue depressor until you have a wet ball of cornstarch.

3. Describe the material you have created. Pick some up and **observe** its properties. **Record** your observations in your *Science Notebook*.

4. Try cutting the material with a plastic knife. Try rolling it into various shapes. Place marbles on the material and describe what happens.

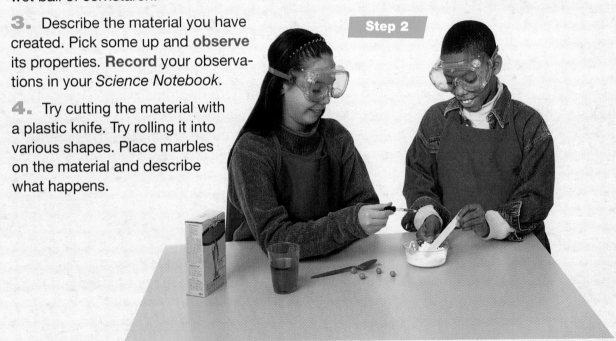

Step 2

Analyze and Conclude

1. Why is the material produced in this activity a mixture?

2. **Describe** the ways that the material acts like a liquid and the ways it acts like a solid.

3. Do you think the mixture can easily be separated into its original parts? Explain your answer.

Mixtures

Reading Focus How is a mixture different from a compound?

The chemical formula for water is H$_2$O. This formula tells you that water is made up of 2 parts hydrogen and 1 part oxygen. Is water a mixture of hydrogen and oxygen? This question may confuse people who are just beginning to study chemistry. The answer to the question is no. About the only thing that compounds and mixtures have in common is that each is made up of two or more different kinds of matter.

Keeping Their Properties

In the activity on pages C44 and C45, aluminum, copper, and sugar are mixed together in a jar. Even after shaking the jar, it is still possible to recognize the different substances that make up the mixture.

This activity provides a clue as to how mixtures are different from compounds. All the substances in a mixture keep their original properties. When substances combine to form a compound, the properties of the substances that make up the compound are gone. The properties of these substances are replaced by the unique properties of the compound.

Suppose you were to mix iron filings with salt. No matter how thoroughly you mixed the two substances, you would still have iron and salt. Both substances would still have their original properties. For example, one physical property of iron is that it is attracted to a magnet.

Mixing the iron with salt has no effect on this property, as the photograph below shows.

◀ Iron is magnetic, and it keeps this property in a salt-iron mixture.

▲ **Is this fruit punch a mixture or a compound?**

When substances combine to form a compound, the substances change. Water, for example, is nothing like the hydrogen and oxygen that combine to make up water. And water's properties are very different from those of hydrogen and oxygen.

The Makeup of a Mixture

Ice cream is a mixture—perhaps one of your favorite mixtures. There are many varieties, or flavors, of ice cream, and each contains different ingredients.

Mixtures, including the various flavors of ice cream, don't have chemical formulas. The reason is that two mixtures of the same materials can be quite different in makeup. This explains why the same flavor of ice cream may taste different from brand to brand.

To understand how mixtures of the same materials can differ, think about two bowls of fruit punch made with the same ingredients. One person might mix two bottles of orange juice, one bottle of club soda, some strawberries, some cherries, and a cut-up orange. Using the same ingredients, someone else might mix one bottle of orange juice, two bottles of club soda, and the same kinds of fruit but in different amounts.

Both would have mixtures of liquids and fruit, but the mixtures would not be the same throughout. So a single formula could not accurately represent the make-up of such a mixture.

Unlike a mixture, a compound *always* has the same composition. For example, no matter where it comes from, salt always contains one part sodium and one part chlorine. Water always contains two parts hydrogen and one part oxygen. That's why you can use a chemical formula to represent a compound. The chemical makeup of a given compound never changes.

Some Common Mixtures

Most matter in the world around you exists as mixtures. You just have to look out the window to see evidence of this. In fact, the glass in your classroom windows is a mixture. Most window glass is made up of silicon dioxide (sil'i kän dī äks'īd) and some other substances. Most glass is pretty much the same, but the amount of each substance in glass can vary from sample to sample without affecting the properties of the glass.

Beyond your classroom window you can probably see a variety of materials, such as bricks, cement, and asphalt (as'fôlt). All these building materials are mixtures. As you observe these mixtures, you are looking through, and are surrounded by, a very important natural mixture—air.

Air is a mixture of gases. This mixture consists of about four-fifths nitrogen gas and one-fifth oxygen gas. But air also contains small amounts of other gases, such as carbon dioxide and water vapor. The percentages of these gases vary from place to place and from time to time.

You don't have to look outside the classroom to find mixtures. In fact, you don't have to look any further than your own body. The human body contains many different mixtures. Blood, sweat, tears, and saliva are a few examples of mixtures that make you what you are.

Separating Mixtures

The different materials in a mixture can almost always be separated from each other by some physical means. For example, a variety of methods are used to

▲ The composition of air changes from time to time and place to place.

separate different mixtures in the activity on pages C44 and C45.

The method used to separate a mixture depends on some difference in the physical properties of the materials in the mixture. One important property used in separating a mixture is the size of the pieces making up the mixture. Suppose, for example, you had a pocketful of coins—pennies, nickels, dimes, and quarters. You could easily separate this mixture by hand.

Now suppose you get a job in a store. At the end of the week, you are asked to separate a shopping bag full of coins. You could do this by hand, but it would take quite a while. A sorting machine like the one shown would make the job of separating the coins easier.

A mixture of salt and sand would be more difficult to separate than a mixture of coins. It would be almost impossible to separate the materials by hand. And a sorting machine wouldn't work, because the pieces of salt and sand are similar in size. So you have to find another method for separating the mixture.

Think about salt and sand. Do either of these materials have some property you could use to separate them? Yes; salt dissolves in water and sand does not. If you

▲ **What properties of coins does this machine use to separate a mixture of coins?**

What property or properties could you use to separate a mixture of coins? ▶

add water to a mixture of salt and sand, the salt will dissolve in the water. You can then pour off the salt water and collect the sand, which remains behind. How might you get the salt back from the salt water? ■

INVESTIGATION 2 WRAP-UP

REVIEW

1. Explain why a mixture cannot be represented by a chemical formula.

2. What is the difference between a mixture and a substance?

CRITICAL THINKING

3. Suppose you had a mixture of iron pellets, pebbles, and small wood spheres, all about the same size. How would you separate this mixture?

4. How can mixtures of the same substances differ?

WHAT ARE LIQUID MIXTURES LIKE?

What do milk, soft drinks, and ocean water have in common? Your first thought may be that they are all liquids. But if you consider it more carefully, you'll realize that they are all liquid mixtures. Study the properties of these mixtures in this investigation.

Activity

Mixing Solids Into Liquids

Sugar dissolves in water and seems to disappear. What factors affect how fast the sugar disappears?

Procedure

1. In your *Science Notebook*, **make a chart** like the one shown.

Conditions	Time
Cold Water	
Water at Room Temperature	
Warm Water	
Warm Water + Stirring	
Warm Water + Crushed Sugar + Stirring	

 See **SCIENCE** and **MATH TOOLBOX** page H11 if you need to review *Making a Chart to Organize Data.*

2. Fill one cup with ice-cold water, a second cup with water at room temperature, and a third cup with warm water. Use equal amounts of water in each cup. Use a marker to label the cups as shown here.

3. Predict which water will most quickly dissolve a sugar cube. Then add a sugar cube to each cup. Time how long it takes for each sugar cube to dissolve. **Record** the times in your chart.

4. Pour out the water and rinse the cups. Refill one cup with warm water and add a sugar cube. This time, stir the mixture until the sugar cube dissolves. **Record** the time.

5. Use a spoon to crush a sugar cube. Repeat step 4, using the crushed sugar. **Record** the time.

Step 4

Analyze and Conclude

1. How did the temperature of the water affect the rate at which the sugar dissolved in it?

2. What effect did stirring have on the rate at which the sugar dissolved in water?

3. What effect did crushing the sugar into small particles have on the rate at which the sugar dissolved?

4. What can you **infer** about the size of the sugar particles that are dissolved in a mixture of sugar and water?

5. Suggest a hypothesis that relates the effects of water temperature, stirring, and smaller pieces of sugar to the rate at which sugar dissolves.

INVESTIGATE FURTHER!

EXPERIMENT

Once salt is dissolved in water, how can you get the salt back? Design an experiment to get the salt out of salt water.

Activity
To Mix or Not to Mix

Shake that bottle of salad dressing before you pour it on your salad. If you don't, you may get only part of the mixture.

Procedure

1. Add water to a jar until it is about one-fourth full.

Math Hint
To estimate the one-fourth line of a container, measure the height of the container and round the height to the nearest whole unit. Then divide by 4.

2. Add a few drops of food coloring to the water. Swirl the jar around until the water is evenly colored throughout.

3. Add the same amount of vegetable oil to the jar as you did water. Screw the lid tightly on the jar.

4. Shake the jar several times and stand it on the table. **Observe** what happens to the liquids in the jar. **Record** your observations in your *Science Notebook*.

5. Turn the jar upside down and hold it that way. **Observe** what happens to the liquids and **record** your observations.

Step 3

Step 4

Analyze and Conclude

1. Does water mix with food coloring? **Give evidence** to support your answer.

2. Do water and oil mix? **Give evidence** to support your answer.

3. What happened when you turned the jar upside down?

4. Based on your observations, what can you **infer** about the ability of different liquids to mix?

Activity

Making Water Wetter

What happens if you try to clean a greasy dish with plain water? The water runs off the dish. The water doesn't seem to wet the dish. Can you mix something with water to make it "wetter"?

Procedure

1. Spread a sheet of wax paper on the table.

2. Use a dropper to carefully place one drop of an unidentified blue liquid on the paper. Use a toothpick to probe the drop and **observe** how it behaves. In your *Science Notebook*, **record** your observations, including the color of the drop and what shape the drop takes.

3. Using a clean dropper, place a drop of an unidentified red liquid on the paper. Use the toothpick to probe the drop and **observe** how it behaves. **Record** your observations.

4. Repeat step 3 with a drop of plain water.

Step 3

Analyze and Conclude

1. **Describe** the shapes of the two colored drops and **compare** their behavior when you probed them with a toothpick.

2. One colored liquid is plain water mixed with food coloring; the other is water mixed with food coloring and detergent. **Infer** which is which. **Give evidence** to support your inference.

3. Which liquid seemed to "wet" the wax paper better?

4. **Suggest a hypothesis** to explain how detergent in water helps clean grease.

Bubbles

Reading Focus How can the force of attraction between water molecules be changed?

Have you ever seen a water strider? A water strider is an insect that is able to walk on water! How does the water strider manage to stay on the water's surface? If you look very closely at the surface, it seems to be covered with a very thin skin. The shape of the water strider's feet allow the insect to glide across this skin without breaking it.

A force of attraction called cohesion exists among water particles. This force produces an effect called surface tension, which is responsible for the "skin" on the water's surface.

Have you ever tried to produce large bubbles like the one shown, using plain water? It's not possible. In fact, because of cohesion, you can't even get water to form a film on the bubble wand. But if you add a little soap to the water, it's a different story. Like the girl in the picture below, you can form delicate bubbles that float in the air.

When soap is added to water, it reduces the forces of attraction among water particles. Surface tension is also greatly reduced. If the water strider stepped onto the surface of soapy water, the insect would enjoy a swim rather than a stroll.

▲ **Reduced cohesion makes it possible for the soap-water mixture to be stretched out into a thin film, or bubble. Some soap bubbles are no more than one or two particles in thickness.**

Alloys

Reading Focus What are some common alloys and how are they used?

Question: When is a metal not an element? Answer: When it's an alloy. An **alloy** is a solution of two or more metals with properties of its own. For example, stainless steel is an alloy made of iron, chromium, carbon, and nickel. Stainless steel is stronger than iron, lighter than iron, and resists rusting.

An alloy is made by melting two or more metals and mixing them together. The mixture is then allowed to cool and harden to a solid. In its final form an alloy consists of a solution in which the metal components are thoroughly mixed with each other.

Some Important Alloys

Alloys have been important to humans for thousands of years. One of the first alloys ever prepared was bronze, which is a mixture of copper and tin. Some bronzes also contain zinc.

The earliest bronze items have been dated at about 3500 B.C. The introduction of bronze was such an important event that a whole period in human history— the Bronze Age—has been named after this alloy.

▲ **These bronze objects are more than 1,000 years old.**

Common Alloys		
Alloy	**Composition**	**Use**
Brass	70% Cu, 30% Zn	hardware, plumbing
Bronze	90% Cu, 10% Sn	artwork, domes of buildings
Gold alloy	70% Au, 15% Ag, 10% Cu, 1% Pt, 1% Zn, 1% Pd	dentistry, jewelry
Pewter	85% Sn, 7% Cu, 6% Bi, 2% Sb	cups, candlesticks
Solder	60% Pb, 40% Sn	connecting metal pieces together
Stainless steel	74% Fe, 18% Cr, 8% Ni	cutlery
Steel	99% Fe, 1% C	bridges, buildings
Sterling silver	93% Ag, 7% Cu	jewelry, tableware

The table above lists some common alloys and tells what metals they contain and how they are used. Refer to the periodic table on pages C36 and C37 for the names of the metals whose chemical symbols are given.

Alloys are useful because their properties are different from those of the metals from which they are made. For example, alloys of gold are much harder and less expensive than pure gold. A unit called a karat (kar′ət) is used to express the purity of a sample of gold.

Amalgams (ə mal′gəmz) are alloys that contain mercury. An amalgam used in dental work consists of 70 percent silver, 18 percent tin, 10 percent copper, and 2 percent mercury. The mercury makes the amalgam soft enough for a dentist to work with it.

Some alloys have unusual properties. For example, Wood's metal is an alloy of bismuth (biz′məth), lead, tin, and cadmium (kad′mē əm). This alloy has a melting point of 70°C. It will melt on your stove at a relatively low temperature setting. Can you see how this alloy can be used in automatic sprinklers?

Another interesting alloy is misch (mish) metal, which is made of cerium (sir′ē əm), lanthanum (lan′thə nəm), and other metals. Misch metal has the unusual property of giving off sparks when it is rubbed. Because of this property, misch metal is used in the manufacture of flints used for lighting butane stoves. ■

INVESTIGATION 3 WRAP-UP

REVIEW

1. Explain why salad dressing is not a solution.

2. What do compounds and mixtures have in common?

CRITICAL THINKING

3. Why is an alloy both a mixture and a solution?

4. What methods would you use to dissolve a large crystal of salt, known as rock salt, in water? Explain all the factors that affect the rate at which the salt will dissolve.

REFLECT & EVALUATE

Word Power

Write the letter of the term that best matches the definition. *Not all terms will be used*.

1. Characteristics that can be measured or detected by the senses
2. The smallest particle of an element that has its chemical properties
3. A group of symbols that show the elements in a compound
4. Characteristics that describe how matter changes when it reacts with other matter
5. A group of atoms that are chemically linked
6. A solution of two or more metals

a. alloy
b. atom
c. chemical formula
d. chemical properties
e. element
f. molecule
g. physical properties
h. solvent

Check What You Know

Write the word in each pair that correctly completes each sentence.

1. Metals, nonmetals, semimetals, and noble gases are four different types of (elements, compounds).
2. When elements are joined in a compound, they (lose, keep) their original properties.
3. Glass is a (mixture, compound).
4. When soap is added to water, its surface tension (increases, decreases).

Problem Solving

1. Explain why all the elements that appear in the same column of the periodic table are commonly referred to as a family.
2. How could you quickly separate a mixture of brass tacks and iron tacks?
3. Explain why salt cannot be removed from a salt-water mixture by pouring the mixture through a paper filter.

Study the section of the periodic table shown. Use the section to determine which elements are more similar in chemical and physical properties—copper and zinc, or copper and silver. Explain how you know.

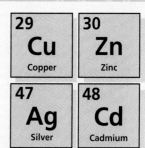

29	30
Cu	**Zn**
Copper	Zinc
47	48
Ag	**Cd**
Silver	Cadmium

CHAPTER 3

HOW MATTER CHANGES

Have you ever been camping? A good campfire may have helped warm you. A campfire builder usually has to cut large pieces of wood into smaller pieces for the fire. When this wood burns, it leaves only ashes. In this chapter you'll find out about the physical and chemical changes that matter undergoes.

PEOPLE USING SCIENCE

Bioprospector Petrona Rios collects plants and insects in the rain forests of Costa Rica. As a bioprospector (bī ō prä'spek-tər), she gathers these specimens so that chemists can analyze them for their potential use in developing new medicines.

Along with other bioprospectors, Petrona Rios continually crisscrosses the rain forest, gathering plant and insect specimens. The collected specimens are processed at INBio (Instituto Nacional de Biodiversidad) and sent to the University of Costa Rica. There, chemists make samples of the materials and send them to a major drug company. Chemists at the drug company thoroughly test the samples, looking for substances that can be used in new medicines.

As the samples are tested, they go through many chemical and physical changes. What chemical and physical changes do you see every day?

Coming Up

Petrona Rios (*center*) with student assistants

INVESTIGATION 1

HOW CAN MATTER CHANGE?

You can tear a piece of paper into hundreds of smaller pieces. Yet each piece, no matter how small, is still paper. You could recycle the small pieces and make new paper from them. But what would you have if you were to burn the paper? Find out about changes that matter can undergo in this investigation.

Activity

Balloon Blower

Blowing up a balloon can be a lot of work. How would you like to have a balloon that inflates by itself? In this activity you can combine some materials and make an automatic balloon inflater with the changes that result.

Procedure

1. Blow up a balloon and let the air out several times. This action will stretch the rubber, making the balloon easier to inflate.

2. Place the stem of a funnel in the neck of the deflated balloon. Pour two spoonfuls of baking soda into the balloon. Gently shake the balloon to make sure the baking soda settles to the bottom of the balloon. Remove the funnel from the balloon.

3. Add several spoonfuls of vinegar to a narrow-necked bottle.

MATERIALS
- goggles
- balloon
- funnel
- measuring spoon
- baking soda
- vinegar
- narrow-necked bottle
- *Science Notebook*

SAFETY
Wear goggles during this activity.

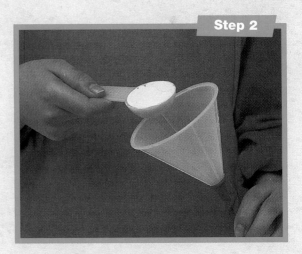

Step 2

4. Stretch the opening of the balloon over the mouth of the bottle, as shown in the picture. Make sure no baking soda escapes from the balloon.

5. Lift the balloon and hold it above the bottle so that the baking soda falls into the bottle.

Step 4

6. Observe the changes that take place when the baking soda mixes with the vinegar. **Record** your observations in your *Science Notebook*.

Analyze and Conclude

1. A **chemical change** involves the formation of new substances. What evidence is there that a chemical change took place inside the bottle after the baking soda dropped into the vinegar?

2. What happened to the balloon? From your observation, what can you **infer** about one of the substances produced when vinegar and baking soda react?

3. Hypothesize about the action of the baking soda and vinegar. Are both substances still present, or have they changed into new types of matter? **Give evidence** to support your hypothesis.

Technology Link CD-ROM

INVESTIGATE FURTHER!

Use the **Science Processor CD-ROM**, *The Nature of Matter* (Investigation 3, More Matter?) to travel back in time to 1789 and visit Antoine Lavoisier's laboratory. Conduct an experiment to find out what happens when you heat tin.

Activity

Making a Fire Extinguisher

In the last activity a chemical change produced a gas. In this activity you can see why this gas makes a useful fire extinguisher.

Procedure

1. Add three spoonfuls of vinegar to one jar and one spoonful of baking soda to another jar.

2. Place a candle in the center of a shallow dish and ask your teacher to light the candle. Ignite a fireplace match by holding it at the end and placing the tip of the match in the candle flame.

3. Insert the burning match first into the jar containing baking soda and then into the jar containing vinegar, as shown in the picture. Do not allow the flame to touch the contents of the jars. Look for any changes in the flame and then blow out the match. **Record** your observations in your *Science Notebook*.

4. Hold the jar containing baking soda firmly on the tabletop while you carefully pour the vinegar into this jar. **Describe** what happens.

5. Light another fireplace match by holding it in the candle flame and then blow out the candle. Insert the tip of the burning match into the jar containing the vinegar and baking soda. **Observe** what happens and **record** your observations.

Analyze and Conclude

1. Oxygen must be present for burning to take place. **Infer** whether oxygen was present above the baking soda and the vinegar in each jar before you mixed these materials. **Explain** what your inference is based on.

2. What **inferences** can you make about the gas released when you mixed the vinegar and the baking soda? **Give evidence** to support your inferences.

Step 3

C66

Activity

Solids From Liquids

If you have ever made water turn into ice, you've made a solid from a liquid. In this activity you'll make a solid from two liquids by causing a chemical change.

MATERIALS
- goggles
- unknown liquids *A* and *B*
- timer
- *Science Notebook*

SAFETY
Wear goggles during this activity. Avoid letting chemicals come in contact with your skin. Do not put any chemicals in your mouth.

Procedure

1. Obtain samples of unknown liquids *A* and *B*. Study the liquids and **record** your observations in your *Science Notebook*.

2. Mix the two liquids by carefully pouring the contents of one container into the other container.

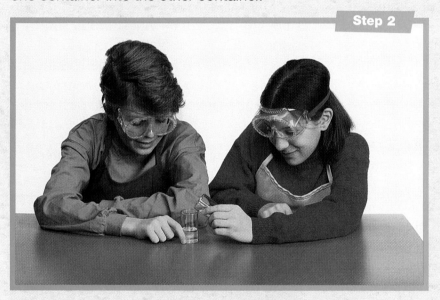

Step 2

3. **Observe** the mixture for five minutes. **Record** any changes you observe.

Analyze and Conclude

1. What did you observe happening when you mixed the two liquids together?

2. What evidence indicates that the change you observed taking place was a chemical change?

3. **Hypothesize** whether liquids *A* and *B* are the same material or different materials. Support your hypothesis.

Physical and Chemical Change

Reading Focus How are chemical changes different from physical changes?

Picture yourself in this situation. You're getting ready to go to a party. You're all dressed except for your favorite wool sweater, which just came from the cleaners. You take the sweater from its protective plastic and pull it on. But it's too small—much too small!

You take the sweater off and hold it up. It's about half the size it's supposed to be! At first you think the cleaners gave you the wrong sweater. But the name tag sewn inside tells you it's your sweater. What went wrong?

Changing but Staying the Same

The case of the shrunken sweater is an example of a physical change. A **physical change** is a change in the size, shape, or state of a material. No new matter is formed during a physical change. The wool of the sweater is still the same. It just takes up less space now!

You see physical changes every day. When you sharpen a pencil or rub chalk on the board, you cause physical changes to take place. The pencil shavings and the chalk dust produced by your actions are different from the objects they came from. But the shavings are still made up of wood, and the dust is still made up of chalk.

In nature, physical changes can turn one kind of landscape into another. For example, over many millions of years, a river can carve its way down through solid rock to form a deep canyon. Pounding waves, over time, can transform rock cliffs into fine sand. In both cases, the rocks may be changed in size and appearance, but they are still made of the same substances.

Water is a good substance to use when studying physical changes. Many substances dissolve in water. The act of dissolving is a physical change. Changes in state—melting, freezing, evaporation, and condensation—are physical changes.

Why is making a baseball bat from a piece of wood an example of a physical change? ▼

Changing but *Not* Staying the Same

Have you ever smelled milk that has turned sour? Do you think that sour milk is the same as fresh milk? Whole milk is a mixture. When bacteria from the air digest part of the mixture, changes occur and a new substance, called lactic acid, is produced. This change is similar to the one that occurs when two liquids are mixed together in the activity on page C67. Any change in which one or more new substances are formed is a **chemical change**.

Water can also be changed chemically. Recall that water is a compound made up of the elements hydrogen and oxygen. The drawing shows how water can be changed into its component elements.

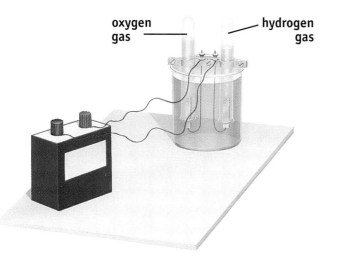

An electric current can be used to separate water into oxygen gas and hydrogen gas. The gases can be collected in test tubes.

Chemical changes are common in nature. The rusting of iron is one example of such a change. Rust is produced when oxygen from the air combines with iron. The product is neither iron nor oxygen, but a new substance called iron oxide, or rust.

Plants use energy from sunlight to change water and carbon dioxide gas into sugar. Plants use the sugar as food.

Animals use plants as food. Chemical changes occur when food is digested. These chemical changes release energy that animals need to grow and be active.

Some chemical changes are not helpful. For example, rusted parts on a bicycle don't move smoothly and may even crumble.

Describing Chemical Changes

Chemical changes are triggered by chemical reactions. In a chemical reaction, one or more substances interact to form new substances. When describing what happens during a chemical reaction, scientists often use symbols and formulas to write "chemical sentences." These sentences are written in the form of equations, much like those used in math problems.

Suppose you wanted to describe the reaction in which water is broken down into hydrogen and oxygen. The chemical equation for this reaction is shown here.

$$2H_2O \longrightarrow 2H_2 + O_2$$

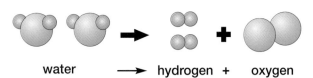

water ⟶ hydrogen + oxygen

If you wanted to express this reaction in words, you would say that two molecules of water break down to produce two molecules of hydrogen gas and one molecule of oxygen gas. In this equation, the arrow is read as *produce*, and the plus sign is read as *and*.

Look at the equation for the reaction in which iron and oxygen combine to produce iron oxide, or rust.

$$4Fe + 3O_2 \longrightarrow 2Fe_2O_3$$

How would you write this chemical sentence in words?

Many changes, such as the freezing of water to form ice, are physical. No new substances are formed. Other changes, such as those that occur when a fuel is burned, or a piece of iron rusts, result in new substances being formed. Such changes are chemical changes. ■

Science in Literature

HOW METALS REACT

"Potassium and tin behave differently when put into contact with water. Potassium . . . reacts vigorously, and so much heat is generated that the hydrogen gas produced catches fire and burns with a lilac flame. Tin . . . reacts hardly at all with water. If diluted acid is used, potassium reacts even more vigorously, and tin reacts very slowly to produce hydrogen."

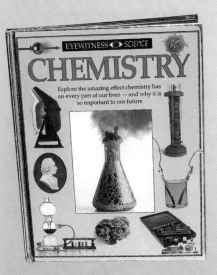

Eyewitness Science: Chemistry
by Dr. Ann Newmark
Dorling Kindersley, 1993

Look at page 25 of *Eyewitness Science: Chemistry* by Dr. Ann Newmark, to see pictures of these reactions. Then read on to find out about many other chemical changes.

Atomic Structure and Chemical Change

Reading Focus What are the parts of an atom and how are they arranged in a Bohr model?

Imagine that the marbles in the picture are elements. Suppose you were asked to arrange the marbles to make as many different substances as possible. You are told that a substance can have as few as one element and as many as five. How many different substances can you make in two minutes?

Now think about the 112 known elements. How many different substances can be made from these elements? Now you have some idea about how it is possible to have so many different kinds of matter on Earth.

What Is a Model?

All chemical changes involve atoms. So if you want to understand what's happening when a match burns, when iron rusts, or when milk sours, you need to know more about atoms.

Atoms, of course, are much too small to be seen, even with the most powerful microscope. How then do scientists learn about atoms? Just about everything known about atoms has been learned from indirect evidence. This evidence is gathered by studying how matter behaves in all kinds of chemical reactions.

Based on this evidence, scientists have developed various models of the atom. In science, a **model** is a way to represent an object or to describe how a process takes place. Models are often used to describe things that are too big or too small to be studied directly. For example, a globe is a model of Earth.

What Is an Atom Like?

Modern scientific models of the atom describe it as being made up of several different tiny parts. These tiny parts are called protons (prō′tänz), neutrons (no͞o′tränz), and electrons (ē lek′tränz).

Most of the mass of an atom is contained in a dense, central core called a **nucleus** (no͞o′klē əs). This nucleus contains protons and neutrons. A **proton** is a particle with a positive electric charge. A **neutron** is a particle with no electric charge.

Traveling around the nucleus, at some distance from it, are one or more electrons. An **electron** is a particle with a negative electric charge.

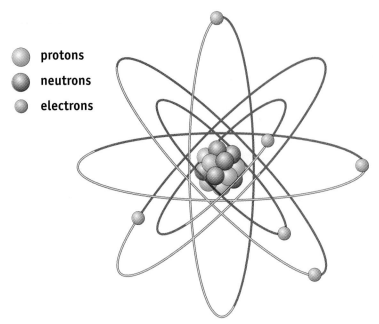

protons
neutrons
electrons

◄ The drawing shows a model of a carbon atom. This atom has six protons and six neutrons in its nucleus and six electrons outside the nucleus. This type of atomic model is known as a Bohr model, after Niels Bohr, the Danish physicist who developed it.

Two Models—Old and New

Look at the Bohr models of a helium atom and a lithium (lith′ē əm) atom below. Notice how the electrons are shown moving around the nucleus in paths called orbits. The helium atom has one orbit and the lithium atom has two orbits. A Bohr model is also called a planetary model of the atom. Why do you think this is so?

Bohr suggested his model in 1913. As scientists learned more about atoms, they found that electrons do not travel in definite orbits. Rather, they "swarm" around the nucleus, much like bees swarm around a hive.

Because electrons travel so fast, they can be thought of as a "cloud" surrounding the nucleus. The drawing below shows an electron cloud model of a helium atom.

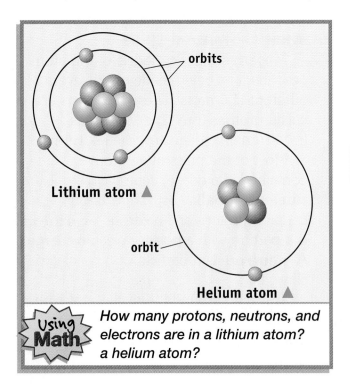

orbits

Lithium atom ▲

orbit

Helium atom ▲

Using **Math** *How many protons, neutrons, and electrons are in a lithium atom? a helium atom?*

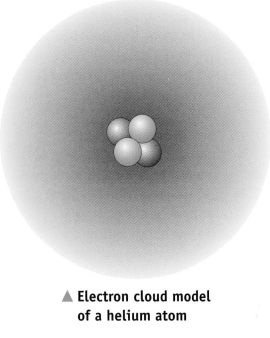

▲ **Electron cloud model of a helium atom**

Roles of Protons and Electrons

The number of protons in the nucleus of an atom gives the atom its identity. An atom of hydrogen has one proton. An atom of oxygen has eight protons. That's what makes hydrogen what it is and oxygen what it is.

Recall from the periodic table on pages C36 and C37 that every element has a different atomic number. The **atomic number** of an element is the number of protons in an atom of that element. The atomic number of hydrogen is 1. Look at oxygen in the periodic table. What is the atomic number of oxygen?

Electrons are the smallest and lightest of the three types of atomic particles. Yet, because electrons move around outside the nucleus, they determine how an atom reacts with other atoms. In other words, the electrons that surround the nucleus of an atom give the atom its chemical properties.

Atoms With a Charge

Usually the number of protons in an atom equals the number of electrons. So the positive and negative charges balance each other. This balance leaves the atom electrically neutral.

Sometimes, however, an atom may capture one or more electrons from another atom. When this happens, both atoms become electrically charged. An electrically charged atom is called an **ion** (ī′ən). The drawing shows how positive and negative ions are formed.

Because they have opposite charges, positive and negative ions attract each other. If the attraction is strong enough, the ions are held tightly together and form an ionic compound, such as sodium chloride. Ionic compounds are not made up of molecules. Instead, the basic unit of any ionic compound is made up of one or more positive ions and one or more negative ions.

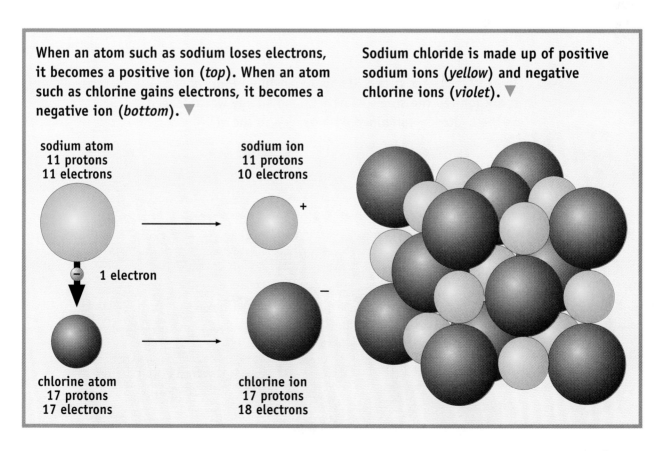

When an atom such as sodium loses electrons, it becomes a positive ion (*top*). When an atom such as chlorine gains electrons, it becomes a negative ion (*bottom*). ▼

Sodium chloride is made up of positive sodium ions (*yellow*) and negative chlorine ions (*violet*). ▼

sodium atom
11 protons
11 electrons

sodium ion
11 protons
10 electrons

+

1 electron

−

chlorine atom
17 protons
17 electrons

chlorine ion
17 protons
18 electrons

Atoms and Molecules

Many compounds, such as water, are made up of molecules. In forming molecules, atoms don't gain or lose electrons. Instead they share electrons. For example, when hydrogen reacts with oxygen to form water, two hydrogen atoms and one oxygen atom join up by sharing electrons, as shown in the drawing.

It is as if the oxygen atom is holding hands with two hydrogen atoms. Think of each hand as an electron. And think of each pair of clasped hands as a chemical bond between the atoms. Chemists call this type of compound a covalent compound.

Making and Breaking Bonds

Energy is always involved in the making or breaking of chemical bonds. Usually when bonds form between atoms, energy is given off. However, sometimes a little energy must be added to get such a reaction started. For example, a little spark is needed to get hydrogen to combine with oxygen. But once the reaction starts,

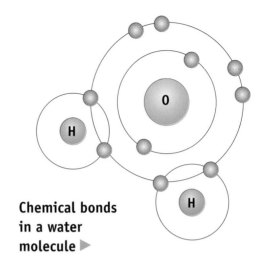

Chemical bonds in a water molecule ▶

energy is given off rapidly, as shown in the photograph below.

Energy is also involved in breaking chemical bonds. Recall the description on page C69 of how water can be broken down into hydrogen and oxygen by passing electricity through it. The electricity provides the energy needed to break the bonds between the hydrogen atoms and oxygen atoms that make up water. ■

Internet Field Trip

Visit **www.eduplace.com** to find out more about chemical bonding.

In 1937, disaster struck the hydrogen-filled *Hindenburg*. A spark ignited the ship's hydrogen, and energy was released as the hydrogen combined with oxygen in the air. ▼

Conservation of Mass

Reading Focus What is the law of conservation of mass?

When a piece of wood burns, the mass of the ashes that remain is less than the mass of the original piece of wood. On the other hand, when a piece of tin is heated, it gains mass. Three hundred years ago, these and similar observations led scientists to wonder: Is matter destroyed when wood burns? Is matter created when tin is heated?

Over the years the work of many scientists provided answers to these and other questions about matter. For example, when wood burns, some of its mass goes into gases that are produced. These gases escape into the air. Today we know that matter cannot be created or destroyed by any chemical reaction. This statement of fact is known as the law of conservation of mass.

Albert Einstein publishes his theory of relativity, which includes the equation $E = mc^2$. This theory establishes the relationship between mass and energy.

1905

Working independently, two scientists—Karl Wilhelm Scheele and Joseph Priestley—discover oxygen.

A.D. 1772–1774

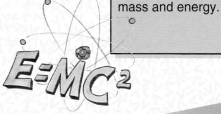

1890–1910
Marie Curie's work with radium leads to a better understanding of radioactivity.

450 B.C.
Greek philosophers Leucippus (lōō sip'əs) and Democritus (di mäk'rə təs) first state the ideas set forth in the law of conservation of mass.

1789
Antoine Lavoisier, a French chemist, discovers that when matter such as tin burns, it combines with oxygen. This discovery leads to the law of conservation of mass.

Radioactive Elements

Reading Focus What is a radioactive element?

On March 1, 1896, French scientist Henri Becquerel wrapped a sheet of photographic film in paper that light couldn't penetrate. He placed the package in a desk drawer, together with a few small rocks, and closed the drawer.

A few days later, Becquerel developed the film, expecting to see an unexposed white negative. Instead he was shocked to see darkened areas on the film. Something had changed the chemicals on the film—but what?

▲ Becquerel discovers radioactivity.

Nuclear Radiation

Becquerel's film had been exposed to nuclear radiation (rā dē ā'shən), invisible energy that came from the rocks. The rocks contained the radioactive element uranium (yo͞o rā'nē əm). A **radioactive element** is made up of atoms whose nuclei (*nuclei* is the plural of *nucleus*)

break down, or decay, into nuclei of other atoms. When a radioactive element decays, it changes into a different element. This happens because some of the radiation released by the decaying nucleus is in the form of protons and neutrons. And when an atom loses protons from its nucleus, its atomic number changes.

Recall that an element is identified by its atomic number. The drawing shows how a uranium nucleus decays to form a thorium (thôr'ē əm) nucleus. Notice how the atomic number changes from 92 to 90.

When a nucleus decays, large amounts of energy are released. The particles released from the nucleus will have lots of energy. Sometimes high-energy rays called gamma rays are produced as well.

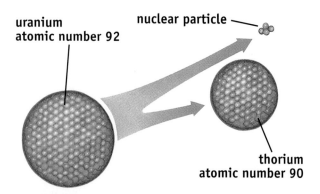

▲ When a uranium nucleus decays, it loses 2 protons and 2 neutrons, leaving a nucleus with 90 protons. The element with atomic number 90 is thorium.

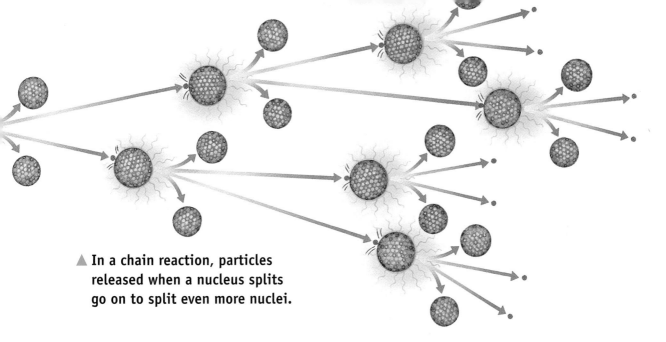

▲ In a chain reaction, particles released when a nucleus splits go on to split even more nuclei.

Using Energy From Atoms

Radioactive elements occur naturally. Scientists have also learned how to split the nuclei of some atoms by bombarding them with neutrons. This reaction is called **nuclear fission** (nōō′klē ər fish′ən). *Fission* means "splitting."

The drawing above shows how neutrons are used to split nuclei of uranium atoms. Two new atoms are produced each time a nucleus splits. Also, some single neutrons and energy are released. Some of these neutrons collide with and split other nuclei, producing a chain reaction.

An uncontrolled nuclear chain reaction releases energy so fast that an explosion takes place. A nuclear reactor is a device in which a nuclear chain reaction is controlled. In a controlled chain reaction, energy is released slowly.

Radiation—Helpful and Harmful

Nuclear reactors provide energy that is used to generate electricity. Reactors are also used to make radioactive forms of many elements. These elements are used in medical research and in the treatment of certain illnesses.

Clearly, nuclear energy has many uses that are beneficial. But nuclear radiation can also damage human tissues. Thus, radioactive materials must be handled safely and must not be allowed to get into the environment by accident. ■

INVESTIGATION 1 WRAP-UP

REVIEW

1. How does heating sugar in a spoon differ from dissolving it in a cup of hot water?

2. Write the following chemical equation in words.

$$2H_2O \longrightarrow 2H_2 + O_2$$

CRITICAL THINKING

3. When might a Bohr model of an atom be more helpful than an electron cloud model?

4. If two neutrons escaped the nucleus of an atom, what would be the effect on the atom's atomic number and its total electric charge?

WHAT ARE ACIDS AND BASES?

Vinegar, orange juice, soap, baking soda, and antacid tablets are all things you can probably find around your home. Some of these materials are acids, and some are bases. In this investigation you'll find out what acids and bases are and how to use some simple tests to tell the difference.

Activity

Cabbage-Juice Science

Some substances, called indicators, are one color in an acid and a different color in a base. In this activity you can see for yourself how an indicator works.

- -

Procedure

1. In your *Science Notebook*, **make a chart** like the one shown.

Cup	Material	Observation
1	Vinegar	
2	Lemon juice	
3	Baking soda	
4	Powdered lime	

See **SCIENCE** and **MATH TOOLBOX** page H11 if you need to review *Making a Chart to Organize Data.*

2. Half fill four small plastic cups with red cabbage juice and number the cups with a marker.

3. Use a dropper to add a few drops of vinegar to the cabbage juice in cup 1. Use a clean dropper to add a few drops of lemon juice to cup 2. **Record** in your chart any changes that you observe.

4. Add a small amount of baking soda to cup 3 and a small amount of powdered lime to cup 4. **Record** any changes that you observe.

5. **Predict** what would happen if you tested red cabbage juice with pineapple juice and with liquid soap. Carry out the tests in clean cups and check your predictions.

6. **Predict** what would happen if you added vinegar to the cup containing the baking soda and cabbage juice. Carry out the test. **Record** your results.

Step 4

Analyze and Conclude

1. In which cups did chemical changes occur? How do you know?

2. Cabbage juice is an indicator. What evidence is there that some of the materials you tested are acids or bases?

3. **Infer** which of the materials is the most similar to vinegar. **Give evidence** to support your inference. These materials are acids.

4. **Classify** all the substances you tested into two groups, based on how they react with the cabbage-juice indicator.

INVESTIGATE FURTHER!

EXPERIMENT

Use additional cabbage juice to test different liquids, including plain water and carbonated water. Group the liquids by the color changes they produce.

Activity
The Litmus Test

Litmus paper is an indicator. Blue litmus paper turns red in an acid. Red litmus paper turns blue in a base. See if you can identify the acids and bases in this activity.

MATERIALS

- goggles
- 3 pieces of red litmus paper
- 3 pieces of blue litmus paper
- 3 liquids in containers—one labeled A, one labeled B, and one labeled C
- *Science Notebook*

SAFETY //////

Wear goggles during this activity. Do not touch or taste any of the chemicals used in this activity.

Procedure

1. In your *Science Notebook*, **make a chart** like the one shown.

Solution	Red Litmus Paper	Blue Litmus Paper
A		
B		
C		

2. Place a piece of red litmus (lit′məs) paper and a piece of blue litmus paper beside three containers labeled *A*, *B*, and *C*. Remember, blue litmus paper turns red in an acid; red litmus paper turns blue in a base.

3. Dip the tip of a piece of blue litmus paper and the tip of a piece of red litmus paper in each liquid. Leave each piece of litmus paper beside the container in which it was dipped.

4. **Observe** each piece of litmus paper for any change in color. In your chart, **record** your observations.

Step 2

Analyze and Conclude

1. Which liquids were acids? How do you know?

2. Which liquids were bases? How do you know?

3. Write a rule for using litmus paper to identify a liquid that is neither an acid nor a base.

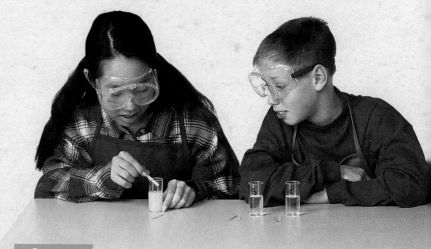

Step 3

C80

Acids, Bases, and Salts

Reading Focus How can you find out if a compound is an acid or a base?

It's a brutally hot day, and you've just finished mowing the lawn. Now you're looking forward to a cool, refreshing drink of lemonade. You take the pitcher from the refrigerator, pour yourself an ice-cold glass, and take a deep gulp. Immediately your mouth puckers and your eyes begin to water. It's not lemonade—it's lemon juice! And is it sour!

Although you didn't mean to, you have just discovered a telltale property of some important chemical compounds—acids. And you used a test that you wouldn't be able to use in the laboratory—the taste test.

Telltale Colors

Compounds have certain properties that can be used to classify them. Acids and bases are two important groups of compounds. As the pictures below show, these compounds are found in many household products.

One property of acids and bases is the effect they have on indicators (in′di kāt-ərz). An **indicator** is a substance that changes color when mixed with an acid or a base. Cabbage juice is used as an indicator in the activity on pages C78 and C79. In the activity on page C80, paper treated with an indicator called litmus is used to test for acids and bases.

ACIDS The substances below are acids. An acid is a compound that turns blue litmus paper red. ▼

BASES The substances below are bases. A base is a compound that turns red litmus paper blue. ▼

As the pictures on page C81 show, the effects of acids and bases on litmus can be used to define these compounds.

Some Properties of Acids and Bases

As you would learn if you drank some lemon juice, acids have a sour taste. Some acids, like the natural acids in foods, are weak. Vinegar and citrus fruits are foods that contain acids. Boric (bôr′ik) acid is safe enough to be used in eyewash solutions.

Strong acids, such as sulfuric (sul-fyoor′ik) acid, are dangerous—they are poisonous and can burn the skin. Many acids, even some weak ones, are *corrosive*—they eat away metals and other substances. Digestive juices produced by your stomach contain a strong acid.

However, the acid is very dilute (di loot′). This means that small amounts of the acid are mixed with large amounts of water. Diluting strong acids helps to reduce their harmful effects.

Bases taste bitter and feel slippery. Like acids, some bases are weak and some are strong. Examples of weak bases include baking soda, which is used in cooking, and antacid tablets, which are used for upset stomachs.

Strong bases, like strong acids, are poisonous and can burn the skin. Sodium hydroxide (hī dräks′īd), commonly known as lye, is an example of a strong base. Sodium hydroxide is used in soap making and in drain cleaners.

The pH Scale

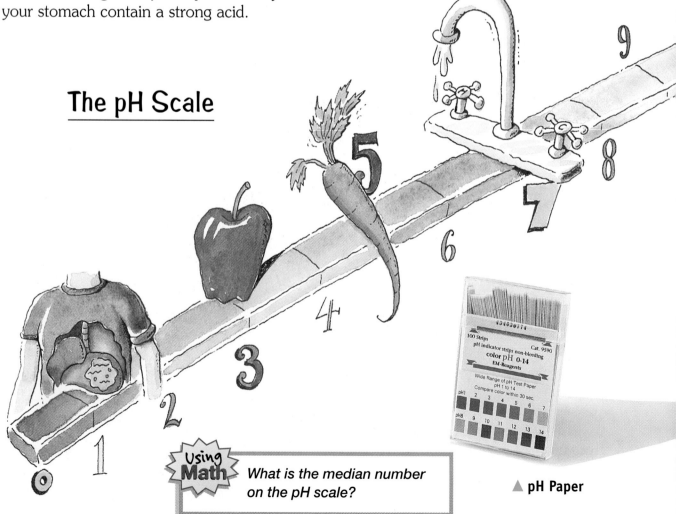

Using Math What is the median number on the pH scale?

▲ pH Paper

The Strong and the Weak

Acids and bases are usually found dissolved in water. For example, lemon juice and orange juice are solutions of citric acid in water. If you add a small amount of acid to a large volume of water, the solution won't be very acidic. On the other hand, if you add a large amount of acid to a small volume of water, the solution might be very acidic.

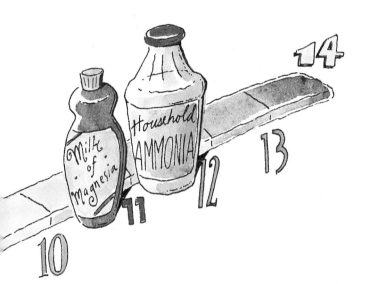

There's a way to measure how acidic or how basic a solution is. The acidic or basic strength of a solution is measured on a scale known as the pH scale.

The pH scale has units from zero to 14. The smaller the unit, the more acidic a solution is. The larger the unit, the more basic it is. So a solution with a pH of 1 or less would be very acidic. On the other hand, a solution with a pH near 14 would be very basic. Solutions with a pH near the middle of the scale are neutral. Pure water has a pH of 7.

How can you find the pH of a solution? Indicator paper made with special dyes is used for this purpose. The paper turns different colors depending upon how acidic or basic the solution is that's being tested.

Canceling Out Each Other

Have you ever heard someone complain of having acid indigestion, or heartburn? This condition occurs when the stomach produces too much acid, resulting in a burning sensation.

Antacid tablets, which are weak bases, are often used to relieve this condition. The word part *ant* in the term *antacid* comes from the prefix *anti-*, which means "against" or "opposed to." The base in the tablet reacts with the acid and cancels out, or neutralizes (no͞o′trə līz əz), its effects.

The reaction between an acid and a base is called **neutralization** (no͞o trə li-zā′shən). When an acid and a base react, two substances—water and a salt—are produced. A **salt** is a compound that can be formed when an acid reacts with a base. The properties of water and salt are very different from those of the acids and bases that react to produce them. ■

Acid Rain

Reading Focus What is acid rain, and how does it damage the environment?

A gentle wind blows constantly across the land. As the wind travels, it sweeps across cities, villages, factories, and power plants like an invisible broom. And like a real broom, the wind carries all sorts of dirt along with it. This dirt includes soot, dust, and smoke. It also includes a number of harmful gases.

Pickup and Delivery

When the wind moves over farm areas, it picks up dust and may pick up traces of fertilizers or chemicals used to control weeds and insects. Over cities and industrial regions, the wind picks up gases produced by the burning of gasoline, coal, and oil. These gases include compounds of sulfur and of nitrogen.

Where acid rain is "born" ▼

Acids From the Sky

As sulfur and nitrogen compounds mix with water in the air, they react to produce two strong acids—sulfuric acid and nitric acid. At first these acids are dissolved in tiny droplets of water that remain in the air. They are part of the clouds that form and drift across the sky. However, over time these droplets begin to collect into larger and larger drops. Eventually the drops are too heavy to stay in the air, and they begin to fall as rain, snow, sleet, or hail.

If you were to measure the pH of this precipitation, you might discover readings as low as 2.0. Acid solutions that are this strong can do serious damage to both living and nonliving things. People in many parts of the world have suffered

**Modern windmills use clean wind
energy to generate electricity.** ▶

from lung, skin, and eye irritations related
to acid precipitation.

The stone and metal of famous statues
and well-known buildings have been damaged or eaten away by acids from the
sky. Forests and lakes in many regions of
the world have been severely affected by
acid rain. In Germany's Black Forest,
acid rain has killed trees covering an area
of more than 5,000 km² (2,000 mi²). In
Sweden, thousands of lakes have become
so acidic that most plants and many
species of fish can no longer live in them.
Similar events and conditions have been
reported in many areas of the world,
including the United States and Canada.

What can be done to stop the destruction caused by acid precipitation? The
obvious answer is to reduce air pollution.
The major source of air pollution is the
burning of fossil fuels—coal, oil, and gas.
These are the fuels we use to run our
cars, heat our homes, produce our electricity, and power our factories.

Scientists and engineers worldwide are
seeking ways to reduce dependency on
fossil fuels. Some promising alternative
sources of energy are being used. These
sources include hydroelectric plants,
which use the energy of moving water to
generate electricity. Other sources of
clean energy being explored are wind
energy and solar energy.

In cases where fossil fuels are commonly used—such as in power plants,
factories, and automobiles—methods
have been developed to keep pollutants
from escaping into the air. Various measures for reducing air pollution are being
used in many countries. After all, sulfuric
acid—or its acidic relatives—belongs in a
container, not in a cloud. ■

INVESTIGATION 2 WRAP-UP

REVIEW

1. How are acids and bases alike? different?

2. When would you use an indicator?

**CRITICAL
THINKING**

3. A solution has a pH of 11. What effect would
such a solution have on litmus paper? How would
you neutralize this solution?

4. What are some ways you and your family can
help prevent acid rain?

WHAT DO CHEMISTS DO?

Suppose you read about a mysterious material beneath the Antarctic icecap that scientists have discovered. How would you learn about such a material? A chemist would study its chemical and physical properties. You can do the same thing.

Activity

Mystery Powders

Imagine that you find six jars, each containing a different powder. On the floor near the jars, you find six labels—sugar, salt, baking soda, cornstarch, powdered milk, and plaster of Paris. How will you identify the powders?

Procedure

1. Study the table on page C87. It contains information about the appearance and behavior of six materials.

2. In your *Science Notebook*, **make a chart** with the same headings as the table on the next page, but don't fill in your chart yet. Instead of names of substances in column 1, **record** the letters *A* through *F*.

3. Sprinkle a sample of one powder on a sheet of black construction paper. **Observe** the powder with a hand lens. Under the heading *Appearance*, In the appropriate row, **record** how the powder looks. Repeat this step for each mystery powder.

MATERIALS

- goggles
- mystery powders in jars labeled *A* through *F*
- black construction paper
- hand lens
- aluminum foil
- 3 droppers
- water
- toothpicks
- plastic spoons
- vinegar
- solution of iodine
- *Science Notebook*

SAFETY /////

Wear goggles during this activity. Do not touch or taste any of the chemicals in this activity.

Name	Appearance	Water	Vinegar	Iodine
Sugar	white; grains of different shapes	dissolves, forming clear solution	no reaction	no reaction
Salt	white; small crystal cubes	dissolves, forming clear solution	no reaction	no reaction
Baking soda	small grains of different shapes	dissolves, forming clear solution	bubbles form	no reaction
Cornstarch	white powder; tiny particles	forms gooey mixture	no reaction	turns dark blue
Powdered milk	white powder; tiny particles	forms cloudy mixture	no reaction	no reaction
Plaster of Paris	white powder; tiny particles	forms cloudy mixture that slowly hardens	no reaction	no reaction

4. Place three small samples of one mystery powder on a piece of foil. Add a few drops of water to one sample and stir the mixture with a toothpick. **Record** your observations. Add vinegar to the second sample and iodine to the third. Mix and **observe** each sample and **record** your observations.

5. Repeat step 4 for each mystery powder.

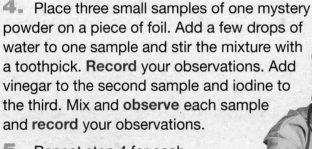

Step 4

Analyze and Conclude

1. Study your chart and **compare** it with the table above.

2. Based on the properties you observed, **identify** each powder. Write the names in your chart.

INVESTIGATE FURTHER!

EXPERIMENT

Think of a powder you did not use in this activity. Check with your teacher to be sure that your choice is safe. Then have your classmates test your mystery powder. Have them tell which of the six powders studied in this activity is most like your mystery powder.

Activity

"Slime" Time

Look around you. Many objects in your classroom are made of materials that were "invented" by chemists working in laboratories. Plastics and synthetic fibers are good examples of such materials. In this activity you'll make some "slime." Is this a good name for your substance?

Procedure

1. Study samples of water, white glue, food coloring, and borax. **List** them in your *Science Notebook*. **Describe** the appearance of each material and **list** as many properties of each material as you can.

2. Add equal amounts of the water and white glue to a plastic cup. Add a few drops of food coloring and stir the mixture thoroughly with a plastic spoon.

3. **Observe** how the mixture looks. If you wish, you may keep adding more food coloring until the mixture is the color you want.

4. Gradually add the borax to the mixture while you stir it. **Observe** and **record** any changes in the appearance of the mixture.

5. Add borax until no more liquid is visible. Touch the mixture and **describe** how it feels. You can adjust the amount of borax to give your slime exactly the slimy feeling you want it to have.

Step 4

Analyze and Conclude

1. Pick up and handle your slime. **Describe** as many of its properties as you can.

2. **Compare** the properties of your slime to the properties of the materials you mixed together to make it.

3. Think of some possible uses for your slime. **Describe** the uses in your *Science Notebook*.

Polymers and Plastics

Reading Focus What are some organic compounds found in nature and some made by scientists?

SCIENCE TECHNOLOGY & SOCIETY

Scientists once believed that compounds containing carbon could only be produced by living things. Because living things are called organisms, compounds containing carbon were called organic compounds. The study of these compounds was, and still is, called organic chemistry.

Carbon, the Supercombiner

All elements are not created equal. Scientists have identified about 11 million different compounds. Of these, more than 10 million contain carbon.

One of carbon's unique properties is its ability to join, or form bonds, with other atoms. Recall that chemical bonding was described in an earlier section as atoms that are "holding hands." Because of the arrangement of its electrons, a single carbon atom is able to bond or "hold hands" with as many as four other atoms.

This bond-forming ability makes it possible for long chains of carbon atoms to form. Each carbon atom in a chain can also form bonds with atoms of other elements. For example, there are hundreds of ways that compounds can form from the elements carbon and hydrogen.

Not all organic compounds are complex. A molecule of methane (meth'ān), the simplest organic compound, is made up of only five atoms. Models of molecules of methane and two other organic compounds are shown below.

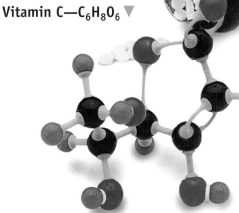
Vitamin C—$C_6H_8O_6$ ▼

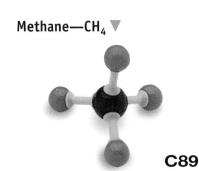

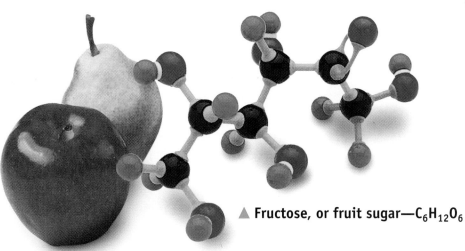
▲ **Fructose, or fruit sugar—$C_6H_{12}O_6$**

Methane—CH_4 ▼

C89

Polymers—Chemical Giants

The next time you sprinkle sugar on your cereal, think of the formula for sugar.

$$C_{12}H_{22}O_{11}$$

Every molecule in those sugar crystals contains 45 atoms! Sounds pretty impressive, doesn't it? Now look at the model of a small part of a protein molecule. Proteins are the building blocks from which your body is made. They are probably the most complex organic compounds found in nature.

Proteins are polymers (päl'ə mərz). A **polymer** is an organic compound made up mainly of a very long chain or chains of carbon compounds. The word *polymer* means "many parts."

Part of a protein molecule ▼

Try to imagine how different your life would be without plastics. Plastics are synthetic polymers. To make a polymer, chemists start with a simple organic molecule. This molecule is one part of the

▲ **Some useful products made of plastic**

polymer. Hundreds or even thousands of these parts are put together to form the carbon chain. At the same time, other molecules are added to the sides of the carbon chain.

The side chains of a polymer determine its properties. For example, side chains can make a polymer hard, flexible, or tough. Just think of all the different kinds of plastics there are and the wide range of properties they exhibit. ■

INVESTIGATE FURTHER!

EXPERIMENT

You can make your own model of a polymer by using paper clips of different sizes and colors, as shown here. Work with a partner to create a paper-clip polymer. When you're finished, describe its properties.

What Chemists Do

Reading Focus What are the two main categories of work that chemists do?

Chemistry is the study of matter—what it's made of and how it behaves. Now think back to the title of this unit—"The Nature of Matter." The unit title could have been "An Introduction to Chemistry." So all this time you have been studying chemistry and doing some of the things chemists do!

Analysis and Synthesis

The things that chemists do can be divided into two large categories—analysis (ə nal'ə sis) and synthesis (sin'thə sis). In simple terms, *analysis* means "taking things apart" and *synthesis* means "putting things together."

Many of the materials you use in everyday life are products of chemical research. Research chemists are constantly inventing and testing new drugs and medicines. The making of polymers, as described earlier, is an excellent example of synthesis.

Types of Chemical Reactions

In conducting their research, chemists observe different types of chemical reactions. Most of those reactions can be classified into one of four major groups—synthesis, decomposition (dē käm pə-zish'ən), single replacement, and double replacement. Take a closer look at these reactions. It might surprise you to know that many of the changes that occur during the activities in this unit involve these reactions.

A chemist at work in the laboratory ▼

SYNTHESIS *Synthesis* means "putting things together." The reaction in which hydrogen gas and oxygen gas combine to produce water is an example of a synthesis reaction in which a water molecule is "put together."

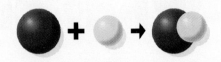

synthesis

DECOMPOSITION Decomposition involves the breaking down of a substance into simpler substances. In the activity on page C33, sugar is heated, causing it to break down into simpler substances—carbon and water.

decomposition

SINGLE REPLACEMENT In this type of reaction, one of the elements in a compound is replaced by another element. Such a reaction can be used to coat a piece of metal, such as copper, with a thin layer of another metal, such as silver.

single replacement

DOUBLE REPLACEMENT In this type of reaction, elements from two different compounds change places, something like two couples changing partners at a dance. Such a reaction produces a solid from two clear liquids in the activity on page C67.

double replacement

Now you know a lot more about matter than you did at the beginning of this unit. You know what matter is made up of. You know what happens when things change. You know what to look for and how to tell whether a change is chemical or physical. And you have an idea of what causes things to change. So congratulations! You are officially a beginning chemist in good standing. ■

INVESTIGATION 3 WRAP-UP

REVIEW

1. What is a polymer?

2. What are four main types of chemical reactions?

CRITICAL THINKING

3. What type of reaction is involved when many small molecules combine to form a polymer?

4. Imagine that a water molecule (H_2O) has undergone decomposition. Explain what happens to the atoms.

REFLECT & EVALUATE

Word Power

Write the letter of the term that best completes each sentence. *Not all terms will be used.*

1. An organic compound made up of a very long chain of carbon compounds is a (an) ___.
2. A substance that changes color when mixed with an acid or a base is a (an) ___.
3. A change from the solid to the liquid state is a (an) ___.
4. One or more new substances are formed in a (an) ___.
5. When an acid reacts with a base, a (an) ___ forms.
6. A negatively charged particle in an atom is a (an) ___.

a. chemical change
b. electron
c. indicator
d. neutron
e. nucleus
f. physical change
g. polymer
h. salt

Check What You Know

Write the word in each pair that correctly completes each sentence.

1. On the pH scale the numbers are higher for solutions that are more (acidic, basic).
2. The number of compounds of carbon is more than 10 (thousand, million).
3. A particle with a positive electric charge is a (proton, electron).
4. The planetary model of the atom was proposed by (Bohr, Einstein).

Problem Solving

1. Tungsten is an element with 74 protons and 109 neutrons. What is tungsten's atomic number? How many electrons does a tungsten atom have?

2. Sodium (an element) reacts with water (a compound) to produce sodium hydroxide (a compound) and hydrogen gas (an element). What kind of chemical reaction is this? Explain how you know.

Study the photographs. Then use the photographs to explain what happens during a physical change and a chemical change.

Using READING SKILLS

Drawing Conclusions

Writers often imply, or hint at, more information than they actually state. They give you clues and expect you to figure out the rest, using what you already know. Suppose an author writes "Ernie the dog awoke suddenly, ran to the door, and stood near it barking furiously." You can conclude that the animal sensed something unusual that alarmed him.

Consider these questions as you draw conclusions.

- What did the author write?
- What do I know?
- What is my conclusion?

Read the paragraphs. Then complete the exercises that follow.

Float or Sink?

Density can be useful in predicting whether an object will sink or float in water. The density of water is 1.0 g/mL. Any material with a density less than 1.0 g/mL will float in water. Anything with a density greater than 1.0 g/mL will sink. How might such information be useful?

Imagine you're going to boil some eggs for breakfast. You want to make sure the eggs aren't spoiled. The density of a fresh egg is about 1.2 g/mL. The density of a spoiled egg is about 0.9 g/mL. If you place an egg in water and it floats, what does this tell you about the egg?

1. Which statement is a conclusion you can draw from the paragraphs? Write the letter of that statement.

   a. The density of water is 1.0 g/mL.

   b. Anything with a density greater than 1.0 g/mL will sink.

   c. A spoiled egg will float in water.

   d. A fresh egg will float in water.

2. What was the most important clue in helping you draw that conclusion?

 **Line Graph**

The line graph shows the result of an experiment. In the experiment, a quantity of tin was heated.

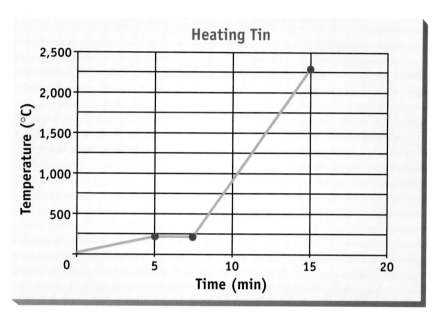

Use the line graph to complete the exercises.

1. After about 5 minutes of heating, the tin melted. Estimate the temperature at which tin reaches its melting point.

2. About how many minutes did it take for the tin to reach a temperature of 1,200°C?

3. The tin boiled at 2,270°C. About how many minutes did it take for the melted tin to begin to boil?

4. Suppose the experiment began at 2:10 P.M. Estimate the time at which the temperature of the tin reached 1,000°C.

5. What did the line graph look like from 0 to 5 minutes compared to the interval from 5 to 15 minutes? How does the graph show what is happening to the tin as it is being heated?

6. Suppose after 16 minutes the tin is no longer heated. Describe what the graph might look like from 16 minutes to 20 minutes.

WRAP-UP!

On your own, use scientific methods to investigate a question about matter.

THINK LIKE A SCIENTIST

Ask a Question

Pose a question about matter that you would like to investigate. For example, ask, "How does the acidity of rainwater in my area compare with the acidity of distilled water?"

Make a Hypothesis

Suggest a hypothesis that is a possible answer to the question. One hypothesis is that the rainwater in my area is more acidic than distilled water.

Plan and Do a Test

Plan a controlled experiment to compare the acidity of rainwater in your area with the acidity of distilled water. You could start with rainwater, distilled water, several clean containers, and pH paper. Develop a procedure that uses these materials to test the hypothesis. With permission, carry out your experiment. Follow the safety guidelines on pages S14–S15.

Record and Analyze

Observe carefully and record your data accurately. Make repeated observations.

Draw Conclusions

Look for evidence to support the hypothesis or to show that it is false. Draw conclusions about the hypothesis. Repeat the experiment to verify the results.

WRITING IN SCIENCE
Summary

Write a one-paragraph summary of "What Chemists Do," pages C91–C92. Use these guidelines in writing your summary.

- Write one sentence stating the main idea or ideas.

- Include only important details for each main idea.

- Sum up the content in a concluding statement.

Compare your summary with that of a partner.

UNIT D

Continuity of Life

Theme: Constancy and Change

THINK LIKE A SCIENTIST

DIG THOSE FOSSILS

The picture on these pages shows fossils of ammonites (am′ə nīts). Ammonites were mollusks, squidlike animals with coiled shells. These creatures became extinct around the same time that dinosaurs became extinct. Many kinds of organisms, both plants and animals, that lived millions of years ago are no longer found on Earth today. The only evidence of their existence are the fossil remains buried deep in rock layers. Paleontologists are scientists that study these fossils to find out about ancient life.

THINK LIKE A SCIENTIST

Questioning In this unit you'll study how different species of living things continue to survive over time. You'll learn how traits are passed on from parents to offspring, and how scientists think species change over time. You'll investigate questions such as these.

- What Are Asexual Reproduction and Sexual Reproduction?
- What Do Fossils Tell Us About Life—Past and Present?

Observing, Testing, Hypothesizing In the Activity "Examine a Fossil," you'll examine two fossils, compare them, and label the parts of each fossil. Based on your observations, you'll infer what kind of environment each organism lived in.

Researching In the Resource "The Geologic Time Scale," you'll find out what the four spans of time in Earth's history are and what kinds of organisms appeared during each.

Drawing Conclusions After you've completed your investigations, you'll draw conclusions about what you've learned—and get new ideas.

CHAPTER 1

REPRODUCTION

An oak tree, a human being, and bacteria can do something that a rock can't do. They can reproduce and grow because they are alive. All living things can reproduce. And with a little luck and the right environment, life will continue through the offspring of the organisms.

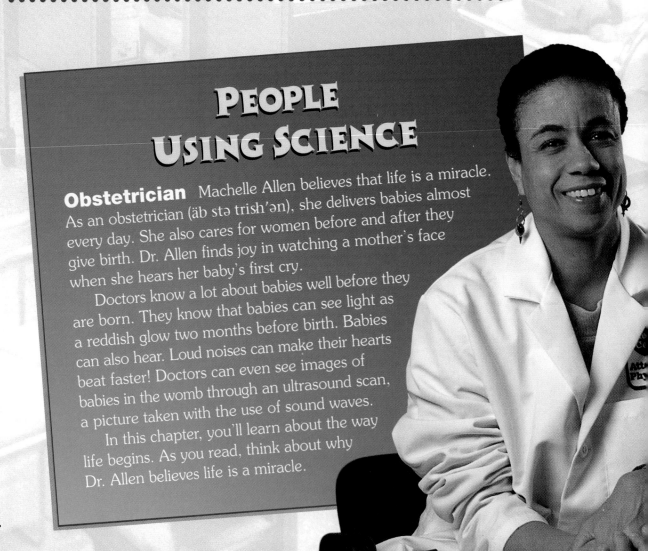

PEOPLE USING SCIENCE

Obstetrician Machelle Allen believes that life is a miracle. As an obstetrician (äb stə trish'ən), she delivers babies almost every day. She also cares for women before and after they give birth. Dr. Allen finds joy in watching a mother's face when she hears her baby's first cry.

Doctors know a lot about babies well before they are born. They know that babies can see light as a reddish glow two months before birth. Babies can also hear. Loud noises can make their hearts beat faster! Doctors can even see images of babies in the womb through an ultrasound scan, a picture taken with the use of sound waves.

In this chapter, you'll learn about the way life begins. As you read, think about why Dr. Allen believes life is a miracle.

Coming Up

◀ Dr. Machelle Allen uses ultrasound technology to "see" babies before they are born.

INVESTIGATION 1

WHAT IS ASEXUAL REPRODUCTION?

One morning you discover that the water in your fish tank has turned green overnight. You think that the green color comes from algae, but how could algae reproduce so quickly? In this investigation you'll find out.

Activity

Divide and Conquer!

Reproduction is the life process by which living things produce more of their own kind. How do some microorganisms reproduce?

Procedure

1. A paramecium is a protist. It is a one-celled organism. Place the first prepared slide of parameciums on the microscope stage.

 See **SCIENCE** *and* **MATH TOOLBOX** page H2 if you need to review *Using a Microscope.*

2. **Observe** the parameciums under low power of the microscope and then switch to high power. Study one paramecium closely. In your *Science Notebook*, **describe** and **draw** what you see.

3. Place the second prepared slide of parameciums on the microscope stage.

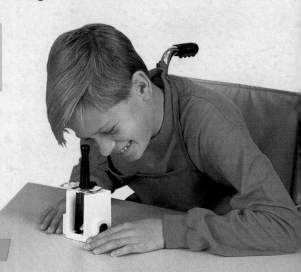

Step 2

D6

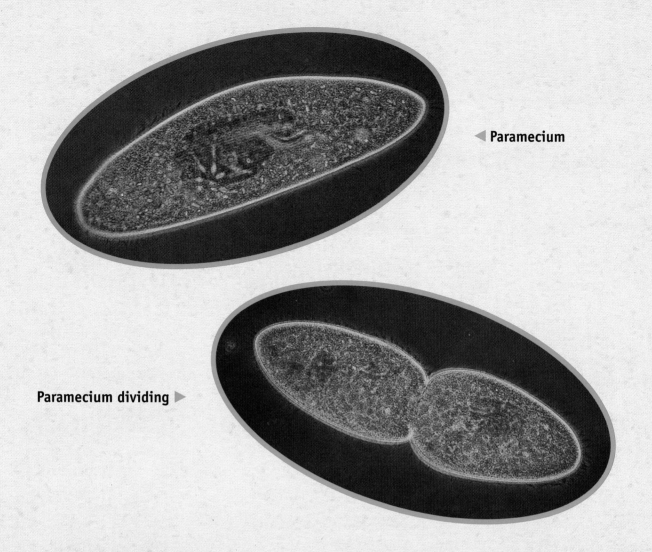

◄ **Paramecium**

Paramecium dividing ▶

4. Choose one specimen to study closely. **Describe** and **draw** what you see.

5. Look again at both prepared slides. **Compare** what you saw on the slides with the photographs of parameciums on this page. **Record** your comparisons.

6. **Suggest a hypothesis** to explain the differences between the first and second slides.

Analyze and Conclude

1. How would you describe the shape of a paramecium?

2. How are the shapes different in the two slides?

3. How can you tell that the paramecium on the second slide is reproducing?

4. On the second slide you saw a paramecium dividing. **Hypothesize** what will happen to the two new cells after division is complete.

Activity

The "Budding" System

Yeasts and hydras are organisms that have an unusual method of reproduction. Yeasts are fungi that can be used to make bread. Hydras are animals that live in pond water. Do this activity to find out how they reproduce.

Procedure

1. Place one drop of yeast culture in the center of a clean slide. Gently add a cover slip.

2. Using your microscope, **observe** the yeasts under low power. In your *Science Notebook*, **describe** and **draw** what you see. How many yeast cells do you see? Note any differences among the yeast cells.

See **SCIENCE** *and* **MATH TOOLBOX** page H2 *if you need to review **Using a Microscope.***

3. Change to high power and **observe** the cells more closely. Look for a cell that seems to have a smaller cell attached to it. Based on your observations, **infer** what is happening to such cells.

4. Wash and dry the slide and cover slip and be sure that the microscope stage is clean before you look at the slide of a hydra.

5. Using the microscope, **observe** the prepared slide of a hydra. **Describe** and **draw** what you see.

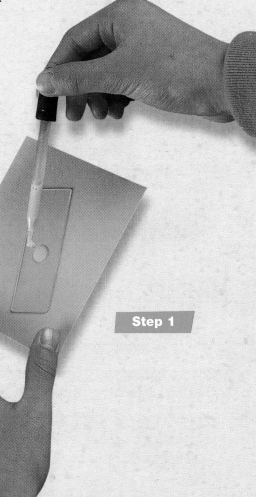

Step 1

Analyze and Conclude

1. A yeast cell can reproduce by forming a bud. What evidence of budding did you observe?

2. A yeast cell that forms a bud is called a parent cell. **Infer** what eventually happens as the bud develops from the parent cell.

3. What evidence did you observe that the hydra reproduces by budding?

4. **Infer** how a hydra bud is like a yeast bud. How are they different?

5. Reproduction involving only one parent is called **asexual reproduction**. How is budding a form of asexual reproduction? Explain your answer.

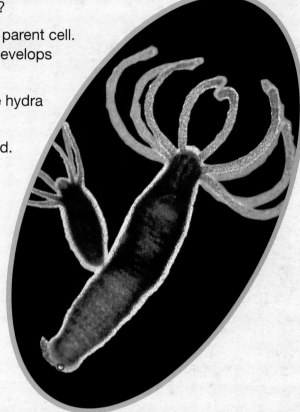

▲ Hydra: What is it doing?

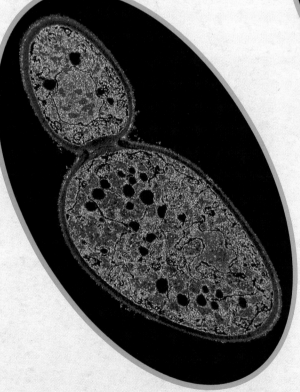

▲ Yeast: What is it doing?

INVESTIGATE FURTHER!

RESEARCH

Now that you have seen how a yeast cell reproduces, do research in the library to find out how yeast budding is important to certain industries. Report on how scientists prepare and store yeasts for use in these industries.

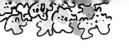

Fission: Splitting Heirs

Reading Focus How does a one-celled organism reproduce?

The activity on pages D6 and D7 shows that **reproduction** is the life process in which organisms produce more of their own kind. Not every organism in a species has to reproduce—but at least some members of a species must reproduce for the species to survive.

One Cell Becomes Two Cells

Imagine that you are 1 cm tall and are the captain of a submarine sent to study how one-celled pond dwellers reproduce. Suddenly, right above you near the surface of the pond, you see some amoebas. When you get closer, you notice that a few of the amoebas seem to be splitting apart. What's going on here?

Many one-celled organisms, including animal-like protists such as parameciums and amoebas, reproduce by splitting in half. When the split is complete, two identical cells result. This process is known as **fission** (fish'ən). Fission is a form of **asexual** (ā sek'shoo əl) **reproduction** because it involves a single parent producing an offspring that is exactly like the parent. Fission is the simplest kind of asexual reproduction. Before it can take place, certain changes must occur within the parent cell.

All organisms contain a chemical code that controls the life processes of the cell. Before a single-celled organism can undergo fission, it must copy the chemical code

that is necessary for life. One copy of this code will become part of one new cell that is formed during fission; the other copy will become part of the second new cell that is formed during fission. Once the two copies of the chemical code are produced, the parent cell begins to divide.

Now imagine that you're back in your submarine, observing the amoebas. Study the diagrams on the next page to see what you would see.

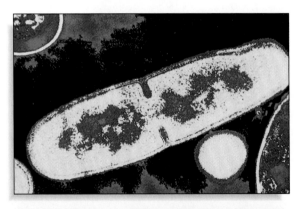

The bacteria shown above are reproducing through fission.

Fission in an Amoeba

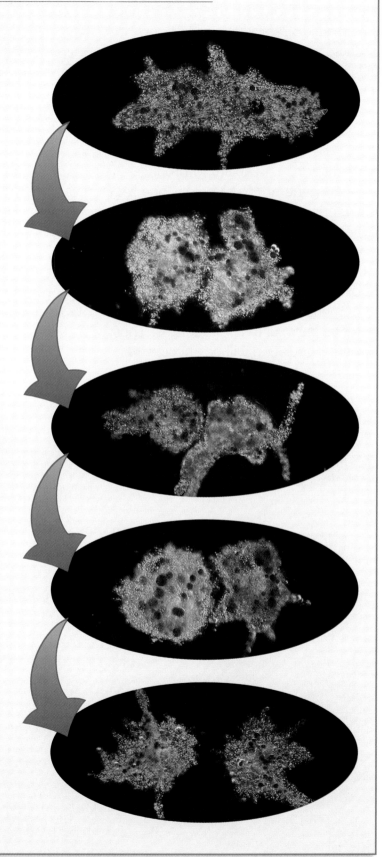

1 The cell material in an amoeba begins to stretch out toward the opposite ends of the cell.

2 Gradually, the center of the cell begins to pinch inward, as if the cell were developing a "waist."

3 The "waist" of the parent cell becomes a dividing line between the two sections of cell material. If you got a little closer in your submarine, you'd begin to see a line forming along the waist of the cell.

4 Once the cell material is about evenly divided between the two newly forming cells, the waistline becomes thicker. In fact, this waistline is actually a new cell membrane forming between the two new cells.

5 Look at that! The cell membrane has completely formed, and the two new "daughter" cells have completely separated. The parent cell no longer exists. In its place are two identical daughter cells.

One of the benefits of reproduction by fission is that it's very rapid. The two daughter cells shown on the previous page will be ready to reproduce in 24 hours. In four days, four generations of amoebas could be produced.

Fission is a quick and efficient method of asexual reproduction. It is the process the algae in a fish tank go through to multiply overnight. Bacteria also reproduce by fission. The ability to produce many new generations rapidly is one reason bacterial diseases are so devastating.

Like all forms of asexual reproduction, fission results in offspring that are exactly like the parent. This may be a disadvantage of fission, since a factor in the environment that is harmful to one organism will be harmful to all organisms. Thus, the entire population will be affected. ■

 Sixty years produces four generations of humans—and 21,900 generations of amoebas! How many years is one human generation?

Science in Literature

WE ARE FAMILY

"You may have noticed many family resemblances yourself. As you look through old family photos, you may see the shape of your face, the cleft in your chin, or the dimple when you smile right there in the features of a distant relative. When you see resemblances that are so obvious in a family, it may seem that these traits are passed along from one relative to another, that they are *inherited*."

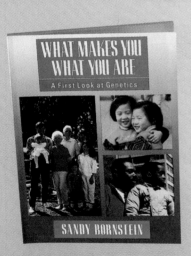

What Makes You What You Are: A First Look at Genetics
by Sandy Bornstein
Julian Messner, 1989

Find out more about why family members may look alike by reading *What Makes You What You Are: A First Look at Genetics* by Sandy Bornstein. You'll also learn how people can select perfect traits for plants and animals.

Reproduction by Budding

Reading Focus How does reproduction by budding differ from fission?

Some organisms reproduce asexually by fission. Other organisms use a form of asexual reproduction called budding. **Budding** begins with a tiny bump, or bud, on the parent's body. Although the bud initially looks like a pimple, it's the beginning of a new organism. As the tiny bump grows, it starts to look exactly like its parent.

Yeast and some other single-celled organisms reproduce asexually by budding. The yeast bud grows out from the parent cell and eventually pinches off.

The activity on pages D8 and D9, shows that the hydra, a many-celled organism, also reproduces by budding. So budding is not limited to single-celled organisms. Follow how a hydra reproduces in the photos to the right.

❶ A projection, or bud, appears on the hydra's body.

❷ The tip of the bud starts to grow what look like long hairs. These "hairs" will continue to develop, becoming the tentacles with which the mature hydra will catch its food.

❸ As the bud continues to grow, one part begins to look like the "stalk" of the hydra's body.

❹ The hydra bud contains all the features that it needs to live as an adult, independent hydra. It breaks free from its parent's body to start life on its own.

Budding in a hydra ▼

D13

New Plants From Old

Reading Focus How does a new plant grow from part of a parent plant?

Have you ever visited a friend or neighbor who had a beautiful plant that you wished you had? Maybe your friend offered to give you a cutting from the plant. Perhaps she snipped off some of the plant stem, including some leaves, and told you how to plant it to grow a plant of your own. Growing a new plant from a part of a parent plant is called **vegetative propagation**. Vegetative propagation is a kind of asexual reproduc-tion, because an identical plant is gener-ated from a part of only one parent—the original plant.

In vegetative propagation, new plants may be grown from a stem, a root, or a leaf of the parent plant. This process is useful in many ways. Gardeners use it to produce new plants faster than growing plants from seeds. They can also grow identical plants from plants that have desirable characteristics, such as resist-ance to disease and drought.

Professional gardeners use vegetative propagation to grow new plants. ▼

Vegetative propagation occurs naturally, too. For example, when a willow tree bends so that it touches the ground, roots may grow into the soil from a part of a branch. The roots then send up shoots of a new, identical willow tree. Other plants that reproduce by using vegetative propagation include onions, artichokes, potatoes, tulips, daffodils, hyacinths, red raspberries, spicebush, and sweet pepper bush.

Kalanchoe (kal an kō'ē), commonly called the air plant, produces new plants from its leaves. Tiny buds, also called plantlets, grow along the edges of its leaves. These plantlets will grow into exact copies of the parent plant. The photos below show how kalanchoe grows new plants through vegetative propagation.

Vegetative propagation allows new plants to be grown from a part of the parent plant. This form of asexual reproduction produces a population of identical copies in a rapid fashion. The parent plant also continues to produce new plants through this process. More examples of how vegetative propagation occurs are shown on the next two pages.

Vegetative Propagation in Kalanchoe

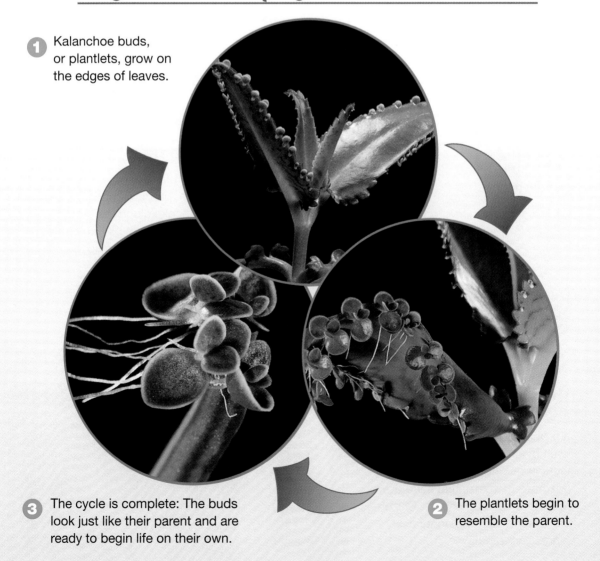

1 Kalanchoe buds, or plantlets, grow on the edges of leaves.

3 The cycle is complete: The buds look just like their parent and are ready to begin life on their own.

2 The plantlets begin to resemble the parent.

Growth resulting from stem damage

Sometimes a plant stem or tree trunk is damaged or completely cut in two. New plants, identical to the original, may grow out of the stem or stump.

Growth from existing root systems

Roots of some plants, such as the poplar tree, may develop tiny sprouts beneath the soil. The sprouts produce shoots that worm their way up out of the soil and roots that push down into the soil, producing many identical poplars very rapidly.

Runners

Some plants, such as strawberry plants, produce runners—stems that snake along the ground away from the parent plant. At some point, a runner begins to grow roots into the ground. A new strawberry plant grows out of the runner above these roots.

Rhizomes

Ever wonder why crabgrass is such a problem? Crabgrass reproduces itself by growing a spreading network of underground stems, called rhizomes (rī′zōmz), that send down roots and send up shoots. Rhizomes can spread and propagate new plants very rapidly.

Grafting

Stems of two plants—two different apple trees, for example—are joined to create a new plant that has characteristics of both parents. The single plant that results produces two different kinds of apples. Grafting—a kind of asexual reproduction controlled by people—is used to improve the number of crops that can be grown in one area.

Tubers

Potatoes are tubers—enlarged underground stem sections that store food. They have "eyes," or indentations from which new potato plants sprout. Potato farmers cut up "seed" potatoes so that each piece contains an eye. Each eye will grow a new potato plant that produces tubers—the potatoes we eat.

INVESTIGATION 1 WRAP-UP

REVIEW

1. What are the advantages of asexual reproduction? What are the disadvantages?

2. Compare and contrast budding and fission.

CRITICAL THINKING

3. Why might a gardener choose to use vegetative propagation rather than planting a garden with seeds?

4. Organism *A* reproduces by budding. Organism *B* reproduces by fission. Each organism can reproduce an offspring in 12 hours. After 36 hours, which organism will have more offspring? Explain why this is so.

INVESTIGATION 2

WHAT IS SEXUAL REPRODUCTION?

The chemical code that controls life processes is found in cells on structures called chromosomes. In sexual reproduction the offspring receives chromosomes from two different cells. How does this happen?

Activity

Splitting Pairs

The cells involved in sexual reproduction are called sperm and egg. In this activity, find out how sperm cells and egg cells differ from other body cells.

MATERIALS

- colored pencils
- large sheet of paper
- compass
- scissors
- yarn of 2 different colors
- metric ruler
- removable tape
- *Science Notebook*

Procedure

1. On a large sheet of paper, use colored pencils to **draw** and **label** two large circles and four small circles, as shown on the next page. Immature sex cells go through a process, called **meiosis**, to produce sperm cells and egg cells. Make a copy of these cell drawings in your *Science Notebook*.

Step 1

2. Cut six pieces of yarn of one color. Two pieces should be about 2 cm long, two should be about 4 cm long, and two should be about 6 cm long.

3. These pieces of yarn represent three pairs of chromosomes. Place them on the sheet of paper in the circle labeled *immature female sex cell*.

4. Repeat step 2 with the yarn of another color. Place these "chromosomes" on the sheet of paper in the circle labeled *immature male sex cell*.

5. **Draw** the chromosomes of the female and male immature sex cells that you've just modeled.

6. Take the two long pieces of yarn from the female cell and place one in each of the circles labeled *egg cell*. Repeat with the other pieces of yarn. Put an *X* through the immature sex cell you drew to show that it has divided to form new cells.

7. Add the chromosomes of the egg cells to your drawing.

8. Repeat step 6 with the yarn from the male cell, placing one piece of yarn from each pair into each of the circles labeled *sperm cell*.

9. Repeat step 7 for the sperm cells in your drawing.

10. Tape the chromosomes in place and save the large sheet of paper for the next activity.

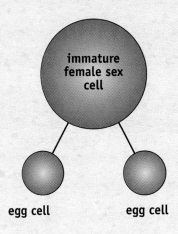

immature female sex cell

egg cell   egg cell

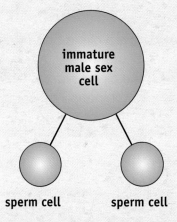

immature male sex cell

sperm cell   sperm cell

Analyze and Conclude

1. In your model, how many pairs of chromosomes are there in each immature male sex cell and each immature female sex cell? How many chromosomes are there in each of these cells?

2. How are the paired chromosomes in the immature sex cells alike?

3. How many chromosomes are there in each sperm cell and each egg cell?

4. Are there any pairs of chromosomes in the sperm and egg cells?

5. From what you have observed, **infer** how immature sex cells differ from sperm cells and egg cells.

INVESTIGATE FURTHER!

RESEARCH

Human sex cells have 23 chromosomes. Do other animals' sex cells have this number of chromosomes? Research your favorite animal in the library (or talk to a veterinarian or zookeeper) to find out.

Activity
Combining Cells

Sexual reproduction involves the joining of a sperm cell and an egg cell. Find out what happens to the chromosomes when these cells join.

MATERIALS
- colored pencils
- large sheet of paper and yarn from the activity "Splitting Pairs"
- *Science Notebook*

Procedure

1. Study the cells you drew on the large sheet of paper in the previous activity. **Predict** what will happen to the number of chromosomes when an egg cell and a sperm cell combine. **Record** your prediction.

2. **Draw** a circle below the sperm cell and the egg cell that are the closest together, as shown in the diagram on the next page. **Label** the circle *zygote*. A **zygote** is the first cell of the offspring of the combination of the sperm cell and the egg cell. Also add a circle to the drawing in your *Science Notebook*.

Step 2

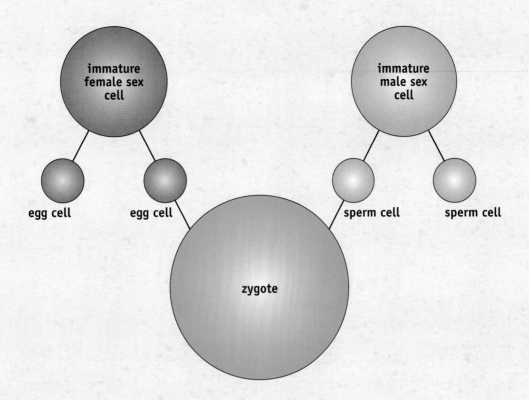

immature female sex cell

egg cell   egg cell

immature male sex cell

sperm cell   sperm cell

zygote

3. Remove the tape that held the yarn in the first activity. Move the yarn chromosomes from one egg cell and one sperm cell into the circle labeled *zygote*. Make sure that the yarn chromosomes are matched in pairs by color and size. Then count the chromosomes in the zygote and **record** them.

4. Add these chromosomes to your drawing.

Analyze and Conclude

1. How many chromosomes does the zygote have? How does this compare with your prediction?

2. How many pairs of chromosomes does the zygote have?

3. How does the number of chromosome pairs that the zygote has compare with the number of pairs in each male and female immature sex cell at the beginning of the activity on pages D18 and D19? **Infer** what has happened.

4. The joining of a sperm cell and an egg cell is called **fertilization**. How do meiosis and fertilization keep a species' chromosome number the same from generation to generation?

Technology Link CD-ROM

INVESTIGATE FURTHER!

Use the **Science Processor CD-ROM**, *Continuity of Life* (Investigation 1, The Great Divide) to learn about the chromosomes in a cow's body cells. Learn how meiosis makes sure that each calf has the same number of chromosomes as its parents.

Meiosis and Fertilization

> **Reading Focus** What is the role of meiosis in sexual reproduction?

Your body is growing—even as you are reading this chapter! And for growth to occur, your body cells must be reproducing. Your bone cells are making more bone cells; your skin cells, blood cells, cheek cells, liver cells, hair cells, and many other specialized cells are reproducing as you grow. This cell reproduction will continue throughout your life.

Body Cells

Each human body cell contains 23 pairs of chromosomes (krō′mə sōmz), or 46 chromosomes. **Chromosomes** are stringlike packets of chemical information that are located in a cell's nucleus. The information, coded by the chemicals, controls everything that a cell does.

When one of your body cells, such as a liver cell, reproduces, it first doubles the number of chromosomes it has (from 46 to 92), then divides into two cells. Each of the two new cells has the 46 chromosomes it needs to function properly. The new cells have exactly the same chemical information that the parent cell had.

Sex Cells

Humans, like most multicellular animals and most plants, reproduce sexually. **Sexual reproduction** involves the joining of **sex cells** from a male and a female. The male sex cell is the sperm cell; the female sex cell is the egg cell.

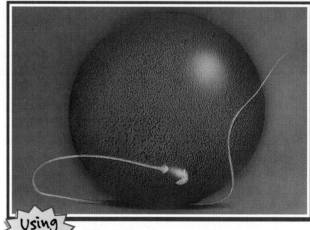

Using Math **What fraction would you use to compare the size of a sperm cell without its tail to the size of an egg cell?**

Since sexual reproduction involves the joining of cells, problems would arise if sex cells were produced in the same way as other body cells. Each would have a full set of chromosomes. Then when an egg cell united with a sperm cell, the resulting cell would contain twice as many chromosomes as it should.

However, this problem does not occur. The activity on pages D18 and D19 shows that through a special type of cell division called **meiosis** (mī ō′sis), sex cells receive only half the number of chromosomes as other body cells. So instead of having 46 chromosomes, human sex cells contain only 23 chromosomes. To understand meiosis, follow the steps in the drawing on the next page.

The Process of Meiosis

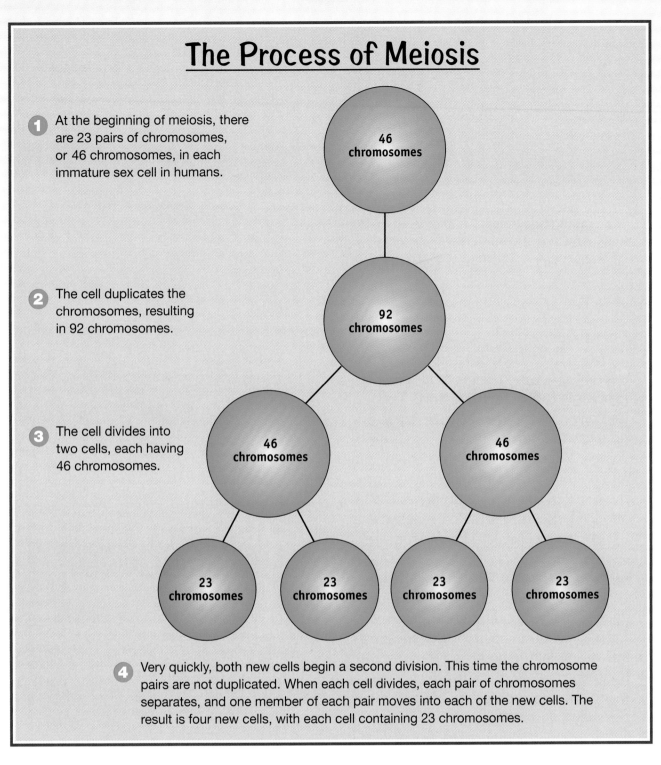

1. At the beginning of meiosis, there are 23 pairs of chromosomes, or 46 chromosomes, in each immature sex cell in humans.

2. The cell duplicates the chromosomes, resulting in 92 chromosomes.

3. The cell divides into two cells, each having 46 chromosomes.

46 chromosomes

92 chromosomes

46 chromosomes

46 chromosomes

23 chromosomes

23 chromosomes

23 chromosomes

23 chromosomes

4. Very quickly, both new cells begin a second division. This time the chromosome pairs are not duplicated. When each cell divides, each pair of chromosomes separates, and one member of each pair moves into each of the new cells. The result is four new cells, with each cell containing 23 chromosomes.

The process of meiosis is complete. What happened was that an immature sex cell with a normal number of body cell chromosomes doubled that number. The cell then divided into two cells, each with the normal number of chromosomes. These two cells then divided, producing four sex cells, each with half the number of body cell chromosomes. Since sex cells contain half the number of body cell chromosomes, when they join, the resulting cell will have the normal number of body cell chromosomes.

Internet Field Trip

Visit **www.eduplace.com** to see how a cell goes through meiosis.

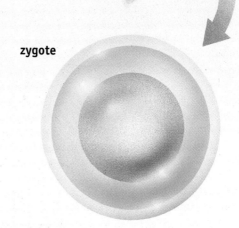

sperm cell

egg cell

zygote

The zygote (*below right*) is the result of the process of fertilization, which occurs when the sperm cell and egg cell unite (*above right*).

Fertilization

When the sperm cell and the egg cell are united, the egg cell is fertilized. This process is called **fertilization**. The fertilized egg cell, called a **zygote** (zī′gōt), now has the normal number of chromosomes, half of which it gets from the male and the other half of which it gets from the female. The activity on pages D20 and D21 shows that the chromosomes the zygote receives are joined in pairs.

Sexual Reproduction and Nature

Millions of kinds of organisms reproduce sexually. Yet different organisms have different numbers of chromosomes. For example, the body cells of a common housefly have 12 chromosomes. How many chromosomes, then, do you think a housefly's sperm cell has?

All organisms that reproduce sexually produce sex cells by meiosis. Sexual reproduction has one great advantage over asexual reproduction—it results in variation in offspring. Among organisms that reproduce sexually, no two offspring are exactly alike. Some individuals may be better adapted to a particular environment than other individuals. As you will see, this variation is important in understanding the history of life. ■

UNIT PROJECT LINK

For this Unit Project you will participate in a class debate about the possible relationships between an organism's method of reproduction and its risk of being endangered. To prepare for the debate, find out whether any species that reproduce asexually are endangered. What advantages or disadvantages could asexual reproduction give a species? Write a short report explaining your views. Share your report or place it in a journal for reference during the debate.

TechnologyLink
For more help with your Unit Project, go to **www.eduplace.com**.

Saving Species

Reading Focus How are endangered species saved from extinction?

Reproduction is supposed to ensure the survival of a species. But sometimes the survival of a species is threatened by the actions of other organisms. Before Europeans settled in North America, there were approximately 75 million American bison roaming the Great Plains. In less than two decades in the mid-1800s, settlers systematically slaughtered the bison. There were so few bison left that this symbol of the American West would have become **extinct**, or would no longer exist, had it not been for the efforts of the New York Zoological Society. Concerned scientists at the society's Bronx Zoo saved the few remaining bison and began breeding them at the zoo. This was one of the first examples of zoos helping to save endangered wildlife. Today the American bison has returned to many western states.

An **endangered species** is a species whose population has become so low that it is in danger of extinction. Species become endangered for many reasons, but in modern times, human destruction of natural habitats is a common cause. The peregrine falcon became endangered because its eggs were harmed by pesticides made by humans.

Sometimes, scientists try to save a species by capturing some or all of the remaining animals of that species. These animals are cared for in zoos or wildlife centers. If conditions are right, the

Using Math *Bison were hunted nearly to extinction. On Earth, one plant or animal species becomes extinct every hour. How many species become extinct every year?*

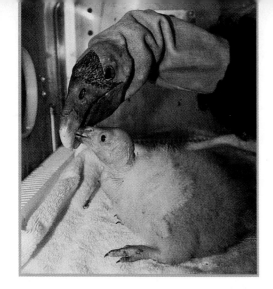

▲ This California condor is fed by a zoo-keeper who is wearing a "condor costume." The costume prevents the condor from becoming attached to its human caregivers.

animals will breed. New generations can then be returned to the wild. Breeding programs at zoos, such as at the San Diego Zoo, helped save the California condor. The San Diego Zoo program began when four eggs were taken from one of the few condor nests found in the wild. The eggs were carefully incubated and cared for.

Even though zoos try to create conditions like those of an animal's natural habitat, some species do not breed well, if at all, in captivity. Even when captive breeding is successful, it is not a complete victory until the animal can be released back to its natural home. Scientists are hard at work trying to preserve the native

habitats of many endangered species. If a new suitable habitat is found or if a wrecked habitat can be restored, scientists must convince people not to disturb it. Only then can the endangered animal be released into the habitat.

For example, black-footed ferrets lived on the Great Plains and hunted prairie dogs. In the nineteenth century many prairie dogs were poisoned by ranchers. The ferrets starved and nearly became extinct. Eventually some ferrets were captured and bred at a wildlife center. Scientists found an unspoiled place where the ferrets might survive and where prairie dogs still lived. The scientists convinced ranchers not to disturb the area, and some ferrets were released back into their natural home. ■

▲ A black-footed ferret

INVESTIGATION 2 WRAP-UP

REVIEW

1. How is meiosis different from fission?

2. How many new cells are produced in meiosis?

CRITICAL THINKING

3. What is the difference between a zygote and an immature sex cell?

4. How does meiosis ensure that a zygote will have the normal number of chromosomes?

REFLECT & EVALUATE

Word Power

Write the letter of the term that best matches the definition. *Not all terms will be used*.

1. Form of reproduction that involves only one parent producing an offspring that is exactly like the parent
2. Species whose population is in danger of extinction
3. Process of uniting the sperm cell and the egg cell
4. Fertilized egg cell
5. Stringlike packets of chemical information that are in a cell's nucleus
6. Process of growing a new plant from part of a parent plant

a. asexual reproduction
b. chromosomes
c. endangered species
d. extinct
e. fertilization
f. sexual reproduction
g. vegetative propagation
h. zygote

Check What You Know

Write the word in each pair that correctly completes each sentence.

1. Through the process of meiosis, sex cells are created with half the number of (chromosomes, genes) as body cells.
2. Kalanchoe can reproduce by (budding, fission).
3. The American bison became (extinct, endangered) when millions of them were slaughtered in the mid-1800s.

Problem Solving

1. A type of bacteria reproduces by fission every 20 minutes. At this rate, how many bacteria will be present after 1 hour?

2. Why might a population of organisms produced through asexual reproduction be in greater danger of extinction than a population of organisms produced through sexual reproduction?

BUILD YOUR PORTFOLIO

Study the photograph. Then identify and describe the process that is taking place.

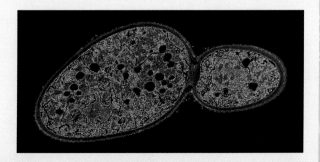

HEREDITY

Why are some roses red and others yellow? How can one puppy in a litter have golden fur when all the others and both its parents are black? You can think of the traits an organism inherits from its parents as items in a salad bar. Each salad that is made is unique, because the vegetables are combined in a different way. In the same way, combinations of inherited traits create unique individuals.

PEOPLE
USING SCIENCE

Plant Geneticist Jack Hearn is a plant geneticist (jə net'ə-sist). He works with a team at the U.S. Horticultural Research Laboratory in Orlando, Florida. Researchers at the laboratory develop new fruits and vegetables by fertilizing one plant species with pollen from another, similar species. The tangelo, a cross between a tangerine and a grapefruit, was made in this way.

Recently Jack Hearn and his team fertilized tangelos with pollen from a type of sweet orange. The result? A new citrus fruit called the Ambersweet. From the tangelo the Ambersweet inherited a tangerine's loose skin and a grapefruit's size. From the orange, the Ambersweet inherited its dark orange pulp.

As you do the investigations in this chapter, think about how parents affect the traits that an individual inherits. What else besides parents influences the traits of living things?

◀ Jack Hearn, plant geneticist, with some of his Ambersweets

WHAT ARE INHERITED TRAITS?

When you describe how someone looks—the person is short or tall, has blue eyes or brown eyes—you are often talking about the traits that the person inherited from his or her parents. Can these traits be changed? Find out in this investigation.

Activity

What Can You Do?

You have learned to do many things. But some things are impossible to learn because they are inherited traits. What kinds of traits are inherited?

MATERIALS
- mirror
- *Science Notebook*

Procedure

1. You and your classmates will collect data on three traits. First, stick out your tongue and try to roll up the edges to form a tube. With the help of your partner, look in a mirror to see if you can do this.

Step 1

▲ **Left-thumb superior**

▲ **Right-thumb superior**

2. After everyone in the class has had a chance to check this trait, **make a chart** in your *Science Notebook* to **record** the class data.

See **SCIENCE** *and* **MATH TOOLBOX** *page H11 if you need to review* **Making a Chart to Organize Data.**

3. Next, fold your hands together and see which thumb naturally falls on the top. Are you left-thumb superior or right-thumb superior? (See the photographs above.) **Record** the class data on this trait.

4. Finally, are you left-handed or right-handed? **Record** the class data in your chart.

Analyze and Conclude

1. Were there more tongue rollers or nonrollers in your class? Were more people left-thumb superior or right-thumb superior? Were there more lefties or righties? **Make a bar graph** to show the number of people with each trait. **Compare** the incidence of each trait.

2. If these three traits are inherited traits, what can you **infer** about the incidence of these traits in the general population? Use the bar graph you created as a guide.

3. **Hypothesize** whether nonrollers can learn to roll their tongues. Can people change which thumb naturally falls on top when their hands are folded? Can righties learn to be lefties and vice versa? Explain your hypotheses.

INVESTIGATE FURTHER!

EXPERIMENT

Poll a random group of 25 people—members of a school club or sports team—and see whether they are tongue rollers or non-rollers, left-thumb or right-thumb superior, and right-handed or left-handed. Draw a bar graph and compare it to the one you drew of your class data.

Genes, Traits, and Environment

Reading Focus How are an organism's traits affected by its genes and its environment?

When friends and family see a new baby for the first time, they may make comments such as "She has her father's eyes" or "Look at that curly hair—just like his mother's!" Are such similarities coincidence, or do parents somehow pass traits to their offspring? And why does a baby look like one parent in some ways and like the other parent in other ways?

The Secret in the Cell

The activity on pages D30 and D31 investigates tongue rolling, which is an inherited trait. **Inherited traits** are traits that are passed on from parents to offspring, from generation to generation. These traits are determined by a chemical code found inside cells. As a baby develops, the code causes cells to develop into the tissues that make up the body's organs and systems. Some cells become heart muscle, for example. Others become part of the body's bones.

This chemical code, called DNA, is transferred from generation to generation by the egg cell and sperm cell that join to form the zygote. If you haven't already guessed it, it is this code that controls the hereditary characteristics of the baby that will develop from the fertilized egg. DNA controls eye color, hair color, height, and weight, as well as thousands of other characteristics of the new baby. Therefore, it makes sense to

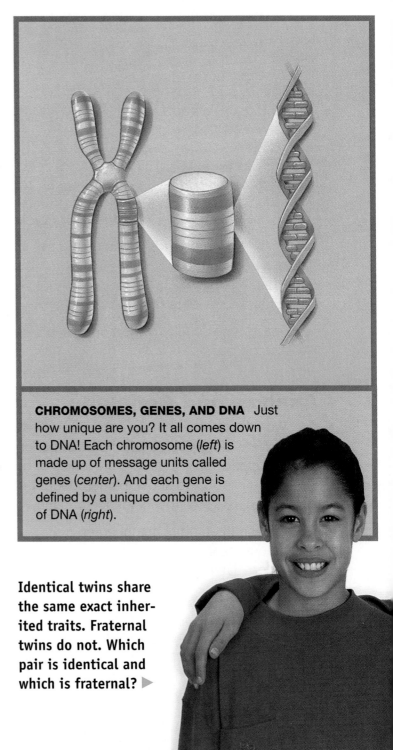

CHROMOSOMES, GENES, AND DNA Just how unique are you? It all comes down to DNA! Each chromosome (*left*) is made up of message units called genes (*center*). And each gene is defined by a unique combination of DNA (*right*).

Identical twins share the same exact inherited traits. Fraternal twins do not. Which pair is identical and which is fraternal? ▶

look closely at how DNA is passed from parents to offspring.

Passing on DNA

Remember that the chromosomes in a cell are duplicated before the cell divides. These chromosomes carry the code that controls the structure and function of each cell. Tiny message units, called **genes**, make up the chromosomes. The genes themselves are made of DNA. So when a cell reproduces by meiosis, half of each gene pair is passed on to each sperm cell or egg cell.

Each chromosome is like a chain made up of many genes. As shown in the illustration on page D32, each gene is a small piece of the cell's total DNA. For example, one gene might carry a code for hair color, another might carry a code for skin texture, and a third might carry a code for tongue rolling.

Genes: A Gift From Your Parents

Genes, too small to be seen even with a microscope, are the units from which your unique inheritance is created. Because half of your genes come from one parent and half from the other, you might have eyes with the shape of your father's and color like your mother's.

But if half your genes and chromosomes come from your father and half from your mother, why don't brothers and sisters in a family all look identical? It's because each new offspring has a new combination of chromosomes and genes. During meiosis, chromosomes are shuffled, mixing the genetic information, and ensuring that different combinations of the parents' genetic information will be passed on. Therefore, each offspring has a unique set of genes. Genes make sure that you have all the right parts doing the right jobs and that you are a designer original.

Is the World Series in Your Genes?

It would be simple if all traits were determined totally by genes! From the moment of fertilization, your traits would be set in stone—your final height, your health, your intelligence, even how long you will live.

But this would be like saying that the look of a new house is the result of only

the architect's blueprint. Many factors actually affect the final look of a new house. The blueprint determines the structural features, but the builder may use cheaper or more expensive materials in constructing it. And the new owner will determine the colors and type of wallpaper. Two houses built from identical blueprints may look—and be—very different when finally completed.

If you think about it, it's pretty obvious that some traits aren't simply the result of orders from genes. The ability to learn to speak is an inherited trait but the language you speak (and how well you speak it) is determined by where you are born and what language your parents speak. Language is a **learned trait**—a trait that is not passed on in DNA.

Sometimes it's difficult to determine to what extent inherited traits are influenced by the environment. For example, if your mother has a stomach ulcer, will you develop stomach ulcers? Did Ken Griffey, Jr., inherit the way he plays baseball from Ken Griffey, Sr.? Or did he inherit certain traits, like muscle structure and coordination, from his father and then learn to love the game and practice hard at it?

Who's in Charge?

The truth is, many traits result from the interaction of genes and environment. Genes provide the opportunity for certain traits to develop. Environment either helps or hinders this development. The environment in which you live influences the way in which many of the traits you inherit will develop. For example, potato plants have genes that enable them to grow green leaves. But without enough sunlight, they will produce leaves

What traits did Ken Griffey, Jr., inherit from his father, and what habits did he learn from him?

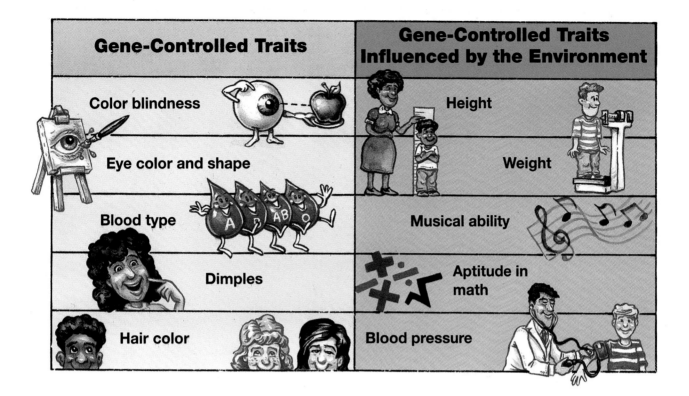

Gene-Controlled Traits	Gene-Controlled Traits Influenced by the Environment
Color blindness	Height
Eye color and shape	Weight
Blood type	Musical ability
Dimples	Aptitude in math
Hair color	Blood pressure

that are colorless (white) or light green. Without light, plants can't develop chlorophyll, the chemical that makes leaves green and that traps the Sun's energy.

Use the chart above to help you see how genes and environment interact to influence the development of traits. Some traits, like eye color, are controlled entirely by genes. Musical ability, however, may be passed from generation to generation, but the ability can only thrive in an environment that teaches a love for music.

For many traits, genes and environmental factors interact in complex ways. For example, genes may give you an ability to burn food quickly. Your tendency would be to remain lean. But overeating may cause you to be overweight.

It's good to know that you can affect certain traits by modifying your environment. For example, you can increase your chances of having a long life by eating properly, getting enough rest, and avoiding dangerous behaviors. ■

INVESTIGATION 1 WRAP-UP

REVIEW

1. Name two inherited traits that can be affected by the environment.

2. Explain why brothers and sisters in a family may not all look alike.

CRITICAL THINKING

3. Explain how muscle structure, a gene-controlled trait, can be influenced by the environment.

4. How does meiosis affect genes?

INVESTIGATION 2

HOW ARE TRAITS INHERITED?

Juan's mother has brown eyes and his father has green eyes. Both grandfathers have blue eyes, while one grandmother has brown and the other has green. How did Juan inherit blue eyes?

Activity

Scrambled Genes

Brothers and sisters in a family get their genes from their parents. How do genes combine to create individuals distinct from one another?

MATERIALS

- 2 paper cups
- 2 sets of disks of 4 different colors
- marker or pencil
- large sheet of paper
- *Science Notebook*

Procedure

1. Divide the disks into two sets, each with the same four colors. One set will represent genes for four different traits from a male parent; the other, genes for these same traits from a female parent.

2. The two sides of each disk represent a gene pair, with each gene controlling a different form of the trait (such as eye color or freckles). Mark one side of each disk with the marker or pencil so that the two forms can be told apart.

3. **Label** one paper cup *male* and the other *female*. Place one set of the gene pairs in the "female" cup. Place the second set of gene pairs in the "male" cup.

4. On a large sheet of paper, **draw** three circles. **Label** one of the circles *sperm cell*; another, *egg cell*; and the third, *zygote*.

5. In your *Science Notebook*, **prepare a data chart** like the one shown. Write one disk color in each row under the column labeled *Disk color*.

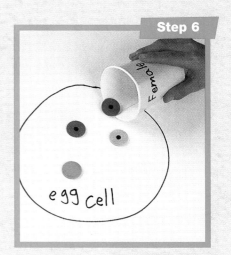

Step 6

Trial 1			
Disk color	**Female gene**	**Male gene**	**Zygote**

6. Hold one hand over the cup marked *female* and gently shake it. Empty the disks into the circle labeled *egg cell*. In your data chart, write *H* for "head side" (the marked side) or *T* for "tail side" (the unmarked side) in the row for that color disk. **Repeat** with the cup marked *male*, emptying the disks into the circle labeled *sperm cell*.

7. Match up the same-colored disk pairs from the egg cell and the sperm cell. Do not turn any of the disks over. Slide the matched pairs of genes into the circle labeled *zygote*. In your chart, **record** the combination of genes in the *Zygote* column.

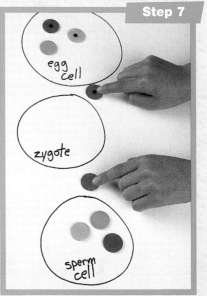

Step 7

8. Make a new data chart titled *Trial 2*. **Predict** what the combination of genes would be if you did steps 6 and 7 again. **Record** your prediction. Then test your prediction. Repeat steps 6 and 7 a total of five times. **Record** the results of each trial in a separate data chart.

Analyze and Conclude

1. Identify and **describe** the processes you were modeling when you shook the cups and emptied the disks onto the paper and then moved the disks into the circle labeled *zygote*.

2. If the six "zygotes" were people, how would they be related? How would they be different?

UNIT PROJECT LINK

The traits of some animals have evolved to make them "specialists": animals that specialize in using one kind of resource efficiently to survive. For example, black-footed ferrets have adapted to eat prairie dogs almost exclusively. Do some research and find out about some endangered plants or animals that are specialists. Decide whether specialists are more likely to be endangered than organisms called generalists, which use many kinds of resources. Organize your data in a poster or large chart.

TechnologyLink

For more help with your Unit Project, go to **www.eduplace.com**.

Activity

Inheriting Traits

Parents often differ for particular traits. As a result their offspring may vary for the trait. Why?

- -

Procedure

1. In this activity, the sperm and egg cells can carry either a dominant gene or a recessive gene. If present, a dominant gene controls the trait in an offspring, masking the recessive gene. If two recessive genes for a trait are passed on, that trait is expressed in the offspring.

2. Make a chart like the one below in your *Science Notebook*. Mark one side of your disk *A*. This will be the "head" side, representing the dominant gene for brown eyes. Mark the other side of your disk *a*. This will be the "tail" side and will represent the recessive gene for blue eyes.

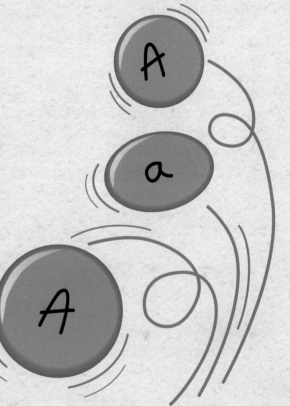

	Sperm cell	Egg cell	Zygote
Trial 1			
Trial 2			
Trial 3			
Trial 4			
Trial 5			
Trial 6			

3. Flip the disk to run the first trial. If the head side comes up, **record** the dominant gene (*A*) in the space for the sperm cell in the chart you copied. If the tail side comes up, **record** the recessive gene (*a*) in the space for the sperm cell.

4. Repeat the trial five more times for the sperm cell, **recording** each time whether the flip of the disk gives you the dominant or recessive gene. Then run the trial a total of six times for the egg cell.

5. **Record** the combination of genes in the zygote that would result from a union of the sperm and egg cells in each trial.

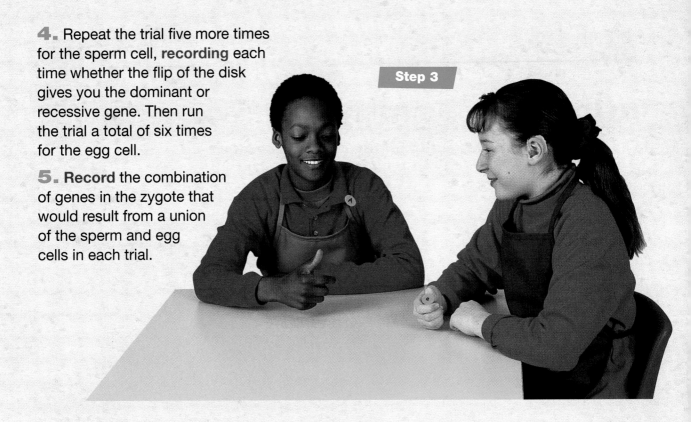

Step 3

Analyze and Conclude

1. Which zygotes carry one or more dominant genes? Which carry one or more recessive genes?

2. In your *Science Notebook*, indicate whether each offspring would be brown-eyed or blue-eyed.

3. **Suggest a hypothesis** to explain how two parents who are both brown-eyed could have a blue-eyed child.

INVESTIGATE FURTHER!

RESEARCH

Research the number of left-handed people versus the number of right-handed people in a population. Find out if hand preference is determined by a single pair of genes or by a combination of genes. Share your results with your classmates.

Activity

All in the Family

The inheritance of traits in a family can be recorded in a pedigree chart. Find out how one works in this activity.

MATERIALS

• *Science Notebook*

Procedure

1. The pedigree chart shown here has information about ear lobes in a family. Ear lobes may be attached or free, depending on whether the individual has genes for attached ear lobes or genes for free ear lobes.

2. On this pedigree chart, circles represent females, and squares represent males. The horizontal lines connect two parents. The vertical and diagonal lines connect parents to children.

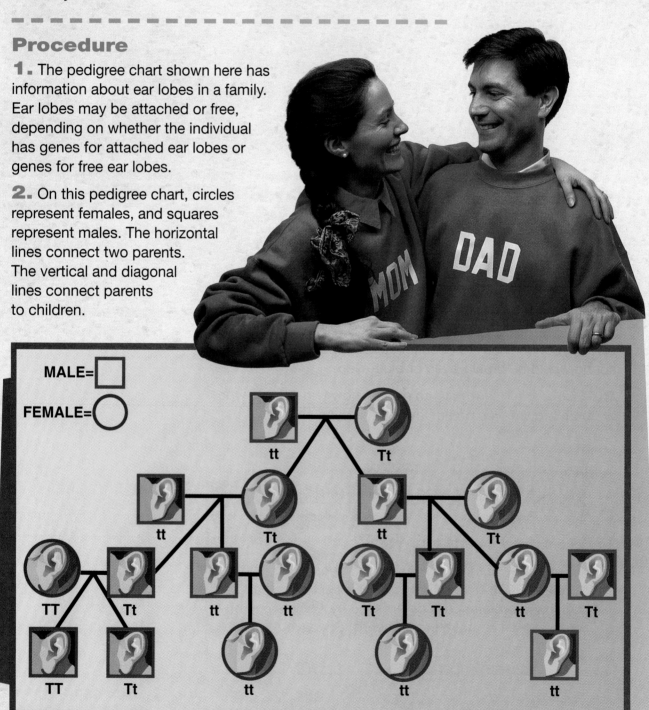

MALE=☐

FEMALE=○

3. Look at the pedigree chart and **identify** the members of the family who have attached ear lobes. Then **identify** the members who have free ear lobes. In your *Science Notebook*, **record** your observations about the ear lobes of each individual in the chart.

Analyze and Conclude

1. Can two parents with attached ear lobes have children with free ear lobes? Explain your answer.

2. Can two parents with free ear lobes have children with attached ear lobes? Explain your answer.

3. Look for patterns in the way ear lobes are inherited. **Write a hypothesis** to explain how attached or free ear lobes are inherited.

4. If an offspring has attached ear lobes, what do you know about the parents' ear lobes?

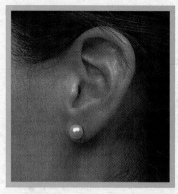

▲ **Free ear lobe**

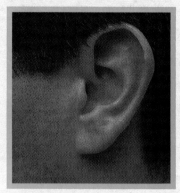

▲ **Attached ear lobe**

Science in Literature

FAMILY TREES REVEAL TRAITS

"By studying many families with the same trait scientists can discover some things about how a trait is passed along from generation to generation. These family studies have taught us a lot about ourselves. To keep records of these interviews, scientists draw a pedigree, or family tree, whenever they investigate a family trait."

Learn more about how pedigrees are drawn and what they reveal about inherited traits by reading *What Makes You What You Are: A First Look at Genetics* by Sandy Bornstein. You'll also find directions on how to make your own pedigree chart.

**What Makes You What You Are:
A First Look at Genetics**
by Sandy Bornstein
Julian Messner, 1989

WHAT MAKES YOU WHAT YOU ARE
A First Look at Genetics
SANDY BORNSTEIN

Laws of Heredity

Reading Focus What did Gregor Mendel discover about genes and hereditary traits?

▲ **A cat may have eight kittens, each different from the others. How can that possibly be the case?**

The activity on pages D40 and D41 shows that offspring from the same parents may not inherit the same traits. The activity on pages D36 and D37 shows that the same combinations of genes are not always passed on when egg cells and sperm cells unite. When an egg cell and a sperm cell are joined, the offspring receives a full set of chromosome pairs, but that set is different from the chromosomes of either parent. The combination of genetic information from an egg cell and a sperm cell leads to a new organism with its own unique set of chromosomes.

If you wanted to look for a pattern in the way traits are passed from one generation to the next, what sort of experiment would you set up? How would you decide on the traits to observe? These are questions a monk named Gregor Mendel asked a century and a half ago.

More Peas, Please

Mendel's love of plants and mathematics led him to discover how traits are passed on. As he worked in the monastery gardens, he noticed that certain traits of pea plants were passed from generation to generation. Curious, he set up experiments to find out why.

At the time, no one knew about genes or chromosomes. Mendel just knew he was looking for "something" that controlled how traits are passed. He made some very smart decisions that would give him good data.

- He chose to observe just a few traits and observed only one at a time.
- He chose traits that were clear-cut and easy to observe.
- He worked carefully and kept good records.
- He used thousands of plants, not just a few.
- He carried out experiments at least to the second generation.

The Tall and the Short of It

One trait Mendel observed was tall-ness. He noted that some pea plants always produced tall offspring; others always produced short offspring. Mendel described these plants as being "pure" for the trait of height.

Mendel wondered what would happen if pure tall plants were crossed with pure short ones. He began by hand-pollinating plants to be sure one parent was tall and one short. You might expect the off-spring of a tall parent and a short parent to be of medium height. Instead, all the offspring were tall! Mendel hypothesized that each parent contributed one unit of heredity for tallness. He called these units T (tall) and t (short). Today, we refer to these units as genes. He used the term **dominant trait** (T) to describe the trait that was expressed. The trait that was not expressed was the **recessive trait** (t). He reasoned that the offspring must have a Tt combination. Mendel allowed the Tt off-spring to self-pollinate. The drawing and table below—known as a Punnett square—will help you understand what happened.

Notice that one fourth of the offspring of Tt plants were short, and three fourths were tall. The two possible genes that each parent may pass on appear at the top and side of the table. The squares in the table show the combinations of genes the offspring may have.

There are three possible combinations of genes (TT, Tt, tt), and on average,

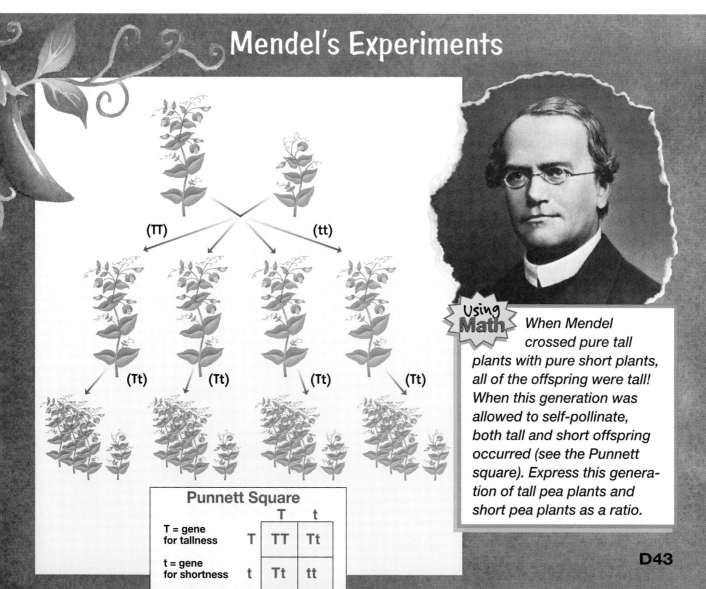

Mendel's Experiments

(TT)   (tt)

(Tt)   (Tt)   (Tt)   (Tt)

Punnett Square

		T	t
T = gene for tallness	T	TT	Tt
t = gene for shortness	t	Tt	tt

Using Math *When Mendel crossed pure tall plants with pure short plants, all of the offspring were tall! When this generation was allowed to self-pollinate, both tall and short offspring occurred (see the Punnett square). Express this genera-tion of tall pea plants and short pea plants as a ratio.*

Amaiz-ing Genes

Barbara McClintock

When she went to college in 1919, Barbara McClintock became excited about the young science of genetics, the study of heredity. (No one understood the significance of Mendel's work until around 1900; the term *genetics* didn't even exist until 1905.) McClintock (*pictured left*) stood out not only because she wanted to become a geneticist, but also because she was the only woman on her team!

In the 1920s, McClintock began her work with maize (corn) plants. She showed how some maize genes act like switches. These genes turn other genes on and off. She also discovered that these controlling genes could rearrange them-selves in response to chemical signals in the cell or in response to environmental influences. Barbara McClintock's tireless research took Mendel's and others' theories many steps further. McClintock was awarded a Nobel Prize in 1983.

three zygotes out of four will inherit a dominant gene (T). Sure enough, three out of the four pea plants proved to be tall. Mendel's results show clearly that a dominant gene masks a recessive one (t) when both are present. Only plants with two recessive genes for shortness (tt) were short. The activity on pages D38 and D39 shows how a dominant gene masks a recessive gene.

Black and White, or Gray?

Some traits may have two different dominant genes. For example, the four o'clock flower may have red flowers (RR—two genes for red flower color) or white flowers (WW—two genes for white flower color). When red and white are crossed, the offspring have pink (RW) flowers. In this case, neither gene is masked; both are expressed in a way that produces a blended effect. This is known as **incomplete dominance**.

Multiple Genes

Is inheritance always so simple? Of course not. Many traits have more than two forms of genes. Eye color is one such trait. There are several genes for eye color ranging from brown, which is most dominant, to blue, which is most recessive. In between are genes for hazel, green, gray, and violet. An individual has only one pair of genes for eye color—but it can be any combination of these colors! Some traits are influenced by two or more pairs of genes. Skin color is determined not by a single pair of genes but by many pairs. Therefore, skin color in humans is quite varied and its inheritance very complex. ■

Technology Link
CD-ROM

INVESTIGATE FURTHER!

Use the **Science Processor CD-ROM**, *Continuity of Life* (Investigation 2, Peas in a Pod) to set up Mendel's crossbreeding experiments. You'll be able to predict and observe pod colors in the offspring.

Designer Genes

Reading Focus How do scientists transfer the genes of one organism to another?

STS
SCIENCE TECHNOLOGY & SOCIETY

The researchers who unlocked the secrets of genes opened a world of possibilities and raised more exciting questions than were even dreamed of years before. Today, genes can be altered and even transferred from one organism to another, a process called **genetic engineering**. One important example of genetic engineering is the use of microorganisms to produce medicines needed by humans. Diabetics, for example, need the protein insulin, which their bodies have stopped producing. Today, bacteria are used to produce human insulin.

How can a gene for producing insulin be removed from one organism and transferred to a bacterium? Think of a precise operation performed in the world's smallest operating room. The diagram on page D46 will help you understand this operation, called **gene splicing**.

What Are the Possibilities?

What would make the process of transplanting genes easier and more useful? What if we could just insert the new genes right into a human cell? This would involve identifying the location of each gene on all 46 human chromosomes, a project currently under way.

Several new techniques of transplanting genes show great promise. The ability to transplant genes directly into human cells has created the field of gene therapy. For example, a gene that produces a cancer-fighting substance can be injected right into a tumor.

Genetic engineering opens a world of fascinating possibilities. Scientists can now turn cells into living factories that can produce medicines, proteins, and drugs. They might one day be able to correct genetic defects before birth. What other possibilities do you see?

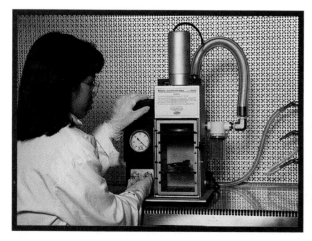

▲ Scientists use genetic engineering to try to discover cures for diseases.

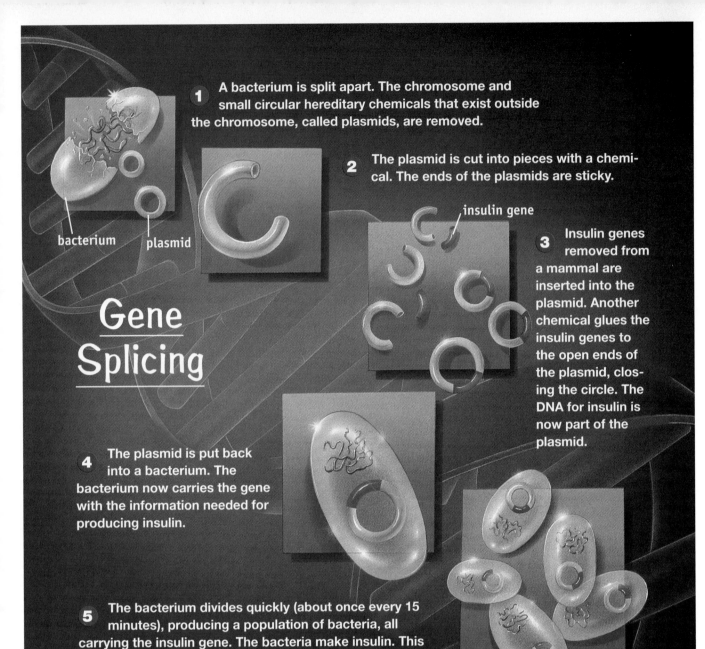

Gene Splicing

1 A bacterium is split apart. The chromosome and small circular hereditary chemicals that exist outside the chromosome, called plasmids, are removed.

bacterium   plasmid

2 The plasmid is cut into pieces with a chemical. The ends of the plasmids are sticky.

insulin gene

3 Insulin genes removed from a mammal are inserted into the plasmid. Another chemical glues the insulin genes to the open ends of the plasmid, closing the circle. The DNA for insulin is now part of the plasmid.

4 The plasmid is put back into a bacterium. The bacterium now carries the gene with the information needed for producing insulin.

5 The bacterium divides quickly (about once every 15 minutes), producing a population of bacteria, all carrying the insulin gene. The bacteria make insulin. This insulin can be harvested for use by people with diabetes.

INVESTIGATION 2 WRAP-UP

THINK IT WRITE IT

REVIEW

1. Distinguish between a dominant gene and a recessive gene for a trait.

2. Name two important methods that Mendel used in his research.

CRITICAL THINKING

3. Mendel crossed tall plants (TT) with short plants (tt). Use a Punnett square to show the possible gene combinations in the offspring.

4. Explain why two blue-eyed parents can never have brown-eyed offspring.

REFLECT & EVALUATE

Word Power

Write the letter of the term that best completes each sentence. *Not all terms will be used*.

1. Traits passed from parents to offspring are called ___.
2. Chromosomes are made up of message units, or ___.
3. The ability to play the piano is a ___.
4. The trait that is expressed is the ___.
5. The process of altering genes is called ___.
6. Two different dominant genes for a trait will result in ___.

a. dominant trait
b. genes
c. genetic engineering
d. incomplete dominance
e. inherited traits
f. learned trait
g. recessive trait

Check What You Know

Write the word in each pair that correctly completes each sentence.

1. Mendel carried out his experiments to at least the (second, third) generation.
2. Many traits are affected by (genes only, genes and the environment).
3. Two parents with attached ear lobes (can, cannot) have children with unattached ear lobes.

Problem Solving

1. Certain diseases are inherited. One example is sickle-cell anemia, a disorder in which red blood cells cannot carry oxygen. How might gene splicing someday help in treating this disease?

2. If you were a chicken farmer, how might keeping records of egg size and production help you to develop the best egg-laying chickens?

BUILD YOUR PORTFOLIO

The incomplete Punnett square to the right shows a cross between a female guinea pig with black fur and a male guinea pig with white fur. Determine the possible gene pairs and fur colors in the offspring. What percentage of the offspring are likely to have white fur?

	Father	
	b	b
Mother B		
b		

CHAPTER 3

CHANGE THROUGH TIME

Can you imagine a horse that's no bigger than a beagle? That was the size of a horse millions of years ago! Those early horses were the ancestors of the horses we know now. All species are forever changing.

PEOPLE USING SCIENCE

Paleontologist   Did you know that the largest dinosaur found so far is Gigantosaurus? Or that the first forms of life were one-celled organisms? These amazing facts lay hidden in fossils, traces or remains of organisms that lived long ago. Scientists called paleontologists (pā lē ən täl′ə jists) study fossils in order to learn about the history of life on Earth.

Jorge Orlando Calvo is a paleontologist at the Geology and Paleontology Museum in Buenos Aires, Argentina. In 1998, Calvo headed a team of researchers that found fossils of an 85-million-year-old dinosaur of unknown species in Argentina. According to Calvo, "It is spectacular when you walk on the desert and suddenly you find something that could be a dinosaur."

In this chapter you will learn how fossils tell us much about the changes that have helped life continue through the years.

Coming Up

◄ Jorge Orlando Calvo studies an ornithopod dinosaur track.

D49

WHAT DO FOSSILS TELL US ABOUT LIFE— PAST AND PRESENT?

Scientists search for clues about organisms that lived long ago. Such clues may include fossil remains, footprints, and other traces, and, in rare cases, the organism itself! What do these fossils tell us about how life has changed over time?

Activity

Examine a Fossil

Fossils are the remains or traces of organisms that lived long ago. What can a fossil tell you about organisms from the past?

MATERIALS
- 2 fossils
- metric ruler
- hand lens
- *Science Notebook*

Procedure

1. **Examine** one of the fossils. Note its size, shape, structure, and texture. Use a metric ruler to take measurements of the fossil. In your *Science Notebook*, **record** your observations.

 See **SCIENCE** *and* **MATH TOOLBOX** page H6 if you need to review *Using a Tape Measure or Ruler.*

2. Use a hand lens to get a closer look at the fossil. **Record** any details you see that you could not see before.

Step 2

3. **Make a drawing** of the fossil, including all the details you see. **Label** any parts you can identify.

4. **Examine** the second fossil, repeating steps 1 through 3. **Compare** this fossil with the first one you studied.

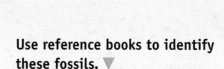

Step 3

Analyze and Conclude

1. **Infer** what the fossils are made of.

2. How are the two fossils similar? How are they different?

3. What organism do you think each fossil is the remains of? Give reasons for your answers.

4. Based on your observations of the fossils, **infer** what you can about the environments in which the organisms lived.

INVESTIGATE FURTHER!

RESEARCH

Use books and other sources to try to identify the fossils in this activity as well as the fossils pictured below. Try to find out when each organism lived, what its diet was, and where it might have lived.

Use reference books to identify these fossils. ▼

Activity

Make a Model Fossil

If you put your hand in wet sand, it will leave an outline of your hand. Some fossils formed in a similar way when they were pressed into layers of sediment, which then hardened into a rock. You can make a model of these types of fossils to see how they formed.

Procedure

1. Press modeling clay into the bottom of a paper cup. Use scissors to cut off the top of the cup about 5 cm above the level of the clay.

2. Coat the outside of a shell with a thin layer of vegetable oil and press that side of the shell into the clay. **Predict** what the clay will look like after you remove the shell.

3. Remove the shell and look at the surface of the clay. You have **made a model** of a **mold fossil**. In your *Science Notebook*, **record** your observations.

4. Use a spoon to mix water and plaster of Paris in a jar. Follow the directions on the package.

 See **SCIENCE** *and* **MATH TOOLBOX** page H7 if you need to review **Measuring Volume.**

5. Use the spoon to cover the clay with the plaster until the cup is almost full.

6. Let the plaster of Paris harden overnight. Peel away the paper cup. Gently separate the layer of clay from the layer of plaster. You have **made a model** of a **cast fossil**. **Record** your observations.

Step 2

Analyze and Conclude

1. How does a mold fossil differ from a cast fossil?

2. How is your mold fossil like the shell? What can you learn about an organism from a mold fossil of it?

3. How is your cast fossil like the shell? What can you learn about an organism from a cast fossil of it?

4. How is your cast fossil different from the original object? What kind of information about an organism can you *not* learn from its cast fossil?

5. **Infer** why a cast fossil might form in one instance and a mold fossil in another.

UNIT PROJECT LINK

As part of your project, make a cast or mold "fossil" of a footprint from an endangered animal you've learned about. Get a field guide to animal tracks from your teacher or librarian. Then find an illustration and a description of the animal's footprint. Assemble all the materials you will need, such as clay and modeling tools. Now use these materials and the illustration of the animal's footprint to create your own "fossil."

TechnologyLink

For more help with your Unit Project, go to **www.eduplace.com**.

How Fossils Form

Reading Focus What are fossils, and how do they form?

Have fossils ever been discovered in your area? **Fossils** are the remains or traces of organisms that lived long ago. Most fossils are found in sedimentary rock, such as sandstone or limestone. This kind of rock formed when sediment—bits of rock and minerals—built up in layers. The tiny particles of sediment on the bottom were squeezed together as layers of sediment formed above. Over millions of years, the particles slowly hardened into rock layers. The fossils that are examined in the activity on pages D50 and D51 may have been discovered in sedimentary rock.

Molds and Casts

The remains of animals and plants that have died can become preserved as fossils in sedimentary rock in several ways. Sometimes after an organism dies, sediments collect and harden into rock around its body. As the organism decays or dissolves, an open space that has the shape of the organism remains in the sedimentary rock. A hollowed space in the shape of a once-living organism or one of its parts is called a **mold fossil**.

Minerals dissolved from the rock surrounding a mold fossil may slowly move into the space left as the organism

This dinosaur's remains began as bones in sediment. Over millions of years the bones became petrified. ▼

decayed. These minerals harden into the shape of the original organism, forming a **cast fossil**. In the activity on pages D52 and D53, plaster of Paris is used to show how a cast fossil is formed.

Sometimes, living things leave behind traces of their activities instead of fossils of their bodies. Some animals, including dinosaurs, walked through soft mud that dried in the sun before the footprints were buried by sediment. These fossilized imprints are a type of mold fossil, and the prints tell us much about the animals and their lives. For example, the size and shape of a dinosaur footprint might give a scientist clues about how tall the dinosaur was, how much it weighed, how it moved, and even what kinds of foods it ate.

Cast in Stone

Another kind of fossil can form from the hard parts of organisms, parts such as bones and wood. For example, a tree may fall into water and be quickly buried in the mud at the bottom. Water and minerals seep into the wood. As the wood decays, the minerals replace the wood, taking the shape of the wood and hardening into stone. The changing of the hard parts of a dead organism to stone is called **petrification**. You may have seen petrified wood that is hard as a rock but still shows the rings of the original tree. The fossilized skeletons of dinosaurs and other animals are often petrified remains. Such remains preserve fine details of these organisms.

Entombed Fossils

Do you think you'd like to wear a fossil as jewelry? Many people do. Amber is fossilized tree resin. Resin is a sticky kind of tree sap. If you've handled pine cones or pine branches, you know how sticky

Petrified Forest National Park, in Arizona, is known for its vast number of trees turned to stone. ▼

A cast fossil of a trilobite, an ancient organism that no longer exists. ▼

PALEOZOIC ERA

600 million to 230 million years ago (mya)

Cambrian Period
(600 mya)

Life exploded into great varieties of forms in Earth's oceans. Many creatures with hard shells are preserved as fossils. There were many life forms, and most of them have no counterparts today. They simply died out.

Silurian Period
(435 mya)

Land plants and such animals as scorpions appeared. The first fish with jaws evolved during this period.

Carboniferous Period
(360 mya)

Tropical climates resulted in swamps that would become coal beds millions of years later. The earliest insects and reptiles appeared. Amphibians thrived.

Ordovician Period
(500 mya)

Fish, the first vertebrates, or animals with backbones, appeared. An ice age occurred, causing the extinction of much ocean life during this period.

Devonian Period
(410 mya)

As Earth's land-masses drifted and ocean conditions changed, many kinds of ocean life became extinct. Many new fish and the first sharks roamed the seas. Amphibians and ferns populated the land.

Permian Period
(290 mya)

Earth's climate became drier, and more and more species lived on land. Reptiles thrived. Toward the end of the Permian Period, many species, particularly in the sea, became extinct, perhaps due to environmental changes.

GEOLOGIC TIME SCALE

Precambrian

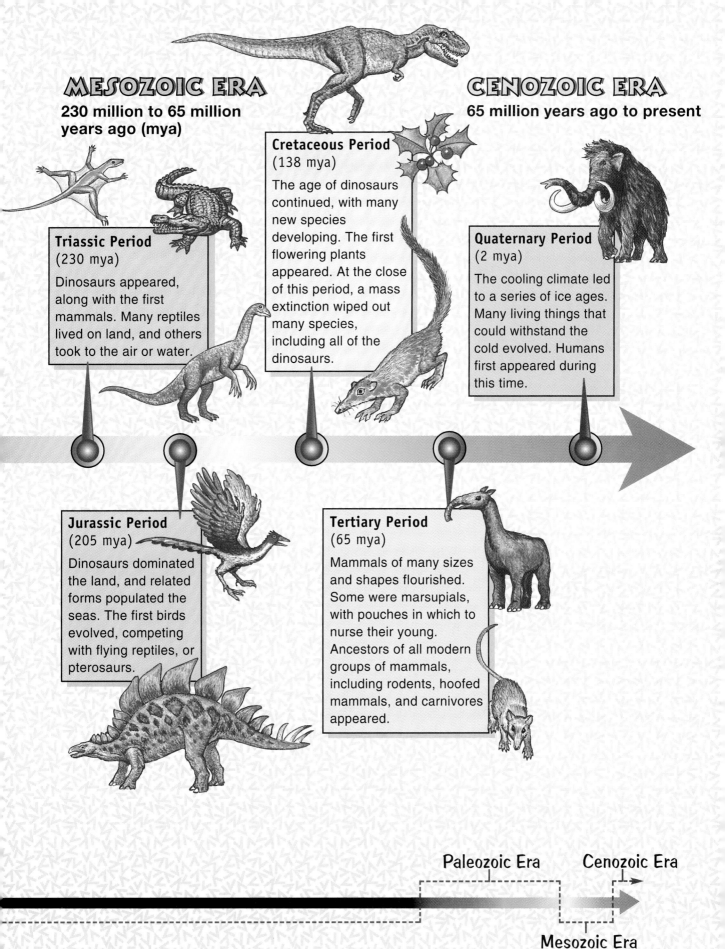

MESOZOIC ERA

230 million to 65 million years ago (mya)

CENOZOIC ERA

65 million years ago to present

Cretaceous Period (138 mya)

The age of dinosaurs continued, with many new species developing. The first flowering plants appeared. At the close of this period, a mass extinction wiped out many species, including all of the dinosaurs.

Triassic Period (230 mya)

Dinosaurs appeared, along with the first mammals. Many reptiles lived on land, and others took to the air or water.

Quaternary Period (2 mya)

The cooling climate led to a series of ice ages. Many living things that could withstand the cold evolved. Humans first appeared during this time.

Jurassic Period (205 mya)

Dinosaurs dominated the land, and related forms populated the seas. The first birds evolved, competing with flying reptiles, or pterosaurs.

Tertiary Period (65 mya)

Mammals of many sizes and shapes flourished. Some were marsupials, with pouches in which to nurse their young. Ancestors of all modern groups of mammals, including rodents, hoofed mammals, and carnivores appeared.

Paleozoic Era

Cenozoic Era

Mesozoic Era

What Happened to the Dinosaurs?

Reading Focus What are some hypotheses that try to explain why dinosaurs became extinct?

Scientists have learned much about dinosaurs, but they still don't know why dinosaurs became extinct. **Extinction** means that a species no longer exists. Scientists do know that the dinosaurs died out at the end of the Mesozoic Era, about 65 million years ago.

Many hypotheses have been suggested to explain the extinction of the dinosaurs. Some scientists proposed that small mammals also living during the Mesozoic Era ate so many dinosaur eggs that the huge creatures became extinct. Others hypothesized that the dinosaurs were poisoned by eating the flowering plants that had evolved near the end of the Mesozoic Era.

Some evidence indicates that at the end of the Mesozoic Era, Earth's climate began to cool down. Did this change in climate kill the dinosaurs? Possibly, but there is also evidence that some dinosaurs were well-adapted to cool climates and thus could have survived.

Today, many scientists think that dinosaurs were wiped out when a large asteroid collided with Earth. An asteroid is a chunk of rock that orbits the Sun. An asteroid that struck Earth would have exploded, sending millions of tons of dust into the atmosphere.

Such a collision could have greatly disturbed the climate. Thick clouds of black smoke and dust in the atmosphere could have blocked sunlight for months or even years. Without sunlight, plants would have died and temperatures would have plunged. The loss of plants would have caused many food webs to collapse.

▲ Artists have imagined what an asteroid's impact on Earth might have looked like.

▲ Iridium: Is it the clue to what happened to the dinosaurs?

Eventually, the plant eaters and the meat eaters would have starved to death.

The asteroid hypothesis is supported by the discovery of the metal iridium (ī rid′ē əm) in the rock layers that formed about 65 million years ago, at the end of the Mesozoic Era. Iridium is very rare on Earth, but it is common in asteroids. If an asteroid collided with Earth 65 million years ago, it could have showered the land with iridium. Evidence for this hypothesis has been found in the rock layer formed at the close of the Mesozoic Era. This layer has 30 times more iridium than is found in other layers.

Some scientists think they have located where such an asteroid may have struck. In Mexico's Yucatán Peninsula, on land bordering the Caribbean Sea, there is a layer of boulders that are different from the rocks above and below them. This type of boulder is common on the *bottom* of the Caribbean Sea. Could the force of the falling asteroid have tossed boulders out of the water and onto the shore?

Although many scientists support the asteroid hypothesis, others say the evidence is not strong enough. Perhaps some day you will help determine what really happened to the dinosaurs. ∎

INVESTIGATION 1 WRAP-UP

REVIEW

1. Describe three ways that fossils can be formed.

2. What can we learn by looking at the fossils of different species?

CRITICAL THINKING

3. Why do you think the petrified remains of complete skeletons of animals are rare?

4. Do you agree with the asteroid hypothesis about dinosaurs becoming extinct? Explain your reasoning.

WHAT EVIDENCE DO SCIENTISTS HAVE THAT SPECIES CHANGE OVER TIME?

The shape and structure of each living thing give scientists clues as to how organisms are related. What other clues to evolution do scientists have?

Activity

Out on a Limb

Your arm bones and leg bones are similar to those of your classmates. Do other animals have bone structures similar to those in humans? Find out!

Procedure

1. Study and **compare** the drawings of the front limbs of four animals—a lizard, a bird, a cat, and a chimpanzee. Look for differences and similarities. **Record** your observations in your *Science Notebook*.

Math Hint
Whenever possible, include measurable characteristics in your observations.

Step 1

D62

2. Working on newspaper, use clay to **make models** of the bones of the lizard's front limb. Use one color for the upper limb, a second color for the lower limb, a third color for the small wrist bones, and a fourth color for the hand and fingers. Arrange the bones on a piece of paper.

3. Using the colors in the same way, **make models** of the bones of the bird's wing. Also **make models** of the bones of the cat's front limb and the chimpanzee's front limb.

4. **Compare** and **contrast** the models of the limb-bone structures of these animals. **Record** your observations.

Analyze and Conclude

1. How did the structures of the limbs compare?

2. Did the same bones occur in more than one of the models? Which bones were they?

3. Which bones were not found in all four models?

4. What do you think the similarities among the models mean in terms of evolution?

5. **Infer** how the differences in your models show that evolution has taken place.

Technology Link CD-ROM

INVESTIGATE FURTHER!

Use the **Science Processor CD-ROM**, *Continuity of Life* (Unit Opening Investigation, Can You Relate?) to group organisms with common characteristics. Then explain why you think the organisms are related.

Comparing Limbs

Reading Focus What do similarities in the limbs of different species tell us about their ancestry?

In 1836 an American naturalist named Constantine Samuel Rafinesque hypothesized that all living things began as varieties of the same species. Through his extensive study of living things, Rafinesque came to believe that gradually, over time, living things evolved into separate species.

The activity on pages D62 and D63 illustrates similarities among the front limbs of four animals. If you were to compare these limbs with the bones in a human's arm, you would see more similarities. In fact, all vertebrates (vur'tə brits), or animals with backbones, have the same basic bones in their front limbs. The term *vertebrate* includes mammals as well as dinosaurs, birds, reptiles, amphibians, and fish.

Differences in the sizes and shapes of bones in the front limbs enable different vertebrates to fly, swim, dig, hang from a tree branch, and applaud their favorite sports heroes.

The similarities in the limb-bone structures of different kinds of vertebrates are evidence that these species are related. At some time in the past, these species had a common ancestor. The more alike the structures, the closer the species are thought to be related. So the study of bone structures not only provides evidence that Rafinesque was correct in his belief that living things evolve into separate species, but it also helps establish relationships among living things.

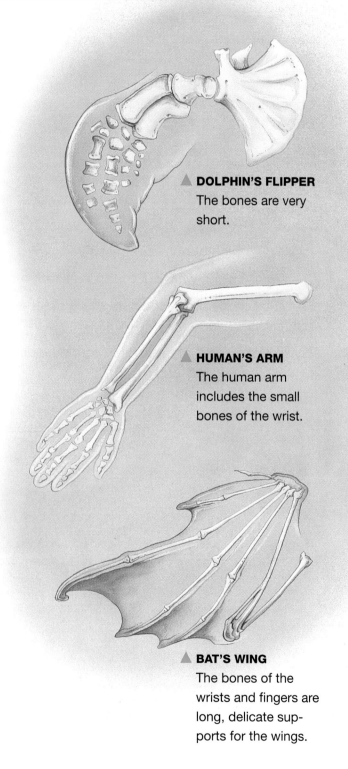

▲ **DOLPHIN'S FLIPPER**
The bones are very short.

▲ **HUMAN'S ARM**
The human arm includes the small bones of the wrist.

▲ **BAT'S WING**
The bones of the wrists and fingers are long, delicate supports for the wings.

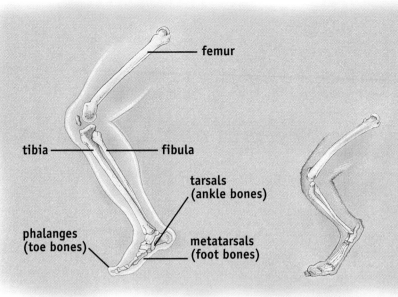

femur

tibia — fibula

tarsals
(ankle bones)

phalanges
(toe bones)

metatarsals
(foot bones)

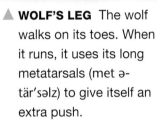

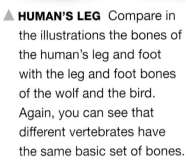

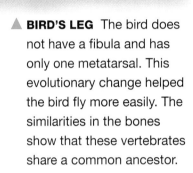

▲ **HUMAN'S LEG** Compare in the illustrations the bones of the human's leg and foot with the leg and foot bones of the wolf and the bird. Again, you can see that different vertebrates have the same basic set of bones.

▲ **WOLF'S LEG** The wolf walks on its toes. When it runs, it uses its long metatarsals (met ə-tär′səlz) to give itself an extra push.

▲ **BIRD'S LEG** The bird does not have a fibula and has only one metatarsal. This evolutionary change helped the bird fly more easily. The similarities in the bones show that these vertebrates share a common ancestor.

Science in Literature

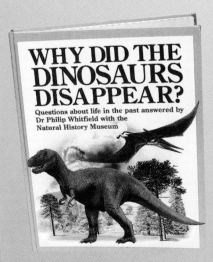

Why Did the Dinosaurs Disappear?
by Dr. Philip Whitfield
Viking, 1991

TRAPPED IN RESIN!

"Some special sorts of fossils give an even more detailed idea of what prehistoric animals looked like. Certain ancient conifers (relations of today's pines and spruces) made a sticky, clear resin when they were cut or damaged. Insects, spiders, and even tree frogs living perhaps 100 million years ago became stuck in this resin, died, and then sank inside."

Read *Why Did the Dinosaurs Disappear?* by Dr. Philip Whitfield and discover more about how scientists learn about prehistoric life forms.

Darwin's Voyage

Reading Focus What observations did Charles Darwin make on the Galápagos Islands?

Charles Darwin's nose almost cost him the most important job of his life. The captain of the ship that Darwin wanted to work on believed he could read a person's character in the shape of his or her head. To him, Darwin's nose showed that he lacked energy and determination.

▲ **Charles Darwin**

The year was 1831, the ship was a British sailing vessel called HMS *Beagle*, and the captain turned out to be quite wrong. Darwin had applied for a full-time job as a seagoing naturalist, to study nature and gather samples of organisms on a voyage around the world. None of this work was easy, but the 22-year-old Darwin got the job and did it well.

Before the *Beagle* sailed from London, Darwin had studied for the ministry. But his real love was nature—especially beetles! His enthusiasm for collecting beetles was so strong that he once stuck one in his mouth to hold it while he caught two more. By squirting a bitter liquid on Darwin's tongue, the captive beetle got itself spit out—and got away!

What Did Darwin Find?

HMS *Beagle* sailed west from England, down the east coast of South America, up the west coast, then west again until it had gone all the way around the globe. During the entire journey, the

HMS *Beagle*'s path through the Galápagos Islands ▼

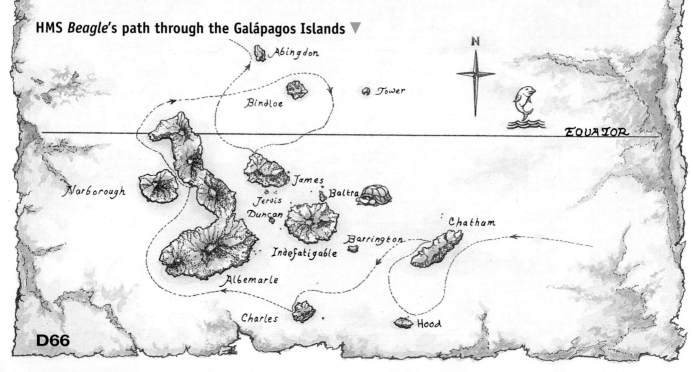

Abingdon
Tower
Bindloe
N
EQUATOR
Narborough
James
Jervis
Duncan
Baltra
Chatham
Barrington
Indefatigable
Albemarle
Charles
Hood

▲ **A variety of finches that Darwin observed on the Galápagos Islands**

Large Insectivorous Tree Finch

Medium Insectivorous Tree Finch

Small Insectivorous Tree Finch

Warbler Finch

Mangrove Finch

Tool Using Finch

Large Ground Finch

Sharp Beaked Ground Finch

Large Cactus Ground Finch

Medium Ground Finch

Small Ground Finch

Vegetarian Tree Finch

Cactus Ground Finch

crew mapped the lands the ship visited. Off the coast of Ecuador, at a group of islands in the Pacific Ocean called the Galápagos (gə lä′pə gōs) Islands, Darwin discovered an incredible treasure-trove of plants, fossils, and living animals.

There, Darwin found the world's only sea-dwelling lizards. These sea iguanas looked like tiny dinosaurs and fed on seaweed growing on underwater rocks. They had blunt snouts, and their strong claws helped them cling to the rocks.

A short distance inland, Darwin also found land-dwelling lizards. They were iguanas, too, but they never mated with the sea iguanas. These iguanas lived in trees and ate cactus plants. The sea iguanas had partially webbed toes and rather flat tails; the land dwellers had normal toes and round tails. Darwin noted, however, that the two species were alike in many ways, as well.

Darwin's most famous discovery was what he called "a most singular group of finches." These birds are found throughout the world. Darwin noted 13 varieties of finches on the Galápagos, and each

variety was adapted to a different way of life. Some finches ate insects, and some ate plants. The tool-using finch even hunted food by holding a cactus spine in its beak and chipping holes in bark. The finches in each group had their own characteristics that were well-suited to the ways they lived. For example, the beaks of plant eaters were different from the beaks of insect eaters.

Charles Darwin certainly found his share of adventure aboard the *Beagle*, yet he found something that to him was a lot more important. He found thousands of unique plants and animals—more than most people of his day and age knew anything about. As he studied his notes and samples, Darwin realized that many of the species he had found and studied seemed to be related to other species. Different species seemed to have evolved from a common ancestor. But how?

From his observations and studies, Darwin proposed a theory to answer this question. You will learn more about Darwin's theory of evolution by natural selection in the next investigation. ■

Selective Breeding

Reading Focus How does selective breeding produce desirable traits?

Long before Charles Darwin sailed around the world, people had discovered that they could tame some wild animals if they caught the animals when they were very young. By breeding such animals, people produced new generations of **domesticated**, or tamed, animals that could be controlled and used by humans. Horses, for example, were tamed and used as pack animals and for transportation.

Other animals were also domesticated, such as the elephant and the water buffalo in India, the camel in Somalia, and the reindeer in Lapland. The musk ox, which is actually a member of the sheep-goat family, was domesticated as recently as the 1950s. It is now raised by native Alaskans for its fine cashmerelike wool.

Along Comes Selective Breeding

People did not stop at domestication. They realized that they could actually direct the development of certain characteristics in plants and animals by breeding individuals that had those characteristics. This is the way certain animals came to be raised on farms. Domestic sheep were developed around 7,000 years ago from a long-horned, hairy beast called the Asiatic mouflon (mo͞of'län). The modern pig was bred from the wild boar. Such breeding of living things to produce offspring with desirable characteristics is called **selective breeding**.

Through the generations, people developed gentler elephants, hardier camels, and faster horses. As many as 20,000 years ago, people domesticated the dog to help with hunting. Since then, more selective breeding has produced hundreds of different kinds of dogs.

People practiced selective breeding of plants, too. By 3600 B.C., some native tribes of North America had developed plants that yielded small ears of corn, most likely from a grasslike plant. Other native tribes in North and South America developed tomatoes, potatoes, and tobacco.

◀ **A sheep (*right*) and its ancestor, an Asiatic mouflon (*left*).**

▲ Corn is an example of a product that has been selectively bred and grown in the Americas for centuries.

Back to the Wild Again!

Charles Darwin knew that humans could cause changes in plants and animals through selective breeding. But as he began working with his notes and samples, he realized that the plants and animals he'd seen had evolved on their own.

He then decided to find out how living things in the wild evolved. In order to do this he learned all he could about selective breeding. He wanted to compare what had been discovered by others with the new things he'd learned. Immediately, he began tracing the wild origins of a number of domesticated plants and animals. These included sheep, cattle, pigs, rabbits, pigeons, goldfish, bees, and silk moths. He also studied cabbages, peas, potatoes, fruit trees, beans, roses, pansies, and dahlias.

After 20 years Charles Darwin understood how the plants and animals in the wild had changed through a natural form of selective breeding. ■

INVESTIGATION 2 WRAP-UP

REVIEW

1. How do structural similarities among organisms support the idea that living things are related?

2. What important discoveries did Charles Darwin make on the Galápagos Islands?

CRITICAL THINKING

3. What characteristics do you think were bred from the wolf into the domestic dog?

4. Write a proposal to selectively breed a new organism from two existing plants or animals. Describe the desirable traits it will get from the original organisms.

HOW DO CHANGES IN SPECIES OCCUR?

You saw in Investigation 2 that there is evidence that changes occur in organisms over time. But how do these changes occur? In this investigation you'll find out some of the answers scientists have for this question.

Activity

A Variety of Peanuts

Differences among organisms of a single species are important in helping them survive in a variety of environments. Sometimes these variations are easy to see. You can study variations in peanuts and draw some conclusions about how those variations are helpful to the plant.

Procedure

1. Peanuts grow to different lengths. Design a method to divide your peanuts into ten groups so that each group of peanuts is a little longer than the previous group. Predict the number of peanuts you will have in each group. Record your sorting method and predictions in your *Science Notebook*.

Step 2

2. **Measure** the length of the peanuts and **sort** them using your procedure. Record the number of peanuts in each group in a data table.

3. **Make a bar graph.** Show the ten groups along the x-axis. Show the number of peanuts in each group along the y-axis.

4. **Make a circle graph.** Each group should make up one section on the graph. Which group has the most peanuts? Which group has the fewest peanuts? Does your circle graph show this?

 See **SCIENCE** *and* **MATH TOOLBOX** *page H12 if you need to review* **Making a Circle Graph.**

Analyze and Conclude

1. What length did you predict would be found most often? Why did you choose this length?

2. Were the lengths of the peanuts evenly distributed, or was there some other pattern to the lengths?

3. Each peanut is a seed that can develop into a new peanut plant. Most of the peanut is stored food for the baby plant. Why might forming large peanuts be helpful?

4. Explain why forming large peanuts might be harmful to the plant.

INVESTIGATE FURTHER!

EXPERIMENT

If your class has a balance that can measure the mass of an object as light as a peanut, find the mass of each of the peanuts. Make a graph, as you did in the activity, to record the masses. Before you begin, hypothesize whether you will find any correlation between peanut length and peanut mass. Did your hypothesis match your results?

This is something like figuring out how to build an automobile before learning how to make an engine work!

As you have learned, living things produce egg cells and sperm cells through the process of meiosis. After fertilization, the new cell has the normal number of chromosomes. And because half of the chromosomes come from each parent, the new organism has a brand-new combination of genes. You learned in Chapter 2 that genes are made of DNA and are passed from parents to offspring.

Changes in DNA

Although sexual reproduction produces a new combination of genes with each new individual, it doesn't change the DNA in the genes. But sometimes genes do change. A change in the gene's DNA is called a **mutation** (myoo ta'-shən). Mutations may be caused by chemicals or radiation in the environment. Some mutations happen for reasons scientists haven't identified. Many are harmful and may make the individual less likely to survive. Some mutations are so severe that the individual quickly dies.

Sometimes, however, a mutation is beneficial. It helps the individual to survive better. Think back to the horse galloping away from its enemies. Fossil evidence suggests that the earliest horses were small forest-dwelling creatures. At some point, perhaps, the forest shrank and grasslands spread. Speed is important on grasslands, since hiding places are scarce. Mutations that favor survival on grasslands—longer legs and faster speed—were beneficial. Over many generations, larger, swifter horses developed. Those horses were favored as the environment changed from a forested area to a grassland full of predators that attacked weaker, slower animals. ■

Technology Link CD-ROM

INVESTIGATE FURTHER!

Use the **Science Processor CD-ROM**, *Continuity of Life* (Investigation 3, Camouflage!) to see the process of natural selection with moths. Play a game with your partner to find out which moths survive better in different environments.

The ancestor of today's horse (*right*) was *Hyracotherium* (*left*), which was the size of a small dog!

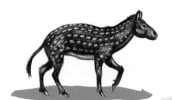

Competition and Isolation

Reading Focus How do competition and isolation affect the way a species evolves?

After his voyage on HMS *Beagle*, Charles Darwin worked for 20 years to be absolutely sure of his two most important conclusions. First, a struggle for existence goes on all the time in nature—day by day, year by year, century by century. Second, in that struggle the most fit are likely to survive and reproduce.

You have already seen how the most fit are defined by natural selection. But **competition**—or lack of competition because of isolation—also plays a big role. On the surface, competition in nature may even resemble the rivalry between tennis players or baseball teams. But competition in nature is not friendly, and often it is a matter of life or death.

Competition in Nature

You see competition at work in nature every time you go outside. The branches of trees spread wide, allowing as many leaves as possible to be in the sunlight. Small bushes below reach out to whatever sunlight passes through the trees. Nearby, grass blades are turned sideways, also to catch sunlight.

But what you see in an ordinary yard is just the beginning. Plants and animals have thousands and thousands of variations on basic ways of competing with one another for sunlight, food, water, and everything else needed for survival.

Throughout the entire world, different plants and animals grow in every possible place—from dark forests to cold ocean floors; from mountaintops to deep valleys; from dry deserts to soggy swamps; from desert sands to frozen tundra. In all these places, different species live in slightly different environments. Each species seems to have the best characteristics to survive in its environment. Thus trees grow tall, and ferns are adapted to a shady environment around the bases of trees.

But individuals within a species compete with their own kind, perhaps by growing bigger and stronger as fast as

▲ **Competition for scarce resources favors the most fit organisms.**

they can. You may not see it happening, but as plants grow, they block each other and send out huge root systems. These are adaptations to obtain as much light and water as possible. When you pull weeds and find the roots of plants all tangled together, you know they were fighting for the same minerals in the soil!

Where Does Isolation Fit In?

Each island of the Galápagos visited by Darwin is isolated from the others by strong winds and rough waters. When he arrived, Darwin found that this isolation had produced an unusual cast of characters. Huge 227-kg (500-lb) tortoises, with shells like upturned bathtubs, grazed like cattle in the fields and lived about 100 years. Many of the islands had populations of these huge tortoises. On each island, however, the population differed from those on the other islands. In fact, each island had a different species of tortoise—all closely related.

The finches on the different islands and in the different environments taught Darwin the most. Though they had the same ancestor, isolation on the different islands prevented them from breeding with each other. Also, because there were different sources of food on each island, mutations allowed the finches to develop different kinds of beaks. There were small, medium, and large versions of each kind of beak. From Darwin's studies and similar studies, scientists have concluded that when populations of the same species are isolated, or separated, over a long period of time, they tend to become separate species. ■

Isolation in nature favors the evolution of new species, such as the giant tortoise. ▼

INVESTIGATION 3 WRAP-UP

REVIEW

1. How did Darwin's theory of natural selection explain how varieties of species evolved?

2. How did isolation affect the finches on the Galápagos Islands?

CRITICAL THINKING

3. How does the work of Mendel help explain Darwin's theory?

4. Give examples of competition in a forest. Explain how different organisms respond to the competition.

REFLECT & EVALUATE

Word Power

Write the letter of the term that best matches the definition. *Not all terms will be used.*

1. Remains or traces of organisms that lived long ago
2. Changing of the hard parts of a dead organism into stone
3. Time spans that geologic eras are divided into
4. Scientist who studies fossils of ancient life
5. Process of taming animals
6. Breeding living things to produce offspring with desired traits
7. Change in a gene's DNA

a. domestication
b. fossils
c. mold fossil
d. mutation
e. natural selection
f. paleontologist
g. periods
h. petrification
i. selective breeding

Check What You Know

Write the word in each pair that correctly completes each sentence.

1. A hollowed space in the shape of an organism or one of its parts is called a (mold, cast) fossil.
2. Animals (with, without) backbones are called vertebrates.
3. Earth's first (4 billion, 600 million) years are referred to as the Precambrian time.

Problem Solving

1. Explain the differences in the way each of these fossils form: dinosaur skeleton; insect encased in amber; shell preserved in rock.

2. Some scientists predict that in the year 3000, Earth will have a hot, dry, and barren environment. How might a present-day organism have to evolve in order to survive?

Study the diagram. Identify the group that each animal belongs to. In what sequence did these groups of animals evolve?

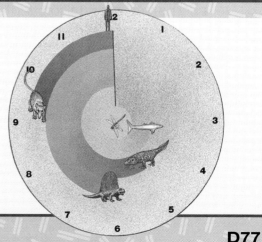

Cause and Effect

When you read, it is important to figure out what happens and why it happens. What happens is called the *effect*. Why it happens is called the *cause*.

Read the paragraphs below. Then complete the exercises that follow.

> Use these hints to determine cause and effect.
>
> • Look for signal words: *because, and so, as a result*
>
> • As you read, ask yourself why something is happening.

Saving Species

An **endangered species** is a species whose population has become so low that it is in danger of extinction. Species become endangered for many reasons, but in modern times, human destruction of natural habitats is a common cause. The peregrine falcon became endangered because its eggs were harmed by pesticides made by humans.

Sometimes scientists try to save a species by capturing some or all of the remaining animals of that species. These animals are cared for in zoos or wildlife centers.

Write the letter of each sentence that states a cause-and-effect relationship. For each sentence you identify, state both the cause and the effect.

   a. An endangered species is a species whose population is in danger of extinction.

   b. One reason why species become endangered is human destruction of natural habitats.

   c. The peregrine falcon became endangered because its eggs were harmed by pesticides made by humans.

   d. Scientists try to save a species by capturing some or all of the remaining animals of that species.

Analyze Data

The table shows the numbers of species of swallowtail butterflies found at various latitudes on Earth.

Swallowtail Butterfly Species	
Number of Species	Latitude Found
131	20°–30° N
167	10°–20° N
240	0°–10° N
261	0°–10° S
161	10°–20° S
92	20°–30° S

Use the data in the table to complete these exercises.

1. What is the range for the number of species?

2. Find the mean number of species. Round your answer to the nearest whole number.

3. What is the median for the number of species? At which latitudes is the number of species greater than the median?

4. Which measure—mean or range—best describes this set of data? Explain.

5. In the Northern Hemisphere, what happens to the number of species as latitude decreases?

6. In the Southern Hemisphere, what happens to the number of species as latitude increases?

7. Based on the data, what would you conclude about the relationship between climate and the number of species of swallowtail butterfly?

UNIT D

WRAP-UP!

On your own, use scientific methods to investigate a question about the continuity of life.

THINK LIKE A SCIENTIST

Ask a Question

Pose a question about inherited traits that you would like to investigate. For example, ask, "What role does the acidity of soil play in the expression of inherited traits in a plant that grows in that soil?"

Make a Hypothesis

Suggest a hypothesis that is a possible answer to the question. One hypothesis is that the acidity of soil will alter the expression of one or more inherited traits in plants that grow in that soil.

Plan and Do a Test

Plan a controlled experiment to test for the role that soil acidity plays in the expression of inherited traits in a plant. You could start with sprouted "eyes" from a single potato, several containers, soil samples of varying acidity, and water. Develop a procedure that uses these materials to test the hypothesis. With permission, carry out your experiment. Follow the safety guidelines on pages S14–S15.

Record and Analyze

Observe carefully and record your data accurately. Make repeated observations.

Draw Conclusions

Look for evidence to support the hypothesis or to show that it is false. Draw conclusions about the hypothesis. Repeat the experiment to verify the results.

WRITING IN SCIENCE
Interview

To learn more about inherited traits of animals, interview a professional animal breeder, such as a dog breeder or a horse breeder. Write up your interview as an entry in your *Science Notebook*. Follow these guidelines.

- Prepare questions before the interview.
- Take notes and, with permission, record the interview.
- Use a question-and-answer format in writing up the main points.

Oceanography

Theme: Systems

THINK LIKE A SCIENTIST

SEA OF SERENITY

The conditions where this underwater photograph was taken are perfect to support a variety of life forms. These life forms range from coral-producing organisms to colorful fish. The conditions include clear, shallow water that allows sunlight to reach the sea floor and warm the water above it. But oceans and seas cover about two thirds of Earth's surface. Places where the conditions are like those shown here make up only a very small part of that area. Exploring the part of Earth's surface that is covered by deep ocean water can be as fascinating and mysterious as walking on the surface of our Moon!

THINK LIKE A SCIENTIST

Questioning In this unit you'll learn about ocean water—what it's made up of, how it moves, the things that live in it, and the resources that come from it—and you'll find out about the features of the ocean floor. You'll investigate questions such as these.

- How Do Scientists Study the Ocean Floor?
- What Resources Can the Oceans Provide?

Observing, Testing, Hypothesizing In the Activity "Lighting the Water," you'll observe how the amount of available light in water changes with depth.

Researching In the Resource "Energy and the Sea," you'll learn about the development and continued improvement of technology to harness the energy of moving ocean water.

Drawing Conclusions After you've completed your investigations, you'll draw conclusions about what you've learned—and get new ideas.

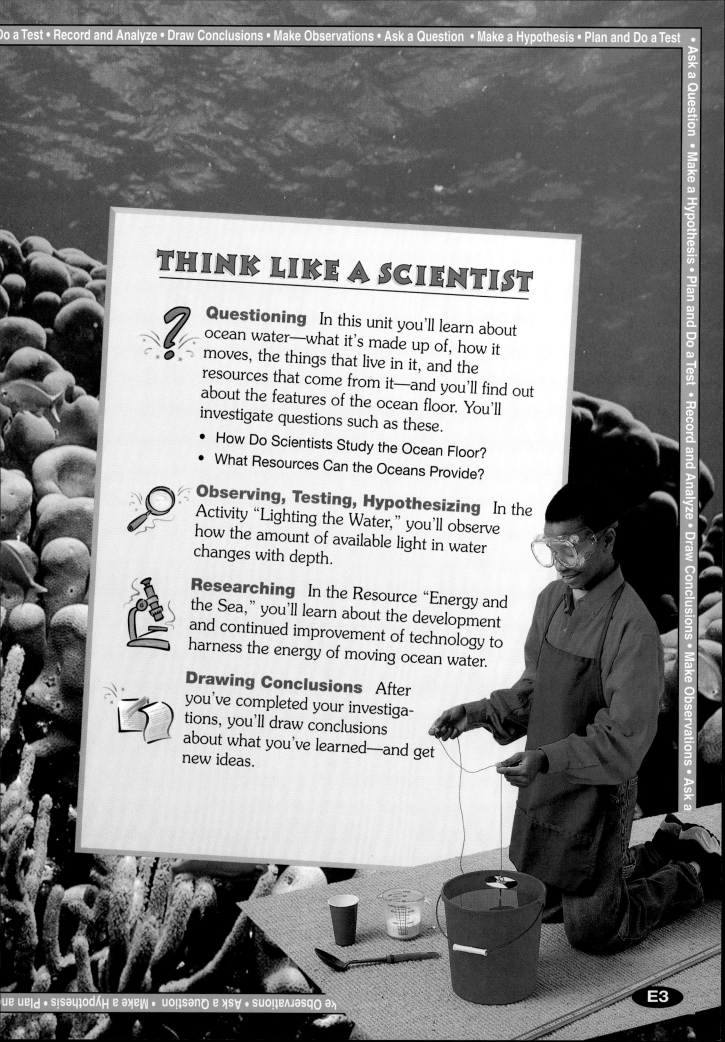

CHAPTER 1

OCEAN WATER

The waters of the oceans are a vast resource with a rich abundance of life. Yet, the exploration of the oceans has really just begun. What would you like to find out about the ocean waters?

PEOPLE USING SCIENCE

Marine Biologist Rose Petrecca says she has wanted to learn more about the ocean ever since she watched the television program *Sea Hunt* as a young girl. Now she is a marine biologist and the lead scientist on LEO-15—the Long-Term Ecosystem Observatory. LEO-15 is one of the world's few underwater laboratories. It is being built off the New Jersey coast in 15 m (49.5 ft) of water.

Petrecca and other oceanographers will use the permanent lab to study ocean conditions over a long period of time. Using video cameras and vehicles operated by remote control, the scientists will observe daily life in the ocean. They will check on how pollution is affecting the sea robins, black sea bass, starfish, and surf clams in the water around LEO-15. What questions would you ask Rose Petrecca about her work?

Coming Up

◀ Rose Petrecca works on LEO-15.

E5

INVESTIGATION 1

WHAT MAKES UP OCEAN WATER?

You probably know that ocean water is not the same as the water that comes from a faucet in your home. What makes ocean water different from the water you drink each day?

Activity

A Closer Look at Ocean Water

How can you use observations to help you infer what's in ocean water?

- -

Procedure

1. Your teacher will give you a sample of ocean water in a clear container. Examine the sample and test for any odor. **Record** your observations in your *Science Notebook*.

2. Use a dropper to place a drop of ocean water on a slide. Place a cover slip over the drop and examine the slide through a microscope. **Record** your observations.

See **SCIENCE** and **MATH TOOLBOX** page H2 if you need to review **Using a Microscope**.

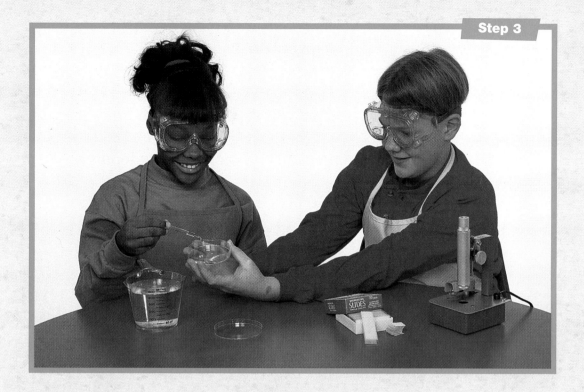

3. Use the dropper to stir the ocean water sample. Then place several dropperfuls of the sample in an empty clear container. Place the container in sunlight and allow the water to evaporate. **Predict** what you will see as the water evaporates. **Record** your prediction. Then **observe** the container periodically as the water evaporates. **Record** your observations.

4. When evaporation is complete, use the hand lens to **observe** any material left behind in the container. **Record** your observations.

5. Add tap water to the container and **observe** what happens. **Record** your observations.

Analyze and Conclude

1. Compare your observation of the drop of ocean water on the slide with what was left behind when the water evaporated.

2. Infer from your observations what was left behind when the water evaporated. **Explain** your inference.

3. What can you **conclude** about ocean water?

4. Why was evaporation important to the results of this activity?

INVESTIGATE FURTHER!

EXPERIMENT

Predict how your observations would differ if you were using fresh water instead of ocean water. Obtain a sample of fresh water and repeat the activity to check your predictions. Record your data.

What's in the Water?

Reading Focus What chemical and biological materials are found in ocean water?

▲ **Water covers two thirds of Earth's surface—from the vast oceans to small mountain streams.**

Someday you may have the chance to peer from the window of a spacecraft and see Earth floating in space. You'll see a brilliant sphere shining blue, green, brown, and white. But mostly you'll see blue—the blue of Earth's oceans covering two thirds of its surface.

A Salty Story

Even people who have never been to the ocean know that ocean water is salty. In the activity on pages E6 and E7, salts dissolved in ocean water are left behind when the water evaporates. It might surprise you to learn that when the oceans formed billions of years ago, they weren't salty. Where did the salt in the present-day oceans come from?

Ocean water is a mixture of the compound water (H_2O) and several salts. The most common salt found in ocean water consists of two elements—sodium and chlorine. These elements are combined in the compound sodium chloride, which you use as table salt.

In nature, sodium chloride, potassium chloride, and magnesium chloride are salts that are present in rocks and soils. When rainwater flows over the land, it dissolves and carries away traces of the salts as well as other elements and compounds. The rainwater drains into rivers and streams, which discharge into the oceans. Each year about 364 billion kilograms (400 million tons) of dissolved salts and other substances are washed into the ocean. Some of these substances stay dissolved in the water. Those that come out of solutions form sediments, which settle on the ocean floor.

Measuring Salt Content

Even though their waters are considered to be "fresh," rivers and streams carry dissolved salts and deposit them in the oceans. Over billions of years the concentration of these salts has built up in the ocean water. On average, 1 kg of ocean water contains 35 g of salt. In other words, 3.5 percent of ocean water is made up of dissolved salts.

The total amount of dissolved salts in ocean water is called **salinity** (sə lin'ə-tē). Because the ocean is so huge, its overall salinity changes very slowly. However, salinity does vary in different parts of the ocean. Around the world, the salinity of the oceans and seas can range from 33 to 40 grams per kilogram of water.

Near the equator, heavy rainfalls over the ocean increase the amount of fresh water in the ocean, so salinity tends to be lower there. Areas where rivers empty into the ocean also have lower salinity.

In those areas of the ocean where rainfall is low, the salinity is higher than average, since evaporation leaves salts behind. For example, the Red Sea, which is surrounded by deserts, receives little rainfall. Hot, dry winds blowing over the water speed evaporation. As a result, 1 kg of water from the Red Sea contains about 40 g of salt instead of the average 35 g.

Using Math

In some bodies of water, the salinity is so great that salt deposits form along the shore and a person floats easily. The salinity of the Great Salt Lake is 20%, and the salinity of the Dead Sea is 28%. How many grams of salt are there in 1 kg of water from the Dead Sea?

Other Dissolved Substances

Ocean water contains substances other than salt. The graph on page E11 shows these substances and their concentrations. Six substances make up about 99 percent of the dissolved materials. The amounts of these six main compounds tend to remain the same in ocean water everywhere in the world.

As you can see from the graph, all other compounds and elements make up about 1 percent of the dissolved materials in ocean water. In fact, 80 of the 112 known elements have been found in ocean water. The percentage of these 80 elements tends to vary from one region to another, depending upon rainfall, evaporation, and outflow of water from rivers and bays.

Dissolved Gases

Ocean water also contains large amounts of dissolved gases, especially nitrogen, carbon dioxide, and oxygen. (The dissolved oxygen is in addition to the oxygen that is part of the water molecules themselves.) The amounts of these dissolved gases depend on many factors, including water depth and temperature. For example, near the surface of the ocean, sunlight helps tiny plantlike organisms in the water grow. As they grow, they release oxygen into the water. As a result, water at or near the surface contains much more oxygen than deeper water does.

Gases dissolve more easily in cold water than in warm water, so ocean water in colder regions of the world contains larger amounts of dissolved gases. Near the equator, the water is warmer, so the amount of dissolved gases is less.

Both plants and animals depend on the dissolved gases in ocean water. Tiny living creatures called **plankton** (plaŋk'tən) float near the surface and drift with the currents. Plantlike plankton, called **phytoplankton** (fīt ō plaŋk'tən), must have oxygen, carbon dioxide, and

Ocean water is a "soup" of living organisms, such as fish, plants, and kelp (_inset_), along with minerals and dissolved gases. ▼

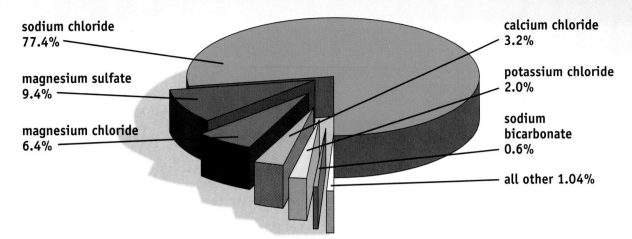

sodium chloride 77.4%

magnesium sulfate 9.4%

magnesium chloride 6.4%

calcium chloride 3.2%

potassium chloride 2.0%

sodium bicarbonate 0.6%

all other 1.04%

▲ This graph shows the breakdown of substances dissolved in ocean water.

other dissolved gases and elements to survive. Animal-like plankton, called **zooplankton** (zō ō plaŋk'tən), feed on the phytoplankton. If a region's water cannot support phytoplankton, the zooplankton cannot survive. If zooplankton cannot survive, then few other organisms can survive there, either.

Sediments and Pollution

Along with dissolved salts and gases and living plankton, ocean water also contains sediments that have been washed into the ocean or stirred up from the bottom. Sediments might include sand particles, bits of shells, and decaying organisms. Unlike salts, sediments do not dissolve in the water.

Unfortunately, ocean water also includes some harmful substances put there by people. We already know what human-caused pollution is doing to the water along our coasts. Now wastes from many coastal communities are being carried far out to sea and dumped. These waste materials are affecting water quality even farther out in the ocean.

Ocean water is much more than a mixture of salt and water. It's a complex and constantly changing mixture of water, elements, and living things. This carefully balanced mixture provides oxygen and food, which support other living things in the ocean. They, in turn, support all the organisms living on the land—including us. ■

───── **INVESTIGATION 1 WRAP-UP** ─────

REVIEW

1. What kinds of materials are found in ocean water?

2. Why does the salinity of ocean water vary in different parts of the ocean?

CRITICAL THINKING

3. You are given two samples of water and told that one is ocean water and one is water from a lake. Without tasting them, how might you determine which is which?

4. Where would you expect to find more living organisms, in cold or warm ocean water? Explain.

WHAT ARE THE PROPERTIES OF OCEAN WATER?

All matter, including ocean water, has physical properties. When you first stick your foot in the ocean, what physical property determines if you'll dive right in or run back to shore? What other properties does ocean water have?

Activity

Lighting the Water

Living things depend on sunlight that moves down through the water. How does the amount of available light change with depth?

MATERIALS
- goggles
- large bucket or trash can
- water
- Secchi disk
- meterstick
- flour
- tablespoon
- *Science Notebook*

SAFETY //////

Wear goggles at all times. To prevent slipping and falling, immediately clean up spills.

Procedure

1. In your *Science Notebook*, **make a chart** like the one shown.

2. Fill a bucket with water. Holding a Secchi disk by its string, lower it 10 cm into the water. **Record** how well you can see the disk.

Water Depth	Observation
10 cm	
20 cm	
30 cm	

3. Lower the disk by 10-cm intervals and **record** how well you can see the disk at each depth.

See **SCIENCE** and **MATH TOOLBOX** page H6 if you need to review **Using a Tape Measure or Ruler.**

4. Add 5 tablespoons of flour to the water. Stir the water-flour mixture with the spoon.

5. Lower the Secchi disk into the water until you can no longer see the disk. Grasp the string at the surface of the water and pull the disk out of the water while you hold this spot. Use the meterstick to **measure** the distance between your fingers and the disk. This measurement represents the depth below the water's surface at which you can no longer see the disk. **Record** the depth.

6. **Predict** the depth to which you would be able to see the Secchi disk if you added 10 more tablespoons of flour to the water.

7. **Test your prediction** by adding 10 more tablespoons of flour and repeating steps 4 and 5.

Step 5

Analyze and Conclude

1. Compare the visibility of the disk at 10-cm intervals beneath the surface.

2. Suggest a hypothesis to explain any change in the visibility of the Secchi disk.

3. What can you **infer** about the available light as depth increases in the ocean?

4. If the water in the bucket models ocean water, **infer** what kinds of particles the flour might represent. How do those particles affect how light penetrates the water?

INVESTIGATE FURTHER!

RESEARCH

Work in groups to research the role light plays in determining the color of ocean water. Write a report on your findings.

Activity
Dense Water

Density is a physical property of matter. It can be thought of as an indication of how tightly packed the particles are that make up a substance. What factors affect the density of water?

MATERIALS
- waterproof marker
- metric ruler
- plastic straw
- modeling clay
- bottom half of a plastic soda bottle (2 L)
- ice cubes
- distilled water
- thermometer
- scissors
- tablespoon
- table salt
- *Science Notebook*

Procedure

1. In your *Science Notebook*, **make a chart** like the one shown below.

	Warm Water	Cold Water	Salt Water
Temperature			
Estimated Length (in cm)			

2. Mark lines at 0.5-cm intervals along a plastic straw.

3. Pack one end of the straw with clay to a length of 3 cm.

4. Half fill a bottle with warm water. Place a thermometer in the bottle. **Record** the water temperature in your chart.

See **SCIENCE** and **MATH TOOLBOX** page H8 if you need to review *Using a Thermometer.*

5. Place the clay-filled end of the straw in the water so that it floats straight up. (You may need to cut off the open end of the straw, 0.5 cm at a time, until it floats properly.) Use the lines on the straw to **estimate** the length of the straw that is under water. **Record** the length in your chart.

6. Remove the straw. Place the thermometer in the bottle. Place the bottle in an ice bath.

Step 2

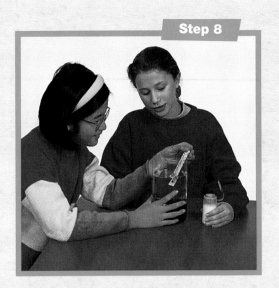

7. When the temperature of the water drops between 5° and 10°C, remove the bottle from the ice bath. **Record** the temperature in your chart. **Predict** how much of the straw will be under water in cold water. **Discuss** your prediction with your classmates. Repeat step 5.

8. Discard the cold water from the bottle. Half fill the bottle with water that is the same temperature as the water used in step 4. **Record** the temperature in your chart and remove the thermometer. Add 3 tablespoons of salt and stir until it dissolves. **Predict** how much of the straw will be under water in salt water. **Discuss** your prediction with your classmates. Repeat step 5.

Analyze and Conclude

1. The deeper the straw sinks, the less dense the water is. Which was more dense, the warm fresh water, the cold fresh water, or the salt water? How do you know?

2. **Suggest a hypothesis** about how temperature and salinity affect the density of water.

 # Science in Literature

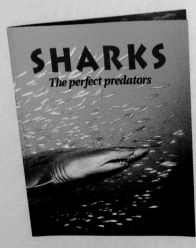

**Sharks:
The Perfect Predators**
by Howard Hall
Silver Burdett Press, 1995

A SHOCKING TALE

"Sharks can sense incredibly weak electrical fields. If you hooked up a single flashlight battery and connected it to two electrodes 1,000 miles apart, its electrical field would be within the shark's astounding sensory range."

This is just one of the amazing facts found in *Sharks: The Perfect Predators* by Howard Hall. The author, a diver and marine biologist, has been up close with sharks many times as an underwater filmmaker and photographer. Find out how the 350 species of sharks alive today are suited to life in the ocean.

Activity

Under Pressure

If you've ever dived deep into the water, you may have felt some pain in your ears. What physical property of water causes this effect?

MATERIALS
- pencil
- milk carton
- metric ruler
- small ball of clay
- sink or basin
- water
- *Science Notebook*

Procedure

1. Use a pencil to make a hole in a milk carton about 2 cm from the bottom, as shown in the photo.

2. Plug the hole with clay.

3. From the hole, measure up 5 cm, 10 cm, 15 cm, and 20 cm. Make a mark at each point.

4. Carefully pour water into the carton up to the 5-cm mark.

5. Hold the carton over a sink or a basin. Your partner should hold the metric ruler below the hole as shown.

6. Unplug the hole and **measure** how far the water squirts out of the carton. In your *Science Notebook*, **record** your results.

7. Replug the hole and fill the carton to the 10-cm mark. Repeat steps 5 and 6.

8. **Predict** how far the water will squirt if you fill the carton to the 15-cm and 20-cm marks. Test your predictions and **record** your results.

Step 1

Analyze and Conclude

1. When did the water squirt farthest? Why do you think this happened?

2. Pressure is the amount of force acting on an area. From your observations, **infer** when the water pressure was the greatest in the carton.

3. **Suggest a hypothesis** that relates water pressure to depth.

Steps 5 and 6

The Bends

Reading Focus How does water pressure affect scuba divers?

People who want to explore the ocean depths need to understand the effects of water pressure. Divers using scuba (**s**elf-**c**ontained **u**nderwater **b**reathing **a**pparatus) equipment receive one to eight weeks of instruction on diving safety. Because of increasing water pressure, most scuba divers venture to depths of no more than 50 m (165 ft). However, some scuba divers have descended to depths of 90 m (300 ft).

The divers wear air tanks and carry depth gauges to tell them how far down they are and pressure gauges to show how much air they have left in their tanks. Some divers now carry tiny computers that figure out how long they can stay at a certain depth.

When divers descend into the water, their bodies naturally adjust to the increasing water pressure. However, after divers spend some time under greater pressure, nitrogen from their air tanks begins to build up in their body tissues. As the divers begin rising to the surface, the decreasing water pressure can cause the nitrogen to form bubbles in their blood and other tissues. This condition, called the bends, can cause problems ranging from itchy skin to brain damage and even death.

▲ Scuba equipment has enabled people to explore shallow ocean depths. Those who go too deep and come up too fast may suffer from the bends.

To avoid the bends, divers must rise slowly to allow the nitrogen to be released safely from their bodies through respiration. A diver who has been at a depth of 90 m (300 ft) for two hours may need five or six hours to rise safely to the surface.

To avoid this long delay, divers who intend to explore deep waters sometimes breathe a mixture of oxygen and helium gas. Helium doesn't dissolve as easily in body tissues as nitrogen, so it doesn't build up quickly and require such a slow return to the surface. ■

Ocean Temperatures and Pressure

Reading Focus How do temperature and pressure change as you go deeper in the ocean?

January 23, 1960—Western Pacific Ocean: For several hours now, Jacques Piccard, an oceanographic engineer, and Lieutenant Don Walsh of the U.S. Navy have been descending into the Mariana Trench in the Pacific Ocean. Inside the deep-diving vehicle *Trieste* the two men have been monitoring the temperature and pressure of the water surrounding them.

Some time ago, the vehicle passed the 9,090-m (30,000-ft) mark. At this depth, the *Trieste*'s walls creak under the nearly 7 T/in.^{2} of pressure. The water temperature has dropped well below what would be freezing at a normal surface pressure of 14.7 lb/in.^{2}. *Trieste* stops at a depth of 10,910 m (35,800 ft)—nearly 7 miles beneath the surface. Piccard and Walsh peer out at the cold dark world surrounding them. Strange-looking fish move slowly through the water, and a "snowstorm" of sediment drifts down past the *Trieste*'s lights as they penetrate the total blackness of the water.

Jan. 23

Trieste is readied for the descent into the trench.

Trieste surfaces and awaits pickup by the mother ship.

On that day in January 1960, Jacques Piccard and Lt. Don Walsh descended into the Challenger Deep, the deepest known part of the ocean. And as you read, most of their descent into the trench was through water that was completely black. Without the lights from the *Trieste*, they would have seen nothing at all. But how can that be? If oceans cover two thirds of Earth's surface, most of the Sun's light that strikes Earth must fall on ocean water.

In the activity on pages E12 and E13, the deeper a Secchi disk is lowered into a bucket of water, the harder it is to see. Visibility worsens with depth because the surface water quickly absorbs much of the light. By the time sunlight penetrates 10 m (33 ft) into the water, the water has absorbed most of the visible light rays. Only a blue-green light is left, which gives the ocean its color.

No sunlight—and no direct heat from sunlight—penetrates deep into the ocean. Although sunlight can heat the water surface near the equator to the bathtub temperature of 30°C (86°F), temperatures in the deepest regions of the ocean stay near or below 0°C (32°F). Only the tremendous pressures at those depths keep the water from becoming solid ice.

Just as temperatures decrease in the ocean depths, water pressure increases. The activity on page E16 illustrates how water pressure increases as the water depth increases. Water pressure can be measured in pounds per square inch. At the ocean's surface, air pressure is 14.7 lb/in.^{2}, but the water pressure is 0 lb/in.^{2}. At great depths, water pressure can reach more than 14,000 lb/in.^{2}. Had the *Trieste* not been specially constructed, the water pressure at the bottom of the Mariana Trench would have crushed it, and everything in it, within seconds. ∎

Technology Link
CD-ROM

INVESTIGATE FURTHER!

Use the **Science Processor CD-ROM**, *Oceanography* (Investigation 1, Hello Down There) to explore the relationships between temperature and depth, and pressure and depth.

E19

That's Dense!

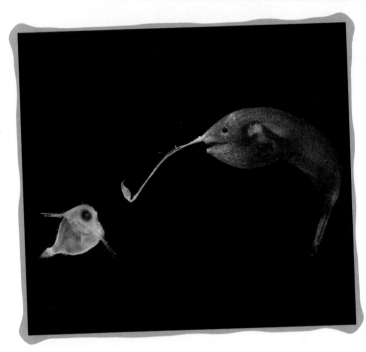

▲ Strange, luminescent creatures are to be found in the cold, dark waters of the Mariana Trench.

When Piccard and Walsh descended into the Mariana Trench, they monitored the increasing pressure and decreasing temperature of the water. They also monitored the water's density. Changes in temperature and pressure are fairly easy to measure and to monitor using thermometers and gauges. However, measuring and keeping track of changes in density is a more complicated matter.

What causes the density of water to change? Generally, as a substance becomes colder, it contracts and becomes more dense. Warming a substance has the opposite effect.

As ocean water is warmed, it expands slightly and becomes less dense. Water near the ocean's surface is generally warmer and less dense than the water at greater depths. However, when surface water is cooled, it contracts and becomes denser. If it becomes dense enough, surface water will sink and be replaced by warmer, less dense water below it.

As water cools, it contracts until its temperature reaches 4°C (39.2°F). At that point the water begins to expand! It continues to expand until its temperature reaches 0°C (32°F). Then it freezes. Think about it. Have you ever seen an ice cube sink?

As an iceberg melts, it releases less-dense fresh water that floats on top of more-dense salt water. ▼

Can you now explain why an ice cube at 0°C floats in water that is substantially warmer than 0°C?

As you have learned, water at the very bottom of the ocean reaches temperatures near or below 0°C (32°F). But it doesn't freeze. Why? Actually there are two reasons. First, the water is salty. Salt water freezes at a lower temperature than fresh water. Second, along with the contraction caused by the coldness at the ocean depths, the water molecules there are also slightly squeezed together by the weight of the water above them. This squeezing helps to increase the water's density. It also helps prevent the water from freezing even though the temperature of the water at great depths is near or below 0°C.

The difference in water density between the surface and the deep ocean is not great. When the *Trieste* descended into the Mariana Trench, Piccard and Walsh discovered that the water there was only 7 percent denser than water at the surface.

However, the density of water is greatly affected by the amount of salt and other substances dissolved in it. Dissolved substances add mass to a given volume of water. Thus, salty ocean water is more dense than the fresh water in rivers and the lakes that feed them.

When fresh water and salt water meet, the less-dense fresh water sometimes floats on top of the more-dense salt water. For example, Hudson Bay in Canada is almost completely surrounded by land. At one end it's fed by freshwater rivers. At the other end it connects with the Atlantic Ocean.

In the bay, salinity and density increase as the water depth increases. When the current is strong and the ice is melting, fresh water is added to the bay. Then the surface of the bay has a salinity level of only 2 g/1,000 g of water. However, salinity and density increase as the water depth increases. At about 25 m (80 ft) down, the salinity increases to 31 g/1,000 g of water. Differences in density are an important factor in the development of some kinds of ocean currents. ■

Internet Field Trip

Visit **www.eduplace.com** to learn more about underwater exploration.

INVESTIGATION 2 WRAP-UP

REVIEW

1. What are the physical properties of ocean water?

2. Why is visibility decreased the deeper you go in the ocean?

CRITICAL THINKING

3. If a bottle of water is placed in the freezer, why does the bottle often burst or the top pop off?

4. What do you think would happen to any organisms found at the bottom of the Mariana Trench if they were brought suddenly to the surface? Explain your answer.

INVESTIGATION 3

WHAT LIVING THINGS ARE IN OCEAN WATER?

The oceans of the world are teeming with life. Some organisms float with the currents; others swim; still others spend their adult lives crawling on or anchored to the bottom. Find out more about living things in the ocean in this investigation.

Activity

Let the Sun Shine

Living things besides humans affect the oceans. Find out one way in which plants change ocean water in this activity.

Procedure

1. Place an aquarium in an area where it will be exposed to strong sunlight for several hours each day.

2. Fill the aquarium with water to within a few centimeters of the top. Roll up your sleeves.

MATERIALS

- goggles
- aquarium
- water
- *Elodea*
- plastic cup
- paper towels
- *Science Notebook*

SAFETY

Wear goggles. Handle any glass equipment with care. Wipe up spills immediately.

3. *Elodea* is a freshwater plant. **Model** a marine plant by placing *Elodea* in the bottom of the aquarium.

4. Completely submerge a plastic cup in the water. Turn it until it is filled with water. If any air bubbles remain inside, push them out with your finger or a straw. Invert the cup. Don't let air get into the cup as you cover the *Elodea* completely.

5. After 10 minutes, **observe** and **record** any changes. **Predict** any changes that will occur over 24 hours. **Discuss** with your group any changes you think might occur during that time. Then let the aquarium sit overnight. The next day, examine the assembly and **record your observations**.

Step 4

Analyze and Conclude

1. Oxygen is produced by organisms that have chlorophyll. What evidence is there that oxygen was produced in this activity?

2. **Make a hypothesis** as to how the oxygen produced by plants affects other ocean life.

UNIT PROJECT LINK

For this Unit Project, imagine you are promoting a brand-new undersea nature lodge. Visitors will get to and from the lodge in a deep-diving vehicle used for ocean research. Your presentation will include a "moving picture" of what visitors will see, a taped narration, and other materials.

Begin preparing by researching how organisms are adapted to different ocean depths. For example, you might focus on phosphorescent fish, which glow in the lightless waters of the deep. How might phosphorescence help the fish survive? Collect or draw pictures of some of these fish. Create "storyboards" for your moving picture.

TechnologyLink

For more help with your Unit Project, go to **www.eduplace.com**.

All Creatures Great and Small

Reading Focus How can ocean organisms be classified?

Sea nettle jellyfish ▽

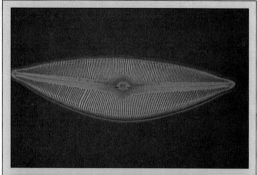

▲ Phytoplankton and zooplankton make up the very bottom of the ocean food chain.

Today, more than 200,000 species of plants and animals live in the ocean. These organisms can be divided into three groups—plankton, nekton, and benthos—according to the depth at which they live.

Plankton

Plankton includes organisms that float on or near the surface and drift with the ocean currents. There are two types of plankton, phytoplankton and zooplankton, but there are billions and billions of individual organisms. Although most phytoplankton are too small to see without a microscope, these tiny organisms produce 80 percent of the oxygen on our planet through **photosynthesis** (fōt ō sin'thə sis). Recall that during photosynthesis, organisms containing chlorophyll use the energy in sunlight to produce sugar and oxygen from carbon dioxide and water. The sugar is used for food, and oxygen is used for respiration. Creatures on land and in the ocean could not survive without the oxygen produced by phytoplankton. Because phytoplankton need sunlight for photosynthesis, these organisms must live near the surface of the ocean.

Zooplankton include larval forms of certain types of ocean creatures. When they mature, the adult organisms will no longer be considered plankton.

▲ **Common green sea turtle**

▲ Nekton includes many varieties of free-swimming organisms like the butterfly fish (*top*) and red soldier fish (*bottom*).

Instead, they will be lobsters, sea cucumbers, jellyfish, corals, or other organisms that belong to either the nekton group or the benthos group.

Nekton

The second main group of organisms, **nekton** (nek'tän), consists of all creatures that swim. It includes invertebrates such as squids and octopuses, all kinds of fish, and mammals such as whales and porpoises. Do you think any plants are considered nekton? Nekton can live at any depth, from near the ocean surface to the ocean floor. However, each type stays mostly at the ocean depth where the water pressure and other conditions are suitable for its needs.

Benthos

The third group of ocean organisms, **benthos** (ben'thäs), consists of plants and animals that live on the ocean floor and do not swim. The ocean floor starts at the shoreline and goes to the deepest parts of the ocean. Think about the different environments this includes, from waves crashing on the sand to the sea floor miles beneath the surface. Can you hypothesize why the benthos group contains the greatest variety of ocean life? (Variety is measured by the number of different species in an environment.)

E25

Benthos

Nekton

Using Math

Ninety-eight percent of the more than 200,000 species of ocean plants and animals live on the ocean floor. Estimate the number of species that do not live on the ocean floor.

Most members of the benthos group live in shallow water, where food is plentiful and the water is warmer. The Benthos group includes shellfish, such as clams, oysters, and mussels, as well as starfish, crabs, barnacles, coral, and many types of seaweed.

Ocean Food Chains

You've probably seen cartoons of a big fish about to eat a small fish that is about to eat a still smaller fish that is about to eat a plant. This is an example of a food chain. All food chains in the ocean start with phytoplankton. In one simple food chain, phytoplankton are eaten by krill, a kind of zooplankton that look like tiny shrimp. The krill are then eaten by enormous baleen whales. These whales swim with their mouths open wide, filtering millions of these tiny krill from the water. You've seen that all creatures need phytoplankton for the oxygen they produce. Additionally, creatures either eat phytoplankton directly, or they eat another organism that has eaten phytoplankton. ■

INVESTIGATION 3 WRAP-UP

REVIEW

1. What organisms might you find as part of the plankton, nekton, and benthos groups?

2. Why are plants not part of the nekton group?

CRITICAL THINKING

3. Why, do you think, are most plantlike organisms found in ocean water no deeper than about 9 or 10 m?

4. How does the oxygen produced by plants affect other ocean life?

REFLECT & EVALUATE

Word Power

Write the term that best matches the definition. *Not all terms will be used.*

1. The plants and animals that live on the ocean floor
2. Any of the usually microscopic plantlike organisms that live near the surface of the ocean
3. The total amount of dissolved salts in ocean water
4. All of the free-swimming animals that live in the ocean
5. The process by which green plants and other producers use light energy to make food

a. benthos
b. nekton
c. photosynthesis
d. phytoplankton
e. plankton
f. salinity
g. zooplankton

Check What You Know

Write the term that best completes each sentence.

1. As you go deeper into the ocean, (water pressure, temperature) increases.
2. Visibility in ocean water (improves, worsens) with depth.
3. (Whales, plankton) are the first links in the ocean food chain.
4. The higher the temperature of ocean water, the (less dense, more dense) it is.

Problem Solving

1. If you had equal volumes of ocean water and fresh water, how could you identify each without tasting them?
2. Explain why members of the nekton group might be more adaptable than those in the benthos group to changes in their environment.
3. If all the phytoplankton in the oceans were to die, how would other living things be affected?

PORTFOLIO

Using pictures cut from magazines or drawings of organisms like the ones to the right, make diagrams that show three possible ocean food chains. Label the organisms in your food chains as examples of plankton, benthos, or nekton.

CHAPTER 2

THE OCEAN FLOOR

Scientists have much to learn about the bottom of the sea,
with its volcanic activity and strange life forms.
There will be many surprises for the explorers who venture there.
How do scientists gather information about the sea floor?

PEOPLE USING SCIENCE

Marine Engineer Graham Hawkes is a marine engineer who is busy designing a new type of submersible to explore the ocean. Unlike existing subs, the new submersible will be light and fast. It will twirl and spin, maneuvering like a dolphin. It will seem to fly rather than float to the bottom of the ocean.

The new submersible will be used in a project called Deep Flight. One of the goals of this project is to explore the 11.2-km (36,900-ft) deep Mariana Trench in the Pacific Ocean. The challenge for the marine engineer is to produce a vessel that can withstand the tremendous pressure at that depth. Graham Hawkes and his team will make the new submersible out of a ceramic material that is light and strong. What else do the designers have to consider as they plan and build this new submersible?

Coming Up

◄ Graham Hawkes in his experimental submersible; submersibles such as this will someday explore the deepest parts of the oceans.

WHAT FEATURES AND SEDIMENTS OCCUR ON THE OCEAN FLOOR?

If you were asked to describe the ocean floor, what would you say? For a long time, people thought the ocean floor was shaped like the bottom of a bathtub. In this investigation you'll see how wrong they were!

Activity

Graphing the Ocean Floor

Scientists use sonar to "see" the ocean floor. In this activity you'll make your own ocean floor profile using depth measurements for an area of the ocean off the east coast of the United States.

Procedure

1. The data in the table provides depth measurements for an area of the ocean off the east coast of the United States. You will make a graph using this data.

2. Prepare a set of axes as shown on page E31. The distance from the coast should be along the *x*-axis and the depth to the ocean floor from sea level should be on the *y*-axis. Notice that the numbers on the *y*-axis are negative.

3. **Graph the data** from the table. Then **use a ruler** to draw lines connecting the points on the graph. When all the points are connected, you will have a profile of the ocean floor.

Distance from coast (km)	Distance from sea level to the ocean floor (m)
610	-5,988
620	-5,840
660	-4,965
695	-4,520
720	-2,333
750	-1,895
775	-1,754
810	-5,110
835	-5,840
850	-5,842

Ocean Floor Profile

Distance From Coast (km)

Analyze and Conclude

1. Describe the shape of your graph.

2. What range of distances from sea level to sea floor is given in the table on page E30?

 See **SCIENCE** and **MATH TOOLBOX** page H14 if you need to review **Finding Range, Median, and Mode.**

3. What would you call the feature you graphed if it were on land?

4. **Infer** from your profile how the shape of the ocean floor might be like that of the continents.

INVESTIGATE FURTHER!

RESEARCH

Use reference materials to find out about some ocean-floor feature, such as a trench or a mid-ocean ridge. If possible, obtain data and use it to graph a profile of the feature.

Features of the Ocean Floor

Reading Focus What features make up the ocean floor?

People build things up and also tear things down. And sometimes nature tears things down for us. Waves wash away sand castles on the beach, for example, and storm waves may wash away homes, boardwalks, and other structures. So it's nice to know that the mountains, valleys, and oceans are forever, right? Wrong! Not even Earth's natural features are forever. Its mountains, its valleys, and even its oceans have been changing continuously since Earth first formed, billions of years ago.

Powerful natural forces pull and wrench at Earth's crust. Earthquakes and volcanoes shift huge masses of rocks on the land and under the sea. Rivers carry weathered rock and deposit it in the oceans. So what natural wonders might you find on the ocean floor? Are there features similar to those on dry land?

The Continental Shelf

Let's start where the oceans begin. The **continental shelf**, which covers about 5 percent of Earth's surface,

The Ocean Basin

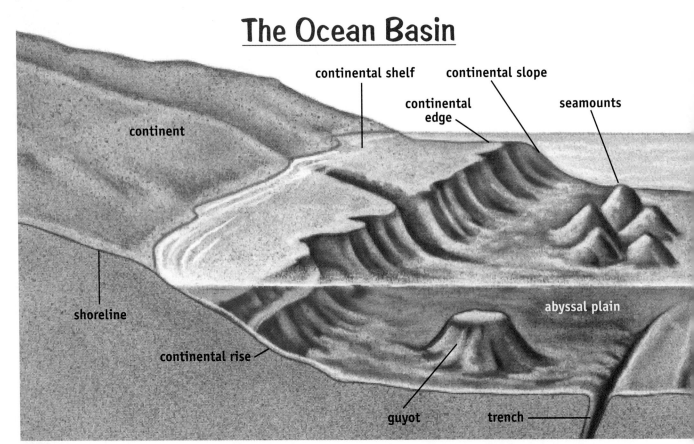

continental shelf · continental slope · continental edge · seamounts · continent · shoreline · continental rise · abyssal plain · guyot · trench

extends in a gentle downward slope from the shorelines of the continents into the oceans. Throughout the world, when you wade into the ocean, you are walking on the continental shelf. At its deepest it is about 365 m (1,205 ft) below the surface, but its average depth is less than 152 m (500 feet).

Although on average the continental shelf extends less than 80 km (50 mi) from shore, it extends about 1,120 km (700 mi) off the coast of Siberia. Off the Atlantic coast of North America, the continental shelf extends 144 km (90 mi) out into the ocean. But off the Pacific coast it extends only 29 km (18 mi).

The continental shelf tends to be widest near the mouths of rivers and off coasts that were formed by glaciers during the ice ages. Rocks, sediments, and other materials carried into the ocean by rivers and glaciers have greatly increased the size of the continental shelf in those areas.

The Continental Edge and the Continental Slope

The **continental edge** is the point at which the shelf surrounding each continent begins to angle sharply downward toward the ocean depths. The clifflike drop beyond the continental edge is called the **continental slope**. The continental slope is the true boundary between the deep ocean floor and the continents.

To help you remember these first three features, think of them as parts of a gigantic bowl. The continental shelf is the rim (or the lip) of the bowl; the continental edge is the inner edge of the lip; and the continental slope is the inside wall of the bowl, leading down to the bottom like a gigantic bluff.

The Continental Rise

The **continental rise** stretches from the lower portion of the continental slope to the deepest part of the ocean.

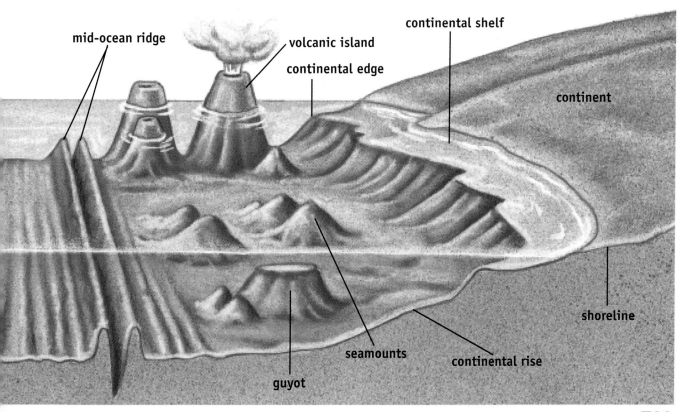

mid-ocean ridge · volcanic island · continental edge · continental shelf · continent · shoreline · seamounts · continental rise · guyot

Although the continental rise slopes downward, it is not nearly as steep as the continental slope. The continental rise usually begins at 1,425 to 1,970 m (4,700 to 6,500 ft) under the ocean's surface. If you again think of the ocean as a giant bowl, the rise is the softly curving link between the flat bottom and the steep, near-vertical sides.

The Abyssal Plain

Typically, the continental rise flattens out completely at about 3,630 m (12,000 ft), leading to the vast ocean bottom itself. The bottom is called the **abyssal** (ə bis′əl) **plain** and covers about 46 percent of Earth's surface.

Parts of the abyssal plain are flat, but for the most part, both the continental rise and the abyssal plain feature caves and deep, steep-walled canyons called trenches. Most of these trenches were formed long ago by undersea rivers and currents, and by the cooling, contracting, and pulling apart of Earth's rocky crust. Even today the ocean bottom is undergoing change. Undersea volcanoes, earthquakes, and powerful deep-water currents continue to alter and reshape the abyssal plain.

Mountains in the Sea

Perhaps the single most startling feature of the abyssal plain is a colossal chain of underwater mountains called the **mid-ocean ridge**. The mid-ocean ridge is the longest mountain range in the world, extending nearly 60,000 km (36,000 mi) and passing through the Atlantic, Indian, and Pacific oceans.

Free-standing mountains, called **seamounts**, formed by volcanoes also exist in the oceans. They are especially numerous in the Pacific, where thousands

Internet Field Trip

Visit **www.eduplace.com** to learn more about the ocean floor.

A diver gets a close-up photo of molten lava cooling on the ocean floor. ▼

of seamounts lie beneath the surface. Some seamounts, which once reached above the surface, have been flattened by wave action. A flat-topped seamount is called a guyot (gē'ō).

Other seamounts rise above the surface, forming islands. A spectacular example is Mauna Kea (mou'nə kā'ə), a volcano forming the island of Hawaii. Rising from the ocean floor, Mauna Kea climbs more than 5,144 m (17,000 ft) to the ocean surface. Then it rises an additional 4,205 m (13,900 ft) to a total height of 9,349 m (31,000 ft).

So, as you can see, the ocean floor certainly doesn't have a flat, bathtub shape. It is made up of some rather spectacular features. ■

Using Math *Would you believe that Mauna Kea, not Mount Everest (8,848 m), is the tallest mountain in the world? And most of it is underwater! Estimate how much taller Mauna Kea is than Mount Everest.*

Science in Literature

LOOK OUT BELOW!

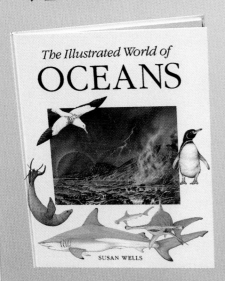

The Illustrated World of Oceans
by Susan Wells
Simon and Schuster Books for Young Readers, 1991

"Underwater avalanches occur when large amounts of sediment resting on the upper continental slope are dislodged by earthquakes or their own weight. This mass of sediment, up to several miles in length and width and several hundreds of feet thick, rolls down the slope at speeds of up to 50 mph."

Learn more about the startling features of the ocean floor, including the mid-ocean ridge, trenches, and seamounts, in *The Illustrated World of Oceans* by Susan Wells.

Sediments on the Ocean Floor

Reading Focus What can scientists learn by studying ocean sediments?

Imagine a long, steady snowfall lasting millions of years. Visualize billions and billions of tiny particles drifting down, some so small they can barely be seen, piling on top of each other hour after hour, day after day, year after year, century after century.

If such a snowfall fell on land, it would cover the entire world with a massive blanket. After thousands of years the blanket would grow so thick, the weight of the snowflakes on top would crush the ones on the bottom and even compress the rocks and soil underneath until everything sank into the crust.

This sounds far-fetched—until one realizes the "snowfall" isn't snow at all, but tiny particles quietly drifting to the ocean bottom. Particles have been settling on the ocean floor since the oceans first formed. Even as you read this sentence, the process continues. The result is a layer of sediments on the ocean floor, forming soft deposits of mud, slime, and decomposed shells that are called ooze. Ooze covers every part of the ocean floor, except where strong currents sweep the bottom bare or where active volcanoes deposit new rock.

Inorganic Sediments

Every time it rains, soil and rock on land are eroded. Some of the particles of soil and rock are washed into the oceans by runoff from the land. Other particles ride the currents of rivers and streams, all of which empty eventually into the oceans.

Other inorganic sediments drifting downward in the oceans include deposits from the thousands of volcanoes rising from the ocean floor. Active volcanoes can contribute great quantities of rock

▲ As this iceberg melts, rocks, soil, and other debris will settle into the ocean as sediments.

and rock particles each time they erupt. But volcanoes need not be spewing lava and scattering debris to add to the sediment layer. Constant friction by the ocean currents, plus the dissolving actions of the water itself, continually erodes ocean volcanoes.

Other inorganic particles reach the ocean floor by way of glaciers that fringe the northern and southern parts of the oceans. As glaciers move slowly toward the oceans, they pick up rocks, soil, and organic deposits—the remains of living things. When the glaciers meet the oceans, pieces break off, or calve, to form icebergs. Gradually, materials that were carried by the glacier are released by the melting iceberg and settle to the ocean bottom.

Another source of inorganic sediments is the burning of meteors in the atmosphere. Fragments of iron, nickel, and other rocky debris settle eventually to the ocean bottom.

Where inorganic sediments are plentiful, they form muds and clays of various consistencies and colors. They cover about a quarter of the ocean floor and build up in the thickest layers near the mouths of rivers and streams.

Organic Sediments

Organic ooze is most abundant in the deeper parts of the ocean. Most of the deep-sea ooze is formed from the shells of protists, particularly the remains of single-celled algae. Some ooze is formed from the shells of tiny snails and other small marine animals. Organic ooze covers about half of the ocean floor. It builds up very slowly, from about 1.3 cm (0.5 in.) to about 10.2 cm (4 in.) in a thousand years.

When organisms in the ocean die, their remains settle to the bottom and become part of the organic sediments. ▶

E37

Chemical and Mineral Deposits

During the nineteenth century, people traveling west across the vast plains and imposing mountains of the United States heard it said that "there's gold in them thar hills!" Well, there's gold in "them thar oceans," too. A cubic mile of sea water contains enough gold to make you rich. Unfortunately, extracting the gold costs more than the gold is worth.

As you know, water moving over the land dissolves vast quantities of chemicals and minerals that eventually end up in the oceans. Many minerals, such as gold, remain suspended in the water. Other minerals build up in the ooze of shallow coastal waters. Although some of the minerals can be mined at a profit, others, like gold and the millions of manganese nodules that litter the ocean floor, aren't yet being reclaimed.

First discovered more than 100 years ago, manganese nodules range in size from 0.5 cm (0.2 in.) to 25 cm (10 in.) across. No one knows for sure how they form, but they seem to grow very slowly from metals dissolved in the water.

Deep Sediments

On the floor of the Atlantic Ocean, the sediment layer is often more than 3,200 m (10,560 ft) thick and millions of years old. Yet it's never more than 303 m (1,000 ft) thick in the Indian and Pacific oceans. The sediment layer also tends to form huge drifts at the bases of seamounts and continental slopes.

What causes such differences in the thickness of sedimentary layers? One possible answer is a turbidity current (tʉr- bid′i tē kʉr′ənt). These currents, which are still barely understood, seem to occur near the mouths of rivers where heavy sedimentary deposits have built up. In time, the sediments become like layers of unstable snow on hillsides, needing only a slight jolt to send them rolling downhill, like an avalanche. Turbidity currents may cause sediment layers to build up more in some places than in others.

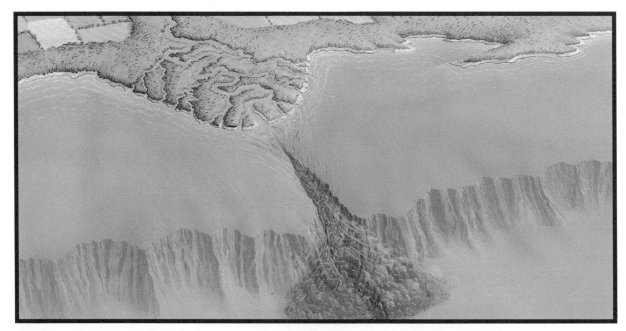

▲ Turbidity currents can carry huge loads of sediments from underwater canyons out onto the ocean floor.

Reading the Past in Sediments

By studying the layers of ocean sediments, scientists can learn much about the past. For example, one layer of sediments that was deposited at the end of the dinosaur era contains unusual quantities of the rare element iridium.

In some places the iridium level is hundreds of times more concentrated than it should be. Some scientists think that the most likely source for such quantities of iridium would be a single gigantic meteorite or a shower of smaller meteorites all striking Earth at the same time. If a huge meteorite actually did strike our planet millions of years ago, its dust could have blotted out the sun. The darkness would have caused the plants to die, and then the dinosaurs would have starved.

The meteorite hypothesis is controversial and may never be accepted by everyone, but it certainly seems possible. It's just about the only explanation scientists have for the unusually high levels of iridium found in sediment layers of the same age all over the world. It's like finding a person's footprints all over town on a single day. Would the footprints prove the person was everywhere in town on that day? What do you think? ■

▲ Uh, oh!

Technology Link CD-ROM

INVESTIGATE FURTHER!

Use the **Science Processor CD-ROM**, *Oceanography* (Investigation 2, Floor Plans) to take sonar readings and map the topographic features of an ocean floor.

INVESTIGATION 1 WRAP-UP

THINK IT WRITE IT

REVIEW

1. Draw and describe the features of the ocean floor.

2. What contributes to inorganic ocean sediment?

CRITICAL THINKING

3. Why is looking at the sedimentary layers of the ocean floor like looking at a time line?

4. The "X" on an old treasure map is on an island that can no longer be found. Explain how this is possible.

HOW DO SCIENTISTS STUDY THE OCEAN FLOOR?

You've been assigned to investigate something you can't see, touch, or even get near. How do you investigate something under those conditions? That's the question scientists have to answer when they study the ocean floor. Find out how they do it in this investigation.

Activity

Modeling Sonar

Sonar waves are sound waves that can be used to probe the ocean. Find out how scientists collect and use data gathered with sonar.

MATERIALS
- goggles
- spring toy
- length of string
- meterstick
- timer
- calculator
- *Science Notebook*

Procedure

1. Work with a partner. Tie one end of a spring toy to a doorknob and pull the spring so that it is parallel to the floor.

2. With your free hand, gather a handful of coils near the end of the spring. Then release them. Have your partner **measure** the time it takes the wave motion to travel to the doorknob and back to your hand. **Record** the time in your *Science Notebook*.

3. **Measure** the distance from your hand to the doorknob. **Record** the distance.

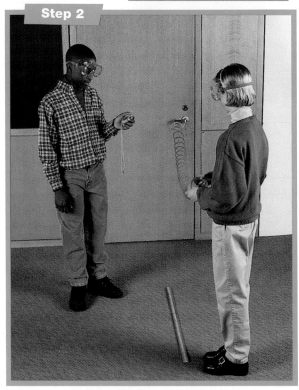

Step 2

4. Repeat step 2 five times and find the average time. To **calculate** the rate of travel, multiply the distance by 2 for the round trip distance and then divide the product by the time. **Record** the rate in your *Science Notebook*.

Analyze and Conclude

1. Sonar waves traveling through ocean water bounce off objects and return. How is your model similar to the way sonar waves behave?

2. Suppose it takes 4 seconds for the wave in a spring to make a round trip. **Calculate** the distance traveled.

3. Dolphins use a form of sonar to locate and track food. Using the drawing below, explain how a dolphin's sonarlike system works.

UNIT PROJECT LINK

An important part of your *undersea lodge* promotion is to show where on the ocean floor the lodge would be. Work with your group to decide at what depth and distance from land you would locate the site. Discuss the safety features you should take into account. Use an ocean map to help you decide where to build. Draw illustrations to show the topography that visitors to the lodge would see. Also, keep gathering data for your taped narration. Remember, your goal is to communicate how unique and interesting an underwater living experience would be.

Technology Link
For more help with your Unit Project, go to **www.eduplace.com**.

Underwater Exploration

Reading Focus What kinds of technological advancements made deep underwater exploration possible?

Explorers have always been fascinated with what could be found beneath the ocean waves. Early in the seventeenth century, inventors began developing diving suits and diving chambers. But it wasn't until the nineteenth century that underwater exploration was really taken seriously.

The *Glomar Challenger* takes up where the HMS *Challenger* has left off. It drills hundreds of deep-water "core samples" from sediment layers all over the world, adding immeasurably to our knowledge of the makeup, age, and natural forces at work in and on Earth. **1968–1983**

Matthew Fontaine Maury, a landlubber from Tennessee, joins the U.S. Navy. He begins gathering information and developing accurate charts of the world's oceans. He becomes the father of modern oceanography. **1825**

Cornelis Drebbel builds the first working submarine. It actually works for a few hours! **1620**

1870 Jules Verne writes *Twenty Thousand Leagues Under the Sea*. This novel revives the ageless dream that safe undersea travel might be possible.

1872 British scientists and the Royal Navy launch HMS *Challenger*. On this voyage, scientists and crew will travel more than 112,000 km (70,000 miles), and collect more than 300 deep-sea samples.

BEYOND 2000

Argo, a complex, advanced underwater survey vehicle, locates the *Titanic.* *Jason Jr.*, a tiny robot submarine, sends back hundreds of high-quality video and still pictures from inside the wreck.

1985

1996

The remains of Alexandria, the royal city of the last Egyptian Dynasty, are discovered underwater. One-of-a-kind mapping technology, including satellite positioning, is used to locate the city which was lost in a series of earthquakes 1,600 years ago.

1979

Off Makapu'u Point, Oahu, Hawaii, Sylvia Earle plants the Stars and Stripes at a depth of 378.78 m (1,250 ft). This marks the deepest untethered solo dive in history.

Exploring the Oceans

Reading Focus Why is it important to explore the oceans?

Why explore the oceans? Why explore anything, for that matter? You might as well ask, "Why eat?" Because, as humans, exploring is something that's in our nature. Soon after we are born, we begin to get curious about our surroundings. So we explore. People have always looked at the oceans and wondered what was under all the water. In recent times people devised some means of finding out.

The first direct observations of what was under all that water began in 1872. The Royal Society of London helped equip the 2,300-ton warship HMS *Challenger* with the most advanced navigating and measuring instruments of the day. During the next three years, the *Challenger* crew sailed about 112,000 km (70,000 miles), measuring ocean depths and collecting deep-sea samples.

What the *Challenger* crew discovered changed the scientific world. In more than 300 locations around the world, the *Challenger* crew dropped a crude dredging device, allowed it to drag along the bottom until it filled with samples, and then hauled it back on deck. A typical drop and retrieval took an entire day. But then, as the dredge was emptied on deck, imagine the scene! Deep into the night, scientists and sailors were still bouncing around on deck, yelling and shaking their heads as they examined by flickering lantern light the day's astonishing finds.

HMS *Challenger* under sail in the Antarctic ▼

A deep-sea lobster brought up by the *Challenger* crew. ▼

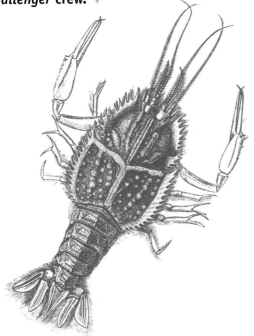

The ocean bottom had been envisioned as barren. Instead, the crew found it to be teeming with life.

The crew of the *Challenger* also took measurements of the ocean depths, using weighted lines. Where they presumed a shallow bottom, the sounding weights fell about 11 km (7 mi) into what became known as the Challenger Deep of the Mariana Trench. At the end of their long voyage, the scientists on board the *Challenger* concluded that they had barely begun to explore the oceans.

Almost 100 years later, the *Glomar Challenger* took up the work begun by the first *Challenger*. Between 1968 and 1983 this highly advanced exploration ship bored hundreds of holes into the ocean floor and collected long core samples of the sediments. Some of these sediments were 140 million years old. Such core samples gave valuable information about the water, the life it supports, Earth's age, how Earth formed, and the forces that still shape our planet today.

Among many other sophisticated instruments, the *Glomar Challenger* had satellite navigation systems that gave it accurate positioning via on-board computers. In the 1980s, the ship *JOIDES Resolution* took over the job of exploration and continues today. *JOIDES* stands for **J**oint **O**ceanographic **I**nstitutions for **D**eep **E**arth **S**ampling.

Mapping the Ocean Floor

Another tool used by ocean explorers is sonar, which comes from the words "**so**und **na**vigation **r**anging." Sonar devices use echoes to map the ocean floor. An echo is a sound wave bouncing, or reflecting, from a surface and returning to its source. In the activity on pages E40 and E41, the back-and-forth movement of the coils of the spring toy model the motion of a sound wave and its echo.

Modern sonar devices include a metal "fish" that is towed through the water by a ship. High-frequency sound pulses are sent out from the fish to scan the ocean floor. The returning echo pulses are picked up by a receiver on the fish and converted to electronic signals. These signals go to a computer on the ship, which prints out visual images of the ocean floor on paper.

A deep-sea animal-like protist brought up by the *Challenger* crew. ▼

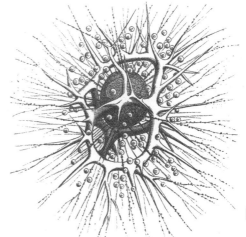

Submersibles, Bathyspheres, and Bathyscaphs

Ocean exploration also has been done by some very daring and brave individuals using a wide variety of specialized equipment. The legendary deep-sea divers with their bulky pressure suits, heavy metal helmets, flexible air hoses, and weighted shoes still exist, and are still in demand for specialized tasks. But much of what such divers once did can now be completed by submersibles.

In modern oceanography a submersible is any self-propelled underwater craft. Most are shaped like submarines, though they are usually smaller. They can carry researchers, but often they carry only robots and sampling equipment controlled by computers and cameras.

An older type of submersible is the bathysphere, such as the one used by Charles William Beebe to descend to 923 m (3,028 ft) in 1934. A bathysphere is usually a heavily reinforced, spherical capsule that is attached to a cable that lowers it into the ocean and brings it back to the surface. However, since the late 1950s, bathyspheres have been replaced by bathyscaphs, such as the *Trieste*. Unlike a bathysphere, a bathyscaph is a free-moving vehicle. It dives and surfaces like a submarine.

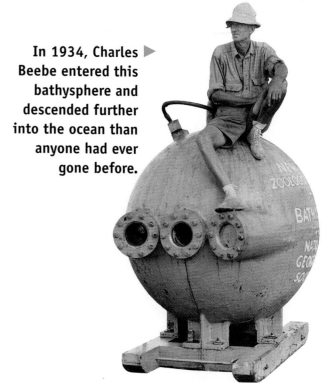

In 1934, Charles ▶ Beebe entered this bathysphere and descended further into the ocean than anyone had ever gone before.

Underwater Housing

Once humans began to explore the oceans, it was only a matter of time before someone began thinking about living there. In the 1960s *Conshelf I* was built by Jacques Cousteau and placed 10 m (33 ft) deep off the coast of France. *Conshelf I* housed two researchers for 7 days. *Conshelf II* housed five researchers for 30 days on the floor of the Red Sea at a depth of 11 m (36 ft). Within your lifetime, researchers and vacationers will probably have the opportunity to spend time on the ocean floor for research and recreation. ■

═══ INVESTIGATION 2 WRAP-UP ═══

REVIEW

1. Describe some methods that have been used to explore the ocean floor.

2. What can be learned from core samples of sediments from the ocean floor?

CRITICAL THINKING

3. What are some reasons that sonar might produce an inaccurate depth reading?

4. What is the likelihood of an underwater housing experiment on the deep ocean floor? Explain.

REFLECT & EVALUATE

Word Power

Write the term that best matches the definition. *Not all terms will be used*.

1. The shallowest part of the ocean floor
2. The longest mountain range in the world
3. Free-standing mountain on the ocean floor
4. The flat ocean bottom
5. Clifflike drop beyond the continental edge

a. abyssal plain
b. continental edge
c. continental rise
d. continental shelf
e. continental slope
f. mid-ocean ridge
g. seamount

Check What You Know

Write the term that best completes each sentence.

1. The (abyssal plain, mid-ocean ridge) is where the continental rise flattens out completely.
2. The shallow, sloping portion of land near the edge of a continent is the (continental rise, continental shelf).
3. The clifflike drop beyond the continental edge is called the (abyssal plain, continental slope).

Problem Solving

1. Sound travels through water at a speed of about 1,531 m/s. If a signal sent from a ship takes four seconds to return, how far away is the ocean floor?

2. Give examples of three substances found in ocean water or on the ocean floor. Why, do you think, are they not being reclaimed?

3. What advantage do bathyscaphs have over bathyspheres?

Imagine you are traveling around the world in a submarine that glides just above a section of the ocean floor like the one pictured in the drawing to the right. Write a short story about your journey that describes at least five features of the ocean floor and some of the organisms you see there.

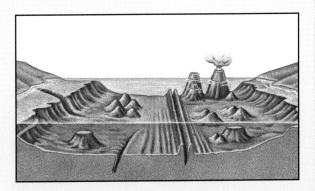

MOVING OCEAN WATER

The waters of the oceans are constantly in motion. You may have enjoyed watching waves breaking on a beach. While on a boat ride, you may have felt the rhythmic motion of the sea. Yet some waves are powerful enough to alter the course of ships at sea. What do we know about ocean water and how it moves?

PEOPLE USING SCIENCE

Seismologist   A *tsunami* (ts$\overline{oo}$ nä'mē) is an earthquake-generated wave that races across the ocean at 800 km/h (500 mph). As it travels, it can be thousands of feet deep and hundreds of miles long. A tsunami slowly builds in size as it approaches land, sometimes to a height of 27 m (90 ft) above sea level. When such a wave hits the shore, it can cause great destruction.

Hiroo Kanamori of Caltech in California is a seismologist (sīz mäl'ə jist), a scientist who deals with earthquakes. He seeks to understand how tsunamis are produced. He believes that mild, hardly noticeable undersea earthquakes slowly move the ocean floor. An enormous amount of water between the ocean floor and its surface is pushed up. Why do you think this would cause tsunami waves to develop on the ocean surface?

Coming Up

◀ Hiroo Kanamori in his lab at Caltech in California

WHAT CAUSES OCEAN CURRENTS?

Thrown overboard by a passenger on a ship, a message in a bottle floats in the ocean for ten years. Then, after being carried thousands of kilometers by ocean currents, it washes onto a lonely shore. How are ocean currents formed?

Activity

Current Trends

A moving stream of air is called wind. In this activity you'll find out how winds and surface currents are related.

Procedure

1. Fill a pan with water to within 2 cm of the top. Sprinkle pepper on the surface of the water.

2. Predict what will happen if you gently blow across the surface of the water through a straw. **Record** your prediction in your *Science Notebook*.

MATERIALS
- goggles
- rectangular pan
- water
- pepper
- straw
- *Science Notebook*

SAFETY //////
Wear goggles during this activity.

Step 1

3. **Test** your prediction by blowing across the water through a straw. In your *Science Notebook*, **sketch** and **record** your observations.

4. **Predict** what will happen if you blow harder across the surface of the water.

5. Repeat step 3, this time blowing harder.

Analyze and Conclude

1. What did you observe when you blew across the surface of the water?

2. How does a stronger "wind" affect the water?

3. Currents are rivers of water in oceans and other bodies of water. **Suggest a hypothesis** to explain the role wind plays in producing currents.

INVESTIGATE FURTHER!

RESEARCH

What is the Sargasso Sea, and how is it connected to ocean currents? Research and write a report of your findings. Be sure to include any interesting superstitions or tales you discover concerning the Sargasso Sea.

Step 3

Activity

Modeling Density Currents

Recall from Chapter 1 that differences in density cause ocean water to move. In this activity you'll make a model of one kind of density current.

MATERIALS
- bottom half of a plastic soda bottle
- water
- table salt
- teaspoon
- food coloring
- plastic cup
- plastic straw
- *Science Notebook*

SAFETY

Wipe up any spills immediately.

Procedure

1. Pour water into a bottle until it is about three-fourths full. Add half a spoonful of salt. Stir the mixture with a plastic straw.

Math Hint *To estimate a three-fourths line, round the height of the bottle to the nearest whole unit. Divide the height by 4, then multiply the quotient by 3.*

2. Half fill a cup with water. Add 4 teaspoons of salt and several drops of food coloring. Stir the mixture well.

3. **Predict** what will happen if you slowly and carefully pour the contents of the cup into the jar. **Test** your prediction.

4. Wait two minutes and **describe** what you observe.

5. **Predict** how the liquid will change in ten minutes. Let the jar of liquid sit for ten minutes. Then **describe** what you observe.

Analyze and Conclude

1. **Describe** what you observed in steps 4 and 5.

2. Which liquid was more dense? How do you know it was more dense?

3. In this activity you made a model of density currents that move water between the ocean's surface and its depths. Based on your observations, **hypothesize** what causes such currents.

Step 2

Step 3

World Currents

Reading Focus What causes ocean currents, and how do these currents influence weather?

The ocean is never still. It's restless and constantly moving, and it's a partner of the land and atmosphere in shaping Earth's surface. So how do we begin to talk about the restless oceans? Let's start with the great rivers of water that move through them. These rivers, called **currents**, move water through all parts of the ocean. Some currents, deep under the surface, move very slowly. Others, near the surface, move very quickly.

What Causes Currents?

The speed and direction of surface currents is determined by two factors—the wind and Earth's rotation. In the activity on pages E50 and E51, blowing on the water causes the surface of the water to move. The same thing happens in the ocean. When the wind blows, it pushes water in the direction it is blowing. Although these water movements are called surface currents, the wind affects water under the surface as well. A surface current often carries more water than the largest rivers and travels at speeds ranging from 10 to 160 km (6 to 100 mi) a day.

Since the wind produces surface currents, the direction of the wind affects the direction of ocean currents. Let's look more closely at Earth's planetary winds.

▲ Even from high above Earth's surface, the Gulf Stream shows up as a dark blue river flowing north off the eastern coast of Florida.

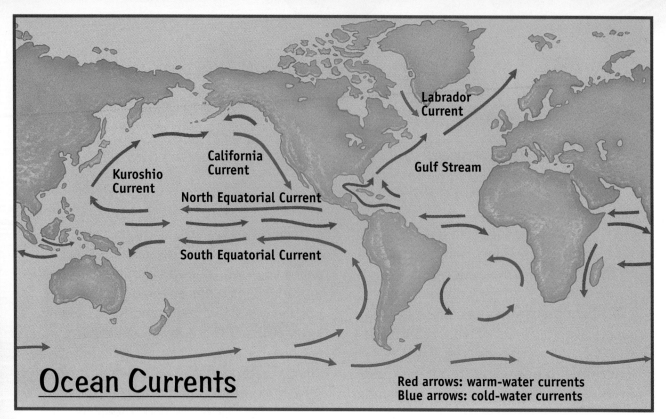

Ocean Currents

Labrador Current

California Current

Kuroshio Current

North Equatorial Current

South Equatorial Current

Gulf Stream

Red arrows: warm-water currents
Blue arrows: cold-water currents

Earth's planetary winds (*below*) are responsible for the movement of the surface currents in the oceans (*above*).

Examine the diagram of Earth's planetary wind belts. You'll notice that the winds tend to blow across the surface in curved paths rather than in straight lines. In the Northern Hemisphere, Earth's rotation causes the motion of the winds to curve and shift in a clockwise direction.

Earth's wind belts ▼

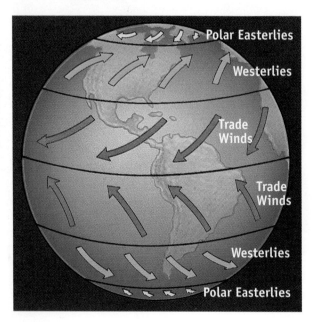

Polar Easterlies

Westerlies

Trade Winds

Trade Winds

Westerlies

Polar Easterlies

In the Southern Hemisphere, Earth's rotation causes the winds to follow counterclockwise paths. The curving motion caused by Earth's rotation is called the **Coriolis effect**. It was named for Gaspard de Coriolis, the French mathematician who explained it.

Some planetary winds, called **trade winds**, move from east to west toward the equator. As the trade winds move over the oceans, they push surface currents from east to west. Other winds, called the **westerlies**, blow from west to east, pushing surface currents along with them.

If you examine the two maps on this page, you will see that the surface ocean currents of the world, like the Gulf Stream and the Kuroshio Current, follow the same general patterns as the planetary wind belts. The prevailing winds push the water in about the same curving pattern as the wind.

On the maps, notice how the surface currents that begin in warm areas carry

warm water, whereas those that begin near the North and South Poles carry cold water. How do you think the temperature of ocean currents affect land areas near the coast?

How Currents Affect Us

Winds cause currents, and currents influence something that affects us each day—the weather. One current that affects weather in parts of North America and Europe is the Gulf Stream.

The Gulf Stream is one of the Atlantic Ocean's main warm-water surface currents. It moves 100 times more water than all of Earth's rivers combined! The Gulf Stream influences the weather on land by bringing warm water from the equator up the eastern coast of the United States. This water warms the air, producing milder weather conditions along coastal areas, particularly in winter. Then the Gulf Stream crosses the Atlantic and produces the same effects along Europe's western coast.

When the pattern of ocean currents changes, the weather on land can change, too. One country that is greatly affected by changes in ocean currents is India. Twice a year, India's coastal currents are affected when winds, called monsoons, change direction. When this happens, the amount of rainfall and the temperature on land also change. The people of India have come to expect this weather change and depend on it for growing their crops.

Large areas of the world are affected by changes in a surface current called El Niño (el nēn'yō). Trade winds blowing across the Pacific Ocean usually keep warm water away from the coasts of North and South America. When these winds weaken, the warm El Niño current reaches these coasts. This current changes position every two to seven years. When it changes position, it causes dramatic changes in the climate, ranging from drought in some areas to frequent storms in others. ■

Although they are at the same latitude, Ireland (*left*) and Newfoundland (*right*) have very different weather because of the Gulf Stream. Both of these pictures were taken at about the same time in winter.

How Deep Water Moves

Reading Focus What factors are involved in causing deep ocean currents?

Did you know that currents deep in the oceans often move in the opposite direction from surface currents? Deep currents also tend to move more slowly than surface currents, traveling from 91 m to 5 km (300 ft to 3 mi) a day. And deep currents are not formed in the same way as surface currents.

You have learned that surface currents are powered by the winds. For the most part, deep ocean currents are driven by differences in water density. Density refers to the mass of a substance compared to the amount of space it takes up. If you have two samples of water that take up the same amount of space, the sample with the greater mass is more dense. Just as dense air sinks in the atmosphere, dense water sinks in the oceans. It's this sinking of dense water that starts deep water currents moving. The density of ocean water depends on three things: salinity, temperature, and sediment content.

Pass the Salt

In Chapter 1 you found that different parts of the ocean contain different amounts of salt. The activity on page E52 illustrates that dissolving salt in water increases the density of the water. In fact, the more salt that is dissolved in a body of water, the more dense the water becomes.

▲ **At the Strait of Gibraltar, less-salty water from the Atlantic flows into the Mediterranean Sea above the saltier water that is flowing out into the Atlantic.**

For centuries, sailors and scientists watched water flow constantly into the Mediterranean Sea without increasing the water depth. They couldn't figure out where the extra water went. It wasn't until the late 1600s that a deep density current moving from the Mediterranean Sea into the Atlantic Ocean was discovered.

What causes this current? The hot, dry air above the Mediterranean Sea makes surface water evaporate. The surface water that remains becomes saltier. This dense, salty water sinks and flows into the Atlantic Ocean. The less salty water of the Atlantic flows into the Mediterranean Sea on the surface. The result is a surface current and a deep current that move in opposite directions.

Running Hot and Cold

If you poured cold water into a tub of warm water, what do you think would happen? Although some mixing occurs, the cold water would tend to sink below the warm water. That's because cold water is more dense than warm water.

Some deep currents begin in the icy-cold waters near the North and South Poles. Water near the poles is very dense, in part because it is so cold but also because it is very salty. When water freezes, as it does near the poles, most of the salt stays behind in the unfrozen water. This dense polar water sinks to the ocean floor and flows under warmer water toward the equator.

Two deep-ocean currents are shown in the diagram at the bottom of the page. Notice that dense, cold water sinks in both polar regions. Deep currents carry this cold water toward the equator. The area of contact between these two currents is indicated by a light-blue wavy boundary. Antarctic Bottom Water, which is the coldest water in the world, flows under the North Atlantic Deep Water for some distance before turning back toward the South Pole.

In equatorial regions, some of the water in these deep currents is warmed enough to rise slowly toward the surface. Then it begins to flow back toward the pole it came from. Because it is so cold and dense, some of the Antarctic Bottom Water remains near the ocean bottom. This water may circulate near the ocean floor for as long as a thousand years!

Here in the Antarctic, the coldest, densest water in the oceans sinks to the bottom and begins to flow north. ▼

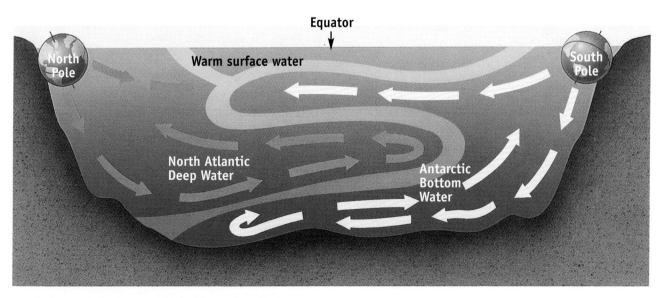

▲ **Deep-water currents in the Atlantic Ocean**

Nutrients such as zooplankton (*inset*) that are brought to the surface by upwelling currents are eaten by some of the world's largest organisms (*above*).

Water From the Depths

In some coastal areas, winds blow surface water away from the shore. This forces deep currents to flow up and replace the surface water. The rising of deep water to the surface is called **upwelling**.

In the ocean, minerals and detritus—bits of shells and dead organisms—constantly drift down to the ocean floor. An upwelling of cold water carries them back up to the surface where they provide phytoplankton and zooplankton with nourishment. The phytoplankton and zooplankton, in turn, nourish many other kinds of ocean life. This is why areas of upwelling often have abundant sea life.

Upwelling is constant in the Antarctic seas, where cooling surface water sinks and is replaced by warmer water from below. Here, upwelling supports a food chain that begins with phytoplankton, zooplankton, and krill. This food chain goes on to include hundreds of thousands of whales, tens of millions of seals, and hundreds of millions of birds.

Off the coasts of Chile and Peru, upwelling supports the fishing industries by bringing up food for fish. But when the warm El Niño current flows in this

UNIT PROJECT LINK

During a stay at the undersea lodge, one-day side trips in the deep-diving vehicle will be offered to visitors. With your group, refer to the world map of ocean currents on page E54. Plan a number of trips from the lodge. Take into account how deep-sea currents affect sea life, visibility, and the stability of the vehicle. Where will you go, and what will be seen? Make a map of the routes and explain your choices.

TechnologyLink For more help with your Unit Project, go to **www.eduplace.com**.

◄ **Since the ocean has been used as a dumping ground for wastes, it's important to know how currents are going to move those wastes.**

area, it prevents the normal upwelling of nutrients since upwelling cannot occur where there is warm surface water. The zooplankton have nothing to feed on, so they die. Once the zooplankton die, small fish have nothing to feed on. They leave the coast, and the fishing business is affected until El Niño shifts again.

Turbidity Currents

Have you ever dropped a pebble into a pond? If so, you know it sinks to the bottom. Pebbles, sand, and other sediments are denser than water. When sediment mixes with ocean water, it can sink to form a **turbidity current**.

Turbidity currents form when earth-quakes or flood waters flowing from rivers into the ocean send large amounts of sediment into the ocean. As the sediment slides down the continental slope toward the ocean floor, it forms an underwater avalanche that can travel up to 80 km/h (50 mph).

As a turbidity current moves, the swirling sediment erodes the ocean floor. According to some scientists, it's possible that turbidity currents actually were responsible for carving out the steep walls of underwater canyons found on the ocean bottom. Unlike other deep currents, turbidity currents are only temporary. After the turbidity current reaches the ocean floor, it slows down, and the sediment settles out.

Scientists study deep currents to learn how they affect surface currents, ocean life, and weather. Since the ocean floor is being considered as a dumping ground for wastes, the more scientists know about deep currents, the better they will be able to predict the possible movement and spread of those wastes. ■

INVESTIGATION 1 WRAP-UP

THINK IT WRITE IT

REVIEW

1. What role does wind play in creating currents?

2. Explain why it would take less time to sail from North America to Europe than from Europe to North America.

CRITICAL THINKING

3. How are surface currents and deep currents alike? How are they different?

4. How does Earth's rotation influence weather?

INVESTIGATION 2

WHAT CAUSES OCEAN WAVES?

You sit on a sandy beach and watch the waves crash against the shore. The next day, the surface of the water is calm, and waves gently lap your feet as you walk along the beach. Why does the force of the waves vary from day to day? How are ocean waves formed?

Activity

Making Waves

You saw in Investigation 1 how steadily blowing winds result in the world's ocean currents. Wind can cause another, more familiar movement of surface water.

Step 1

MATERIALS

- rectangular pan
- water
- cardboard
- metric ruler
- *Science Notebook*

Procedure

1. Fill a pan with water until the water reaches a level 2 cm from the top.

2. Hold a piece of cardboard at about a 45° angle to the water's surface. Blow gently down the side of the cardboard. **Record** your observations in your *Science Notebook*.

Math Hint *Remember, a 45° angle is one half of a 90° angle.*

3. **Predict** what would happen if you blew harder down the side of the cardboard. **Test** your prediction and **record** your observations.

4. **Predict** how the waves will be affected if you blow on the water for a longer period of time. **Test** your prediction and **record** your observations.

Analyze and Conclude

1. How were waves produced?

2. How did the waves vary in steps 2, 3, and 4? What caused the variation?

3. Based on your observations, **hypothesize** how the creation of waves differs from the creation of currents.

4. **Name** two factors that affect the size of ocean waves.

INVESTIGATE FURTHER!

EXPERIMENT

Predict how an island might affect the size of waves. Use a larger or smaller pan and add an "island." Then redo the activity and describe what happens.

Activity
Wave Motion

How do the particles of water move within a wave?

MATERIALS
- goggles
- spring toy
- string
- ribbon
- tape
- meterstick
- *Science Notebook*

SAFETY

Wear goggles during this activity.

Procedure

1. With a piece of string, tie one end of a spring toy to a doorknob.

2. Pull the spring so that it is as taut and parallel to the floor as possible. Have your partner tie a short piece of ribbon to one of the loops in the middle of the spring. Mark the position of the ribbon by placing tape on the floor beneath the ribbon. **Measure** the height of the ribbon knot above the floor.

 See **SCIENCE** and **MATH TOOLBOX** page H6 if you need to review *Using a Tape Measure or Ruler.*

3. Slowly shake the spring up and down to form a wave. Watch the movement of the ribbon as the wave moves along the spring. **Observe** how the ribbon moves relative to the tape. Form waves of different heights to confirm your observations. Each time, have a partner **measure** the height of the wave. **Record** these observations in your *Science Notebook* in a chart like the one below. **Sketch** what you observe.

Step 2

Wave Trial	Height	Observations
1		
2		
3		

Analyze and Conclude

1. How did the ribbon move with the wave?

2. **Infer** how the water particles in a wave move.

3. How did the height of the wave affect the movement of the ribbon?

What Are Waves?

Reading Focus How do the strength and duration of wind affect wave size?

If you've ever jumped into a pool or visited the ocean, you've seen the surface of the water move up and down. These up-and-down movements in the ocean are called **waves**.

Measuring Waves

The top of a wave is called the **crest**. A wave's height is the distance from the crest to the level ocean surface. The distance between two successive waves is the **wavelength**.

It is possible to measure how fast a wave is moving. A **period** is the time it takes for two successive wave crests to pass the same point. The periods for ocean waves range from 2 to 20 seconds. This means that the speeds of waves range from 11 to 113 km/h (7 to 70 mph). Most ocean waves travel at about 56 km/h (35 mph).

Movement of Waves

How do the water particles in a wave move? In the activity on page E62, a ribbon tied to a spring models one of these particles. The model shows that particles (the ribbon) do not move forward with a wave. Look at the particles represented by circles in the diagram. As the wave passes by, the particles roll in a somersault but end up back where they started. Water particles near the surface turn the biggest somersaults. The motion of the particles decreases as the depth increases.

What controls how big waves get? In the activity on pages E60 and E61 that models wind blowing on the ocean, the strongest winds create the biggest waves.

The harder the wind blows, the higher the waves become. A wind of 48 km/h (30 mph) can cause waves 4.5 m (15 ft) high. The highest wave ever measured

As a wave approaches shore, the wave falls over, or breaks. ▼

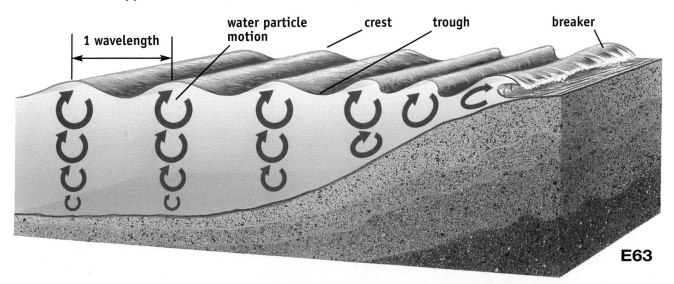

1 wavelength

water particle motion   crest   trough   breaker

was produced during a severe storm with winds of more than 88 km/h (55 mph). The wave reached 34 m (112 ft) high, as tall as a ten-story building.

The size of a wave also depends on how long the wind blows and how far it blows. The distance the wind blows over open water is called the **fetch**. The longer the wind blows and the greater the fetch, the bigger the waves become. When the wind blows hard, the crest of a wave can outrun the lower part of that wave. This makes the crest fall forward and break into foam, called a whitecap.

When waves travel from a windy part of the ocean to a calmer area, their crests may become lower and smoother. These waves, called swells, are far apart and can have a wavelength of as much as 1 km (0.6 mi). Swells can travel long distances,

▲ **Wind can generate huge storm waves.**

even passing from one ocean to another, since all oceans are connected.

Science in Literature

AN ENORMOUS WAVE

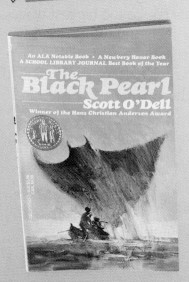

The Black Pearl
by Scott O'Dell
Dell Publishing, 1967

"At that moment a thunderous sound engulfed the canoe. It was as if the sky had fallen in upon us. Then mounds of water rose on both sides of us and met over our heads and filled the air with spray. There followed a groan, a rending of timbers, and the canoe rose crazily and tipped and I was pitching slowly sidewise into the sea."

Ramón Salazar's search for the Pearl of Heaven brings him face to face with the power of the ocean in *The Black Pearl* by Scott O'Dell. You will learn of the destructive power of water as well as about people who live off the bounty of the sea.

▲ Unless protected, homes near the shoreline are often in danger from storm-generated waves.

Waves and Land

Waves pick up and deposit sediment. Even gentle waves can combine with surface currents to move huge amounts of sand from place to place on beaches. During the winter, strong waves may wash away most of a beach's sand, leaving only gravel. The following summer, the waves slowly replace the sand.

During storms, waves can bring hundreds of tons of water crashing onto the shoreline, greatly eroding it. In France, storm waves once moved a 59,000-kg (65-T) concrete block 20 m (65 ft). Powerful waves have been known to toss rocks weighing 45 kg (100 lb).

Waves can be fun for surfing, for swimming, or just for watching. But because of all the energy they carry, they can also be very destructive. Later in this unit you'll find out how we have learned to harness the energy of waves. ■

Internet Field Trip

Visit **www.eduplace.com** to learn more about tsunamis.

INVESTIGATION 2 WRAP-UP

REVIEW

1. How are waves formed?

2. What causes waves to break?

CRITICAL THINKING

3. Would you expect larger waves to form from a wind with a fetch of 1 km or 3 km? Explain your answer.

4. Explain how the particles of water move within a wave.

WHAT CAUSES TIDES?

What never stops moving, is always going through a phase, is billions of years old, and yet becomes new again each month? If you know the answer to this riddle, then you know what causes the tides to rise and fall each day!

Activity

Making a Tide Model

What does the Moon's position have to do with the tides?

Moon

Procedure

1. **Label** one side of the larger of two cardboard circles with the numbers 1–4, as shown in the picture.

Steps 1 and 2

Math Hint *Use perpendicular diameters to divide the circle into 4 equal parts.*

2. Use the larger circle to model Earth and the smaller circle to model the Moon. Then place the model of Earth on a level surface, with number 1 facing right. Tie the ends of a piece of string together and position it so the string evenly circles Earth. The string represents the ocean water on Earth.

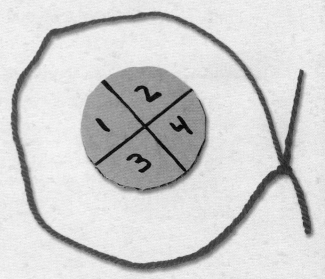

Step 3

3. Place the Moon outside the string 2–3 cm to the right of number 1. The Moon's gravity pulls on Earth's oceans, causing them to bulge outward on the side where the Moon is located and on the side away from the Moon. What results is that the oceans take on a different shape, shown in the picture. **Model** this by repositioning the string as shown.

4. On which two numbered sides of Earth is the ocean deepest (in other words, bulging out farthest)? **Record** your answer in your *Science Notebook*. These sides are experiencing high tide. The two sides of Earth where the ocean is shallowest are experiencing low tide.

5. Rotate the model of Earth counterclockwise until 1 moves to the position 3 used to be in. Be careful to keep Earth in the same location without disturbing the string. You have just **modeled** the passing of about 6 hours in Earth's rotation.

Analyze and Conclude

1. In step 3, what was the relationship between the Moon's position and the high tides?

2. **Describe** how the tide changed at position 1 on Earth in step 5.

3. **Predict** how many high tides position 1, starting from its current location, will experience after one complete rotation of Earth occurs. **Test** your prediction.

4. **Suggest a hypothesis** to explain how the Moon causes tides.

Technology
Link
CD-ROM

INVESTIGATE FURTHER!

Use the **Science Processor CD-ROM**, *Oceanography* (Investigation 3, The Tide's In) to identify the relationship between the positions of the Sun, Moon, and Earth and the height of the tides.

E67

During World War II, the timing of the tides determined the date and time of the D-Day invasion. On June 6, 1944, the Allied forces landed on the beaches at Normandy, France. The invasion was planned for the time of the lowest tide possible. Under such conditions, most of the beach would be exposed, thus making the landing safer.

The difference between the water levels at high tide and low tide is called the tidal range. In the open ocean, the tidal range is about 0.55 m (1.8 ft). Where the incoming tide has room to spread out, as in the Gulf of Mexico, the tidal range may be only a few centimeters. In some places, the incoming tide is forced into a small bay with steep sides. In such cases the water level may rise as much as 18 m (60 ft) during high tide. In addition, the tidal range at one place can change from one season to the next.

Century after century, the tides follow their own schedules, determined by the relative positions of the Moon, the Sun, and Earth. They are one of nature's tremendous forces, powerful enough to move entire oceans of water. ■

The tidal range at the Abbey of Mont-St.-Michel in France is particularly dramatic. Twice a day, the abbey becomes an island.

INVESTIGATION 3 WRAP-UP

REVIEW

1. Use a sketch to show how the Moon's gravity causes tides on Earth.

2. What causes extreme tides?

CRITICAL THINKING

3. How many low tides do most coastal areas experience during two days and two nights? Explain your answer.

4. What variables besides the Moon's gravity affect tides on Earth?

Coming Up

◀ Ready for market, these threadfin fish were raised and harvested at the Natural Energy Laboratory of Hawaii Authority (*below*).

WHAT RESOURCES CAN THE OCEANS PROVIDE?

There are many useful things that come from the sea. Did you know that ice cream and pudding contain a product that comes from plantlike organisms in the ocean? There are even farms floating on the sea that may provide some of your food. Find out about resources from the ocean in this investigation.

Activity

What You See From the Sea

Materials made from ocean resources are all around you. How many can you spot?

MATERIALS
- magazines
- newspapers
- scissors
- glue
- markers
- posterboard
- *Science Notebook*

Procedure

Look around the classroom. Do you see anything you use that comes from the sea? Can you think of anything else you use that comes from the sea? Look around the rest of the building and your home. In your *Science Notebook*, **make a list** of everything you find that comes from the sea. Be creative and make a poster to present your list.

Analyze and Conclude

1. How many items were you able to think of? How do the items on your list compare with the items other students listed?

2. Make an **inference** regarding the importance of the sea to your life, based on your observations.

Activity

Desalination

The ocean can be used as a freshwater resource. How difficult is it to remove salt from ocean water?

- - - - - - - - - - - - - - - - - -

MATERIALS

- goggles
- sample of ocean water
- glass bowl or beaker
- clear glass plate
- lamp
- *Science Notebook*

SAFETY ///////

Wear goggles during this activity. The lamp will get very hot. Avoid touching the bulb or the lampshade at all times.

Procedure

1. Pour a small amount of ocean water into a beaker. Cover the beaker with a clear glass plate.

2. Place the beaker under a lamp so that the beaker is just below the bulb. Turn on the lamp. Be careful not to touch the bulb or the lampshade. Leave the lamp on for 30 minutes.

Step 2

3. Turn the lamp off and allow the setup to cool for 15 minutes. In your *Science Notebook,* **record** any changes you observe in the setup.

Analyze and Conclude

1. What collected on the plate? **Infer** how the matter differs from the ocean water and how it got on the plate.

2. How do you think your setup differs from a large-scale method to produce fresh water from ocean water? Could you use your method to efficiently produce fresh water from sea water? Why or why not?

Activity
Obtaining Energy

What kinds of energy might the oceans provide?

MATERIALS
- posterboard
- markers
- construction paper
- cardboard
- wood splints
- glue
- tape
- scissors
- *Science Notebook*

SAFETY /////

Use care when handling scissors.

Procedure

1. Think of all the ways energy is produced. What raw materials are needed? What kinds of equipment are used to change the raw materials to usable forms of energy? In your *Science Notebook,* list as many forms of energy as you can.

2. Think about oceans and their resources. Hypothesize about what untapped forms of energy there might be in the ocean. Be creative when listing ideas for obtaining energy from the oceans.

3. Choose one energy-source idea and create a model or a poster about it. Use any materials available. Be prepared to present your model or poster to the class. Explain what you are using from the ocean and how you plan to convert it to energy that people can use.

Analyze and Conclude

1. Describe any problems you think your energy source may have that might keep it from being used. For example, is it practical for people living far inland as well as for people living near the ocean?

2. Which idea presented by your classmates do you think is the best idea? Explain your answer.

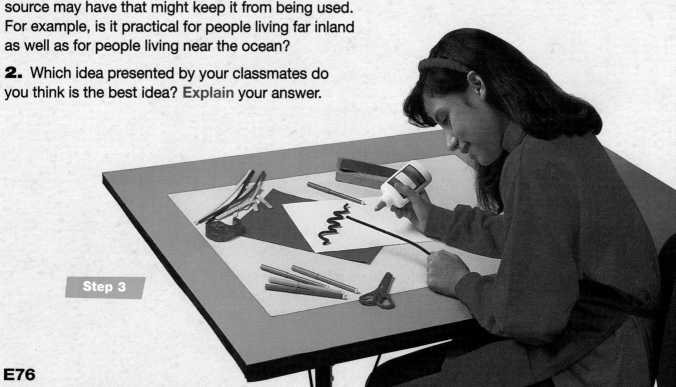

Step 3

Treasures From the Sea

Reading Focus What are some valuable resources that come from the sea?

With some practice, most people can learn to catch a fish. All you have to do is stand in the water, wait until a big one swims by, and scoop it up. That's how bears catch salmon in Alaska; it's also how early humans caught fish.

Food From the Sea

Today commercial fishing is much different from what it was in the past. If you were the captain of a modern fishing boat, you'd use sonar to find a school of fish, such as herring. The crew would spread huge nets in the water and then haul the whole school on board at once. Your ship could catch up to 36,400 kg (about 40 T) in one grab, enough to make fish dinners for 40,000 people! That school of herring has met its match!

What's the point? Well, seafood is probably the single most important resource we obtain from the ocean. In fact, more than half the protein eaten in Japan comes from the ocean.

Although some countries, such as the United States, may not depend on the ocean quite so heavily, the ocean is still an important source of food. What different kinds of seafood could you include on the list in the activity on page E74?

Modern fishing methods, including those that use sonar, have made us almost *too* good at fishing. Many species of sea life have been overfished, placing them in danger of becoming extinct. Today many fishing countries are reducing the amount of fish taken to protect this food resource before some species are gone.

▲ Humans are not alone in harvesting the treasures of the sea. We share what is available with a wide variety of plants and animals.

▲ Increasing demand for food worldwide has created a need for fish farming.

▲ Increasing need for fresh water will probably force us to rely on desalination plants.

In addition to reducing the rate at which some species are being depleted, scientists hope to find alternative methods of obtaining ocean resources for food. A method called **aquaculture** (ak'wə kul chər), or ocean farming, will help the world meet growing food needs without overfishing. Aquaculture involves raising animals and seaweed in closed-off areas of the oceans and other waters. Organisms being farmed include lobsters, salmon, kelp, oysters, and mussels.

"Water, water everywhere, nor any drop to drink."

As Earth's population continues to increase, the rate at which fresh water is being used also is increasing. That's why, with so many oceans surrounding us, getting fresh water from salt water seems like a reasonable goal.

Obtaining fresh water from salt water is called **desalination** (dē sal ə nā'shən). However, only a few nations currently operate desalination plants. In the activity on page E75, the method for removing salt from water is not very efficient. Large-scale operations are more efficient, but they are very expensive. Often the cost of the energy needed to desalinate the ocean water would make the fresh water too expensive.

There is another possible source of fresh water in the oceans. Less than 3 percent of Earth's water is fresh, and 77 percent of this fresh water is locked up in icecaps and glaciers. So it might make sense to attach cables to icebergs, tow them to where the water is needed, and pump the ice ashore as slush.

Using Math
What percent of all Earth's water is not locked up in icecaps and glaciers?

Common Chemicals From the Sea

In addition to water, what other chemicals do the oceans provide? About 30 percent of the world's salt supply comes directly from sea water. Giant factories along some coasts extract it by evaporating the ocean water.

More than 99 percent of the world's supply of bromine comes from the oceans. It's used in the manufacture of gasolines, dyes, medicines, and metals.

Even ocean food sources provide more than just food. For example, seaweed and kelp have been important foods in the Far East for hundreds of years. But seaweed provides other valuable products, too. Red seaweed yields agar, a product that dissolves in boiling water to make a clear gel. As a food additive, agar is used in canned meat, cake icing, candy, pet food, and any number of other foods. It's good for coating pills and for making cosmetics and is used in medical laboratories to grow bacteria, molds, and tissues.

Brown seaweed produces alginic acid, which is used as a thickener in ice cream, jellies, pie fillings, salad dressings, fabric dyes, shampoos, plastics, rubber, and certain kinds of paints.

Animals from the sea make many non-food contributions. Blowfish toxin is a perfect example. If eaten, it can kill in 30 minutes. Yet when used medically, it is an extremely powerful painkiller. Another substance, produced by sea cucumbers, reduces tumors and may someday be used to fight cancer. The inedible parts of fish, including bones, are ground up for use in fertilizers and livestock feed.

▲ Alginic acid, which is obtained from brown kelp (*inset*), is used in the manufacture of products such as those shown here.

Minerals and Fossil Fuels

Even the mud and ooze on the bottom of the oceans and seas are rich in resources. The floor of the Red Sea is covered with mud that contains tons of iron, zinc, copper, and silver, worth billions of dollars. Although these resources can't yet be mined because of the expense, scientists are researching ways to remove these materials cheaply.

When you ride in a car, you may be using another ocean resource. More than 20 percent of the world's oil and gas reserves are located under the ocean floor. From offshore oil rigs, workers drill down through sediment and rock to reach reserves of these fossil fuels. In addition to gasoline, chemicals taken from oil are used to make more than 3,000 products, including heating oil, plastics, detergents, and shampoos. ■

◀ Agar, which is obtained from red kelp (*inset*), is used in the manufacture of products such as those shown here.

Treasures Through Time

You may enjoy eating fish or even wearing jewelry made from shells. But did you know that people have been mining the oceans for thousands of years? Ocean resources have been considered valuable treasures for a very long time! Explore some of them in this time line.

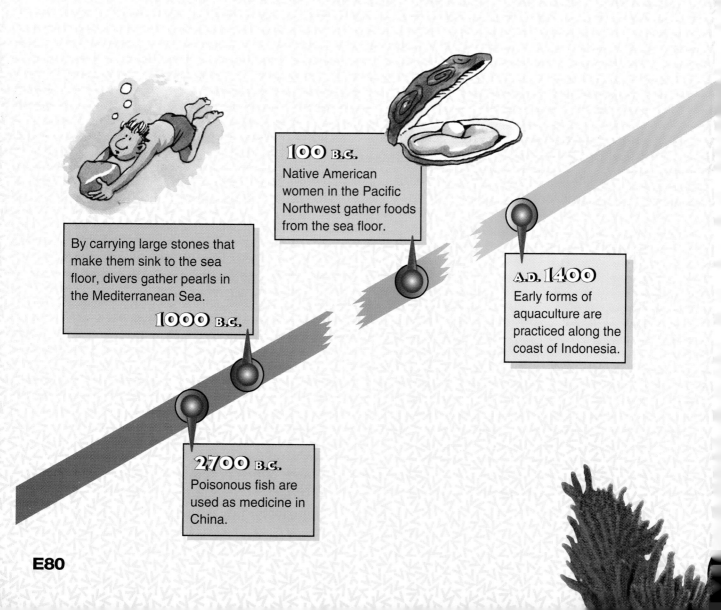

100 B.C.
Native American women in the Pacific Northwest gather foods from the sea floor.

By carrying large stones that make them sink to the sea floor, divers gather pearls in the Mediterranean Sea.
1000 B.C.

A.D. 1400
Early forms of aquaculture are practiced along the coast of Indonesia.

2700 B.C.
Poisonous fish are used as medicine in China.

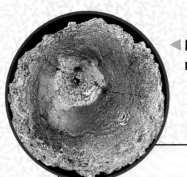

◄ **Manganese nodule**

An international ban on whaling, first enacted in 1985, is continued.
1993

BEYOND 2000

Manganese nodules are first discovered during the scientific voyage of the HMS *Challenger*.
1872–1876

1976
Salmon fishing off Greenland is banned in an attempt to protect ocean salmon feeding grounds.

1896
The world's first offshore oil well is dug off the coast of California, using wooden jetties that extend from the land.

1492
Christopher Columbus crosses the Atlantic Ocean.

UNIT PROJECT LINK

The oceans provide a great variety of food products. Research which life forms thrive near the site of your undersea lodge. Could some of these forms of life provide ocean farming products? Which ones? Why do you think so? Add pushpins and labels to your map to show possible areas for ocean farms. Also, diagram an idea you have for aquaculture technology.

TechnologyLink

For more help with your Unit Project, go to **www.eduplace.com**.

RESOURCE

Energy and the Sea

Reading Focus What are the obstacles to using the energy from the ocean as an alternative source of energy?

▲ Just standing in a breaking wave can give you an idea of the tremendous energy that waves contain.

For centuries, people have stood on the ocean shore, marveled at the majesty of the waves, and dreamed of using that raw power. But other energy sources were cheaper and easier to use. Over the last few decades, however, some people have started looking to the sea for new sources of energy.

Power From the Waves

The Sun, winds, and oceans all produce enormous amounts of energy. So how do we harness all of this power? Recall that waves form when ocean water receives energy from the wind.

SALTER'S DUCKS

1 **The ducks** ride the ocean surface, with the angled sides facing incoming waves. A rounded bottom dangles beneath the surface.

2 **Incoming waves** hit the hollow concrete ducks; the angled sides tilt up, absorb the wave's energy, and then drop back down. So much of the wave's energy is absorbed that calm water is left behind the ducks. The energy of the bobbing movement turns a shaft running through a line of ducks.

If you have ever been swimming in the ocean, you know about the energy and power of waves. Water in a breaking wave can knock you over! So it makes sense to conclude that there is usable energy in waves. Modern computers can calculate how much energy a moving section of ocean water should be able to provide.

The energy stored in 1 m (3 ft) of a typical wave in the Atlantic Ocean could provide about 70 kilowatts (kW) of power, enough to run 70 electric heaters. But several problems must be solved before that energy can be used.

First, obtaining energy from waves is 10 to 20 times more expensive than obtaining energy from other sources. Second, waves are rarely of a constant size for long periods of time, so their power is never constant. Additionally, even in calm areas of the ocean, storms can create waves capable of destroying even the strongest of energy-collection devices in just a few minutes or hours. Third, no one has yet thought of a way to store wave energy for later use.

Nevertheless, many ideas for harnessing wave energy are being tested. A promising one involves Salter's ducks, devices named after their inventor, Stephen Salter. Study the diagrams to see how these devices work.

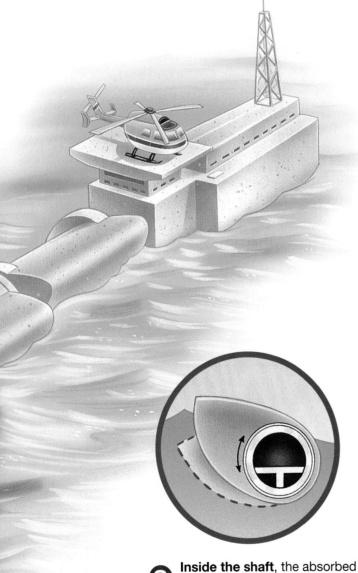

3 **Inside the shaft,** the absorbed energy moves oil through an engine, driving an electric generator. An 800-m (0.5-mi) string of ducks could supply energy for a city of 85,000 people.

OTEC

Other devices now being tested can take advantage of relatively small differences in ocean water temperatures. The method of using temperature differences to get energy from ocean water is called Ocean Thermal Energy Conversion, or OTEC.

In tropical areas the Sun may heat the ocean surface water to 27°C (81°F). But ocean water found at a depth of 610 m (2,000 ft) or more may be much colder. As shown in the drawing, the difference in temperature between the water at the ocean's surface and the deep water can be harnessed to power an engine that produces electricity.

Methane

As you have learned, the oceans are a major source of oil and natural gas. These fossil fuels are found in sediments and rocks below the ocean floor. But another kind of gas may be obtained from organisms living in ocean waters. This gas is called methane.

Methane is a colorless, odorless, burnable gas. Methane is produced from the decomposition of organic matter. Rotting seaweed (such as kelp) and other kinds of algae are especially good sources of methane gas, since these organisms are rich in hydrogen and carbon, the components of methane.

A Navy scientist, Howard Wilcox, has come up with a plan for growing kelp for use in making methane gas. He proposes that kelp be grown in open-ocean farms anchored on a series of plastic lines up to 31 m (102 ft) below the ocean surface. Wilcox believes that up to 50 percent of the energy in the kelp can be turned into methane fuel. An ocean farm with an area of about 400 km² (154 mi²) could provide enough methane gas to power a city of 500,000 people.

In the activity on page E76, a poster is made to illustrate an energy source from the ocean. What would you include in a poster of one of the energy sources that are discussed here?

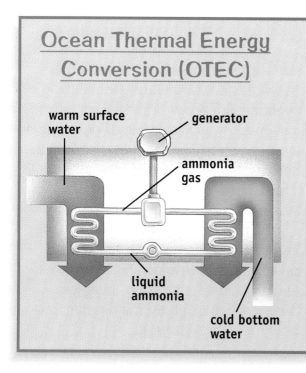

Ocean Thermal Energy Conversion (OTEC)

warm surface water

generator

ammonia gas

liquid ammonia

cold bottom water

1. The OTEC process is quite simple. Warm surface water is pumped through an evaporator. In the evaporator, liquid ammonia is heated by the surface water until it boils to form ammonia gas.

2. Ammonia gas travels through pipes to turn a generator that produces electricity.

3. The ammonia gas then passes through a condenser, where it is cooled and turned back into a liquid by the colder deep-ocean water. The liquid then returns to its starting point, and the cycle starts over.

▲ As you can see in these pictures, the power of water cannot be overestimated. How can tidal energy be harnessed?

Tidal Energy

An ancient myth tells of a king who thought he had grown so powerful he could command the seas. So he went to the ocean's edge, told the tide to stop moving . . . and drowned.

Unlike the king, modern scientists know they can't control the tides. But they have made astonishing progress toward finding ways to use tidal energy. If there is at least a 4.6-m (15-ft) difference between low and high tide, scientists think that the ebb and flow can be harnessed to produce usable energy.

The best-known use of tidal energy is a power plant built at the mouth of the Rance (räns) River in France. Known as the Rance Tidal Power Station, the plant consists of 24 separate tunnels, each

facing the sea and built into a dam stretching 702 m (2,303 ft) across the river. As the tide moves upriver, the tidal water flows through the tunnels and builds up behind the dam. At peak high tide the water is released and flows back to the sea, turning turbines connected to massive generators.

The Rance Power Station can generate up to 608 million kilowatt-hours (kWh) of electrical energy a year. However, the plant didn't pay its way at first and was almost shut down. Then in the 1970s, rising energy prices made its production costs seem more reasonable. ■

Internet Field Trip

Visit **www.eduplace.com** to learn more about ocean resources.

INVESTIGATION 1 WRAP-UP

REVIEW

1. Name six resources that come from the oceans.

2. What are the obstacles to using the energy from the ocean as an alternative source of energy?

CRITICAL THINKING

3. Would tidal energy be a good source of energy for the town you live in? Why or why not?

4. How does polluting and overfishing affect the cost of fish at the market?

E85

HOW DOES POLLUTION AFFECT THE OCEANS AND THEIR RESOURCES?

INVESTIGATION 2

You now know that the oceans are a very large and very valuable resource. Now consider that pollution is damaging large parts of that resource. Explore the effects of ocean pollution in this investigation.

Activity

Investigating Oil Spills

What problems do oil spills create? To find out, observe how oil affects water and a feather.

Procedure

1. Work with a partner. Half fill one container with water.

2. **Predict** what will happen if you place a small drop of oil in the water. **Record** your prediction in your *Science Notebook*.

3. **Test your prediction.** Using a spoon, place a small drop of oil in the water. How does the oil behave? **Record** what you observe.

MATERIALS

- goggles
- 3 small clear plastic containers
- water
- vegetable oil
- spoon
- lids for containers
- feather
- hand lens
- paper towels
- *Science Notebook*

SAFETY

Wear goggles. Clean up spills immediately.

Step 1

4. Place several more drops of oil in the water. Put the lid on the container, then carefully shake the container so that the water moves around. How do the oil and water interact? **Record** your observations. Save this container for the activity on page E88.

5. Use a hand lens to examine a feather. **Record** your observations.

6. Fill another container with water. Soak the feather in the water for one minute. Remove it and blot it dry with a paper towel. Repeat step 5, using this feather.

7. Fill another container with oil to a depth of 1 cm. Soak the feather in the oil for one minute. Remove it and blot it dry with a paper towel. Repeat step 5, using this feather.

8. Dispose of the oil and water as directed by your teacher. Do not pour the oil and water down the drain.

Analyze and Conclude

1. From your observations, **infer** why it might be important to begin cleaning up an oil spill as soon as possible. What problems might a delay create?

2. What effect might an oil spill have on coastal birds?

3. Based upon your observations, **infer** why it is important to properly dispose of the oil used in this and the next activity. Why shouldn't you just pour it down the drain?

INVESTIGATE FURTHER!

EXPERIMENT

Predict the effect an oil spill might have on bird eggs in nests along the coast. Then test your prediction by soaking a hard-boiled egg in oil for 20 minutes. Remove the egg and blot it dry with a paper towel. Peel the egg and record your observations. Do not eat the egg.

Activity

Cleaning Up the Mess

You've seen some of the problems oil spills create. What is the best way to clean up an oil spill?

MATERIALS

- container of oil and water from previous activity
- spoon
- vegetable oil
- drinking straw
- plastic container
- paper towels
- cotton balls
- fabric scraps
- any other absorbant materials
- *Science Notebook*

SAFETY

Clean up spills immediately.

Procedure

1. Use the container of oil and water from step 4 of the previous activity as your model oil spill. Add a few more drops of oil to the water.

2. **Hypothesize** as to a method you might use to clean up the oil. **Record** your hypothesis in your *Science Notebook*.

3. **Experiment** to test your cleanup method. Begin by describing the procedure in detail. Then use any of the materials available to test your method.

4. As you test your method, place any oil or oily materials in the empty container. **Record** in a chart how effective your method was.

> See **SCIENCE** and **MATH TOOLBOX** page H11 if you need to review **Making a Chart to Organize Data.**

5. Repeat steps 2 and 3 two more times, using either different materials or procedures. If needed, add more oil to the water.

Analyze and Conclude

1. **Describe** how difficult it was to clean up the oil spill.

2. Which method worked best? Why?

3. **Infer** how difficult it might be to use your method or one similar to it to clean up an oil spill in the ocean.

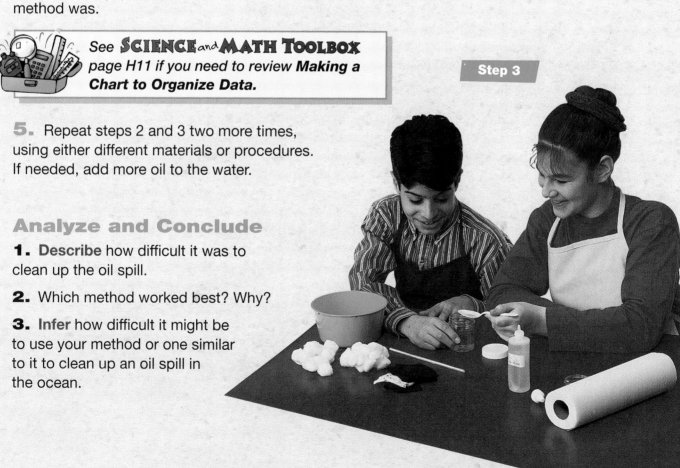

Step 3

Pollution of the Oceans

Reading Focus What are some sources of ocean pollution?

▲ This water may look pure, but the chances are very good that this water is polluted to some extent.

Pollution is the contamination of the environment with waste. When you realize that the water in practically every lake, river, and stream in the world eventually reaches the sea, it's not hard to figure out how our oceans become polluted.

For thousands of years, wastes, both liquid and solid, have been dumped into bodies of water. Even waste materials thought to have been safely buried have found their way into underground streams and eventually to the oceans.

Since the nineteenth century, when people began mass-producing most goods, wastes from manufacturing have been dumped into the oceans in larger and larger amounts. As a result, the

Scenes like this provide vivid evidence of the harmful effects of careless disposal of waste materials. ▼

oceans and the life forms that depend on the oceans have been disturbed in very serious ways.

The Chain of Ocean Life

The oceans contain important ecosystems in which all organisms and the wastes of some varieties of life are used by other organisms. At the beginning of the ocean food chain are microscopic organisms called phytoplankton. They float in the ocean and use sunlight to produce oxygen, absorbing carbon dioxide from the ocean water and the water itself in the process. Microscopic animal-like organisms, called zooplankton, eat the phytoplankton and then are eaten in turn by small fish and some whales. The small fish are consumed by larger fish, which may then be consumed by even larger

fish, seals, dolphins, some whales, birds, and humans.

Pollutants taken in by some ocean organisms can be passed to others through the ocean's food chains. Thus the harmful effects of pollution spread through ocean ecosystems, and may eventually move to terrestrial, or land, ecosystems.

Pollution Sources

There are many different sources and kinds of ocean pollution. Ordinary people are responsible for pollution. Think about the different materials you throw away every day. And all towns and cities produce sewage, both treated and raw. Few, if any, major industries in the world are entirely nonpolluting—almost all generate waste. Even farmers contribute dangerous

Science in Literature

PLASTIC TOY FOOLS WHALE

"Plastic containers, packaging, and a wide variety of toys float to remote areas on the ocean currents. Turtles and whales die from eating floating plastic that looks like jellyfish."

Read *The Illustrated World of Oceans* by Susan Wells to find out how people around the world are taking action to reduce ocean pollution and preserve ocean animals that are in danger. What actions can you take to help reduce ocean pollution?

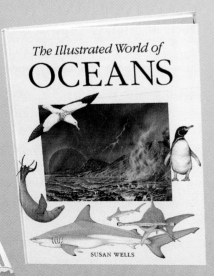

The Illustrated World of **OCEANS**
— SUSAN WELLS

The Illustrated World of Oceans
by Susan Wells
Simon & Schuster Books for Young Readers, 1991

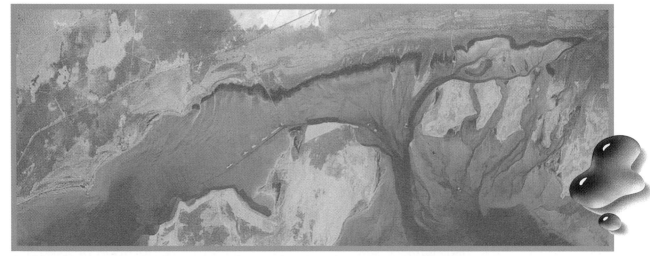

▲ This photo, taken in the spring of 1991 by shuttle astronauts 256 km (138 mi) above the Strait of Hormuz, dramatically shows the extent of oil spilled during the Gulf War. The light sheen on the water is oil that has been dumped into the Strait.

chemicals in the form of pesticides and fertilizers that eventually make their way into the oceans by way of streams and rivers. Pesticides are chemicals used by farmers to kill insects. These substances can be very harmful to marine organisms.

The element mercury is a highly toxic pollutant. Toxic pollutants are poisonous chemicals that can cause serious illness or even death. In the 1950s, mercury was dumped from a factory into the ocean near the fishing village of Minamata, Japan. Contaminated fish that were caught and eaten by people of the village caused brain damage, physical deformities, and birth defects.

Ocean Oil Spills

Seemingly worst of all—but only because they are so much more visible than most forms of pollution—are the

▲ Not all pollution is this obvious. Sometimes, pollution is dissolved in the water and is impossible to see.

gigantic ocean spills of oil. The oil spill modeled in the activity on page E86 illustrates how oil spills can affect oceans.

Between 1967 and 1989, the fifteen largest oil spills in the world spewed more than 14 million barrels of oil into the oceans. Most of the oil came from huge tankers rupturing on rocks or reefs. The best known occurred in 1989, when the *Exxon Valdez*, in a navigational error, ripped itself open on a reef in a huge, unspoiled bay in Alaska. Thousands of birds, fish, whales, sea otters, and dolphins died almost immediately by swallowing the oil. Others died slow deaths caused by respiratory distress or contamination of their fur or feathers.

Reducing Pollution!

Thankfully, many of the antipollution laws passed since the 1960s have had good results. Many industries have become extremely careful about adding pollution to the oceans after realizing how serious the problem was.

Today, many areas along ocean shores once badly polluted are free of waste contamination. The pollution problem is not hopeless, though at times the outlook may seem bad. As many people have noted, the only good way to deal with ocean pollution is to make sure it never happens. ■

Much of the pollution resulting from the *Exxon Valdez* accident has been cleaned up through the efforts of volunteers.

INVESTIGATION 2 WRAP-UP

THINK IT WRITE IT

REVIEW

1. Name three kinds of pollution that affect the oceans.

2. Discuss some of the ways that oil can harm ocean organisms.

CRITICAL THINKING

3. How do you think the growth in the human population will affect the ocean? Give specific examples.

4. Describe why you do or do not think ocean pollution threatens the quality of all life on Earth.

REFLECT & EVALUATE

Word Power

Write the letter of the term that best matches the definition.

a. aquaculture
b. desalination
c. pollution

1. Obtaining fresh water from salty ocean water is called ___.

2. The raising of crops or animals in ocean water is called ___.

3. The addition of harmful materials to the environment is called ___.

Check What You Know

Write the term that best completes each sentence.

1. Salter's ducks convert energy of (waves, tides) into useful energy.

2. (Aquaculture, Desalination) will help the world meet growing food needs.

3. International bans protecting (whales, blowfish) help prevent them from becoming extinct.

4. In the past century, industrial processes have been a major source of ocean (pollution, desalination).

Problem Solving

1. If you were trapped on a desert island, how might you use a variety of ocean resources in order to survive?

2. How might toxic ocean pollution and overfishing have a similar effect on ocean life?

3. Compare and contrast the way we use ocean resources today with the way people in the past used ocean resources.

BUILD YOUR PORTFOLIO

The photograph to the right shows one event involving pollution that might affect ocean life. Describe how this might even affect the entire food chain. Draw a diagram if you wish.

Using READING SKILLS

Compare and Contrast

Making comparisons when you read is a good way to understand new ideas. As you read, compare each new idea to an old, familiar idea.

Read the passages and complete the exercise that follows.

Look for these signal words to help you compare and contrast.

- To show similar things: *like, the same as*

- To show different things: *different from, instead*

Sea Life

Plankton includes organisms that float on or near the surface and drift with the ocean currents. There are two types of plankton, phytoplankton and zooplankton, but there are billions and billions of individual organisms. Although most phytoplankton are too small to see without a microscope, these tiny organisms produce 80 percent of the oxygen on our planet. . . .

Zooplankton include the larval form of certain types of ocean creatures. When they mature, the adult organisms will no longer be considered plankton. Instead, they will be lobsters, sea cucumbers, jellyfish, corals, or other organisms that belong to either the nekton group or the benthos group.

The second main group of organisms, nekton consists of all creatures that swim. It includes invertebrates such as squids and octopuses, all kinds of fish, and mammals such as whales and porpoises. . . . Nekton can live at any depth, from near the ocean surface to the ocean floor.

The third group of ocean organisms, the benthos, consists of plants and animals that live on the ocean floor and do not swim. . . . Most members of the benthos group live in shallow water, where food is plentiful and the water is warm. Shellfish, such as clams, oysters, mussels, and scallops, are members of the benthos group.

Make a chart like the one shown to compare and contrast the plankton, nekton, and benthos groups.

Plankton	Nekton	Benthos

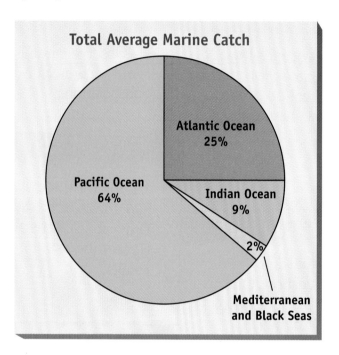

Use the data in the table to complete these exercises.

1. What is the sum of the percents displayed by the graph?

2. What percent of the catch is from the Indian Ocean?

3. Suppose the total marine catch was 2,000 tons. How many tons would be caught in the Atlantic Ocean?

4. If marine catch from the Pacific Ocean was 4,000 tons, how many tons would the *total* marine catch be?

5. Suppose the percents displayed by the graph were changed to fractions. Which fractions could be used to approximate 25%, 64%, and 9%?

6. How can you check that the fractions you chose in Exercise 5 are reasonable to represent the percents displayed by the graph? Explain.

7. Write a question about the marine catch that cannot be answered by the data shown on the graph.

WRAP-UP!

On your own, use scientific methods to investigate a question about the world's oceans.

THINK LIKE A SCIENTIST

Ask a Question

Pose a question about oceans that you would like to investigate. For example, ask, "What effect do ocean waves of different heights have on beach erosion?"

Make a Hypothesis

Suggest a hypothesis that is a possible answer to the question. One hypothesis is that the higher the wave, the greater is the amount of beach erosion.

Plan and Do a Test

Plan a controlled experiment to find the relationship between wave height and amount of beach erosion. You could start with a large pan, sand, water, and a tool for making waves. Develop a procedure that uses these materials to test the hypothesis. With permission, carry out your experiment. Follow the safety guidelines on pages S14–S15.

Record and Analyze

Observe carefully and record your data accurately. Make repeated observations.

Draw Conclusions

Look for evidence to support the hypothesis or to show that it is false. Draw conclusions about the hypothesis. Repeat the experiment to verify the results.

WRITING IN SCIENCE
Persuasive Essay

Write a persuasive essay that argues against dumping pollutants in the ocean. Use these guidelines.

- Describe the importance of ocean resources.

- Identify ways that pollution harms ocean resources.

- Suggest alternative ways for disposing of pollutants.

Present your essay orally to a group of classmates. Invite suggestions for making your argument more persuasive.

Forces and Motion

Theme: Scale

THINK LIKE A SCIENTIST

THINK LIKE A SCIENTIST

FOLLOWING "BIG BIRD"

As you look at the photograph on these pages, you might think that the birds in the picture are chasing the strange-looking aircraft. In fact, the birds are following it. The pilot of the bird-shaped, ultralight airplane is Joseph Duff. He is part of a unique program called Operation Migration. The goal of the program is to teach large endangered water birds, such as whooping cranes, to migrate. The airplane and the birds rely on the design of their wings and on air resistance to remain aloft. They use air resistance to work against gravity, a force that acts to pull them toward Earth's surface.

THINK LIKE A SCIENTIST

Questioning In this unit you'll study the relationship between the motion of an object and the forces that act on the object. You'll investigate questions such as these.

- How Do Forces Affect Motion?
- How Do Heavy Things Fly?

Observing, Testing, Hypothesizing In the Activity "Making a Paper Glider," you'll make and test paper gliders to find out how design affects the ability to fly.

Researching In the Resource "Forces in Fluids," you'll learn how to determine if an object will float in water without actually placing the object in water.

Drawing Conclusions After you've completed your investigations, you'll draw conclusions about what you've learned—and get new ideas.

CHAPTER 1

MOVING ON

People today are fascinated with how fast things can go. We give trophies and money to the owners of the fastest cars and swiftest horses. Bicyclists compete for prizes. Quick-footed athletes are in demand. What does it take to make an object go really fast?

PEOPLE USING SCIENCE

Automotive Engineer   As the eldest of ten children of migrant workers, Tiajuana James learned the value of hard work at an early age. Perhaps more important, she learned that education was the key to improving her life. As a student at Florida A & M University, her interests in math and science led her to a career in engineering.

Today, Tiajuana James is a project engineer for General Motors Powertrain Division. Part of her responsibility is to design, validate, and implement components for automatic transmissions. The transmission of an automobile transfers energy from the engine to the wheels, making it possible for the automobile to move. In this chapter, you will learn about motion and measuring those changes.

Coming Up

◀ Tiajuana James working on a design for a transmission component.

F5

INVESTIGATION ①

HOW DO YOU DESCRIBE MOTION?

The terms *up, down, backward, forward, right,* and *left* all describe directions in which an object can move. In this investigation you'll find out that you may also need to measure in order to describe the motion of an object.

Activity

The Ant Maze

In this activity you'll see how distance and direction are needed to describe the motion of an object.

MATERIALS
• 1 sheet of graph paper
• 2 colored pencils, in different colors
• metric ruler
• *Science Notebook*

Procedure

1. **Draw** an ant inside the bottom left-hand square of a sheet of graph paper. **Label** the top of the grid *North*, the bottom *South*, the right side *East*, and the left side *West*.

2. Using a colored pencil, plot a path for the ant to follow square to square—up, down, across, diagonally—and finally off the paper. The path should include three turns.

3. With a metric ruler, **measure** the length of the path in each direction.

 See **SCIENCE** and **MATH TOOLBOX** page H6 if you need to review **Using a Tape Measure or Ruler.**

Step 2

F6

4. In your *Science Notebook,* write a description of the ant's path. Indicate the distance and compass direction for each part of the path.

5. Exchange descriptions with your partner. Do not look at his or her graph paper.

6. Using a different-colored pencil, **draw** the path of your partner's ant on your sheet of graph paper.

Step 6

Analyze and Conclude

1. **Compare** your drawings with those of your partner. How well did the drawings match?

2. If the drawings did not match, **hypothesize** what you think went wrong.

3. What two factors did you have to include to describe the path of the ant?

4. Decide whether it is easier to interpret descriptions or to write them. When reading or writing descriptions, which are you more likely to make mistakes with—compass directions or distances?

INVESTIGATE FURTHER!

EXPERIMENT

Using compass directions and distance measurements in meters, write a description for going to a specific place in your school or on the playground. Give a classmate a starting place and your description and have your classmate try to find the place.

From Feet to Fathoms

Reading Focus What are some advantages of the metric system of measurement over the English system?

"Why, when I was your age, I had to walk to school. It was three miles, up-hill each way, through snow 30 inches deep!"

Have you ever heard something like this from an older relative who was teasing you about how easy you have it today? If you have, you've probably wanted to respond with a statement to prove that you don't have it quite that easy after all. Well, next time, say this: "That's nothing! When I walk to school, I have to walk 4.8 kilometers, uphill each way, through snow 76.2 centimeters deep!" Should your teasing relative be impressed by these large numbers—and by your efforts?

How far do you live from your school? If you had to give someone directions to your school, what information would you have to provide? Just as in the ant maze activity on pages F6 and F7, your directions to your school should include distances and compass directions.

The compass directions you would use —N, E, W, and S—would be the same as anyone else's. But the distances might be very different, depending upon how far you live from the school and what system of measurement you use. Students who

live near their schools could possibly answer this question in feet or yards. Students who live farther away might answer the question in miles. A science teacher might use a different unit of measurement—the meter or the kilometer—to express the distance from home to school. How would you answer the question about distance from school?

Units of Measurement

People use many kinds of units to make measurements of distance: inches, feet, yards, miles, millimeters, centimeters, meters, and kilometers, to name a few. The unit of measurement that a person chooses depends on what is being measured. It makes sense to measure the length of a pencil in centimeters or in inches but not in kilometers or in miles. On the other hand, you would probably use kilometers or miles rather than centimeters or inches to describe the distance from New York City to Los Angeles, or from your home to school.

If you were talking about distances from Earth to the other planets in our solar system, you could use kilometers or miles. However, most astronomers

measure these distances in astronomical units (AU). An **astronomical unit** is equal to the average distance from Earth to the Sun, or about 150 million km (93 million mi).

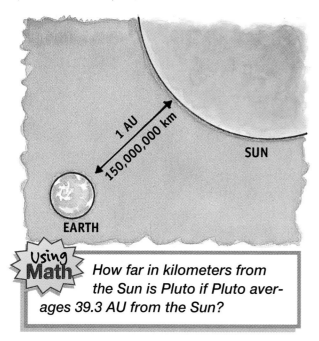

Using Math: *How far in kilometers from the Sun is Pluto if Pluto averages 39.3 AU from the Sun?*

What would you do if you didn't have a system by which to measure distance? Imagine that you and a classmate are stranded on an island. After several days you both become bored, so you decide to map the island. You have food, water, shelter, a small notebook, two pencils, a compass, and matches. But you have no ruler, no tape measure, not even a meterstick! How are you going to map something without being able to measure distances? After some thought, you and your fellow castaway decide to use the length of your stride as your standard unit for measuring distance. Now that you can measure distance, what else do you need to know to map your movements on the island? Where can you get that information?

Inventing Measuring Units

Just as a system of measurement had to be invented by the castaways on the imaginary island, all existing systems of measurement were invented out of need. The English system of measurement is used by most people in the United States. Miles, yards, feet, inches, pounds, gallons, and pints are all examples of English units.

Many units used in the English system originated at a time when there was no consistent system of measurement. In trying to develop a system of measurement that would be convenient, people invented units based upon body parts. For example, one early English measurement—the *yard*—was equal to the distance from the tip of the nose to the tip of the extended forefinger. What do you think happened if people had arms of different lengths?

▲ **One yard (Old English measurement)**

Another unit is the fathom, which is often used to describe the depth of water. The fathom is about 6 feet. The term *fathom* comes from the Old English word *faethm,* meaning "two arms outstretched to embrace." Therefore, a fathom came to mean the distance from the tip of a person's left forefinger to the tip of the right forefinger when the person's arms are fully extended to the sides.

▲ One fathom (Old English measurement)

How many different values for a fathom can you find among your classmates?

Now back to the island. You have just about finished mapping it when you and your partner discover that you are not alone. There are two more people on the island, and they too have been mapping it. But when you compare your distances with those of the other people, you find differences. How can you make your two systems of measurement agree?

The Metric System

Throughout history, many different systems of measurement have been developed. Until the late eighteenth century, systems of measurement were very confusing.

Every nation—and sometimes every town or village—had its own unique system of measurement. If you moved from France to England, you had to learn a whole new system of measurement.

Science in Literature

FROM LIFTOFF TO LANDING

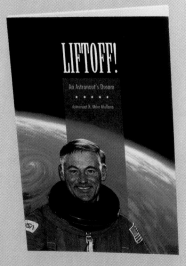

**Liftoff!
An Astronaut's Dream**
by R. Mike Mullane
Silver Burdett Press, 1995

"'Seven . . . six . . . main engine start.' The three liquid-fueled engines ignite, and there is a deafening noise in the cockpit. A growling, wrenching vibration shakes us. I have to force myself to keep watching the instruments. It's like trying to read a book on a theme park ride. The noise and vibration and the thrill and fear make it impossible to concentrate."

In *Liftoff! An Astronaut's Dream*, astronaut R. Mike Mullane provides a vivid description of a mission in the space shuttle *Atlantis*, from the nerve-wracking wait for liftoff to the thrill of touchdown.

In addition, a unit of measurement did not always mean the same thing to everyone within the same country.

Metric and English measures of the Statue of Liberty ▼

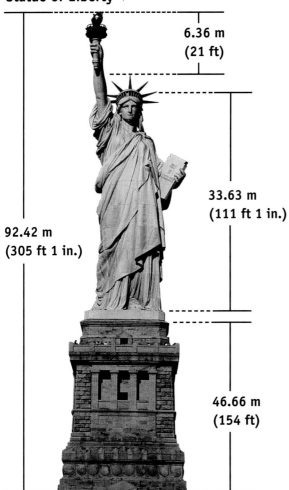

6.36 m
(21 ft)

33.63 m
(111 ft 1 in.)

92.42 m
(305 ft 1 in.)

46.66 m
(154 ft)

To solve this problem, in the 1790s the French National Assembly ordered the development of a new system of measurement, which has come to be known as the **metric system**. This system is based on the number 10 and multiples of 10. The units of measurement in the metric system include the meter, kilometer, centimeter, liter, gram, and kilogram. These units are based on standards that don't vary. So, regardless of whether you are in France, Mexico, or Japan, if you are given directions to go south for 2 km, you can be sure that you know exactly how far to move. ■

Metric Units	
Measurement	**Unit**
Length and distance	meter
Mass	kilogram
Volume	liter

Metric Conversions for Length	
1,000 m	1 km
100 cm	1 m
10 mm	1 cm

INVESTIGATION 1 WRAP-UP

REVIEW

1. What two factors would you include in a description of the route you take from your home to school?

2. How does having a set of standards make a system of measurement more reliable?

CRITICAL THINKING

3. Would you measure the length of a pencil in meters or centimeters? Explain.

4. Since one complete turn of a compass needle describes a circle, how many degrees of direction are shown on a compass?

How Do You Measure Speed?

In addition to compass direction and distance, motion is also described by how fast an object is moving. Suppose a car's speed is 55 miles per hour. What two measurements are needed to describe the speed?

Activity

Speeding Marbles

How fast can you roll a marble? Your answer must include two measurements. Find out how to measure a marble's speed.

Procedure

1. In a gym or hallway of your school, use a metric tape measure to identify a distance of 25 m from a wall. With chalk, mark a line at that point on the floor.

2. Kneel 2 m behind the chalk line. While your partner holds a stopwatch, roll a marble at the wall. When the marble crosses the

MATERIALS

- metric tape measure
- chalk
- stopwatch
- 3 marbles
- pencil
- *Science Notebook*

SAFETY

Be sure to pick up all the marbles to prevent falls.

Step 2

chalk line, your partner should start the stopwatch. When the marble hits the wall, your partner should stop timing. In your *Science Notebook*, record your time in a chart similar to the one below.

Trial Number	Distance of Roll	Elapsed Time	Speed (Distance/Time)
1	25 m		
2	25 m		

3. Roll a second marble, then a third marble, trying to roll each one at about the same speed.

4. Predict how elapsed time will vary as the speed of the marbles is changed. **Record** your prediction. Then repeat steps 2 and 3, this time trying to roll each of the three marbles at a consistently *slower* speed than in the first three trials.

5. Repeat steps 2 and 3, this time trying to roll each of the three marbles at a consistently *faster* speed.

6. For each of the trials, **calculate** the speed by dividing the distance the marble had to roll (25 m) by the time it took for the marble to hit the wall. **Record** the speed for each trial in meters per second (m/s).

 See **SCIENCE** and **MATH TOOLBOX** page H10 if you need to review *Using an Equation or a Formula.*

Analyze and Conclude

1. Which trial had the fastest speed? Which trial had the slowest speed? What was the average speed of all the trials?

2. How would the speed be affected if the distance were decreased, but the time remained the same?

3. How would the speed be affected if the time were increased, but the distance remained the same?

4. What two factors, or measurements, are used to express an object's speed?

INVESTIGATE FURTHER!

RESEARCH

Which ride at an amusement park is the fastest? Contact an amusement park or theme park and ask for fact sheets on the most popular rides. Report the top speed of each ride.

Bicycle Cyclometers

Reading Focus How does a cyclometer measure distance traveled on a bicycle?

How far did you go on your last bicycle trip? How fast did you go? A bicycle cyclometer can give you this information. A cyclometer is a small device that is attached to a bicycle's handlebars. A wire connects the cyclometer to a sensor on your bike frame. A tiny magnet fits on the spoke of a wheel.

CYCLOMETER The cyclometer multiplies the number of times the wheel goes around by the distance around the outside of the wheel (the wheel's circumference). The result is the distance that you have traveled. (Each time the wheel goes around, your bike moves forward a distance equal to one circumference of the wheel.)

CABLE The cable transmits the electric impulses from the sensor to the cyclometer.

SENSOR The sensor counts the number of times the magnet goes around on the wheel as you ride.

MAGNET Each time the magnet passes the sensor, the magnetic field around the magnet induces a small current in the sensor.

Some cyclometers keep track of the total distance you have ridden on your bicycle as well as the distance you have ridden on a particular trip. Cyclometers also keep track of total riding time. To compute average speed, the cyclometer divides distance traveled by total riding time.

F14

What Is Speed?

Reading Focus What defines speed, and how is it measured?

Using Math — *Traveling at 1,183 km/h, this car went faster than the speed of sound. At that speed, how many meters did the car travel each second?*

The expression "Faster than a speeding bullet" does not only apply to Superman. It can also be used to describe the amazing speeds reached by today's fastest racing cars.

Racing Speed

One of the first automobile races took place in 1909 between Count Gaston de Chasseloup-Laubat of France and Camille Jenatzy of Belgium. Jenatzy was clocked at 105.26 km/h (65.79 mph) in that contest. Less than ten years after that first automobile race, a speed of 165.69 km/h (103.56 mph) was recorded by Louis Rigolly of France.

In almost every year since that time, speed records have been broken on speedways around the world. Cars racing in the Indianapolis 500 each year have no trouble exceeding speeds of 352 km/h (220 mph). Drag racers attain even faster speeds on tracks that have no curves. In fact, Jenatzy's 1909 winning speed is close to the legal speed limit on many interstate highways today.

Just how fast do you have to travel to be the fastest? As of 1990, the fastest official time recorded for a land vehicle was 1,183.466 km/h (739.666 mph). That record was set by Stan Barrett in a jet-powered car driven at Edwards Air Force Base in California. Barrett's car, which looked like a rocket on wheels, was designed and shaped so that it had very low wind resistance.

Comparing Speeds

8 km/h	32 km/h		104 km/h	112 km/h		192 km/h

Edwards Air Force Base was selected for the record-breaking attempt because the land is so flat and smooth. There, the speed a car reaches depends entirely on the car and not on any uphill or downhill slope of the land. For similar reasons, another popular site for attempts at breaking the land speed record is the Bonneville Salt Flats in Utah. Like Edwards Air Force Base, the Bonneville Salt Flats are level and smooth, making it possible for jet-powered cars to reach the highest attainable speeds.

Defining Speed

What is speed, and how is it measured? The activity on pages F12 and F13 shows what factors are used to determine speed. **Speed** is defined as the distance traveled in a given amount of time. If you are able to walk 4.8 km (3 mi) in an hour, you are moving at a speed of 4.8 km/h (3 mph). Suppose you continue to walk for another two hours. In the second hour you walk 3.2 km (2 mi), but by the third hour you're really getting tired and you walk only 1.6 km (1 mi). What is your average speed for the three-hour walk? See if you can figure your average speed, using the table and formula in the next column.

Hour	Distance Walked (km)
1	4.8
2	3.2
3	1.6

$$\text{Average Speed} = \frac{\text{Total Distance}}{\text{Total Time}}$$

$$\text{Average Speed} = \frac{d \text{ (distance)}}{t \text{ (time)}}$$

What was your average speed for the three-hour walk? Obviously, you attained a relatively low average speed for your three-hour effort. However, the formula that you used to calculate your speed would be the same regardless of how fast you were going.

So how fast is fast? A fast human might reach a maximum speed of about 32 km/h (20 mph) running. When swimming, the best a human can attain is about 8 km/h (5 mph). By comparison, a running cheetah can attain a speed of 112 km/h (70 mph), and a sailfish can reach speeds of 104 km/h (65 mph)!

Some speeds are actually too fast to visualize. If you enjoy playing with numbers, try figuring out how far a jet, a

320 km/h	360 km/h	4,800+ km/h	28,800+ km/h

space shuttle, and light travel in just a minute or just a second. How long does it take for each of the entries in the drawing across the top of these pages to travel a distance of one kilometer?

Think about riding in a vehicle moving faster than the speed of sound. People who have traveled at these tremendous speeds describe feeling as if a great weight were pressing down on them as they sped up and then slowed down.

Rapid acceleration can place great stress on the human body. As you accelerate, forces on your body may compress your chest, making breathing difficult. Your arms and legs will feel very heavy, and you will have difficulty lifting your head off the back of your seat. Your heart will have difficulty pumping enough blood to your head, and you may feel as if you're going to black out.

Moving at such high speeds can be extremely exciting, but it also can be quite uncomfortable. People such as race-car drivers, jet pilots, and astronauts must be in very good physical condition to handle these speeds. In fact, jet pilots and astronauts wear special suits that help them counteract the forces experienced when flying at such tremendous speeds. ■

Internet Field Trip

Visit **www.eduplace.com** to learn more about designing and testing race cars.

INVESTIGATION 2 WRAP-UP

REVIEW

1. If you want to measure the speed of a car, what two factors do you need to know?

2. If an airplane flies 500 miles in $2\frac{1}{2}$ hours, what is its average speed?

CRITICAL THINKING

3. Why do you have to know the circumference of your bicycle's wheel in order to set a cyclometer?

4. How can the average speed of an object be used to determine an unmeasured distance?

HOW DO YOU DESCRIBE CHANGES IN MOTION?

You're leaving for vacation, and you're riding in the back seat of the car. You can't see the dashboard dials or the steering wheel, but you certainly know when your motion changes. In this investigation you'll find out how to describe those changes.

Activity
Swinging Speeds

In this activity you'll observe and then try to describe changes in the motion of swinging washers.

Procedure

1. Place two chairs or ring stands about 30 cm apart and tie a piece of string between them. The string should be pulled tight between the two chairs or ring stands, as shown.

2. Take a second piece of string. Tie one end of it around a washer. Tie the other end to the string that is connecting the chair legs or ring stands.

MATERIALS
- goggles
- 2 chairs or 2 ring stands
- metric ruler
- string (about 75 cm long)
- metal washer
- scissors
- *Science Notebook*

SAFETY //////
Wear goggles for this activity. Do not swing the washer violently.

Step 2

F18

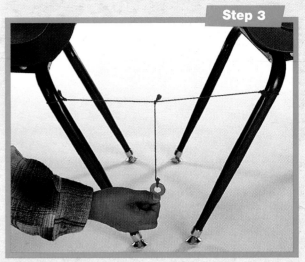

3. **Predict** how the speed of the washer will change as it swings back and forth. Pull the washer back as shown and release it. Notice how its speed changes as it swings.

4. In your *Science Notebook*, **draw** the washer swinging. Label the place where the washer has the greatest speed. Then label the place where the washer is traveling the slowest.

Analyze and Conclude

1. At what point in its swing is the washer gaining speed? Why, do you think, is the washer gaining speed?

2. At what point in its swing is the washer losing speed? Why, do you think, is the washer losing speed?

3. At what point in its swing is the washer changing its direction of motion? How do you know it is changing its direction of motion?

4. *Accelerate* means "to change speed or direction." As the washer swings, when is it accelerating? Explain your answer.

UNIT PROJECT LINK

For this Unit Project you'll build a miniature amusement park for marbles. The first thing you should do is draw a Marble Park map. Leave room for all the rides, games, and restaurants that a big theme park has. Transfer your drawing to large sheets of heavy posterboard.

Now design and build some ways to move your marbles around the park. Include a train that circles the park. Design a chair lift, using tiny drink cups, string, and straws. Each chair should be able to carry at least one marble across the park. Design walkways that lead from one ride to another.

Technology Link

For more help with your Unit Project, go to **www.eduplace.com**.

Activity
Twin Pendulums

What changes in motion would you observe if you were to hang two pendulums from the same horizontal string and swing one of them?

MATERIALS
- same as those for "Swinging Speeds" activity
- additional 30 cm of string
- additional washer
- *Science Notebook*

SAFETY /////
Wear goggles throughout the procedure. Do not swing the washer violently.

Procedure

1. Make two pendulums of exactly the same length—about 15 cm each.

2. Attach both pendulums to a horizontal string so that they are about 5 cm apart.

3. Start one pendulum swinging while holding the other still in its down postion.

4. **Predict** what would happen to the still pendulum if you released it. Stop the moving pendulum. Pull back one pendulum and release it. **Record** what happens to the second pendulum in your *Science Notebook*.

5. Repeat this experiment twice. **Observe** carefully and **record** your observations.

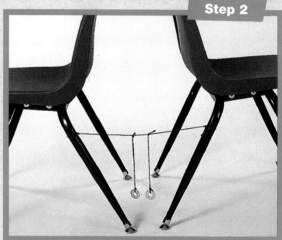

Step 2

Analyze and Conclude

1. How was the second pendulum affected by the swing of the first?

2. Describe how the speed of both pendulums changed. In which pendulum did the speed increase? In which pendulum did it decrease?

3. How can the motion of one pendulum affect the other if the pendulums never touch each other?

4. Did both pendulums accelerate? Explain your answer.

Step 3

Acceleration

Reading Focus What are some different ways a moving object can accelerate?

Go Faster!

At the top of the hill, you look down the steep slope to the bottom. Your stomach tightens just a little as the sense of impending thrill builds inside you. Then you push off. Skimming over the thin film of water, you speed through twists and turns, going faster and faster until you splash down into the pool at the bottom of the hill. Whether it's the thrill of a water slide, a roller-coaster ride, or a ski run, the increase in speed that you experience can be exciting!

Scientists use the term **velocity** to describe speed and direction. Thus, a measurement of your velocity down the water slide would include both your speed and your direction.

Scientists use the term **acceleration** to describe the rate at which velocity changes. But acceleration varies according to the circumstances. On a steep water slide, your speed will increase quickly; you will accelerate rapidly. On a water slide with a gentler slope, your speed will not increase as quickly. Therefore, your acceleration will be less. And even when your speed is constant, you are accelerating if you are changing direction. In the activity on page F20, the pendulums accelerate every time they slow down, speed up, or change direction.

Examples of Acceleration

The acceleration you experience when sliding down a hill is only one example of acceleration. Your muscles accelerate your body when you run, skate, or even walk. A baseball pitcher uses muscles to accelerate a ball toward home plate.

Chemical reactions can also cause objects to accelerate. When a space shuttle's engines fire, fuel begins to burn and hot gases are produced. These gases push against the walls of the engines, causing the shuttle to move. It moves slowly at first, and then gains speed steadily. This acceleration is caused by the chemical changes taking place in the fuel as it burns.

Units of Acceleration

Suppose you are riding a bicycle at a speed of 10 km/h (6.25 mph). As you gradually increase your speed, one minute later you are riding at 15 km/h (9.38 mph). How fast did you accelerate? To figure out your rate of acceleration, you must first answer two questions.

- How much did your speed increase?
- How long did it take for your speed to increase?

Your rate of acceleration is equal to your change in speed divided by the time it took you to accelerate.

$$a = \frac{s_2 - s_1}{t}$$

In this example your increase in speed was 5 km/h (15 km/h − 10 km/h). It took one minute to make that increase. Your rate of acceleration, then, was

$$a = \frac{(15 \text{ km/h} - 10 \text{ km/h})}{1 \text{ min}}$$

$$a = 5 \text{ km/h/min}$$

▲ In the first few moments after liftoff, the shuttle is accelerating to speeds that will place it in orbit around Earth.

The units of acceleration can seem confusing. But the units simply describe how speed is changing with time. In the example given, the speed in kilometers per hour is changing each minute. In this case you would read the answer as "5 kilometers per hour per minute."

Deceleration

Objects in motion usually slow down because of gravity or friction. For example, your speed on the water slide is reduced quickly once your body encounters the friction of the water in the pool. This decrease in speed is sometimes called **deceleration**. But since any change in speed or direction is defined as an acceleration, deceleration is just a type of acceleration.

Many things can cause an object to decelerate. In a car, for example, brakes are applied to cause the car to decelerate. Gravity also can cause deceleration. A ball thrown upward begins to decelerate because of both gravity and friction of the air. Of course, on the way down, gravity causes the ball to accelerate. ∎

▲ When a diver hits the water, he or she decelerates rapidly because the water is much more dense than the air.

INVESTIGATE FURTHER!

RESEARCH

From the earliest days of the space program, acceleration related to launch and reentry has been known to produce incredible stress on the human body. Find out what astronauts experience during launch and reentry, and report on how they are related to acceleration.

Stopping Power

Reading Focus What is the role of friction in making brakes work?

▲ **An early attempt at developing brakes**

Humans have long understood something very basic about moving heavy objects—that is, it's just not easy to push or pull a heavy object over the ground. And if you happen to be pushing or pulling that object up a hill, the job becomes almost impossible.

At some point in prehistory, someone discovered a way to make the job of moving heavy objects much easier. Perhaps this discovery was accidental, or perhaps it was the result of careful consideration. No one will ever know. But at some point, humans discovered that when a narrow log was placed beneath a heavy object, the log rolled and the object was easier to move. The wheel had been invented!

The wheel is the most commonly used device for reducing friction and increasing the speed of an object. Unfortunately, heavy objects rolling on wheels are not always easy to stop once they start moving, so brakes had to be invented to slow and stop wheels once they started turning. Brakes are used to decelerate cars, bicycles, trains, and most other objects that have wheels.

How Brakes Work

Many kinds of brakes exist, but almost all brakes work on the same principle. Some stationary object is brought into contact with a rotating wheel. Friction between the stationary object and the rotating wheel causes the wheel to slow down and come to a stop.

Most cars today have disc brakes. A car with disc brakes has a large metal disc attached to each wheel. As a wheel

turns, so does the metal disc attached to it. Suspended above the disc is a metal housing that holds the rest of the brake system. This part of the system contains the brake fluid, a set of pistons, and the brake shoes.

When a driver wants to stop a car, he or she depresses the brake pedal. This action increases pressure on the brake fluid. That pressure forces the pistons to push the brake shoes against the sides of the rotating discs. Brake linings, or pads, on the face of the brake shoes rub against the discs and slow their rotation. As the discs slow down, so do the wheels to which they are attached.

When a driver pushes forcefully on the brake pedal during a panic stop, normal brakes clamp down hard on the discs. The possible result is "locked" brakes and a dangerous, uncontrollable skid. To prevent this, engineers designed an anti-lock braking system. If a car has this kind of braking system, when the driver pushes forcefully on the brake pedal a computer controls the amount of pressure exerted by the brake pads on the rotating discs. The computer causes the brake pads to pulse rapidly on and off. This pulsing action keeps the brakes from locking and enables the driver to bring the car to a safe stop.

Braking Distance

Brakes do not stop a car immediately. From the instant that the brakes are

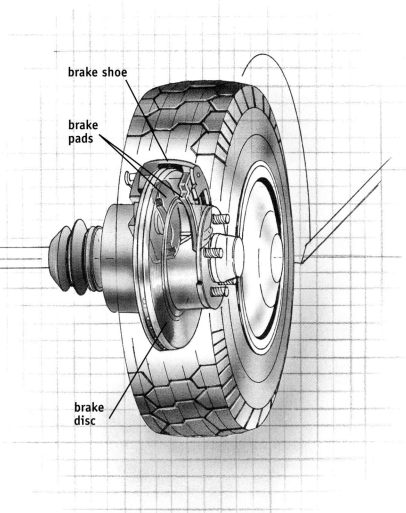

▲ On most automobiles built today, disc brakes are installed at least on the front wheels. They provide an efficient system for stopping a car.

applied, the vehicle will travel some distance. The distance needed to bring a moving object to a complete stop is called the braking distance.

Braking distance and stopping distance are not the same. Stopping distance depends on several factors in addition to braking distance.

- the reaction time of the driver
- the condition of the road surface
- the kind of tire
- the speed of the car

▲ As speed increases, so does braking distance.

Reaction time is the time that elapses between the moment the driver realizes that the brakes must be applied and the moment when the brakes are actually applied. What do you estimate would be your own reaction time for an emergency stop if you were driving a car?

The most important factor in determining actual braking distance is speed at which a vehicle is traveling. The table shows the braking distance for an average-sized car traveling at different speeds. If you were to construct a graph for these figures, what would the graph show about the relationship between car speed and braking distance?

Suppose the average car is 5 m long. How many car lengths should a driver stay behind the car in front of him or her when traveling at 30 km/h? at 60 km/h? at 90 km/h? ■

Car Speed (km/h)	Braking Distance (m)
30	8
45	18
60	32
75	50
90	72

─────── **INVESTIGATION 3 WRAP-UP** ───────

REVIEW

1. When is an object accelerating?

2. You observe a ball bouncing down a long staircase. In what ways is the ball accelerating?

CRITICAL THINKING

3. Use the terms *velocity* and *accelerate* to describe the motion of a race car moving on an oval track.

4. How is it possible for gravity to cause both acceleration and deceleration of an object?

F26

REFLECT & EVALUATE

Word Power

Write the letter of the term that best completes each sentence. *Not all terms will be used.*

a. acceleration
b. astronomical unit
c. deceleration
d. metric system
e. speed
f. velocity

1. A system of measurement based on the number 10 and multiples of 10 is called the ___.
2. The speed and direction of an object describe the object's ___.
3. When you coast down a hill on a bicycle, you experience ___.
4. Dividing the distance traveled by the time spent in traveling will give you the average ___.
5. A decrease in speed is sometimes called ___.

Check What You Know

Write the term in each pair that best completes each sentence.

1. In the metric system, length can be measured in (meters, grams).
2. Automobile brakes depend on (gravity, friction) to work.
3. *Velocity* is a term used to describe speed and (time, direction).
4. One factor that affects braking distance is (time of day, velocity).

Problem Solving

1. Draw a floor plan of your school. Then write a description to show how to go from your classroom to the cafeteria. Be sure to include distances and compass directions.

2. You have just received a radio-operated model car as a gift, and you want to know how fast it will go. What steps would you take to find out?

What unit of measure is the person in the picture finding? Have several classmates do this activity and record the results. Use the results to explain why such measurements make poor standards for a measurement system.

CHAPTER 2

GETTING A GRIP ON GRAVITY

It certainly seems that what goes up, must come down—birds, planes, and all manner of balloons. Even a basketball player on a slam dunk can't stay in the air forever. What do you know about the force that brings you back down to the ground?

PEOPLE USING SCIENCE

Aerobatic Pilot Do you like gymnastics? Perhaps you are good at somersaults, back flips, and dramatic dismounts. Imagine what it would be like to do moves similar to these with an airplane!

Patty Wagstaff, an aerobatic pilot, flies her Extra 260 aircraft through breathtaking maneuvers. In 1991, Wagstaff became the first woman to win the United States National Aerobatic Championship.

In 1993, Patty Wagstaff watched as her famous airplane became part of the National Air and Space Museum in Washington, D.C. This was a tribute, both to the airplane and its history-making pilot. What do you think Wagstaff had to know about forces that act on an aircraft in order to do her dramatic flying?

Coming Up

◀ Patty Wagstaff and the Extra 260

How Can the Force of Gravity Be Measured?

You've had the experience many times. An object slips from your hand. Wouldn't you be amazed if it floated to the ceiling? But it doesn't. It falls toward the ground. Gravity wins again. In this investigation you'll find out how to describe and measure the force of gravity.

Activity

Measuring Gravity's Pull

How strong is the force that holds you to Earth's surface? Is the force of gravity the same on all objects? Take some measurements and find out.

Procedure

1. Hold each object, one at a time, in your hand. Which object feels heaviest?

2. Place the object that you think is heaviest on the balance and determine its mass in kilograms. In your *Science Notebook*, **record** the balance reading under *Mass* in a chart similar to the one on the next page.

 See **SCIENCE** and **MATH TOOLBOX** page H9 if you need to review **Using a Balance.**

3. Repeat this procedure with each object.

Step 1

F30

4. Now place the object you think is heaviest in a mesh bag and hang the mesh bag from a spring scale. **Record** the scale reading under *Force of Gravity*.

See **SCIENCE** *and* **MATH TOOLBOX** *page H15 if you need to review* **Using a Spring Scale.**

5. Repeat this procedure with each object.

6. **Calculate** the ratio of the force of gravity acting on each object to the mass of that object by dividing the force of gravity by the mass. **Record** this information in your chart.

Name of Object	Mass (kg)	Force of Gravity (newtons)	Ratio = Force of Gravity/Mass

Analyze and Conclude

1. Is there a pattern in the relationship of an object's mass to the force of gravity acting upon it? Explain. What do the numbers in the right-hand column represent?

2. **Convert** your own weight to kilograms (1 kg = 2.2 lb). **Calculate** the force of gravity on your body. **Record** this information in your table.

INVESTIGATE FURTHER!

EXPERIMENT

Invent a scale. Use rubber bands, rulers, hooks, and any other equipment you think is necessary. Use the same mesh bag and objects you worked with in this activity. Wearing goggles, experiment to get readings similar to those obtained with the spring scale.

Weighing In

Reading Focus How can the mass of an object stay the same while its weight changes?

Want to lose weight? Walk to the top of the nearest mountain. Want to gain weight? Walk to the bottom of the nearest valley. Does this sound crazy to you? It probably does, but it works. To understand how this method of weight loss or weight gain works, you have to understand what scientists mean when they use the terms *weight* and *mass*.

Mass

The term *mass* describes the amount of "stuff" in an object. That "stuff," of course, is matter. **Matter** is anything that has mass and takes up space.

Suppose you have a pile of 400 gold coins. The mass of the pile is the amount of gold in the pile. In the metric system, mass is usually measured in grams (g) or kilograms (kg). Using a balance, you determine that each coin in your pile has a mass of 0.25 kg. The total mass of the gold is 100 kg. When you place the pile of gold on a scale at sea level, you find that it weighs 980 newtons. A newton (N) is a unit in the metric system that is used to measure weight. You will learn more about the newton later in this unit.

For some reason, you feel that your pile of gold has too much mass. So you decide to move the pile to the top of a mountain. You've heard somewhere that things weigh less on a mountaintop than they do at sea level. You reason that if something weighs less, it must have less mass. Makes sense, right?

You put all the coins in a wagon and haul them to the top of a mountain. Once there, you check the mass of the gold. You place one coin on a balance. Its mass is still 0.25 kg. You count the coins—400. You still have 100 kg of gold! Its mass didn't change.

Then you stop and think about mass. **Mass** is the amount of matter—in this case, gold—in the pile of coins. No matter was lost coming up the mountain. So no mass was lost. In fact, the gold would have the same mass no matter where you moved it, even if you took it to the Moon or to the bottom of the ocean!

Weight

Apparently you hauled all that gold up the mountain for nothing. Or did you?

Amazingly, someone has left a scale on the mountaintop. So you haul the pile of coins over to the scale and weigh it. The scale reads slightly less than 980 N. Perhaps a few of the coins dropped off the cart. You count the coins. You still have 400 coins. What's going on here?

With the balance you found the *mass* of the gold—how much matter it contains. With the scale you found the *weight* of the gold. **Weight** is a measure of the force of gravity on an object—in this case, the gold. In science, a **force** is a push or a pull. **Gravity** is the attractive force exerted by a body or an object on all other bodies or objects.

The strength of an object's gravitational (grav i tā′shən əl) force depends on the object's mass. Very massive bodies, such as Earth, act on nearby objects almost as a magnet acts on a piece of iron. For example, when you throw a ball into the air, gravity pulls the ball back to Earth. Any object near Earth's surface will be pulled toward the surface by Earth's gravitational force. It is this force that keeps all of us from flying off Earth's surface into space.

The weight of your pile of gold, then, is a measure of Earth's gravitational pull on it. The most common units for measuring weight are the pound (lb) in the English system and the newton in the metric system. But what about the "missing" weight of the gold on the mountaintop?

The Effect of Volume

The "missing" gold wasn't missing at all. The confusion was caused by a common misunderstanding. People often use the terms *mass* and *weight* interchangeably, but they mean quite different things. Think about the following situation.

Suppose that as you were struggling to move your pile of gold to the mountaintop, a friend walked by carrying a large, bulging sack. The sack was at least as big as your pile of gold, but your friend carried it easily. You wonder if you're that much weaker than your friend. A couple of hours later, you reached the top of the mountain to find your friend taking a nap, using the sack as a pillow. The sack was filled with goose feathers!

Although your friend's sack of goose feathers and your pile of gold are about the same size, the mass of your gold is obviously much greater than the mass of the feathers. To make sure, you put the sack of feathers on a balance and find its mass to be 1 kg. The mass of your gold is 100 times that of the feathers. Next you weigh the feathers and find that they weigh slightly less than 9.8 N.

After you and your friend return to the base of the mountain, you find that the

Science in Literature

Eyewitness Science: Force and Motion
by Peter Lafferty
Dorling Kindersley, 1992

A Long-Range Force

"The force that makes objects fall to the ground is also the force that keeps the planets in their orbits around the sun. Isaac Newton was the first person to realize this. The ancient Greeks thought that objects fell because they were seeking their natural places, and that the planets were moved by invisible crystal spheres."

In *Eyewitness Science: Force and Motion* by Peter Lafferty, you can also find out how gravity causes high and low tides along Earth's seashores. And if you really want to "bend" your mind, find out what Albert Einstein thought about the powers of gravity.

masses of your gold and the feathers are still the same—100 kg of gold and 1 kg of feathers. But the weights have gone up! Your gold weighs 980 N again, and the feathers weigh 9.8 N.

No matter where you make the measurements, the gold will always weigh 100 times more than the feathers. That's because the mass of the gold is 100 times that of the feathers. And mass never changes. The weight of an object is directly related to its mass. The greater its mass, the stronger the gravitational pull on the object will be.

What happened up there on the mountaintop? Why did your pile of gold weigh less, even though its

mass stayed the same? If you had carried a scale with you, you would have found that as you moved up the mountain, your pile of gold lost weight. And so did you! You were moving farther from Earth's center, and Earth was not able to pull as strongly on the gold, or on your body. The masses of the two objects didn't change, but their weights decreased. ■

▲The same volume of two different substances can have very different masses and weights.

INVESTIGATION 1 WRAP-UP

REVIEW

1. What is the difference between mass and weight?

2. Why does an object "lose" weight as you carry it up a mountainside?

CRITICAL THINKING

3. If a bag of feathers has the same mass as a bag of gold coins, what will be true about the sizes of the two bags?

4. Your bag of gold coins has been stolen, but the police may have found it in Death Valley. When you report the weight of your coins as 980 N, the officer says that this bag of coins can't be yours because it weighs more than 980 N. What has happened?

DO ALL OBJECTS FALL AT THE SAME RATE?

Which is heavier, a pound of lead or a pound of feathers? Yes, it's an old joke, but if both the pound of lead and the pound of feathers were dropped from a 20-m tower, would they fall at the same rate?

Activity

The Great Gravity Race

Suppose a heavy object and a light object fall to Earth from the same height. Which will reach the ground first?

MATERIALS
- heavy ball and light ball (golf ball and table-tennis ball, for instance)
- spring scale and mesh bag
- *Science Notebook*

SAFETY
Don't throw the balls or bounce them in the classroom.

Procedure

Using a spring scale and mesh bag, weigh each ball and **record** each value in your *Science Notebook*. Place both balls on the edge of a table or cabinet. **Predict** which ball will hit the ground first if they both roll off the table together. Try it. **Record** your observations. Repeat the activity several times.

Analyze and Conclude

1. If all objects fall the way these two balls do, what rule could you write about falling objects?

2. Imagine sky divers jumping from a plane at the same time and falling through the sky before they open their parachutes. Will they fall at the same rate? Explain.

F36

Activity
Falling Together

MATERIALS
- index card
- 2 pennies
- quarter
- *Science Notebook*

If two pennies are at the same height and one is dropped straight down while the other is tossed across the room, which hits the ground first?

Procedure

1. Fold an index card in half. Then fold each half toward the center fold, as shown.

 Math Hint *The card will be folded into four equal parts.*

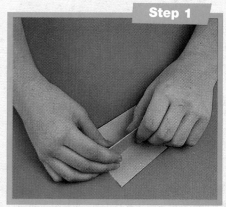
Step 1

2. Place the card on the edge of a table, as shown, and put a penny on each side of the center fold.

3. **Predict** which penny will hit the ground first if you flick the edge of the card with your finger. **Record** your prediction in your *Science Notebook*.

4. Flick the edge of the card and listen for the sounds of the pennies hitting the floor. **Record** which penny hits the ground first.

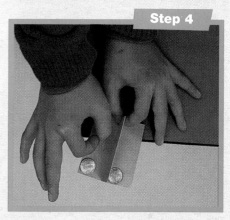
Step 4

5. Repeat the experiment three times.

6. Replace one penny with a quarter. Repeat the experiment. Then put the quarter in the other position and repeat the experiment.

Analyze and Conclude

1. How do you know that gravity is pulling both pennies toward the floor?

2. Does the sideways motion of a falling object have an effect on the rate of its fall?

3. Does the weight of the falling object have an effect on the rate of its fall?

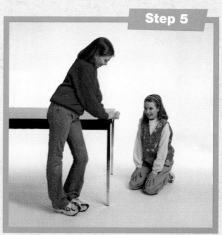
Step 5

F37

Galileo's Great Gravity Discovery

Reading Focus How does the weight of an object affect the rate at which it will fall?

A basketball is heavier than a soccer ball. If you drop both at the same time from the same height, which will hit the ground first? If you answered "the basketball," you're in agreement with the Greek philosopher Aristotle (ar'is tät'l), one of the greatest thinkers of all time. However, you are wrong! About 350 B.C., Aristotle taught that Earth was the center of the universe and that the heavier an object is, the faster it will fall toward Earth.

For nearly 2,000 years, Aristotle's teachings went almost unchallenged. Then, in the late sixteenth century, an Italian scientist named Galileo Galilei (gal i lē'ō gal i lē'ē) decided to test Aristotle's theory that heavy objects fall faster than light objects. Legend has it that Galileo simply climbed to the top of the Leaning Tower of Pisa, held a large cannonball and a small cannonball at arm's length, and dropped them at the same time. An observer, wisely standing well out of the way at the bottom, observed that the cannonballs hit the ground at the same time! While Galileo may not have actually done *this* experiment, he did experiments that showed that objects fall at the same rate.

It wasn't long before other scientists began supporting Galileo's findings. About 1665, Sir Isaac Newton discovered that the force keeping Earth in its orbit around the Sun is the same force that causes all objects to fall at the same rate. That force is gravity!

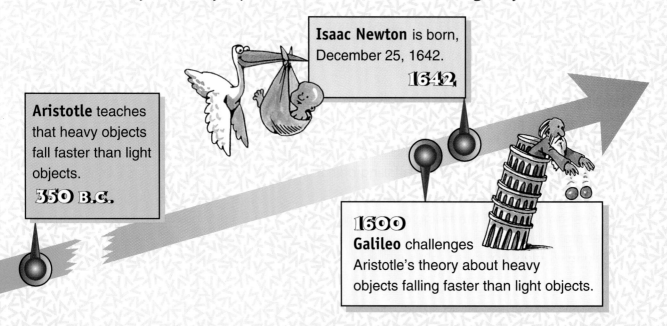

Isaac Newton is born, December 25, 1642.

1642

Aristotle teaches that heavy objects fall faster than light objects.

350 B.C.

1600
Galileo challenges Aristotle's theory about heavy objects falling faster than light objects.

F38

How High?

Reading Focus How are gravity, distance, and the acceleration of a falling body related?

▲ **How does gravity affect the flight of a batted ball?**

"Two out; bases loaded; bottom of the ninth; everything's tied up, two all. Ramirez steps up to the plate, and Johnson looks in for the sign. Ramirez needs only a single to put this game away. Johnson goes into the stretch, and here's the pitch.

"Ramirez swings and smashes a hanging curve! The runners are going, and that ball is almost out of sight! Jefferson is looking for it. He's all the way back at the left-field wall. He's going up. He reaches halfway over the wall . . . and he's got it!

He pulls it back in and robs Ramirez of a grand slam home run! What a catch! That ball must have been coming down like a rocket! At the end of nine, this game is all tied up and we're going into extra innings!"

If you have ever listened to a baseball announcer call a game, you may have heard commentary like this. Think for a moment about the player who caught the ball. How hard was the ball hit? How fast was the ball moving as it came down toward the player? With how much force did the ball hit the player's glove?

Graphing Acceleration

The graph below shows the distance that an object dropped from some point above Earth's surface falls over time. The line of the graph is curved, indicating that the distance a falling object travels does not increase at a steady rate.

The upward curve of the line indicates that during each successive second, the object falls farther than it did during the previous second. According to the graph, how far does an object fall during the first second? the third second? the fifth second?

In order for an object to move farther with each succeeding second, it must be speeding up, or accelerating. Gravity causes an object to accelerate as it falls toward Earth's surface.

Making Predictions About Falling

The information on the graph is accurate for any place on Earth. You can use the graph in two ways. If you know how much time an object has fallen, you can find the distance it has fallen. If you know how far the object has fallen, you can determine how much time it took for the object to fall. For example, suppose you

▲ **With the help of a teacher or another adult, you could launch your own rocket.**

want to know how far an object has fallen five seconds after it was dropped. Read across the horizontal (time) axis to 5. Then read up the 5 line until you come to the curve. Next, read to your left (blue arrow) across the graph to the vertical (distance) axis. Reading up the scale of the vertical axis (red arrow), you should find a distance of about 120 m (400 ft). How far would the same object have fallen after six seconds?

Scientists can use a graph like this to calculate distances that might be difficult to measure otherwise. Suppose, for example, that a rocket is fired straight up and then falls back to Earth. You know that the rocket took eight seconds to come down after reaching its maximum height. Use the graph to find how far the rocket fell in those eight seconds.

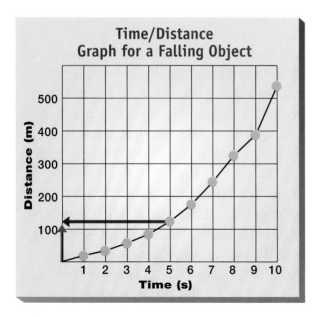

Time/Distance Graph for a Falling Object

UNIT PROJECT LINK

Design two different roller coasters for your amusement park. Then build a three-dimensional model of each that will fit on your posterboard. Be sure each coaster can carry at least one marble. Experiment to determine how fast the coaster can go. Then, beside each coaster, give its name and information about how high and how fast it goes.

TechnologyLink

For more help with your Unit Project, go to **www.eduplace.com**.

▲ Using a stopwatch and the graph on the previous page, you can calculate the height that a model rocket reaches by determining how long it takes to come down.

You can use the same graph to find the time it takes for an object to fall. How long would it take for a baseball to fall 170 m (about 560 ft) from the top of the Washington Monument? Do you think catching a ball dropped from the top of the Washington Monument is a good test of a baseball player's ability? Explain. ■

INVESTIGATION 2 WRAP-UP

REVIEW

1. Would the graph on page F40 be useful in predicting the fall of both a marble and a baseball? Explain.

2. Use the graph on page F40 to find out how long it will take an object dropped from a height of 310 m to fall to Earth.

CRITICAL THINKING

3. How would the graph on page F40 be different if an object fell at a constant speed rather than accelerating?

4. An astronaut standing on the Moon and a scientist standing on Earth drop identical hammers from identical heights at exactly the same moment. Which will hit the surface first? Explain your answer.

F41

INVESTIGATION 3

HOW DOES AIR CHANGE THE RATE AT WHICH AN OBJECT FALLS?

An acorn and a leaf both fall from the same branch at the same moment. What prediction would you make concerning which one will hit the ground first? In this investigation, find out about a force you must consider when making your prediction.

Activity

Paper Race

MATERIALS
- 2 sheets of notebook paper
- spring scale
- *Science Notebook*

Can similar objects fall at different rates? It doesn't take sleight of hand to make it happen.

- -

Procedure

1. Crumple up a sheet of paper into a small ball. Leave a second sheet flat.

2. Using a spring scale, weigh each sheet of paper. **Record** the weights in your *Science Notebook* in a chart similar to the one below.

Step 1

Object	Weight	Description of Results
Crumpled paper		
Flat paper		

See SCIENCE and MATH TOOLBOX page H11 if you need to review **Making a Chart to Organize Data.**

3. **Predict** what will happen if both sheets of paper are dropped from the same height at the same time. **Test your prediction**.

4. **Record** which one reaches the ground first.

5. Repeat the experiment three times and **record** your results.

Step 3

Analyze and Conclude

1. Which sheet of paper experiences a stronger gravitational pull? How do you know?

2. How can the difference between the open paper and the paper ball be used to explain your results?

3. How might the results of this activity have been different if you had dropped both pieces of paper in a vacuum (a space containing no matter)?

INVESTIGATE FURTHER!

RESEARCH

Trees release seeds every year. These seeds are found in various kinds of protective coverings. Collect seeds in their coverings of different shapes. Compare the ways they fall. How might the shapes affect the rates of fall? How might these different rates be advantageous for the trees?

Activity
Parachuting

How does the design of a parachute affect the rate at which it falls?

MATERIALS
- thin plastic garbage bags (for parachute material)
- scissors
- string
- tape
- small action figure
- stopwatch
- *Science Notebook*

Procedure

1. Cut two parachute shapes from a thin plastic bag as shown. Make one much larger than the other.

2. Cut pieces of string and use them to attach an action figure to one of the parachutes. The strings should be attached with tape at the edges of the parachute and then attached to the action figure.

3. Make a mark high on the wall. You will drop the action figure with the parachute from that height every time.

4. Drop the action figure wearing the parachute. **Record** the drop time in your *Science Notebook* in a chart similar to the one below. Repeat the experiment three times. **Record** your data.

5. **Predict** how drop times of the second parachute will compare with those of the first one. Repeat step 4, with the action figure wearing the second parachute.

Step 1

Step 2

Step 4

Parachute Size	Height of Drop	Drop Time
Small		
Large		

F44

Analyze and Conclude

1. What effect did the size of the parachute have on the drop time? Suggest a **hypothesis** to explain any differences you observed in the rates of fall.

2. Parachutes come in many different sizes, for use with people, packages, machinery, and vehicles. How should parachute designs change for different uses?

3. Sky divers wear loose-fitting, baggy clothes. What, do you think, would be the benefit of wearing clothes like this?

INVESTIGATE FURTHER!

EXPERIMENT

What might happen if you parachute on a windy day? Repeat the activity, but add a wind factor by turning on a fan. Try tilting the fan at different angles. Does the direction of the wind have an effect? Do your observations support your explanation of how a parachute works?

Feather Falling on the Moon

> **Reading Focus** Why do some objects fall faster than others?

As you know, there is a legend that Galileo dropped two cannonballs from the Leaning Tower of Pisa. Although Galileo may never have done this particular experiment, he did experiment with the rates of fall for a variety of objects.

As you read earlier, Galileo concluded that all objects fall at the same rate, regardless of their weight. What do you think might have happened if Galileo had experimented with a cannonball and a golf ball? What about a golf ball and a baseball, or a hammer and a feather? In each case, do you think he would have gotten the same result?

Air Resistance

If all objects fall at the same rate, Galileo could have dropped any two objects, including a hammer and a feather, and both would have reached the ground at the same time. But perhaps Galileo suspected that a hammer and a feather dropped from a tower would not hit the ground at the same time. In fact, they wouldn't. Why not?

The additional factor in this experiment is air resistance. Air resistance is the force exerted by air against objects that are moving through the air. If you drop a metal ball from a tower, air resistance does not slow the ball very much. But if you drop a feather, air slows the feather so much that it drifts to Earth's surface at a leisurely rate. So to be scientifically precise, Galileo's theory was that all objects fall at the same rate in a vacuum. In a vacuum there is no air, so there is no air resistance.

Scientists have used vacuum chambers to test Galileo's theory many times since 1642, the year that he died. Each time, scientists have shown that Galileo was correct about the rate at which objects fall in a vacuum.

▲ **July 30, 1971—Galileo is proven right as astronaut David Randolph Scott drops a hammer and a feather on the Moon. They hit at the same time.**

▲ No photographs exist of an actual landing on the Moon. In this picture drawn by NASA artists, what is being used to lower the Lunar Module to the Moon?

But the most dramatic test of Galileo's theory occurred on July 30, 1971, during the voyage of *Apollo 15* to the Moon. During that voyage, astronaut David Randolph Scott dropped both a hammer and a feather at the same time while standing on the Moon's surface. Millions of television viewers saw Galileo's theory confirmed. The two objects struck the Moon's surface at exactly the same time.

Worlds Without Air

The success of Scott's experiment was due to the absence of air on the Moon. With no air resistance to hold the feather afloat, it followed the same law of acceleration as the hammer did. The difference in their masses had no effect on the way the objects fell.

The lack of air helped astronauts prove Galileo's theory once they had landed on the Moon. The lack of air also created a major headache for the scientists on Earth responsible for designing a system for safe landing on the Moon. On Earth, parachutes were used to lower spacecraft to the surface. But parachutes certainly were not going to work on the Moon. Can you explain why not?

Without a parachute, the astronauts had to use a different method for landing on the Moon's surface. What do you think they did? ■

Internet Field Trip

Visit **www.eduplace.com** to learn more about travel in space, where there is no air resistance.

Sky Divers

Reading Focus How do parachutes work?

When referring to U.S. Army Airborne troops, a pilot once said, "I will never understand why anyone would want to jump out of a perfectly good airplane!" Yet every day, people strap parachutes on and jump out of airplanes. Some do it as part of their jobs, and some do it for fun.

Imagine standing at the open door of an airplane and then jumping out into the empty sky. Now imagine free-falling toward Earth, reaching a speed of about 192 km/h (120 mph). This is what sky divers do just for fun!

Patterns in the Sky

Frequently, sky divers jump individually, but sometimes they jump in large groups to create formations as they fall to Earth. As the divers leave the airplane, they don't open their parachutes. Instead,

These sky divers had less than 45 seconds to get into formation, separate, and pull their ripcords. ▼

▲ A parachute without control slits will rock back and forth to allow some trapped air to escape. The result will be a very airsick parachutist.

▲ A parachute with control slits is more stable. It can also be steered so that the parachutist has more control over where he or she lands.

they free-fall. They can change their speed and direction by spreading their arms and legs to increase air resistance. As the divers fall, they reach out and grip each other's arms and legs to form a chosen design.

As sky divers create their formation, they often fall 2.4 km (about 1.5 mi) in 45 seconds. When they are no less than 670 m (about 2,200 ft) above the ground, they release their grips on one another and pull ripcords that open their parachutes. Some divers wear devices that pull their ripcords automatically when they are a certain distance above the ground. The large inside surface of an open parachute offers a great deal of air resistance and slows the diver's fall to 32 km/h (about 20 mph) or less.

A parachute is actually easier to control when it has holes in it. If the parachute has no holes, the air trapped in it tries to escape through the sides. This causes the parachute to tip first one way and then another.

A small hole in the top of a parachute allows some air to escape and stops the parachute from tipping from side to side. Slits in the sides of the parachute let more air escape. Sky divers can open and close the slits by pulling cords. This enables them to change speed and steer to a safe landing place, where they land about as hard as if they had jumped off a platform 2.6 m (9 ft) above the ground.

Sky diving is much safer now than it used to be because of the diver's ability to steer the parachute and the automatic opening feature. In 1991, around 125,000 sky divers made 2.25 million jumps. About 100,000 of these jumpers were sky diving for the first time. Some

◄ Parachutes are nothing new. In the early 16th century, Leonardo da Vinci envisioned a primitive type of parachute.

parachute centers now offer six hours of classroom training and a jump from an airplane on the same day.

Parachutes in History

Parachutes have a long history. When the great inventor Leonardo da Vinci died, in 1519, he left behind the first drawings of a parachute. In 1797, André-Jacques Garnerin of France was the first person to use a parachute more or less successfully. Jumping from a hot-air balloon, he used a parachute that had no control slits. He was tossed around so much that he ended up airsick.

In 1917 during World War I, parachutes were used by pilots to bail out of planes that had been shot down. In World War II, parachutes were also used to drop men and equipment into enemy territory. Soldiers who did this were called paratroopers. Paratroopers attach the ripcord from the parachute to the inside of the plane. As they jump, the ripcords are pulled, and the parachutes open.

Paratroopers usually need larger parachutes than do sky divers because paratroopers often carry heavy equipment and need more air resistance to slow their fall. Even bigger chutes or clusters of chutes are used for dropping cargo. For sky divers, though, one small parachute is big enough for an exciting afternoon of free-falling. ■

INVESTIGATION 3 WRAP-UP

REVIEW

1. Could you sky-dive on the Moon? Why or why not?

2. What are some ways that air resistance is helpful?

CRITICAL THINKING

3. During free fall, what might parachutists do to speed up their rate of fall?

4. If an astronaut released a helium-filled balloon on the Moon's surface, what would happen to the balloon? Explain your answer.

REFLECT & EVALUATE

Word Power

Write the letter of the term that best matches the definition.

1. Force exerted by a body on all other bodies
2. Property not affected by gravity
3. A push or a pull
4. A measure of Earth's gravity on an object
5. Anything that has mass and takes up space

a. force
b. gravity
c. mass
d. matter
e. weight

Check What You Know

Write the word in each pair that correctly completes the statement.

1. The mass of an object is usually measured in (newtons, kilograms).
2. As an object moves farther from Earth's center, its weight (decreases, stays the same).
3. Two things that affect falling objects are gravity and (mass, air resistance).
4. Earth exerts a strong gravitational force because of its great (size, mass).

Problem Solving

1. How are mass and weight related?
2. Would an object be apt to weigh more on the top floor of a skyscraper or in its basement? Explain.
3. If all objects near Earth's surface fall at the same rate, why would a larger parachute be needed for a car than for a human dropped from a plane at the same time?

Study the graph. Describe how the graph can be used to find out how long it would take an object to fall to Earth's surface from a height of 450 m. Then draw a graph showing your data.

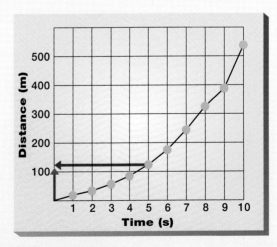

CHAPTER 3

MAKING AND MEASURING MOTION

Look around you on a busy street, and you'll see all sorts of motion. Cars are speeding up and slowing down. People stop at curbs and then walk briskly across the street. Papers on the ground suddenly fly into the air in the breeze. What does all this changing motion have in common?

• •

Connecting to Science
ARTS

Poetry in Motion Have you ever watched professional dancers perform? If so, you have probably been impressed by how graceful the dancers' movements are and how easy they make it seem. In truth, of course, it isn't "easy" at all! Every step, every movement of the arms and body, has been carefully planned. Then, after the planning is done, the dancers spend many hours and weeks of practice, coordinating their movements with the music and with each other. Finally, the dancers are ready. And no matter if they are in the elegant costumes of a ballet company or the jeans and work boots worn by the group known as Tap Dogs, the end result is truly "poetry in motion."

In this chapter, you will learn about the laws that govern motion and how to measure different kinds of motion.

Coming Up

INVESTIGATION 1

HOW ARE OBJECTS AT REST AND OBJECTS IN MOTION ALIKE?

INVESTIGATION 2

HOW DO FORCES AFFECT MOTION?

INVESTIGATION 3

HOW DOES FRICTION AFFECT THE MOTION OF OBJECTS?

◀ Tap Dogs is a popular tap-dance group from Australia.

HOW ARE OBJECTS AT REST AND OBJECTS IN MOTION ALIKE?

A magician approaches a table set with fine china and crystal glassware. She grabs the tablecloth and quickly pulls it from the table, leaving the dishes and glasses upright and undisturbed. How did she do it? To answer, you'll need to know how objects at rest behave.

Activity

Rider Moves

What do you feel when the car in which you are riding changes its motion suddenly?

MATERIALS
- 2 toy pickup trucks
- small block of wood
- *Science Notebook*

Procedure

1. Place two toy pickup trucks, one in front of the other, on a flat hard floor. Place a wood block as a "rider" in the center of the first truck's bed. In your *Science Notebook*, **draw** a picture showing the positions of the trucks and the block.

2. **Predict** what will happen if you hit the first truck sharply from behind. Use the second truck to **test your prediction**. On your picture, show where the first truck was hit and what happened to it and the block.

Step 2

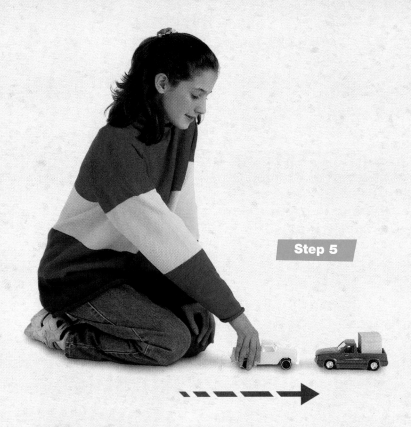

Step 5

3. Repeat the activity two more times to be sure of your results.

4. **Predict** what will happen if the truck carrying the block is struck from the front instead of the back. **Record** your predictions.

5. Repeat the activity, this time hitting the first truck from the front. **Record** your observations.

Analyze and Conclude

1. **Describe** what happened to the block when the truck was hit from the rear.

2. **Describe** what happened to the block when the truck was hit from the front.

3. **Infer** what would happen to the block if the truck carrying the block were to suddenly move forward and then backward.

INVESTIGATE FURTHER!

EXPERIMENT

Repeat the activity, using "riders" of different shapes and materials. Does the shape of the rider have any effect on the outcome? Does the material from which it's made have any effect? Report your results.

Activity

Crash-Test Dummies

When you ride in a car, you wear a seat belt to protect yourself from injury. How can you protect a crash-test dummy when a truck stops suddenly?

Procedure

1. Select a block of wood that will fit in the back of a toy truck. This will be a crash-test dummy.

2. Carefully place the crash-test dummy in the back of the truck. Study its position and decide what safety equipment is needed.

3. Protect the crash-test dummy with one type of material used as safety equipment.

4. Set up a ramp as shown below so that the lowest part ends at a wall.

Step 2

Step 4

F56

5. Place the truck and crash-test dummy at the top of the ramp and release them.

6. Observe what happens to the crash-test dummy as a result of the collision. **Record** your observations in your *Science Notebook*. If the dummy flips out of the truck, tips over, or slides around in any way, you must consider the accident to be serious.

7. After the first test, **evaluate** your safety equipment and make revisions if necessary.

8. Repeat the activity, using any improved safety equipment. **Record** your observations and results.

9. Raise the ramp to make it steeper and repeat the test. **Record** your observations.

Step 5

Analyze and Conclude

1. Make a list of all the safety devices you tried. **Describe** how well each device worked.

2. Add to your list the successful safety devices your classmates used.

3. From your observations, recommend new safety devices for real cars.

4. Why do you think the crash-test dummy tends to move around when the truck crashes into the wall?

5. What function do safety devices such as seat belts serve in car accidents?

INVESTIGATE FURTHER!

RESEARCH

Assume that your truck and dummy must ride on a track that turns upside down like a loop ride in an amusement park. Obtain some books on thrill-ride design and contact an amusement park to find out what kinds of safety devices are built into the designs of such rides. Describe the safety devices that amusement parks use on loop rides.

Sir Isaac Newton's First Law

Reading Focus What is inertia?

Isaac Newton was born in England in 1642, just a few months after the death of Galileo. As a young man, Newton spent most of his time working on his inventions. These included kites, a sundial, and a water clock.

Newton graduated from Cambridge University in 1665, but he made no particular impression on his teachers. As a student, he did not seem destined to become one of the great scientific geniuses of all time.

Newton's Thoughts About Motion

Shortly after his graduation, Newton's life suddenly changed. A terrible epidemic known as the plague swept through Cambridge in 1665. To avoid the disease, Newton moved from Cambridge to his mother's farm near London. During the next 18 months, he made some of the most important discoveries in the history of mathematics and science.

Among Newton's discoveries were his hypotheses about the nature of motion. Until this time, scientists thought that a constant force was needed to keep an object in motion. It seemed obvious to them that if a force stopped acting on an object, the object slowed down and eventually stopped.

Newton thought differently. A story is often told that while sitting under a tree,

▲ Between 1665 and 1667, Isaac Newton revolutionized science with discoveries regarding gravity, motion, light, and mathematics.

he was struck on the head by a falling apple. While we don't know that this actually happened, we do know that late in his life Newton himself told the story to a friend. He explained that he had wondered what caused the apple's motion. Before long, Newton was looking beyond the problem of a single apple dropping from a tree. He extended his inquiries to include the causes of the movement of Earth, the Moon, the planets, and the stars.

The Concept of Inertia

Over time, Newton worked out a number of hypotheses explaining the nature of motion. The basis of all these hypotheses is now known as Newton's **first law of motion**. According to this law, objects at rest tend to remain at rest. Objects in motion tend to stay in motion, traveling at a constant speed and in the same direction. The tendency of an object to remain at rest or to remain in motion is called **inertia**.

We expect a rock to remain sitting at the top of a hill. Similarly, a ball rolling across a table top might be expected to continue rolling in the same direction; no force is needed to keep it in motion.

What we *do* have to explain are changes in the conditions that influence an object's motion. For example, suppose that the rock starts rolling down the hill. The problem is to explain why the rock changed its state. What change in conditions made the rock start rolling down the hill?

Or suppose that a rolling ball speeds up, slows down, or changes direction. You'll discover Newton's explanation for those changes in the ball's condition in the next investigation.

Examples of Inertia

You can find many examples of inertia in everyday life. In the activity on pages F56 and F57, for example, inertia causes the crash dummy to change position when the truck stops suddenly. Similarly, suppose you are standing in the aisle of a bus that is traveling at a constant speed of 40 km/h (25 mph). What would happen if the driver suddenly slammed on the brakes? Chances are you'd fall forward as the bus came to a stop. This would happen because your body has

▲ Unless acted on by some force, this rock will forever balance on top of the other rock. What measurable forces could affect the balance of the rock?

inertia while the bus is traveling forward. Your body is moving in the same direction and at the same speed as the bus. When the driver hits the brakes, the bus comes to a stop, but inertia keeps your body moving forward.

A similar explanation applies to sudden starts by the bus. You stand quietly in the aisle while the bus driver waits for the last passenger to board. At some point, the driver suddenly steps on the accelerator. The bus lurches forward. What happens to you and the other passengers? How does inertia explain the changes that occur? ■

Seat Belts and Air Bags

Reading Focus How does inertia influence the design of automobile safety devices?

STS
SCIENCE
TECHNOLOGY
& SOCIETY

An automobile can provide a frightening lesson in inertia. A person in a car traveling at 88 km/h (55 mph) is also traveling at 88 km/h. If that person is unrestrained and the car is suddenly stopped by a wall or telephone pole, the person will continue to move forward at 88 km/h until stopped by the steering wheel, dashboard, or windshield.

Automobile Safety Systems

Automotive engineers have long been aware of the hazards associated with traveling in a car. Over time, they have developed a number of different systems to overcome inertia and prevent or reduce crash-related injuries.

Newer vehicles are equipped with head restraints. In a rear-end collision a passenger's head is thrown back and hits the head restraint. This support prevents serious injury by stopping the backward motion of the head. Look at the photos on the next page of other automobile safety systems.

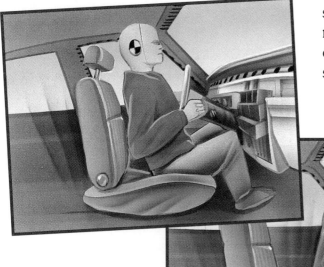

▲ When a car stops suddenly in a crash, inertia will cause an unrestrained person to travel forward at the car's original speed. The person stops when he or she strikes the wheel, dashboard, or windshield.

One of the great safety inventions of recent decades is the air bag. Stored in the dashboard or steering column of a car, the bag prevents the driver from being thrown into the steering wheel or dashboard. ▷

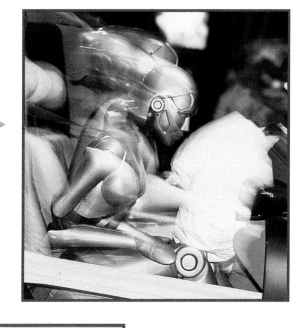

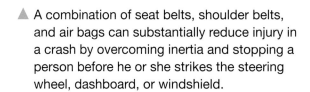

▲ A combination of seat belts, shoulder belts, and air bags can substantially reduce injury in a crash by overcoming inertia and stopping a person before he or she strikes the steering wheel, dashboard, or windshield.

INVESTIGATION 1 WRAP-UP

THINK IT
WRITE IT

REVIEW

1. In terms of inertia, compare a car sitting in a driveway with a car rolling along a level street.

2. What is Newton's first law of motion?

CRITICAL THINKING

3. You bump into a table, and a glass vase on the table tips toward you. What made the vase tip? Why did it tip toward you and not away from you?

4. In a head-on collision of two cars, occupants first move forward and then backward. Explain.

HOW DO FORCES AFFECT MOTION?

Two bike riders meet on James Street. One is coasting along and brakes to slow down. The other is pedaling hard to speed up. What forces are causing both of these changes in motion?

Activity

Starting and Stopping

What happens to the motion of a ball when you push it gently? What happens when you push it harder?

Step 2

MATERIALS

- ball
- sheet of butcher paper
- ruler
- crayon
- *Science Notebook*

Procedure

1. Place a sheet of butcher paper on the floor. **Draw** a dot in the center of the paper. Place a ball on top of the dot.

> **Math Hint** *The center of the paper will be the point where two diagonals intersect.*

2. Use a ruler to **draw** a line extending away from the dot.

3. Hold a crayon over the line and behind the ball, aiming at the center of the ball. **Predict** the direction in which the ball will move if you gently push it with the crayon.

Step 4

4. Push the ball. **Observe** the ball's path. Then **draw** the ball's path on the butcher paper.

5. Repeat steps 4 and 5, this time pushing the ball with more force. **Draw** the path of the ball on the paper.

6. Place the ball on the dot again. **Draw** another line on the paper, extending from the ball in a different direction.

7. Put the crayon over this line and gently strike the ball. **Draw** the ball's path on the paper.

Analyze and Conclude

1. When you push the ball with the crayon, you are applying a force to the ball. **Suggest a hypothesis** that describes the relationship between the strength of the force applied and the resulting behavior of the ball.

2. The lines you drew on the butcher paper in steps 4, 5, and 7 show the direction in which the force acts. **Suggest a hypothesis** that describes the relationship between the direction of each force and the resulting behavior of the ball.

INVESTIGATE FURTHER!

EXPERIMENT

In soccer most players can kick the ball in a straight line along the ground, and they can make the ball rise into the air. Skillful players can put sidespin on the ball to make it curve right or left. Really skillful players also can put backspin on a ball to make it stop dead or roll backward when it lands. Experiment to find out what you have to do to a soccer ball to make it curve or spin backward. Report your results to the class.

Activity

The Problem With Big Trucks

How is the motion of objects that have different masses affected by equal forces?

MATERIALS

- 2 toy trucks, one with a heavy load
- short wooden board
- metric ruler
- calculator
- smooth wooden board
- several books
- block of wood
- *Science Notebook*

Procedure

1. Place two toy trucks, one carrying a heavy load, on a level floor. Place a small wooden board behind both trucks.

2. **Predict** how the trucks will move if you apply equal force to each. Use the board to give both trucks a sudden, sharp push. Do not follow through with your motion.

3. **Measure** the distance that each truck moved and **record** the data in your *Science Notebook*. Repeat the experiment twice. Use a calculator to determine the average distance moved by each truck.

 See **SCIENCE** and **MATH TOOLBOX** page H4 if you need to review **Using a Calculator.**

4. Build a ramp by propping up one end of a long wooden board on a stack of books. Place the empty truck at the top of the ramp. Place a block of wood at the bottom.

5. Release the truck so that it hits the block of wood squarely. **Measure** how far the truck travels after hitting the block. **Record** your measurement.

6. Repeat steps 4 and 5, using the loaded truck.

Analyze and Conclude

1. How does an equal force applied to two objects of different mass affect the acceleration of each?

2. What forces were acting to stop the trucks as they came down the ramp?

3. In which case was a greater force required to stop the truck? How do you know?

Step 1

Step 2

Step 6

Sir Isaac Newton's Second Law

Reading Focus Under what condition will the motion of an object change?

When Isaac Newton left Cambridge, he was just looking for a way to avoid the plague. But during the next 18 months, Newton made observations that enabled him to explain the relationship between light and color and to invent a form of mathematics called calculus. He also explained how the universe is held together in his theory of gravitation and laws of motion.

Although Newton completed his early investigations in 1666, his theory of gravitation and laws of motion were not published until 1687. Newton's first law of motion states that all bodies have inertia. A body at rest tends to remain at rest, and a moving body will travel at a constant speed in a constant direction.

Newton's second law of motion picks up where the first law leaves off. This law states that an object at rest or in motion will not change its condition unless something causes the change. What might make an object move, speed up, slow down, stop, or change direction?

Force, Mass, and Acceleration

Newton hypothesized that the answer to the question asked above is "a force." Remember that, in science, a force is a push or a pull. Newton's **second law of motion** states that an object begins to move, speeds up, slows down, comes to a stop, or changes direction only when some force acts on that object.

For example, a rock on top of a hill might begin rolling down the hill if someone exerted a force on it. Once started down the hill, the rock would continue to gain speed because of the force of gravity

A push and a pull are both forces, and both can result in a change in motion. ▼

F65

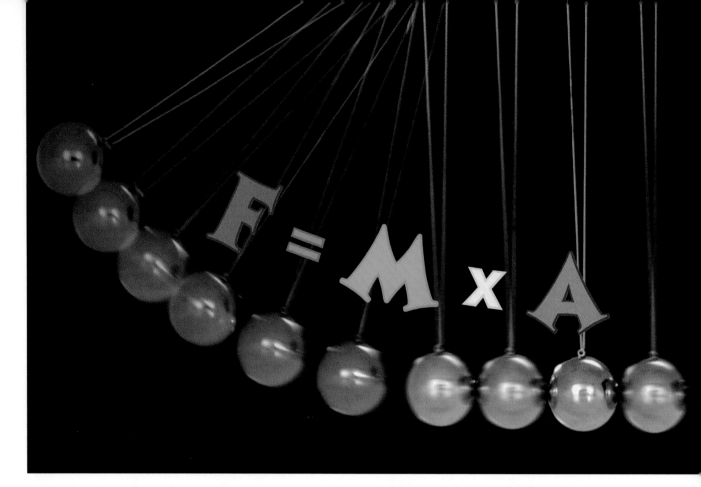

acting on it. The rock would continue moving along a straight course down the hill until some new force acted on it. This new force could change its direction, slow it down, speed it up, or stop it.

Consider a ball rolling across a billiard table. The ball might speed up, slow down, or change direction. Why? The second law says that such a change

The rocks in this picture moved down the hill because a force acted on them. ▼

occurs when a force acts on the ball. What might provide the necessary force on a billiard ball to change its motion?

Perhaps the billiard ball is hit by another ball from behind, from in front, or from the side. If the contact with the other ball is from behind, a pushing force changes the speed of the first ball. If the contact is from the side or front, a pushing force changes not only the speed of the ball but also the direction in which the ball is moving.

Calculating Force

Newton discovered a mathematical formula that shows how force causes a change in the speed or direction of an object. That formula is

$$\text{Force} = \text{mass} \times \text{acceleration}$$
$$F = m \times a$$

The units used in this formula are newtons (N) for force, kilograms (kg) for mass, and meters per second per second (m/s^2) for acceleration. As you learned in the

▲ **"Newton's cradle"** provides another good example of force changing motion. The force is generated by the first ball striking the second ball, the second striking the third, and so on. Finally, when the force is passed on to the last ball, the ball bounces away from the others. When the ball falls back and strikes the one before it, the process is repeated in the opposite direction.

previous chapter, the newton is a unit of weight in the metric system. A **newton** is defined as the force needed to accelerate a 1-kg object 1 meter per second every second.

$$N = kg \times m/s^2$$

The formula for force tells us many things about the way in which a force acts on an object. For example, suppose an object with a mass of 2 kg accelerates at 5 m/s². What force was needed to achieve that acceleration? To answer that question, first write the formula for Newton's second law.

$$F = m \times a$$

Then substitute the values you know for this question.

$$m = 2 \text{ kg}; a = 5 \text{ m/s}^2$$

Using Math *Look at the engines in these two cars. The larger car requires a larger engine because it has a larger mass. How can you use Newton's second law to find out which car requires the greater force to accelerate it to a speed of 88 km/h (55 mph) in 10 seconds?*

F67

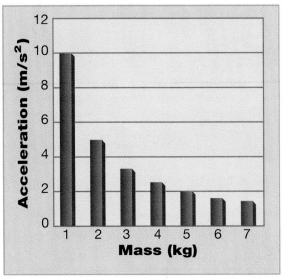

▲ Figure 1: Force = 10 N

▲ Figure 2: Acceleration = 5 m/s²

Finally, use the formula to find the unknown quantity—force.

$$F = m \times a$$
$$F = 2 \text{ kg} \times 5 \text{ m/s}^2$$
$$F = 10 \text{ kg} \times \text{m/s}^2$$
$$F = 10 \text{ N}$$

It would require a force of 10 N to make a 2-kg object accelerate at the rate of 5 m/s every second, or 5 m/s².

What happens if the same force acts on a body of greater mass, one of 5 kg, for example? To find the answer to this question, use the bar graph in Figure 1. Notice that the x-axis of the graph shows seven different masses that are acted on by a force of 10 N. The y-axis shows the resulting acceleration.

When you solved this problem, you discovered an important general rule. A constant force, such as 10 N, causes greater acceleration in a smaller mass than it does in a greater mass.

Other Applications of the Second Law

Suppose you wanted to give the same acceleration to two bodies of different mass. You can use $F = m \times a$ to find out

how to do that, too. Look at the bar graph in Figure 2. Notice that the force required to produce an acceleration of 5 m/s² increases as mass increases. For example, a 4-kg mass requires a force of 20 N to accelerate to 5 m/s². A 2-kg mass only requires a force of 10 N to achieve the same acceleration.

Perhaps you'd like to find out what happens to the acceleration of a 10-kg object if you change the force applied to it. Look at the bar graph in Figure 3. If you increase the force on a 10-kg mass, how is acceleration affected?

Finding the Mass of an Object

How can you find the mass of an object? Easy, you say—just put it on a balance and read the value. Scientists know another way to answer this question. If they know the rate at which an object is accelerated by a given force, they can calculate the mass of the object. They find the object's mass by using Newton's second law: $F = m \times a$.

Suppose you apply force of 15 N to an object of unknown mass, giving that object an acceleration of 5 m/s². Look at

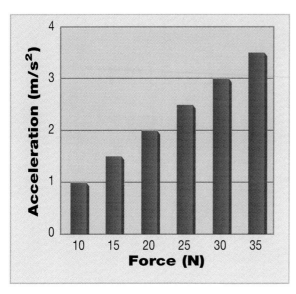

▲ Figure 3: Mass = 10 kg

▲ How are force, mass, and acceleration related in a BMX race?

the bar graph in Figure 2. Can you use any of the information in this graph to solve the problem? You probably can. You can also try to rearrange the second law's formula to solve for mass. If you determined that the mass of the object is 3 kg, you're right on the mark! Congratulations!

In fact, the second law gives us a new way of thinking about mass. Mass is a measure of a body's inertia. If a large force is required to overcome the inertia

of a body and get that body moving, the body has a lot of mass. If only a small force is needed to move a body, the body has a small amount of mass. Now you can find an exact number for the mass of a body, using Newton's second law of motion. ■

Internet Field Trip

Visit **www.eduplace.com** to learn about how the laws of motion influence the design of rides in an amusement park.

INVESTIGATION 2 WRAP-UP

REVIEW

1. What is Newton's second law of motion?

2. When a force is applied to an object, what determines the object's acceleration?

CRITICAL THINKING

3. What can you infer about the force needed to accelerate a ball at a rate of 5 m/s^2 compared to the force needed to accelerate the same ball at a rate of 10 m/s^2?

4. Two children ride in a wagon having a mass of 20 kg. One child has a mass of 30 kg, and the other child has a mass of 40 kg. What force is needed to accelerate the wagon and its passengers at a rate of 5 m/s^2?

HOW DOES FRICTION AFFECT THE MOTION OF OBJECTS?

A race car traveling at 240 km/h (150 mph) suddenly runs out of fuel. In less than 1 km, the car coasts to a stop. What slowed the car to 0 km/h so quickly? In this investigation you'll find out about the force that did it.

Activity

Friction Floors

According to the principle of inertia, a rolling car should roll forever. But it doesn't. Why not?

Procedure

1. In your *Science Notebook*, **make a chart** in which you will list different materials and how far a toy car travels on each.

2. Raise one end of a ramp 5 to 8 cm, as shown in the photograph. Place a piece of sandpaper at the bottom of the ramp.

MATERIALS

- toy car that rolls well
- smooth board that is at least as long as 5 toy cars
- several books
- pieces of sandpaper, aluminum foil, wax paper, and a towel, each at least as long as 5 toy cars
- metric tape measure
- *Science Notebook*

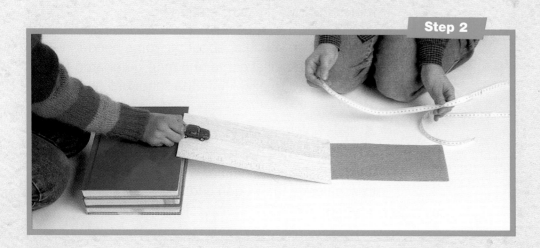
Step 2

3. Place a car in the middle of the ramp. Release the car and watch it roll off the ramp onto the sandpaper.

4. **Measure** how far the car traveled on the sandpaper. **Record** this information in the chart. Repeat the activity twice and **record** the distances.

See **SCIENCE** and **MATH TOOLBOX** page H6 if you need to review *Using a Tape Measure or Ruler.*

5. Repeat steps 2, 3, and 4, using aluminum foil, wax paper, and a towel. **Record** in the chart the distance the car travels over each material.

Step 5

Analyze and Conclude

1. **Rank** the four materials in order, from the one on which the car rolled farthest to the one on which the car rolled the shortest distance.

2. Each material is applying a force to the car to slow it down. Which material applied the most force? What evidence do you have to support your answer?

3. **Compare** the materials. What characteristics make some materials better than others at making the car stop?

INVESTIGATE FURTHER!

EXPERIMENT

When water freezes on a road, the road becomes slick. Freeze some water in a flat pan, then experiment with different materials to make the ice less slippery. Which materials are most effective?

Activity
Wheel Power

How do wheels help vehicles stay in motion?

Procedure

1. Tilt a ramp as shown in the photo.

2. Place a toy truck on the ramp. Release it and **observe** what happens. **Record** your observations in your *Science Notebook*.

3. Place a box on the ramp. Release the box and **observe** what happens. **Record** your observations.

Step 3

Analyze and Conclude

1. When two objects rub as they move past each other, friction is generated. Where does friction occur as the truck moves down the ramp? Where does friction occur when the box is on the ramp?

2. **Explain** what you observed in this activity in terms of friction. What are some ways of reducing friction between objects?

INVESTIGATE FURTHER!

RESEARCH

Wheels are designed to minimize friction between objects. Look around for other objects and substances that reduce friction, such as ball bearings. Write a report about things that reduce the friction between moving objects.

Friction

Reading Focus In what ways can friction be useful, and how can it be harmful?

▲ Spinning rapidly, the wheels of a drag racer rub against the surface of the track. Because the drivers smear a sticky material on the tires, they grip the track better and the car can accelerate faster. During competition, drag racers reach speeds of about 500 km/h (310 mph).

The driver pushes down on the accelerator, and the engine roars. The signal light turns green, and the driver releases the clutch. The car's wheels spin and scream. As smoke pours from the rapidly spinning tires, the car leaps forward. Less than four seconds later, the car reaches the end of the quarter-mile track, the driver hits the brakes, and a parachute pops out in back to stop the car.

Drag racing is an exciting sport. Car drivers compete with each other to see who can travel a quarter-mile course in the shortest time. Drivers usually smear a sticky material on the wheels of their cars at the beginning of the race. The sticky

material increases the friction between tire and pavement. It helps cars grip the road and get off to a faster start.

What Is Friction?

Friction is a force that occurs between surfaces that are in contact with each other. Friction resists the motion of one surface over another. When a race car is at rest on the track, it has no motion. There is no friction between the car's tires and the track. But when the driver steps on the accelerator, the car's tires begin to rotate. Friction begins to develop between the tires and the track beneath them.

The amount of friction between two bodies depends on many factors but especially on the properties of each surface. Rough surfaces generally result in more friction than do smooth surfaces. Imagine sliding an ice cube across the frozen surface of a lake. Ice is usually very smooth, so there is little friction between the ice cube and the ice on the lake. The ice cube will slide a long way before coming to rest. What would happen if you slid the ice cube across a rough surface, such as concrete?

Friction also varies with the kind of motion taking place. Objects that roll over a surface produce less friction than objects that slide. Ball bearings are small metal balls inserted between two surfaces that rub against each other. There is

▲ Bearings are used inside skateboard wheels to reduce the friction caused by pieces turning against one another.

much less friction with the ball bearings rolling between the surfaces than with the two surfaces rubbing directly against each other.

Lubricants are liquids or fine powders used to reduce the friction between two surfaces. In many types of machinery,

Science in Literature

The River
by Gary Paulsen
Dell Publishing, 1991

AN OBJECT IN MOTION ...

"The current was not fast—as he had guessed earlier it was about the speed of a person walking—but it was steady and strong. The logs were heavy and once they were moving in a direction they were hard to turn.

"As a matter of fact, Brian thought, watching the bank at the end of the curve come at him, they were impossible to turn."

As you enjoy the adventures of Brian and Derek in *The River* by Gary Paulsen, look for applications of Newton's first law and the concept of inertia.

metal surfaces rub against each other. A lot of friction results. The friction produces heat, which can damage the machinery. A few drops of oil can reduce this friction. If the friction is reduced, there is less damage to the machinery.

Friction in Sports

In many winter sports, participants want to reduce friction as much as they possibly can. Downhill skiers often put wax on their skis. The wax reduces the friction between the skis and the snow, and the skier's speed increases.

Friction slows speed, but it can also be helpful. Walking is possible, for example, because friction prevents your feet from simply sliding back over the ground. In some sports, players want to increase friction. Someone who runs the 100-m dash wants the maximum possible amount of friction between his or her feet and the running track. What would happen if that friction suddenly disappeared? Why would friction be good for a basketball player or football player?

Shoes and Tires

In the last 50 years, a giant industry has developed that makes the right kind of shoe for each type of sport. In many cases, the right kind of shoe means a shoe that gives an athlete just the right

▲ **The shoes worn by a sprinter contain sharp spikes that penetrate the running surface. The spikes create greater friction between the runner and the track surface.**

amount of friction to do well in his or her particular sport.

Athletic shoes may have studs, cleats, or spikes on their soles to prevent the shoes from sliding over the ground. The bottom of a golfer's shoes, for example, are covered with metal or plastic spikes. The spikes are designed to grip the ground and increase friction between the

Various types of athletic shoes are designed to provide the proper amount of friction for athletes perform at their best. ▼

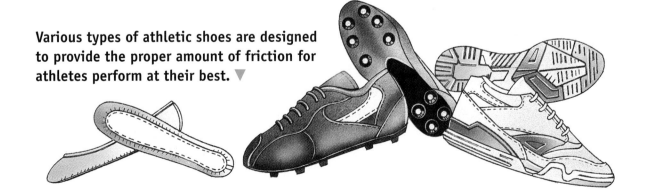

ground and the golfer's feet. This helps to prevent the golfer from slipping as he or she swings the club.

Athletic footwear manufacturers produce several major kinds of shoes: those for running, walking, and training; for tennis and other court sports; for soccer, rugby, and other field sports; for track and field; and for specialty sports such as bowling and aerobics. In each case, the shoe's sole is designed to provide the right amount of friction between the shoe and the surface on which it is intended to be worn.

Interesting comparisons can be made between shoes, designed for human feet, and tires, designed for motor vehicles. Tires are not designed to slide over the pavement. Wheels and tires are meant to roll. The treads on a tire are designed to provide friction between the tire and the road. Friction is needed to get a car moving, to bring it to a stop, and to keep it from sliding on curves.

Different kinds of tires and different tread patterns have been designed to provide more or less friction, depending on the driving conditions. Snow tires, for example, are heavier, wider, and have deeper treads than regular tires. These features increase the friction between the tire and the driving surface. What can happen if there's not enough friction between the tires of a car and the surface over which they travel? ■

UNIT PROJECT LINK

Choose two different motion rides to design. The rides should start, stop, and carry at least one marble. One of the rides should turn in circles. The other should use a swing. Give each ride a name. Then experiment with your rides to determine how fast each goes and the safety features each needs. Display this information beside each ride.

 **Technology**Link
For more help with your Unit Project, go to **www.eduplace.com**.

INVESTIGATION 3 WRAP-UP

REVIEW

1. How does friction help the movement of a car? How does friction hinder the movement of a car?

2. During the winter, road crews often spread sand on icy roads. Why do they do this?

CRITICAL THINKING

3. As a skater glides across the ice, a thin film of water forms beneath the blades of his or her skates. How might this affect the skater's speed? Explain.

4. How might the soles of a pair of bowling shoes be different from the soles of a pair of basketball shoes?

REFLECT & EVALUATE

Word Power

Write the letter of the word that best matches the definition.

1. States that the condition of an object will not change unless something causes it to change
2. Tendency of an object in motion to stay in motion
3. Resists the movement of one surface across another surface
4. States that objects at rest tend to stay at rest
5. Unit that describes force in the metric system

a. first law of motion
b. friction
c. inertia
d. newton
e. second law of motion

Check What You Know

Write the word in each pair that correctly completes the statement.

1. Seat belts reduce the dangerous effects of (friction, inertia).
2. The force needed to overcome the inertia of an object depends on the object's (mass, shape).
3. Because it exerts a pull, gravity is considered a (newton, force).
4. Lubricants are used to (increase velocity, reduce friction).

Problem Solving

1. If the wheels of your skates strike an obstacle and stop, what happens to your body? Explain.

2. Two books fall from a shelf and hit the floor at the same time. Because of gravity, both books had an acceleration of 9.8 m/s^2. If the mass of one book was 1.8 kg and the other was 3.0 kg, what was the force, in newtons, that acted on each book?

BUILD YOUR PORTFOLIO

The bar graph shows the acceleration of two objects. What can you infer about

(a) The masses of the two objects if equal forces had been applied to each?

(b) The forces applied if the two objects have equal masses?

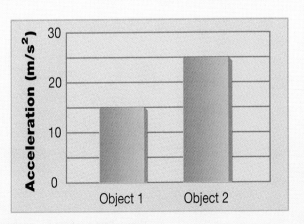

CHAPTER 4

FORCES IN PAIRS

Some objects at rest require little force to move them. Other objects need a great deal of force to be influenced. What do you know about the forces that objects exert on each other?

PEOPLE USING SCIENCE

Demolition Expert How do you demolish a nine-story building in ten seconds? You "let physics do the work," says Anna Chong, president of Engineered Demolition of Minneapolis. The laws of physics cause the building to implode and fall down in a pile of rubble.

In 1994, Anna Chong's company was responsible for imploding the Sears complex in Philadelphia, Pennsylvania. The enormous structure consisted of a nine-story merchandise building and a fourteen-story clock tower.

Using 5,400 kg (12,000 lb) of dynamite, the blasters caused the building to implode instead of explode. The result was a towering heap of steel and concrete that took two months to cart away. How do you think engineers of the demolition company got the building to crumble in this way?

Coming Up

◀ Anna Chong placing dynamite in the
Philadelphia Sears complex

INVESTIGATION 1

WHAT PROPERTY DO ALL MOVING OBJECTS SHARE?

Traveling at 156.8 km/h (98 mph), a baseball streaks toward the player at bat. The batter swings hard and sends the ball sailing toward the stands 121 m (400 ft) away. What has happened to change the ball's speed and direction? In this investigation you'll find out what is shared by the bat and ball.

Activity

Marble Collisions

At one time or another, you've probably run smack into a person who was standing still. What happened? Use marbles to find out!

MATERIALS
- 2 small marbles
- 2 large marbles
- *Science Notebook*

SAFETY
Always direct the marbles away from yourself and others.

Procedure

1. **Predict** what will happen in each of the collisions indicated in the tables below. Then cause the collisions to occur on a smooth, flat surface, and **describe** them in your *Science Notebook*.

Large Moving Marble Colliding With
a small stationary marble
a small moving marble
a large moving marble
the first marble in a row of two small stationary marbles

Small Moving Marble Colliding With
a small stationary marble
a small moving marble
a large moving marble
a small stationary marble that is directly in front of, and touching, a large stationary marble

2. Cause each collision to occur two more times to be certain of the results.

Analyze and Conclude

All moving objects have momentum. Momentum is a property related to the motion of an object. In a collision between a moving object and an object at rest, some of the momentum of the moving object is transferred to the object that is at rest.

1. Describe what happens to the momentum of a small marble when it hits another small marble at rest.

2. Describe what happens to the momentum of a large marble when it hits a small marble at rest.

3. Describe what happens to the momentum of a large marble when it hits two small marbles at rest.

4. What evidence did you find that momentum can be transferred during collisions?

INVESTIGATE FURTHER!

EXPERIMENT

Design an experiment to study momentum, using a beach ball and a basketball. Under exactly the same conditions, which ball has the greater momentum? What two things does momentum depend on?

Step 1

Playing Pool

Reading Focus What is momentum, and how can it be transferred?

"Rack 'em up!" Anyone who has ever played pool has probably heard these words at the beginning of a game. To begin a game of pool, players rack, or arrange, 15 colored balls into the shape of a triangle at one end of the pool table.

Then one player uses a cue stick to strike a white cue ball, sending it speeding at the triangle of balls. When it hits the colored balls, they scatter across the surface of the pool table. The game continues as players take turns trying to knock the colored balls into the pockets of the table by hitting them with the cue ball.

The game of pool depends on the momentum of moving objects, namely pool balls. **Momentum** is a property a moving object has due to its mass and velocity. When a cue ball is set in motion, it has momentum. When it strikes a stationary colored ball, some, if not all, of this momentum is transferred to the colored ball. In the activity on page F80, moving marbles are used to show the effects of momentum.

A good pool player seems to sense how momentum works. The player knows that if a cue ball hits a single colored ball directly, the cue ball will stop. All of its momentum will be transferred to the colored ball.

Pool players often send a colored ball into a pocket by hitting it at an angle. Some of the momentum is maintained by the cue ball and some is transferred to the colored ball. The place where the cue ball hits the colored ball determines the direction in which the colored ball will roll. The path of the cue ball also changes because of impact. The game of pool is not as scientific as this description makes it sound. However, a better understanding of the principle of momentum might just help you play the game better.

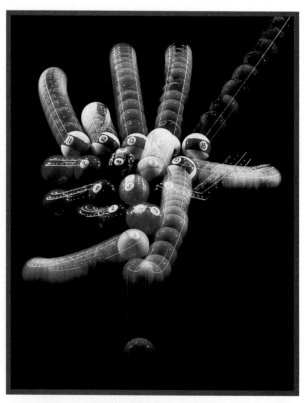

▲ **In pool, momentum is transferred from the cue stick to the cue ball and from the cue ball to the balls it strikes.**

Momentum Sharing

Reading Focus How is the momentum of an object calculated?

▲ **Would you like to catch this baseball with your bare hand?**

Suppose a baseball and a tennis ball are thrown to you at fairly high speeds. You must decide which one to catch barehanded. Which one will you choose?

Now suppose the baseball is lobbed underhand to you, and the tennis ball is served to you by a professional tennis player. Which ball will you choose to catch barehanded this time?

Were your answers to the two questions the same or different? Why? What was the difference between the baseball and the tennis ball in the two situations?

Momentum

The ability of a moving object to make something happen depends on its mass and how fast it's moving. In the

original question, suppose both balls were thrown at speeds of 5 m/s (about 5 yd/s). Which ball do you think would sting more if you caught it with a bare hand?

Now suppose the tennis ball moves toward you at 45 m/s (49 yd/s) and the baseball at 1 m/s (1 yd/s). Which ball do you think would sting more? Another way to ask this question would be: Which ball has more momentum? The momentum of a body can be found by multiplying its mass by its velocity. In mathematical terms, momentum would be expressed as

$$p = m \times v$$

Note that the symbol p is used to represent momentum.

How would you feel about catching this tennis ball? ▶

In the formula shown on page 83, mass (*m*) should be expressed in kilograms (kg), and velocity (*v*) in meters per second (m/s). Then, the unit of measure for momentum (*p*) is kilograms multiplied by meters per second.

You can use this formula to calculate the momentum of any object. For example, suppose that the baseball mentioned has a mass of 0.15 kg. What will be its momentum when traveling at a velocity of 6 m/s? To answer that question, write the formula for momentum.

$$p = m \times v$$

Then substitute the values for the mass (*m*) of the baseball and its velocity (*v*).

$$p = 0.15 \text{ kg} \times 6 \text{ m/s}$$
$$p = 0.90 \text{ kg} \times \text{ m/s}$$

What would be the momentum of the same baseball traveling at 8 m/s?

Conservation of Momentum

Some of the most interesting examples of momentum come from the world of sports. Think about the situation in which a pitcher throws a ball to a batter, who then hits a home run. When the ball was thrown, it had a momentum determined by its mass and velocity. It also had momentum after being hit, determined by its mass and its new velocity. In addition, the bat had momentum determined by its mass and the speed with which the batter swung.

Scientists can analyze such situations by using the **law of conservation of momentum**. This law states that momentum can be transferred but can't be lost. When two or more objects collide, the total momentum at the end of the collision is the same as the total momentum at the beginning. When a bat hits a ball, the sum of the momentum of the bat and of the ball as it rebounds from the bat is equal to the sum of the momentum of the bat as it was swung and of the ball as it approached the bat. Could this law be applied to the marble activity on page F80?

The Rocket's Red Glare

Another example of the law of conservation of momentum is found in a rocket launch. Imagine a rocket whose mass is 100,000 kg (220,000 lb) sitting on a launch pad. What is the rocket's momentum? Since the rocket isn't moving, its momentum is zero.

But what happens once the engines fire? If you've ever seen a rocket launch,

◀ Whenever objects collide, the resulting momentum of the objects is equal to the total momentum of the objects before the collision.

The momentum of a rocket in one direction is equal to the momentum of the burning gases in the opposite direction. ▶

you know that the situation changes quickly once the fuel ignites. As fuel burns, expanding gases move downward, and the rocket moves upward.

Consider launching a model rocket with a total mass, including fuel, of 1 kg (2.2 lb). Assume 0.1 kg (0.22 lb) of fuel is burned quickly, and the gases produced leave the rocket with a speed of 300 m/s (about 330 yd/s). How fast does the rocket go upward?

Remember that the total momentum before launch was zero. The law of conservation of momentum tells us that the total momentum after launch also is zero because the rocket goes in one direction and the gases go in another direction. Mathematically, different directions are represented by opposite signs: a plus sign for the rocket's momentum and a minus sign for the momentum of the gases.

rocket momentum − gas momentum = 0
$(0.9 \text{ kg} \times v) − (0.1 \text{ kg} \times 300 \text{ m/s}) = 0$

Note that since 0.1 kg of fuel has burned, the total mass of the rocket has been reduced to 0.9 kg. What is the value of v?

If you calculated that $v = 33.3$ m/s, you were correct. Remember that this is the value for the first moments of a liftoff. The rocket will gain velocity and lose mass as more fuel is burned. ■

INVESTIGATION 1 WRAP-UP

REVIEW

1. What two factors contribute to the momentum of a moving object?

2. If two baseball bats are swung at the same velocity, how will the momentum of a 1-kg bat compare to that of a 1.5-kg bat?

CRITICAL THINKING

3. A cue ball strikes a rack of 15 stationary pool balls and comes to a complete stop. The pool balls, however, scatter in all directions. Explain what takes place in terms of conservation of momentum.

4. If the total momentum of a rocket and its fuel remains at zero after being launched, why does the rocket still move upward?

How Do Actions Cause Reactions?

A child is roller-skating. Without thinking, he pushes on a wall, rolls backward, loses his balance, and falls into a puddle. You'll be able to explain what happened when you explore the relationship between action forces and reaction forces.

Activity
Bouncing Balls

When you drop a ball, it strikes Earth. What causes the ball to bounce back?

- -

Procedure

1. Drop a large ball on a hard, flat floor. **Observe** the ball's speed. **Record** in your *Science Notebook* the point at which the ball is traveling fastest and the point at which it is traveling slowest.

2. Drop the ball again. This time, **observe** its direction. At what point does the ball's direction of motion change?

3. **Predict** what will happen if you bounce the ball harder against the floor.

4. **Test** your prediction and **observe** the ball's motion. **Record** the results.

MATERIALS
- basketball or other large ball that bounces
- *Science Notebook*

SAFETY
Don't bounce the ball too hard. You don't want to hit other people or the ceiling.

Step 1

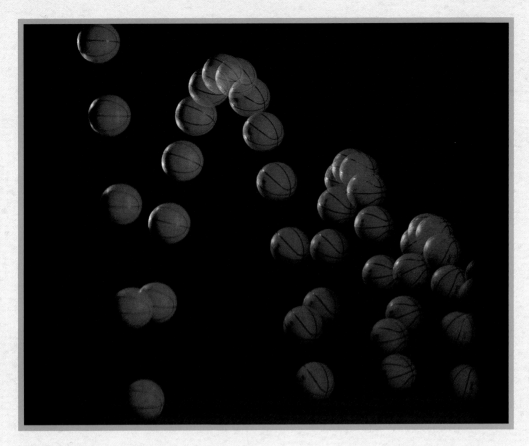

Analyze and Conclude

1. What exerted a force, or pushed back, on the ball when it hit the floor, causing the ball to change speed and direction?

2. How did bouncing the ball harder affect the force that changed the ball's speed and direction?

3. Identify two forces that act when the ball hits the floor.

UNIT PROJECT LINK

Bumper cars are a very popular amusement park attraction. Imagine one bumper car colliding with a second bumper car that is touching a third bumper car. Describe what happens to the cars.

Using three marbles of the same size, create a model of this crash. Describe what happens to each "car" during the collision. Test as many different types of collisions as you can think of. Describe the result of each collision on a card next to a drawing of it.

Technology Link

For more help with your Unit Project, go to **www.eduplace.com**.

Activity
Double-Ball Bounce

How can you use action and reaction forces to make a clay ball bounce?

MATERIALS
- modeling clay
- basketball
- metric tape measure
- *Science Notebook*

SAFETY

Don't throw the basketball or clay at anyone.

Procedure

1. Form some clay into a ball and drop it onto a hard floor. **Observe** the clay. What happened to it after it hit the floor? How did the clay change when it hit the floor? **Record** your observations in your *Science Notebook*.

2. Place the clay ball on top of a basketball.

3. Carefully drop the basketball so that the clay ball remains on top of the basketball.

4. **Make a drawing** of the basketball. **Draw** the location of the clay ball at the point when the basketball hits the ground.

5. **Draw** the path of the clay ball after the basketball has hit the floor and rebounded.

6. **Observe** how high the basketball bounces.

7. **Predict** how high the basketball will bounce without the clay ball on top of it. **Test your prediction** and **record** how high the basketball bounces.

Step 1

Step 2

Analyze and Conclude

1. What happened to the clay ball when it hit the floor? Why did this happen?

2. What happened to the clay ball when it was sitting on top of the dropped basketball? Why did this happen?

3. **Identify** the forces involved in this activity. What is the clay ball pushing against? What is the basketball pushing against?

4. **Compare** the height of the basketball's bounce with and without the clay sitting on the ball. How did the bounces differ? Why do you think they differed?

Actions Cause Reactions

> **Reading Focus** What is Newton's third law of motion?

The basketball is passed to you, and you dribble down the court. The score is tied. There's only one defender between you and the basket. You hear the fans cheering and chanting. They're counting down the clock! "Ten, nine, eight, seven! . . ." This is your moment. You break left. The guard is right in your face. You break right. "Six, five, four. . ." She's still in your face. Cutting left again, you catch her off balance, but she recovers and is coming back at you. "Three, two . . ." At the top of the key, she's right on you! With one second to go, you push off the floor and rise high in the air with your head, arms, and hands well above the defender. With a flick of your wrists, you launch the ball toward the basket. The fans chant, "One!" The buzzer sounds, and silence falls throughout the arena as the ball arcs toward the basket.

What happened? How did you get into the air above the defender? What forces were involved in your last-second heroics?

Newton's Third Law of Motion

Had Sir Isaac Newton been watching you, he would have been happy to explain that you had just provided a wonderful demonstration of his third law of motion. Once he stopped chanting with the crowd, he might have said, "Ah, my young friend, don't you know that for every action force there is an equal and opposite reaction force?" In this case, the action force was your feet pushing against the floor.

When you shoot a basketball, the ball pushes on you just as hard as you push on it. ▶

F89

The reaction force was the floor pushing against your feet. Because you exerted a force, the floor pushed back against you. This caused you to jump high above the defender trying to block you.

Newton's **third law of motion** states that for *every* action force there is an equal and opposite reaction force. Two important things to remember about Newton's third law are: (1) forces always occur in pairs made up of an **action force** and a **reaction force**; (2) the action force and the reaction force always act on different bodies.

When you made your spectacular jump, you might have felt the action and reaction forces between your feet and the floor. But on a hard surface like a basketball court, it's difficult to see these forces work. If you jumped on a trampoline, though, it would be easy to observe the trampoline pushing back on you as you pushed on it.

Mass Matters

Suppose that the defending player had jumped high enough to block your shot. Let's also suppose that she had pushed off the floor with a force exactly equal to the force you used to push off, but that she had less mass than you. The third law explains that the reaction force of the floor would be equal to this player's action force. The reaction force, however, would be acting on a smaller mass. According to Newton's second law, this player would have a greater acceleration and would, therefore, go higher than you. If that had happened, she probably would have blocked your shot. But we

Science in Literature

COMING DOWN TO EARTH

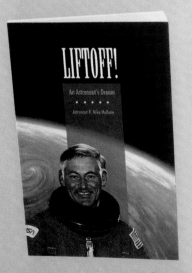

Liftoff! An Astronaut's Dream
by R. Mike Mullane
Silver Burdett Press, 1995

"Five...four...three...two...BOOM!

The OMS engines fire. *Atlantis* is pointing backward in orbit, so the engines are now slowing us down. The shuttle is doing the same thing that you do when you try to stop yourself on a water slide or a snowy sled ride."

Liftoff! An Astronaut's Dream by R. Mike Mullane contains many descriptions of actions and events involving Newton's laws of motion. Try to identify these actions and events as you read this book.

+ momentum

- momentum

action

+ momentum

- momentum

reaction

Using Math *If two people of different masses jump with the same force, which one is going to jump higher? Many basketball players can jump more than one meter straight up. About how many inches is this?*

know that wasn't the case, because the basketball is still arcing toward the basket as if in slow motion.

The Third Law and Earth's Surface

Think again about your leap. You already know that when your feet push against Earth, Earth pushes back. Your momentum is equal to your mass multiplied by your takeoff speed. Suppose you have a mass of 50 kg (110 lb) and jumped with a speed of 10 m/s (11 yd/s). Then your momentum would be

$$p = m \times v$$
$$p = 50 \text{ kg} \times 10 \text{ m/s}$$
$$p = 500 \text{ kg} \times \text{m/s}$$

What is Earth's reaction to your action? As you push against Earth, it

pushes back, causing you to jump into the air. Since your momentum when you jumped is 500 kg × m/s, Earth's momentum must be −500 kg × m/s, the opposite of your momentum. Remember, momentum is conserved. How fast does Earth move backward in reaction to the action of your jump? You don't even have to calculate that number to know that Earth's backward velocity is very, very small. No one watching your jump shot will have any idea that Earth has moved at all! Actually, all the fans care about is whether or not the ball goes through the hoop!

So, what do you think? You took a shot at the last second. Are you a hero, or is the score still tied? ∎

Trampoline Fun

Reading Focus Why can you jump higher on a trampoline than on a hard surface?

▲ **A gymnast uses stored energy to jump higher on a trampoline.**

A gymnast bounces up and down on a trampoline. With each bounce the trampoline surface bends downward and then springs back. The gymnast rises high into the air and executes a beautiful midair somersault with a twist before landing again on the trampoline. Quickly her body again springs high into the air, and she completes another difficult maneuver.

Gymnasts practice for years and years to develop the body control necessary for a near-perfect gymnastics routine. A trampoline helps a gymnast sail much higher than he or she could if jumping from the ground. Is magic at work here? Or does Newton's third law still apply?

The third law of motion is still at work here. As you push down on the surface of a trampoline, the springs around the edges stretch and store energy. As the springs contract, the surface of the trampoline moves upward and the energy is returned to you. The trampoline pushes on you for a longer time than the ground would have, transferring a greater amount of energy to your body.

As you bounce higher and fall from a greater distance, you hit the trampoline with more force, storing more energy in the springs. The reaction force also increases and pushes against you even longer, sending you still higher into the air. Experts warn, though, that inexperienced bouncers should avoid high bounces.

1 When you bounce on a trampoline, you begin by pushing against the trampoline's surface, which bends downward under you.

2 Eventually you and the trampoline's surface come to a stop and begin moving upward. Now the force that the trampoline exerts on you causes you to speed up.

3 Of course, you are exerting an equal and opposite force on the trampoline. Finally you leave the trampoline's surface and sail back into the air.

INVESTIGATION 2 WRAP-UP

REVIEW

1. What happens when you blow up a balloon and let it go? Explain in terms of Newton's third law.

2. A girl wearing in-line skates stands facing a wall. She pushes as hard as she can against the wall. Explain what happens in terms of actions and reactions.

CRITICAL THINKING

3. You're standing in the back of a rowboat. You try to jump from the boat to a dock about one meter away, but you find yourself in the water instead! What happened?

4. Can you jump as high on a sandy beach as you can on a basketball floor? Explain why or why not.

HOW ARE ACTION-REACTION FORCES USED?

Roaring to life, the rocket engines create an action force that causes hot gases to stream from the rocket. The restraining bolts explode free, and the reaction force thrusts the shuttle off the launch pad. In this investigation you'll examine some other ways that action-reaction forces make things move.

Activity

Action-Reaction Wheels

Have you ever noticed in which direction a car's wheels turn when the car moves? What gives a car its forward motion?

MATERIALS

- toy car with a pull-back friction engine
- clay
- *Science Notebook*

Procedure

1. With one hand, push a toy car backward on a table to activate its friction engine.

2. Hold the car up and watch its wheels spin.

Step 2

3. **Predict** which way the wheels will push against your hand. **Test** your prediction. **Record** your observations in your *Science Notebook*.

4. Activate the car's engine one more time and release the car on the table.

5. **Make a drawing** of the car resting on the table. With one arrow, show the direction that the car traveled. With another arrow, show in which direction the wheels pushed against the surface of the table.

6. **Predict** how adding mass to the car would affect its motion. Add a lump of clay to the car and **test** your prediction.

Analyze and Conclude

1. **Analyze** your drawing. What gives the car its push to move forward? Remember that the car moves in the direction in which the force pushes it.

2. **Identify** two forces that act between the car and the surface.

3. How did adding mass to the car affect its motion? Explain.

INVESTIGATE FURTHER!

RESEARCH

What would happen if you changed the surface under the car? Try running the car on a soft pillow. Compare this to how the car runs on carpet or tile. Explain why you think the surface underneath is important.

Civilization and the Wheel

Reading Focus Why was the invention of the wheel such an important occurrence?

The name of the man or woman who invented the wheel will never be known. Perhaps the inventor was a warrior devising a chariot. The inventor might have been a hunter, tired of carrying the bodies of large animals. Or perhaps the inventor was a mourner, who sought

▲ The earliest wheels were probably solid wooden wheels like the ones on this ancient toy.

a smoother ride for a loved one on the way to the grave. What *is* known is that the wheel was probably invented about 5,500 years ago.

In fact, the earliest picture we have of a wheel was drawn by a Sumerian accountant. It shows four rough-shaped wheels mounted on a funeral wagon pulled by oxen. The Sumerians lived in a part of the world known as the Fertile Crescent, between the Tigris and Euphrates rivers, in the country we know today as Iraq.

A Good Idea Spreads Quickly

If the ancient Sumerians invented the wheel, other people quickly adopted it. About 4,000 years ago, tribes from the steppes near the Black Sea appeared in the Tigris-Euphrates Valley. They brought with them strange animals called horses that were used to pull carts rolling on wheels. But these wheels were made with wooden rims and sturdy spokes fastened to a central hub. Soon the wheel with spokes found its way to Greece, China, and Egypt, where it first appeared about 3,750 years ago. The ancient Celts of Western Europe also had the wheel by about this time.

As time went on, wheels became lighter and more efficient for speed. ▼

A Little Bit of Effort Does a Lot of Work

The wheel made life better and easier. It enabled people to accomplish more work with less effort. Before the wheel, some people used sledges, or dry-land sleds, to drag whatever they could not carry. Other people used travoises—two long poles tied together so that loads could be slung between the poles.

But the wheel greatly reduced friction and saved energy over the sledge and

▲ **Before the introduction of the wheel, transporting large objects meant pushing or pulling them on sledges or travoises.**

travois. Thus, the wheel offered a way to carry greater weight over a longer distance, at greater speeds, and with far less effort. A person on foot might be limited to traveling only about 56–64 km (35–40 mi) a day, carrying no more than 40 kg (88 lb). The wheel, however, enabled farmers, merchants, armies, and even whole towns to carry vast loads of food, trading goods, and other supplies over much longer distances. In time

the wheel linked together settlements and speeded up the spread of civilization.

A Good Idea Gets Better

Make no mistake about it, a wheel is a machine that works on the principle of Newton's third law of motion. A wheel pushes on the ground; the ground pushes on the wheel. The result is motion. Along with the lever, inclined plane, and wedge, the wheel is one of the four simple machines on which modern civilization has been built. And through the ages, the wheel has been improved many times.

At first wheels were mounted on axles, or rigid poles, which in turn were connected to the undersides of carts. The wheels and axles turned together as a unit. In time, the axles became fixed in position on the underside of the cart, and the wheels revolved around them.

The ancient Celts developed a crude forerunner of the roller bearing. They simply hollowed out separate channels inside the wheel's hub and lined each channel with hard wooden sticks. When the hub was mounted on the axle, the wheel and the sticks all turned together. As a result, the wheel turned more easily

It's very likely that rollers—a type of wheel—were used to move the Easter Island statues. ▼

and with less friction and wear on all its critical parts. The Celts were also the first to mount the front wheels on a movable platform so that a wagon could be turned and steered by its driver.

▲ **The wheel became important to recreation, transportation, and work, as can be seen in this antique farming tractor.**

The Pace of the Wheel Is the Pace of the Civilization

From the day the wheel was introduced, civilization has owed a huge debt to its inventor. The wheel has been used in hundreds of thousands of inventions that have improved civilization. Social scientists sometimes say that the pace of the wheel is the pace of the civilization. This means that the faster we travel on wheels, the faster we move ahead in other ways, too.

This certainly seems true in this country. People moved westward in covered wagons. They built many of our cities around railroad stations, and then tied

Internet Field Trip

Visit **www.eduplace.com** to learn more about Easter Island and how its early inhabitants may have used wheels to move their statues.

the cities together with a vast network of highways when the automobile appeared. We have even put wheels on our airplanes and moved our moon rockets and space shuttles into launching position on gigantic wheeled contraptions.

Can you imagine a world without wheels? From doorknobs to watches; from bicycles and baby buggies to trains, planes, and automobiles; from simple conveyor belts to the treads on gigantic military machines—almost every modern device with parts that move uses wheels in one way or another.

Beyond that, practically everything you eat, wear, play with, or live in was either produced, transported, or prepared for you by someone or something using wheels. It's probably fair to say that civilization could not exist without the wheel. Certainly the kind of society we're accustomed to would not be possible. ■

Even a shuttle depends on wheels to get it to the launch pad. ▼

Faster Fins

Reading Focus How do different body parts help fish and marine mammals move through water?

SCIENCE
TECHNOLOGY
& SOCIETY

What do you use to move through the water when you swim? If you're like most people, you cup your hands and pull them backward against the water. You probably also kick your feet to help you move through the water. As you pull your hands backward against the water and kick your feet against the water, these action forces are responded to with the reaction force of the water pushing against you. The result of these forces is forward motion.

If you have ever watched championship swimmers in a race, you may have noticed that their movements are very similar to the movements you use. The only difference is that their movements are more efficient than yours. But even the best swimmers only reach speeds of about 8 km/h (5 mph) for fairly short periods of time.

Most swimmers have one thing in common: They usually splash a lot of water around, especially with their feet. But do fish splash a lot of water? Except when they jump, fish very seldom splash.

Did you ever wonder how a fish swims? It swims by moving its tail and the middle section of its body back and forth. The fish's body and tail push against the water, first on one side and then on the other. This motion is an action force against the water. The water in turn produces a reaction force that pushes the fish forward. In this way a sailfish can reach speeds of 108.8 km/h (68 mph).

Some marine mammals, such as seals, swim like fish. They move their rear flippers back and forth in a powerful action force against the water. Other mammals, such as whales, porpoises, and dolphins, swim by moving their tails up and down rather than back and forth.

Humans aren't built for speed in the water. ▼

Using Math *Using their powerful tails, dolphins swim at speeds up to 40 km/h. About how fast is this in miles per hour?*

Having watched fish and marine mammals swim, humans invented something to make swimming more efficient. Swim fins, which mimic the tail actions of fish and marine mammals, are worn by snorkelers and scuba divers to push against the water. The reaction force—the water pushing against the swim fins—pushes the diver through the water.

Long stiff fins push harder against the water than do short flexible fins. Long fins bend slightly as divers move their legs up and down. However, a stiff fin will straighten itself out. The movement gives the diver a little extra push forward.

Snorkelers and scuba divers also can use their fins to help them tread water. They simply stand in the water and "walk" in place. The action force of their fins pushes down on the water. The reaction force is the water pushing the snorkelers and divers up.

With swim fins, humans become much more efficient swimmers. However, their efficiency does not come close to that of a trout, let alone a sailfish! ■

INVESTIGATION 3 WRAP-UP

REVIEW

1. Draw a car and its wheels. Diagram the action force and the reaction force needed to move the car forward.

2. You use action-reaction forces all the time. Explain how action-reaction forces affect you when you walk, climb stairs, roll over, or do a push-up.

CRITICAL THINKING

3. Ducks and other waterfowl have webbed feet. How is this adaptation similar to fins on a fish?

4. On a vehicle with wheels, does the circumference of its wheels affect the velocity of the vehicle? Explain.

REFLECT & EVALUATE

Word Power

Write the letter of the term that best completes each sentence.

1. When riding a bicycle, your push on the pedals is an example of a/an ___.
2. All moving bodies have ___.
3. Momentum is never lost, according to the ___.
4. When you jump on a diving board, the push of the board on your feet is a/an ___.
5. For every action there is an equal and opposite reaction, according to the ___.

a. action force
b. law of conservation of momentum
c. momentum
d. reaction force
e. third law of motion

Check What You Know

Write the term in each pair that best completes each sentence.

1. In the equation used to find momentum, p represents (velocity, momentum).
2. The momentum of a 10-kg mass with a velocity of 2 m/s is (5 kg × m/s, 20 kg × m/s).
3. When a tennis racquet strikes a ball, the racquet provides the (action force, reaction force).

Problem Solving

1. You're playing pool. You want to send a colored ball to a pocket on a sharp angle to your left. On what part of the colored ball do you want the cue ball to strike?
2. Object A has momentum of 200 kg × m/sec. It strikes stationary object B, which moves away with momentum of 150 kg × sec/m. What happens to object A?

Look at the two pictures. Use Newton's third law to describe what is happening in each picture.

5

REAL-WORLD FORCES

Forces are at work in the world. Planes, rockets, and space shuttles may seem to move in different ways, but the laws of motion apply to all of them.

• •

PEOPLE USING SCIENCE

Astronaut Since Michael E. Lopez-Alegria became an astronaut in 1992, he has orbited Earth 256 times and traveled over 6 million miles through space. In 1995, as a mission specialist and flight engineer aboard the space shuttle *Columbia*, Commander Lopez-Alegria assisted in a series of scientific experiments on the physics of fluids, combustion, and other topics.

Originally from Spain, and equally at home in California, Michael E. Lopez-Alegria enjoys sports, traveling, and cooking. Before becoming an astronaut, he trained as a naval aviator and learned to fly over 30 different aircraft. Recently, Lopez-Alegria has assumed new responsibilities as a NASA director of operations at a cosmonaut training center in Russia.

Coming Up

Michael E. Lopez-Alegria changes film in a 35-mm camera aboard the space shuttle *Columbia*.

HOW DO HEAVY THINGS FLY?

Engines screaming, the powerful aircraft thunders toward the end of the runway. Nearly out of room, the pilot pulls back on the stick, and the jet streaks into the sky. What forces are at work to get something so heavy to take off?

Activity

Making a Paper Glider

Under what conditions can the air support a paper glider—or a real glider?

MATERIALS
- sheet of notebook paper
- paper clips
- *Science Notebook*

SAFETY
Don't throw your plane at anyone.

Procedure

1. Using the following diagram, make a paper airplane.

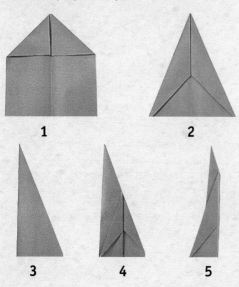

1   2   3   4   5

Step 4

F104

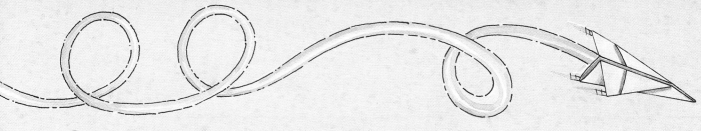

2. **Predict** how your airplane will fly. **Record** your prediction in your *Science Notebook*.

3. In your *Science Notebook*, **create a chart** like the one below. **Record** all your results in this chart.

Description of Flight Test	Result of Test
Forward glide test	
Spiral glide test	
Backward glide test	
Dropping test	

See **SCIENCE** *and* **MATH TOOLBOX** *page H11 if you need to review **Making a Chart to Organize Data**.*

4. Practice tossing the airplane to make it glide forward.

5. Try creasing the wings until the plane turns in a spiral when you throw it.

6. Try throwing the plane backward. Does it fly as well backward as it does forward?

7. Drop the airplane without throwing it forward. Does it still float in the air?

Analyze and Conclude

1. Why do you think an airplane has to move forward through the air to fly?

2. Why is the shape of the airplane important? **Describe** the best shape for an airplane to have.

3. What must you do if you want a plane to spiral?

4. What do you think would make the plane turn to the left or right?

5. What conclusions can you draw about the forces that keep a glider in the air? Write your conclusions in your *Science Notebook*.

INVESTIGATE FURTHER!

EXPERIMENT

Create your own airplane. Make one that glides farther than the one you used in this activity. Use a full piece of paper in your design. Then have an air show with your classmates.

Activity

Propeller Power!

Helicopters don't have wings—they have large fast-spinning propellers. Try experimenting with some paper spinners to see what makes them stay in the air longer.

MATERIALS
- square sheets of paper
- penny
- tape
- *Science Notebook*

- -

Procedure

1. Follow the diagrams below to make two paper spinners, one with wide wings and one with narrow wings.

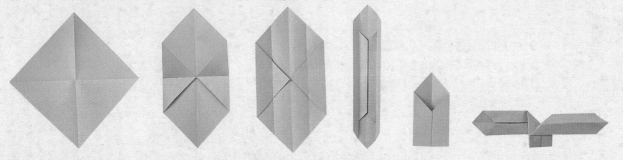

2. **Predict** what will happen when you drop the spinners from the same height. **Record** your prediction in your *Science Notebook*.

3. Drop both spinners from a selected height. **Record** what happens as they fall to the ground.

4. Select a new height. Repeat steps 2 and 3.

5. Make another narrow spinner and tape a penny to the bottom.

6. Drop the two narrow spinners—one with the penny and one without the penny—from the same height. **Record** what you observe.

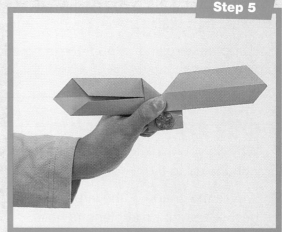

Step 5

Analyze and Conclude

1. Do the spinners always turn in the same direction? Look at the wings and **infer** what causes the spinners to turn the way they do.

2. What effect does the wider wing have?

3. What effect does adding the extra weight have?

Designing Flyers

Reading Focus Who were the Wright brothers?

The Wright brothers flew their first plane at Kitty Hawk, North Carolina. Models tested in a wind tunnel helped them discover that twisted propellers work better than flat ones. On December 17, 1903, their plane, the *Flyer*, made four flights. The longest flight lasted less than one minute.

The Wright brothers build a plane capable of extended periods of flight. They demonstrate figure-eight flights.

1908

The Wright brothers obtain the most scientific knowledge available on aeronautics and flight. They build several successful gliders, improving on Lilienthal's designs.

1900

1903

The Wright brothers announce that their new airplane has flown for 59 seconds. Many newspapers ignore the achievement. Some papers joke about it because everyone "knows" that flight is impossible.

1896

Orville and Wilbur Wright become interested in flying when they read about the death of Otto Lilienthal, a German engineer who built and flew the world's first successful gliders.

Flying Forces

Reading Focus What forces are acting on an airplane in flight?

Greek mythology tells of an Athenian craftsman named Daedalus who went to the island of Crete. While in Crete, he and his son Icarus were imprisoned by the king. To escape, Daedalus built two sets of wings from wax, feathers, and string. He and Icarus flew from the prison out over the sea. But when Icarus flew too close to the Sun, the wax in his wings melted, and he fell to his death in the sea. Although saddened by the loss of his son, Daedalus flew on and eventually returned to Greece.

From the earliest times of recorded history, humans have dreamed of flying. With envy and wonder, people have looked to the skies and have searched for ways to join the birds. Early attempts at flying were not much more successful than Icarus' effort and some proved just as deadly.

LIFT Once the airplane is moving, lift causes the airplane to rise into the air. **Lift** is the upward force caused by the differences in air pressure above and below the wings, produced by the shape of the wings.

DRAG AND WEIGHT The two forces working against flight are the airplane's drag and weight. **Drag** is the resistance to forward motion caused by the air. Weight is the force of gravity acting on the airplane. While the engines and wings are trying to lift an airplane, air is slowing it down, and Earth's gravity is pulling it back to Earth.

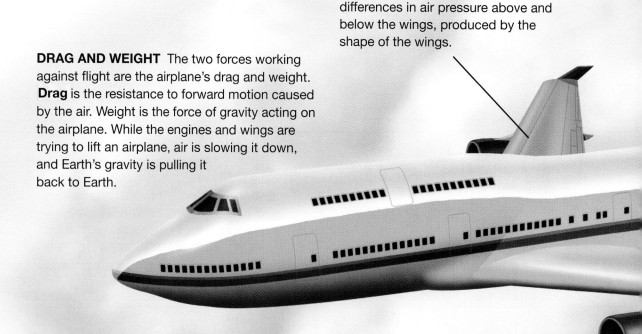

It wasn't until the Wright brothers mastered the forces required for flight that sustained-power flight became possible. However, the Wright brothers' first flight lasted just 12 seconds and covered a distance of only 37 m (120 ft)—a distance shorter than the wingspan of some modern aircraft!

Thrust and Lift

The whole idea of an airplane's design is to get a heavy piece of machinery off the ground and moving through the air. The first step in that process is to move the airplane forward on the ground. The airplane's engines do that job.

The wings of an airplane are curved on the top and flat on the bottom. Air passing over the top of a wing moves faster than air moving across the bottom of a wing. As a result of the higher speed on the top of the wing, air pressure is less in that area. Stronger air pressure on the bottom of the wing lifts the wing— and the rest of the airplane—upward.

You can easily observe this effect with a simple experiment. Hold a sheet of paper with both hands along one edge. Then blow over the top of the paper. In this experiment the paper is the wing of an airplane, and your breath is the wind blowing over it.

How can thrust and lift of airplanes be improved? Larger, more efficient engines are one way to increase thrust. Changing the shape, number, and location of the

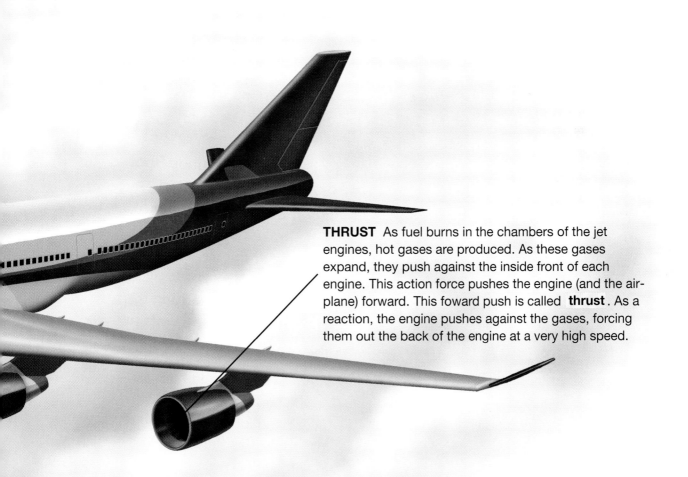

THRUST As fuel burns in the chambers of the jet engines, hot gases are produced. As these gases expand, they push against the inside front of each engine. This action force pushes the engine (and the airplane) forward. This foward push is called **thrust**. As a reaction, the engine pushes against the gases, forcing them out the back of the engine at a very high speed.

F109

wings increases lift. In fact, one interesting and unique design for an airplane, called the flying wing, is in its shape—a large wing. The larger the wing, the greater the lift. So why not make the wing the size of the airplane itself? Some military planes have been designed in this way. While these planes do have a great deal of lift, they are very awkward to fly.

Drag

Since drag (the resistance between the plane and air) is a force that operates in the opposite direction of thrust, it would not seem to be desirable. However, drag is very important. For a plane to slow down and come to a stop, it must have some way to increase its drag. Most airplanes have flaps along the back edge of the wings. When flaps are lowered, they increase both lift and drag, allowing the aircraft to fly and land at slower speeds. Wheel brakes, lift spoilers, and reverse thrust add drag to stop the plane on the ground.

Airplane Design and Testing

Modern airplanes are complicated machines. Engineers must test their designs long before the planes are built. One way to test new designs is to write computer programs that contain all the design features. The computer can then predict what will happen when the plane attempts to take off, fly, and land.

Another step in airplane design is the use of the wind tunnel. Research involving wind tunnels was pioneered by the Russian physicist Konstantin Tsiolkovsky before the turn of the twentieth century.

Science in Literature

UP, UP, AND . . . DOWN!

"No one had ever seen what Amos Root saw on that September afternoon in 1904. Standing in a cow pasture near Dayton, Ohio, he looked up and saw a flying machine circle in the sky above him. He could see the bold pilot lying facedown on the lower wing, staring straight ahead as he steered the craft to a landing in the grass."

THE WRIGHT BROTHERS
How They Invented the Airplane

Russell Freedman
With Original Photographs by Wilbur and Orville Wright

**The Wright Brothers:
How They Invented the Airplane**
by Russell Freedman
Holiday House, 1991

Thus begins *The Wright Brothers: How They Invented the Airplane*, by Russell Freedman. Read this fascinating account and look at the pictures taken by the Wright brothers as they tackled and solved the problems of flight.

▲ A computer program determines the flight capabilities of the design and enables the engineer to make adjustments before actual construction of a new aircraft begins.

A wind tunnel consists of a small chamber in which air is moved rapidly from one end to the other to simulate air rushing over an airplane's body. A small model of the airplane to be tested is placed inside the wind tunnel. Then the plane's behavior in a stream of air can be studied. Smoke is often introduced into the airstream to make it easier to see how air flows over the model. Information collected in the wind tunnel is analyzed by engineers. The data is then used to make design changes that will improve the flight characteristics of the airplane. ■

Internet Field Trip

Visit **www.eduplace.com** to learn more about the forces of flight and how airplanes fly.

INVESTIGATION 1 WRAP-UP

REVIEW

1. How does an airplane wing provide lift?

2. When an airplane is in flight, which is greater—the combined forces of lift and thrust or the combined forces of weight and drag? How do you know?

CRITICAL THINKING

3. Explain why the wings of a space shuttle are useless for most of its mission.

4. To make an airplane turn, a pilot increases the drag on one wing. On which wing would a pilot increase drag to make the plane turn to the right? Explain.

HOW DO ROCKETS USE ACTION-REACTION FORCES?

In space, there is no air, water, or ground to push against. How does a shuttle orbiter use its rockets to change direction in order to return to Earth? In this investigation you'll find out how rocket gases are involved in action-reaction forces.

Activity

Balloon Rocket Race

An inflated balloon can be a model for a rocket. Experiment with its action-reaction forces.

MATERIALS
- goggles
- string
- plastic straw
- long balloon
- tape
- metric tape measure
- *Science Notebook*

Procedure

1. Run a string through a straw and then stretch the string across the classroom.

2. Tie each end of the string to something at opposite ends of the classroom. Clothing hooks and doorknobs work well.

3. Inflate a balloon and hold the end closed with your fingers. Do not inflate the balloon to its full size.

4. With the help of a group member, tape the balloon to the straw so that the straw runs along the length of the balloon.

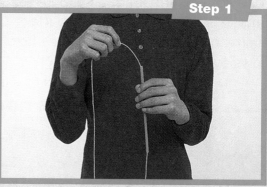

Step 1

Step 3

Step 5

5. Move the straw and balloon on the string to one end of the room.

6. **Predict** what will happen if you release the end of the balloon. **Record** your prediction in your *Science Notebook*. **Test your prediction** and **observe** what happens.

7. **Measure and record** how far the balloon traveled on the string.

 See **SCIENCE** *and* **MATH TOOLBOX** page H6 if you need to review *Using a Tape Measure or Ruler.*

8. Inflate the balloon again; this time, make the balloon as big as you can.

9. Repeat the activity and **record** the distance the fully inflated balloon traveled.

Analyze and Conclude

1. In your *Science Notebook*, **draw a picture** of the inflated balloon on the string. Draw arrows on your picture showing how the air in the balloon is pushing on the inflated balloon. Draw other arrows to show how the balloon is pushing back on the air inside.

2. Have an arrow show the direction in which the air moved as it escaped from the balloon. Draw another arrow to show the direction in which the balloon moved.

3. How did you increase the action force?

4. What happened to the reaction force when you increased the action force? What evidence can you cite?

INVESTIGATE FURTHER!

EXPERIMENT

Have a balloon race. Stretch several strings across the classroom. Be sure that each is level and stretched equally tight. Experiment with balloons of all sizes. Race several balloons at the same time. Draw the shape of each balloon and record the distance that it traveled.

Activity
Straw Rockets

Here's how the result of action-reaction forces can be directed to control movement.

Procedure

1. Insert about 5 cm of a straw into a balloon, leaving the flexible bend outside the balloon. Use a rubber band to hold the straw tightly in place.

2. Inflate the balloon by blowing through the straw. Hold your finger over the end of the straw to prevent the air from escaping.

3. As shown at right, bend the flexible end of the straw so that it forms a right angle to the rest of the straw.

4. Use tape to attach string to the balloon. Have a group member hold the string so that the straw is at a right angle to the string, as shown on the facing page.

Step 3

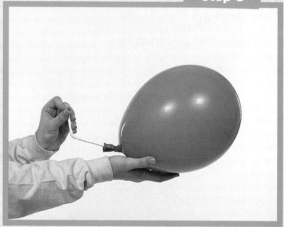

Step 2

5. **Predict** what will happen if you release the air from the balloon. **Record** your prediction in your *Science Notebook*.

6. While a group member holds the string at arm's length, release the air inside the balloon. **Record** what happens.

Analyze and Conclude

1. In your *Science Notebook*, draw the balloon and straw as if you were looking down on them.

2. With an arrow, show the direction that the air moves as it escapes from the balloon. With another arrow, show the way the balloon moves.

3. Draw arrows to indicate the action force and the reaction force that cause the motions of the balloon and straw. Label the arrows.

4. Explain how Newton's third law applies to this activity.

INVESTIGATE FURTHER!

EXPERIMENT

For this experiment, you need an empty milk carton, string, water, and a bucket. Punch a hole in the lower-right corner of each side of the milk carton. Also punch a hole through the center of the top of the carton. Thread the string through the hole in the top of the carton, and hang the carton over the bucket. While two group members cover the holes in the sides, fill the carton with water. Uncover the holes and watch what happens to the carton.

Rocket Launch

Reading Focus How do the space shuttle's booster engines differ from the main engines?

The rockets developed by Goddard (*left*) and Tsiolkovsky (*center*) led directly to the powerful Saturn 5 (*right*).

At about the same time that the Wright brothers were experimenting with powered flight, Russian physicist Konstantin Tsiolkovsky and American physicist Robert Goddard were experimenting with rocket-powered flight. Tsiolkovsky and Goddard each knew that a rocket would operate under the principles of Newton's third law. Working independently of one another, thousands of miles apart, Tsiolkovsky and Goddard both developed the foundation for space exploration.

The early rockets of Tsiolkovsky and Goddard seem simple compared to today's rockets. But the experiments of these men led to the eventual development of the mighty Saturn 5 rocket. In 1969, Saturn 5 would launch Michael Collins, "Buzz" Aldrin, and Neil Armstrong on the Apollo 11 mission to the Moon.

Space-Shuttle Engines

In the more than 25 years since Apollo 11, no rocket produced has been as powerful as the Saturn 5. However, the rockets that lift the space shuttle are the most efficient ever produced.

The shuttle's solid-fuel boosters each contain 500,000 kg (1.1 million lb) of aluminum metal, aluminum perchlorate, and a plasticlike material that holds these together. When the boosters ignite, the aluminum and aluminum perchlorate react to produce very hot gases that are pushed out of the engine nozzles.

The main engines of the shuttle operate on a mixture of liquid hydrogen and liquid oxygen. The liquid fuels are stored in a huge external fuel tank, which holds 550,000 L (143,000 gal) of hydrogen and 1.5 million L (390,000 gal) of oxygen. When ignited, the two liquid

elements react to form steam. The steam exits the main engines at a temperature of about 2,000°C (3,600°F), providing a powerful thrust.

Shuttle Action and Reaction

As the space shuttle sits on its launch pad, its momentum is zero. At the moment the engines ignite, all that changes. The effect of the shuttle engines firing is a stream of hot gases escaping from the engine nozzles at very high speeds. At that time the space shuttle begins ascending.

When the shuttle's engines fire, the hot gases push against the walls of the engine chamber. This action force pushes the chamber and the whole shuttle upward. At the same time, the walls of the chamber push back on the hot gases. This reaction force pushes the hot gases out of the bottom of the shuttle at high speed. The result is that the shuttle lifts off the pad and heads for orbit.

Since the shuttle has such a large mass, its velocity is small at first. As the engines continue to fire, the speed of the shuttle increases. By the time the main engines cut off, the shuttle has a velocity of about 27,000 km/h (16,200 mph). ■

INVESTIGATION 2 WRAP-UP

REVIEW

1. How are action-reaction forces involved in launching a rocket?

2. How is releasing an inflated balloon similar to launching a rocket in terms of action-reaction forces?

CRITICAL THINKING

3. Hydrogen and oxygen react chemically to produce water. How does this fact help explain why these elements are used as fuels in the space shuttle's main engines?

4. The space shuttle spends much of its time in near empty space. Yet its streamlined shape is designed to reduce air resistance. Explain.

HOW DO THINGS FLOAT?

April 15, 1912—Hours ago, the luxury liner *Titanic* floated high in the water. Now she has sunk beneath the waves, down to the bottom of the Atlantic Ocean. What force keeps a ship afloat? What changes occurred to make this ship sink?

Activity

Clay Boats

What happens when you try to float a piece of clay on water? Does the object's shape have any effect on its ability to float? Experiment to find out.

Procedure

1. Roll the clay into a ball. Place it in a container that is partly filled with water. What happens?

2. Form the clay into a boat shape. Put your boat into the water to see if it floats.

Step 2

3. **Draw a picture** of your boat in your *Science Notebook*.

4. **Predict** what will happen if you add marbles to your boat. **Record** your prediction.

5. **Test your prediction** by adding marbles to your boat one by one. Continue adding marbles until your boat sinks.

6. **Record** the number of marbles your boat held before it sank.

7. Redesign your boat to hold more marbles before sinking and repeat the experiment.

Analyze and Conclude

1. Describe how you increased the carrying capacity of your boat in step 7 without using more clay.

2. How did the shape of the boat affect its ability to float?

3. A boat floating in water is moving neither up nor down. Based on Newton's first two laws, what can you **infer** about the forces acting on the boat?

4. A boat floating in water is exerting a downward force on the water. Based on Newton's third law, what is causing the boat to float?

UNIT PROJECT LINK

Make a water ride for your park. Use a pan of water to create the splash pool at the end of the ride. After you complete your design, make a three-dimensional model of the boat and the ride and place it in your park. On your model, show how many passengers will fit in the boat. Place a card next to the ride describing how fast the boat moves and what factors affect the size of the splash the boat makes.

TechnologyLink
For more help with your Unit Project, go to **www.eduplace.com**.

Activity
Floating Egg

Do objects float better in fresh water or salt water? You'll find out in this activity.

MATERIALS
- goggles
- large plastic container
- water
- raw egg
- large spoon
- table salt
- *Science Notebook*

Procedure

1. Half fill a container with water.

 Math Hint *To find the half-full line, measure the height of the container and divide that value by 2.*

SAFETY //////

Wear goggles during this activity. Clean up spills immediately. If you must clean up a broken egg, wash your hands thoroughly.

2. Predict what will happen if you place an egg in the water. **Record** your prediction in your *Science Notebook*. Using a spoon, carefully lower the egg into the container. **Record** what happens.

3. Predict what will happen if you add salt to the water. **Record** your prediction. Gradually add salt to the water and **record** what happens.

Analyze and Conclude

1. In your *Science Notebook*, describe what happened to the egg during this experiment.

2. What else changed during the experiment?

3. How can you explain what you observed?

Step 2

Forces in Fluids

Reading Focus What is Archimedes' principle?

▲ Thousands of tons of steel, aluminum, wood, cargo, and people float easily because the density of the ship is less than the density of the water.

What would happen if you placed a piece of iron in a pan of water? Would the iron sink or float? Iron is denser than water—it has more mass per given volume than does water. So, you might expect the iron to sink. But could it float?

The iron is caught in a battle of two natural forces—gravity and buoyancy. Gravity is the force that tends to pull all objects toward Earth's center. **Buoyancy** (boi'ən sē) is the upward force exerted by a fluid on objects submerged in the fluid. This force tends to keep objects afloat. Which force will win out on the piece of iron—gravity or buoyancy?

Archimedes' Principle

Some questions about buoyancy were answered more than 2,200 years ago by the Greek scientist Archimedes. He found the answers while working on another problem. Archimedes was working for Hiero, king of Syracuse, the largest Greek city in Sicily. The king suspected that his new crown was not made of pure gold. He asked Archimedes to find out.

While trying to solve the problem, Archimedes found that an object submerged in water will displace, or push aside, a volume of water equal to its own volume. He then compared the volume of water displaced by the crown with the volume of water displaced by an equal mass of pure gold. When the crown displaced more water than the pure gold, Archimedes knew that the crown was not pure gold.

▲ A penny sinks in water, but it doesn't sink in all liquids.

▲ When placed in mercury, a penny floats because it is less dense than mercury.

While working to solve the king's problem, Archimedes made another important discovery. He found that when an object placed in water pushes water aside, the water pushes back! The water exerts a force on the object equal to the weight of the water the object displaces. This is known as Archimedes' principle. Today we call the force buoyancy.

Archimedes' principle can be used to explain why some objects float and others do not. If the weight of an object is equal to the weight of the water it displaces, the object will float. If the weight of the object is greater than the weight of the water it displaces, the object will sink.

This explains why a pebble will sink in water but a huge ocean liner will float. The small amount of water displaced by a pebble does not weigh as much as the pebble itself. So, the pebble sinks. As an ocean liner settles into the water, it displaces a huge amount of water. At some point the weight of the displaced water becomes equal to the weight of the liner, the liner floats.

Buoyancy and Density

Water has a density of 1 g/mL. (The density of ocean water is slightly greater.) Any object that has a density less than 1 g/mL will float in water. Consider a piece of wood with a density of 0.7 g/mL. When placed in water, it will sink until it has displaced its own weight of water, at which point it remains afloat.

Mercury is a very dense liquid. Its density is 13.5 g/mL. Most common materials are less dense than mercury and would float in it. For example, the density of iron is 7.9 g/mL. Iron will float in mercury.

Now think back to the piece of iron described at the beginning of this resource. If you placed it in water, would it sink or float? With a density of 7.9 g/mL, you would expect it to sink. But let's think about this for a minute. Suppose you could change the density of the piece of iron so that it was less than the density of water. Then the iron would float.

But how can you change the density of a material? Recall that the formula for

finding density is $D = m/v$. If you could increase the volume of the iron without changing its mass, you would decrease the density of the iron. In the activity on pages F118 and F119, a ball of clay is made to float by flattening the clay and shaping it into a boat, thus increasing the volume of the clay. Will the same idea work with a piece of iron?

A piece of iron will sink in water. But suppose you hammer the piece of iron into a thin sheet and then shape the sheet into a boat. As you increase the volume of the iron without changing its mass, you decrease its density. When the density becomes less than that of water, the iron boat will float.

An ocean liner is basically a huge metal shell filled with air. The density of the liner and all of its contents is less than 1 g/mL—hard to believe! What would happen if that shell was filled with some denser material, such as water? Think of the *Titanic*! In the activity on pages F118 and F119, the density of the clay boat is increased by adding marbles. When the boat becomes denser than water, it sinks.

Underwater Diving

Humans have long been fascinated by the underwater world. However, two factors have limited our ability to explore that world. First, breathing underwater requires special equipment. People can not hold their breath long enough to do much exploring underwater. A breakthrough in solving this problem was made

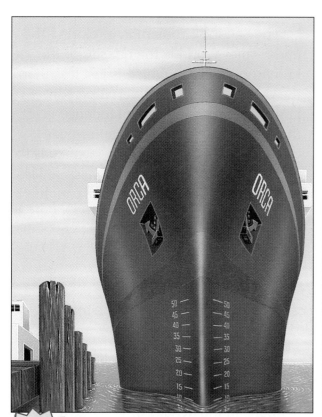

Using Math *How much higher above the surface is one ship floating than the other? What factors might account for this difference?*

▲ Scuba divers attach weights to their bodies to stay below the water.

by Jacques Yves Cousteau and Emile Gagnan in 1943. They developed the Aqua-lung, one of the first breathing devices that allowed the user to remain underwater for an extended time. Their invention is a type of self-contained underwater breathing apparatus.

Scuba equipment consists of a tank of compressed air for the diver to breathe and a system for regulating the intake of the air. Cousteau and Gagnan found designing the system difficult because the amount of air a diver needs changes as the depth of the water increases.

Therefore, the regulating system has to continually adjust the amount of air released to the diver.

The second problem in exploring the underwater world is the density of the human body itself, which is just less than the density of water. When a person jumps into the water, the tendency is for the person to float. One way of overcoming the body's natural buoyancy is to add weights to the person's waist, ankles, or wrists. By adjusting the total weight attached, the diver can go as deep into the water as he or she wants to. ∎

INVESTIGATION 3 WRAP-UP

REVIEW

1. How can changing an object's shape make it more or less buoyant?

2. How can Archimedes' principle be used to find the volume of an object?

CRITICAL THINKING

3. What happens to the density of water as it freezes to form ice? How do you know?

4. Why do objects tend to feel lighter under water than they do in air?

REFLECT & EVALUATE

Word Power

Write the letter of the term that best matches the definition.

a. buoyancy
b. drag
c. lift
d. thrust

1. Upward force on an airplane wing
2. Tendency of fluids to keep things afloat
3. Push on an airplane produced by engines
4. Caused by air resistance

Check What You Know

Write the word in each pair that correctly completes the statement.

1. Wood floats in water because it is (less dense, denser) than water.
2. A parachute slows a falling object by increasing (drag, thrust).
3. Two factors that tend to keep an airplane from falling are lift and (drag, thrust).
4. You can lower the density of a body by increasing its (volume, mass).

Problem Solving

1. How do the forces of lift and gravity on an airplane compare when the airplane is increasing in altitude?
2. How can you compare the densities of several different liquids, using only a tall glass cylinder?
3. A stone and a cork are placed in a container of water. They both displace the same amount of water, yet the stone sinks and the cork floats. Explain.

BUILD YOUR PORTFOLIO

Make a copy of the drawing in your Science Notebook. Then use the drawing to explain, in your own words, how a jet-powered airplane works. Label your drawing and include the labels *drag*, *lift*, and *thrust*.

Summarizing

Summarizing helps you remember what you have read. A summary is a short paragraph that states the main points of a selection. Follow these guidelines to write a good summary.

Read the paragraphs. Then complete the exercises that follow.

Use these guidelines to write a summary.

- List topic sentences.
- Restate main ideas.
- Group similar ideas.
- Omit unimportant ideas.

Inventing Measuring Units

Just as a system of measurement had to be invented by the castaways on the imaginary island, all existing systems of measurement were invented out of need. The English system of measurement is used by most people in the United States. Miles, yards, feet, inches, pounds, gallons, and pints are all examples of English units.

Many units used in the English system originated at a time when there was no consistent system of measurement. In trying to develop a system of measurement that would be convenient, people invented units based upon body parts. For example, one early English measurement—the yard—was equal to the distance from the tip of the nose to the tip of the extended forefinger.

1. **Write the letters of the two statements that you would put in your summary.**

   a. All systems of measurement were invented out of need.

   b. The English system of measurement is used by most people in the United States.

   c. Many units of measurement originated at a time when there was no consistent system of measurement.

   d. One early English measurement—the yard—was equal to the distance from the tip of the nose to the tip of the extended forefinger.

2. **Write a summary of the paragraphs, using the guidelines.**

Equations and Formulas

Data related to two space shuttle missions are shown in the table.

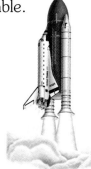

Selected Space Shuttle Missions			
Mission Number	Duration of Mission	Distance Traveled (km)	Number of Orbits
STS-7	6d, 2h, 23 min, 59s	4,048,907	97
STS-51-G	7d, 1h, 38 min, 52s	4,666,100	111

To find the average cirumference of an orbit, use this equation.

average circumference = distance traveled ÷ number of orbits

To find the radius of an orbit, use this formula. Use 3.14 for π.

radius = circumference ÷ 2π

As needed, use formulas to complete the exercises that follow. Round your answers to the nearest whole number. You may wish to use a calculator for some of the exercises.

1. During STS-7, what was the average circumference of each orbit?

2. During STS-51-G, what was the average circumference of each orbit?

3. Use the average circumference you found in Exercise 1 to find the average radius of the orbit of STS-7. That is, find the average distance of STS-7 from Earth's center.

4. Make a sketch of Earth and label Earth's radius 6,371 km. Now, using the average radius you found in Exercise 3, label your sketch to show the average height of the STS-7 shuttle above Earth's surface.

5. Suppose you calculate the average radius of the orbit of STS-51-G to be 4,780 kilometers. Is this answer reasonable? How do you know?

6. On one mission the shuttle traveled 1,502,415 kilometers in 36 hours. What was its average speed?

WRAP-UP!

On your own, use scientific methods to investigate a question about forces and motion.

THINK LIKE A SCIENTIST

Ask a Question

Pose a question about forces and motion that you would like to investigate. For example, ask, "How is the air pressure inside a basketball related to the height that the ball will bounce?"

Make a Hypothesis

Suggest a hypothesis that is a possible answer to the question. One hypothesis is that the greater the air pressure inside a basketball, the higher the ball will bounce.

Plan and Do a Test

Plan a controlled experiment to find the relationship between the air pressure inside a basketball and how high the basketball will bounce. You could start with an air pump, an air pressure gauge, a basketball, and a metric tape measure. Develop a procedure that uses these materials to test the hypothesis. With permission, carry out your experiment. Follow the safety guidelines on pages S14–S15.

Record and Analyze

Observe carefully and record your data accurately. Make repeated observations.

Draw Conclusions

Look for evidence to support the hypothesis or to show that it is false. Draw conclusions about the hypothesis. Repeat the experiment to verify the results.

WRITING IN SCIENCE
Giving Instructions

Write a set of instructions for making a simple paper airplane of your own design. Use these guidelines for writing your instructions.

- Keep in mind the person, or audience, who will read your instructions.

- Write your instructions in the order in which they should be carried out.

- Include simple diagrams, as needed, to go with your written instructions.

SCIENCE and MATH TOOLBOX

Using a Microscope

A microscope makes it possible to see very small things by magnifying them. Some microscopes have a set of lenses that magnify objects by different amounts.

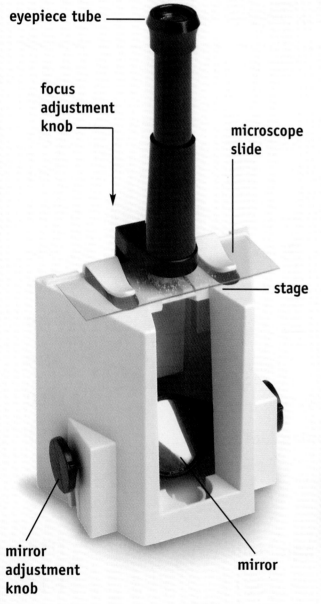

eyepiece tube

focus adjustment knob

microscope slide

stage

mirror adjustment knob

mirror

Examine Some Salt Grains

Handle a microscope carefully; it can break easily. Carry it firmly with both hands and avoid touching the lenses.

1. Turn the mirror toward a source of light. **NEVER** use the Sun as a light source.

2. Place a few grains of salt on the slide. Put the slide on the stage of the microscope.

3. Bring the salt grains into focus. Turn the adjustment knob on the back of the microscope as you look through the eyepiece.

4. Raise the eyepiece tube to increase the magnification; lower it to decrease magnification.

Salt grains magnified one hundred times (100X)

Making a Bar Graph

A bar graph helps you organize and compare data. For example, you might want to make a bar graph to compare weather data for different places.

Make a Bar Graph of Annual Snowfall

For more than 20 years, the cities listed in the table have been recording their yearly snowfall. The table shows the average number of centimeters of snow that the cities receive each year. Use the data in the table to make a bar graph showing the cities' average annual snowfall.

Snowfall	
City	Snowfall (cm)
Atlanta, GA	5
Charleston, SC	1.5
Houston, TX	1
Jackson, MS	3
New Orleans, LA	0.5
Tucson, AZ	3

1. Title your graph. The title should help a reader understand what your graph describes.

2. Choose a scale and mark equal intervals. The vertical scale should include the least value and the greatest value in the set of data.

4. Carefully graph the data. Depending on the interval you choose, some amounts may be between two numbers.

3. Label the vertical axis *Snowfall (cm)* and the horizontal axis *City*. Space the city names equally.

5. Check each step of your work.

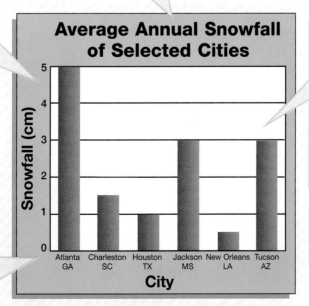

Average Annual Snowfall of Selected Cities

Using a
Calculator

After you've made measurements, a calculator can help you analyze your data. Some calculators have a memory key that allows you to save the result of one calculation while you do another.

Add and Divide to Find Percent

The table shows the amount of rain that was collected using a rain gauge in each month of one year. You can use a calculator to help you find the total yearly rainfall. Then you can find the percent of rain that fell during January.

1. Add the numbers. When you add a series of numbers, you need not press the equal sign until the last number is entered. Just press the plus sign after you enter each number (except the last).

2. If you make a mistake while you are entering numbers, press the clear entry (CE/C) key to erase your mistake. Then you can continue entering the rest of the numbers you are adding. If you can't fix your mistake, you can press the (CE/C) key once or twice until the screen shows 0. Then start over.

3. Your total should be 1,131. Now clear the calculator until the screen shows 0. Then divide the rainfall amount for January by the total yearly rainfall (1,131). Press the percent (%) key. Then press the equal sign key.

214 ÷ 1131 % =

The percent of yearly rainfall that fell in January is 18.921309, which rounds to 19%.

Rainfall	
Month	**Rain (mm)**
Jan.	214
Feb.	138
Mar.	98
Apr.	157
May	84
June	41
July	5
Aug.	23
Sept.	48
Oct.	75
Nov.	140
Dec.	108

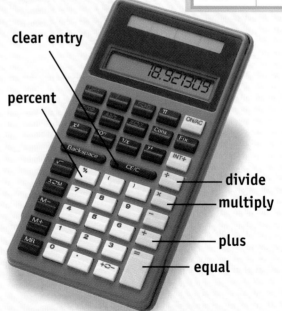

clear entry

percent

divide

multiply

plus

equal

Finding an Average

An average is a way to describe a set of data using one number. For example, you could compare the surface temperature of several stars that are of the same type. You could find the average surface temperature of these stars.

Add and Divide to Find the Average

Suppose scientists found the surface temperature of eight blue-white stars to be those shown in the table. What is the average surface temperature of the stars listed?

Surface Temperature of Selected Blue-white Stars

Blue-white Star	Surface Temperature (°F)
1	7,200
2	6,100
3	6,000
4	6,550
5	7,350
6	6,800
7	7,500
8	6,300

1. First find the sum of the data. Add the numbers in the list.

$$
\begin{array}{r}
7,200 \\
6,100 \\
6,000 \\
6,550 \\
7,350 \\
6,800 \\
7,500 \\
+\ 6,300 \\
\hline
53,800
\end{array}
$$

2. Then divide the sum (53,800) by the number of addends (8).

$$
\begin{array}{r}
6,725 \\
8\ \overline{)\ 53,800} \\
-\ 48 \\
\hline
5\,8 \\
-\ 56 \\
\hline
20 \\
-\ 16 \\
\hline
40 \\
-\ 40 \\
\hline
0
\end{array}
$$

3. $53{,}800 \div 8 = 6{,}725$
The average surface temperature of these eight blue-white stars is 6,725°F.

Using a Tape Measure or Ruler

Tape measures, metersticks, and rulers are tools for measuring length. Scientists use units such as kilometers, meters, centimeters, and millimeters when making length measurements.

Use a Meterstick

1. Work with a partner to find the height of your reach. Stand facing a chalkboard. Reach up as high as you can with one hand.

2. Have your partner use chalk to mark the chalkboard at the highest point of your reach.

3. Use a meterstick to measure your reach to the nearest centimeter. Measure from the floor to the chalk mark. Record the height of your reach.

Use a Tape Measure

1. Use a tape measure to find the circumference of, or distance around, your partner's head. Wrap the tape around your partner's head.

2. Find the line where the tape begins to wrap over itself.

3. Record the distance around your partner's head to the nearest millimeter.

Measuring
Volume

A graduated cylinder, a measuring cup, and a beaker are used to measure volume. Volume is the amount of space something takes up. Most of the containers that scientists use to measure volume have a scale marked in milliliters (mL).

Measure the Volume of a Liquid

1. Measure the volume of some juice. Pour the juice into a measuring container.

2. Move your head so that your eyes are level with the top of the juice. Read the scale line that is closest to the surface of the juice. If the surface of the juice is curved up on the sides, look at the lowest point of the curve.

3. Read the measurement on the scale. You can estimate the value between two lines on the scale to obtain a more accurate measurement.

▲ The bottom of the curve is at 35 mL.

This beaker has marks for each 25 mL. ▶

This graduated cylinder has marks for every 1 mL. ▶

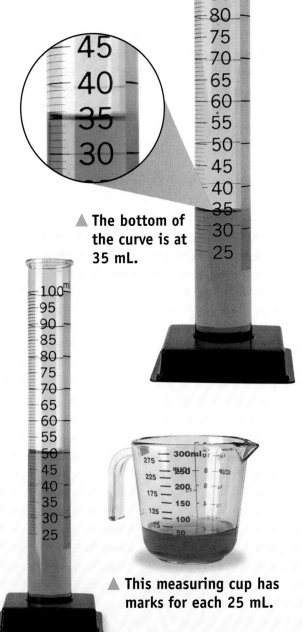

▲ This measuring cup has marks for each 25 mL.

Using a Thermometer

A thermometer is used to measure temperature. When the liquid in the tube of a thermometer gets warmer, it expands and moves farther up the tube. Different scales can be used to measure temperature, but scientists usually use the Celsius scale.

Measure the Temperature of a Cold Liquid

1. Half fill a cup with chilled liquid.

2. Hold the thermometer so that the bulb is in the center of the liquid. Be sure that there are no bright lights or direct sunlight shining on the bulb.

3. Wait until you see the liquid in the tube of the thermometer stop moving. Read the scale line that is closest to the top of the liquid in the tube. The thermometer shown reads 21°C (about 70°F).

Using a Balance

A balance is used to measure mass. Mass is the amount of matter in an object. To find the mass of an object, place the object in the left pan of the balance. Place standard masses in the right pan.

Measure the Mass of a Ball

1. Check that the empty pans are balanced, or level with each other. The pointer at the base should be on the middle mark. If it needs to be adjusted, move the slider on the back of the balance a little to the left or right.

2. Place a ball on the left pan. Notice that the pointer moves and that the pans are no longer level with each other. Then add standard masses, one

at a time, to the right pan. When the pointer is at the middle mark again, the pans are balanced. Each pan is holding the same amount of matter, and the same mass.

3. Each standard mass is marked to show its number of grams. Add the number of grams marked on the masses in the pan. The total is the mass of the ball in grams.

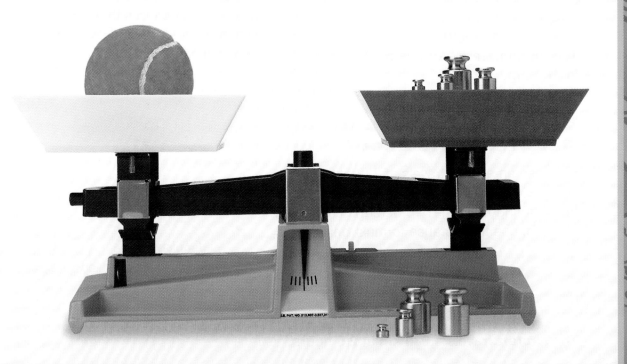

Using an Equation or Formula

Equations and formulas can help you to determine measurements that are not easily made.

Use the Diameter of a Circle to Find Its Circumference

Find the circumference of a circle that has a diameter of 10 cm. To determine the circumference of a circle, use the formula below.

$$C = \pi d$$

$$C = 3.14 \times 10$$

$$C = 31.4 \text{ cm}$$

π is the symbol for pi. Always use 3.14 as the value for π, unless another value for pi is given.

The circumference of this circle is 31.4 cm.

The circumference (C) is a measure of the distance around a circle.

10 cm

The diameter (d) of a circle is a line segment that passes through the center of the circle and connects two points on the circle.

Use Rate and Time to Determine Distance

Suppose an aircraft travels at 772 km/h for 2.5 hours. How many kilometers does the aircraft travel during that time? To determine distance traveled, use the distance formula below.

$$d = rt$$

$$d = 772 \times 2.5$$

$$d = 1{,}930 \text{ km}$$

d = distance

r = rate, or the speed at which the aircraft is traveling.

t = the length of time traveled

The aircraft travels 1,930 km in 2.5 hours.

Making a
Chart to Organize Data

A chart can help you record, compare,
or classify information.

Organize Properties of Elements

Suppose you collected the data shown at the right. The data presents properties of silver, gold, lead, and iron.

You could organize this information in a chart by classifying the physical properties of each element.

My Data

Silver (Ag) has a density of 10.5 g/cm³. It melts at 961°C and boils at 2,212°C. It is used in dentistry and to make jewelry and electronic conductors.

Gold melts at 1,064°C and boils at 2,966°C. Its chemical symbol is Au. It has a density of 19.3 g/cm³ and is used for jewelry, in coins, and in dentistry.

The melting point of lead (Pb) is 328°C. The boiling point is 1,740°C. It has a density of 11.3 g/cm³. Some uses for lead are in storage batteries, paints, and dyes.

Iron (Fe) has a density of 7.9 g/cm³. It will melt at 1,535°C and boil at 3,000°C. It is used for building materials, in manufacturing, and as a dietary supplement.

Create categories that describe the information you have found.

Give the chart a title that describes what is listed in it.

Properties of Some Elements

Element	Symbol	Density g/cm³	Melting Point (°C)	Boiling Point (°C)	Some Uses
Silver	Ag	10.5	961	2,212	jewelry, dentistry, electric conductors
Gold	Au	19.3	1,064	2,966	jewelry, dentistry, coins
Lead	Pb	11.3	328	1,740	storage batteries, paints, dyes
Iron	Fe	7.9	1,535	3,000	building materials, manufacturing, dietary supplement

Make sure the information is listed accurately in each column.

Reading a Circle Graph

A circle graph shows the whole divided into parts. You can use a circle graph to compare parts to each other or to compare parts to the whole.

Read a Circle Graph of Land Area

The whole circle represents the approximate land area of all of the continents on Earth. The number on each wedge indicates the land area of each continent. From the graph you can determine that altogether the land area of the continents is 148,000,000 square kilometers.

Together Antarctica and Australia are about equal to the land area of North America.

Africa accounts for more of the Earth's land area than South America.

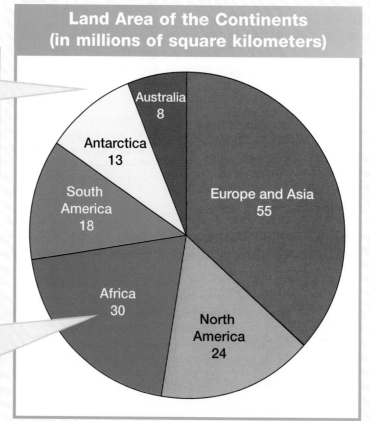

Land Area of the Continents (in millions of square kilometers)

Australia 8

Antarctica 13

South America 18

Europe and Asia 55

Africa 30

North America 24

Making a Line Graph

A line graph is a way to show continuous change over time. You can use the information from a table to make a line graph.

Dallas–Fort Worth Airport Temperature	
Hour	Temp. (°C)
6 A.M.	22
7 A.M.	24
8 A.M.	25
9 A.M.	26
10 A.M.	27
11 A.M.	29
12 NOON	31
1 P.M.	32
2 P.M.	33
3 P.M.	34
4 P.M.	35
5 P.M.	35
6 P.M.	34

Make a Line Graph of Temperatures

The table shows temperature readings over a 12-hour period at the Dallas–Fort Worth Airport in Texas. This data can also be displayed in a line graph that shows temperature change over time.

1. Choose a title. The title should help a reader understand what your graph describes.

2. Choose a scale and mark equal intervals. The vertical scale should include the least value and the greatest value in the set of data.

3. Label the horizontal axis *Time* and the vertical axis *Temperature (°C)*.

4. Write the hours on the horizontal axis. Space the hours equally.

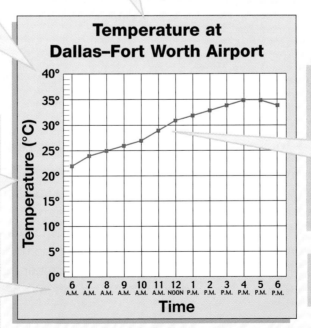

5. Carefully graph the data. Depending on the interval you choose, some temperatures will be between two numbers.

6. Check each step of your work.

Finding
Range, Median, and Mode

You probably know that an average is a way to describe a set of data. Other ways to describe a set of data include range, median, and mode. The data in the table show the speeds at which various animals can run.

Speeds of Animals	
Animal	**Speed (km/h)**
White-tailed deer	48
Hyena	64
Cheetah	113
Squirrel	19
Zebra	64
Rabbit	56
Human	45

Finding the Range

The **range** can tell you if the data is spread far apart or clustered. To find the range, subtract the least number from the greatest number in a set of data.

$$113 - 19 = 94$$

The difference, or range, of the data is 94.

19 45 48 56 64 64 113

Finding the Median

The **median** is the middle number or the average of the two middle numbers when the data is arranged in order. The middle or median of the data set is 56.

Finding the Mode

The **mode** is the number or numbers that occur most often in a set of data. Sometimes there is no mode or more than one mode. The number that occurs most often is 64.

Using a Spring Scale

A spring scale is used to measure force.
You can use a spring scale to find the weight
of an object in newtons. You can also use
the scale to measure other forces.

Measure the Weight of an Object

1. Place the object in a net bag and hang it from the hook on the bottom of the spring scale. Or, if possible, hang the object directly from the hook.

2. Slowly lift the scale by the handle at the top. Be sure the object to be weighed continues to hang from the hook.

3. Wait until the indicator inside the clear tube of the spring scale has stopped moving. Read the number next to the indicator. This number is the weight of the object in newtons.

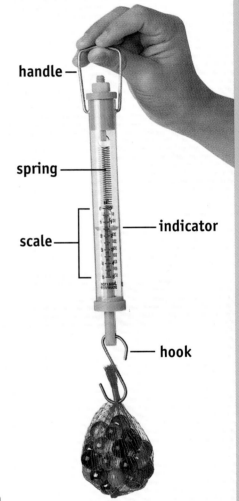

handle

spring

scale

indicator

hook

Measure Friction

1. Hang the object from the hook at the bottom of the spring scale. Use a piece of string to connect the hook and object if needed.

2. Gently pull the handle at the top of the scale parallel to the floor. When the object starts to move, read the number of newtons next to the indicator on the scale. This number is the force of friction between the floor and the object as you drag the object.

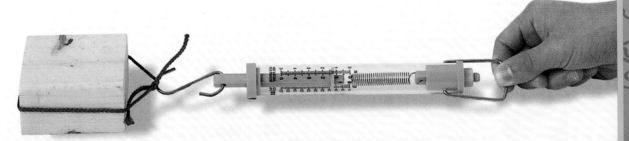

MEASUREMENTS

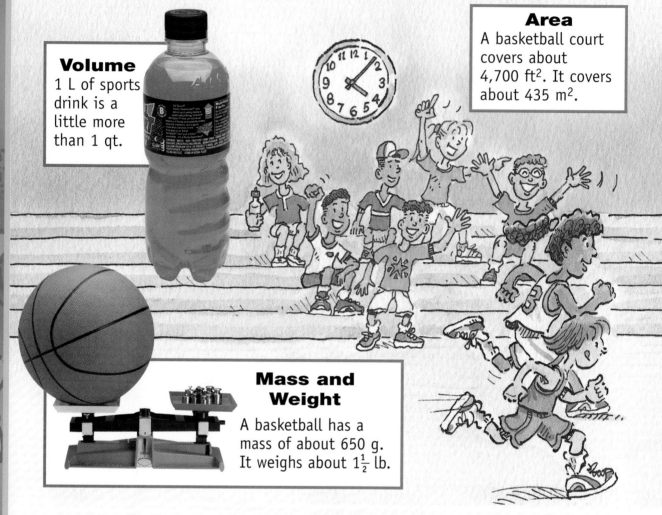

Volume
1 L of sports drink is a little more than 1 qt.

Area
A basketball court covers about 4,700 ft². It covers about 435 m².

Mass and Weight
A basketball has a mass of about 650 g. It weighs about $1\frac{1}{2}$ lb.

Metric Measures

Temperature
Ice melts at 0 degrees Celsius (°C)

Water freezes at 0°C

Water boils at 100°C

Length and Distance
1,000 meters (m) = 1 kilometer (km)

100 centimeters (cm) = 1 m

10 millimeters (mm) = 1 cm

Force
1 newton (N) =
   1 kilogram x meter/second/second
   (kg x m/s²)

Volume
1 cubic meter (m³) = 1 m x 1 m x 1 m

1 cubic centimeter (cm³) =
   1 cm x 1 cm x 1 cm

1 liter (L) = 1,000 milliliters (mL)

1 cm³ = 1 mL

Area
1 square kilometer (km²) = 1 km x 1 km

1 hectare = 10,000 m²

Mass
1,000 grams (g) = 1 kilogram (kg)

1,000 milligrams (mg) = 1 g

Temperature
The temperature at an indoor basketball game might be 25°C, which is 77°F.

Length/Distance
A basketball rim is about 10 ft high, or a little more than 3 m from the floor.

Customary Measures

Temperature
Ice melts at 32 degrees Fahrenheit (°F)
Water freezes at 32°F
Water boils at 212°F

Length and Distance
12 inches (in.) = 1 foot (ft)
3 ft = 1 yard (yd)
5,280 ft = 1 mile (mi)

Weight
16 ounces (oz) = 1 pound (lb)
2,000 pounds = 1 ton (T)

Volume of Fluids
8 fluid ounces (fl oz) = 1 cup (c)
2 c = 1 pint (pt)
2 pt = 1 quart (qt)
4 qt = 1 gallon (gal)

Metric and Customary Rates
km/h = kilometers per hour
m/s = meters per second
mph = miles per hour

GLOSSARY

Pronunciation Key

Symbol	Key Words	Symbol	Key Words
a	cat	g	get
ā	ape	h	help
ä	cot, car	j	jump
		k	kiss, call
e	ten, berry	l	leg
ē	me	m	meat
		n	nose
i	fit, here	p	put
ī	ice, fire	r	red
		s	see
ō	go	t	top
ô	fall, for	v	vat
oi	oil	w	wish
ᴏᴏ	look, pull	y	yard
ᴏ̄ᴏ̄	tool, rule	z	zebra
ou	out, crowd		
		ch	chin, arch
u	up	ŋ	ring, drink
ʉ	fur, shirt	sh	she, push
		th	thin, truth
ə	a in ago	*th*	then, father
	e in agent	zh	measure
	i in pencil		
	o in atom		
	u in circus		

A heavy stress mark (′) is placed after a syllable that gets a heavy, or primary, stress, as in **picture** (pik′chər).

b	bed
d	dog
f	fall

abyssal plain (ə bis'əl plān) The broad, flat ocean bottom. (E34) The *abyssal plain* covers nearly half of Earth's surface.

acceleration (ak sel ər ā'shən) The rate at which velocity changes over time. (F21) The spacecraft's *acceleration* increased as it soared into the air.

acid (as'id) A compound that turns blue litmus paper to red and forms a salt when it reacts with a base. (C81) *Acids* have a sour taste.

action force The initial force exerted in a force-pair. (F90) When you push against something, you are applying an *action force*.

active transport The process by which the cell uses energy to move materials through the cell membrane. (A17) Food molecules are moved into a cell by *active transport*.

aftershock A less powerful shock following the principal shock of an earthquake. (B56) Many *aftershocks* shook the ground in the days after the major earthquake.

algae (al'jē) Any of various mostly single-celled plantlike protists. (A34) Diatoms and seaweed are kinds of *algae*.

alloy (al'oi) A solution of two or more metals. (C59) Bronze is an *alloy* of copper and tin.

antibiotic (an tī bī ät'ik) A substance, often produced by microbes or fungi, that can stop the growth and reproduction of bacteria. (A57) Doctors prescribe *antibiotics* to treat various diseases.

antibody (an'ti bäd ē) A protein produced in the blood that destroys or weakens bacteria and viruses. (A57) *Antibodies* are produced in response to infection.

aquaculture (ak'wə kul chər) The raising of water plants and animals for human use or consumption. (E78) Raising catfish on a catfish "farm" is a form of *aquaculture*.

archaeologist (är kē äl'ə jist) A scientist who studies ancient cultures by digging up evidence of human life from the past. (B90) *Archaeologists* discovered human remains in the ancient city of Pompeii.

asexual reproduction (ā sek'shoo al rē prə duk' shən) Reproduction involving a cell or cells from one parent that results in offspring exactly like the parent. (D10) The division of an amoeba into two cells is an example of *asexual reproduction*.

asthenosphere (as then'ə sfir) The layer of Earth below the lithosphere; the upper part of the mantle. (B36) The *asthenosphere* contains hot, partially melted rock with plasticlike properties.

astronomical unit A unit of measurement equal to the distance from Earth to the Sun. (F9) Pluto is 39.3 *astronomical units* (A.U.) from the Sun.

atom The smallest particle of an element that has the chemical properties of that element. (C35) An *atom* of sodium differs from an *atom* of chlorine.

atomic number (ə täm'ik num'bər) The number of protons in the nucleus of an atom. (C73) The *atomic number* of oxygen is 8.

B
---

bacteria (bak tir'ē ə) Monerans that feed on dead organic matter or on living things. (A49) Diseases such as pneumonia and tuberculosis are caused by *bacteria*.

base A compound that turns red litmus paper blue and that forms a salt when it reacts with an acid. (C81) *Bases* have a slippery feel.

benthos (ben'thäs) All the plants and animals that live on the ocean bottom. (E25) The *benthos* group include oysters, crabs, and coral.

blue-green bacteria (blo͞o grēn bak tir'ē ə) Monerans that contain chlorophyll. (A49) Like plants, *blue-green bacteria* carry out photosynthesis and make their own food.

budding A form of asexual reproduction in which a new individual develops from a bump, or bud, on the body of the parent. (D13) Some one-celled organisms, such as yeast, reproduce by *budding*.

buoyancy (boi'ən sē) The upward force exerted by a fluid on objects submerged in the fluid. (F121) Objects float better in salt water than in fresh water because salt water has greater *buoyancy*.

C
---

caldera (kal der'ə) A large circular depression, or basin, at the top of a volcano. (B102) The eruption formed a *caldera* that later became a lake.

cast fossil (kast fäs'əl) A fossil formed when minerals from rock move into and harden inside the space left by a decaying organism. (D55) *Cast fossils* of shells can provide information about the animals from which the fossils formed.

cell The basic unit that makes up all living things. (A9) The human body is made up of trillions of *cells*.

cell differentiation (sel dif ər en-shē ā'shən) The development of cells into different and specialized cell types. (A25) Through *cell differentiation*, plant cells and animal cells develop into tissues.

cell membrane (sel mem'brān) The structure that surrounds and encloses a cell and controls the movement of substances into and out of the cell. (A10) The *cell membrane* shrank when the cell was placed in salt water.

cell respiration (sel res pə rā'shən) The process in cells in which oxygen is used to release stored energy by breaking down sugar molecules. (A19) The process of *cell respiration* provides energy for a cell's activities.

cell theory A theory that explains the structure of all living things. (A10) The *cell theory* states that all living things are made up of cells.

cell wall The rigid structure surrounding the cells of plants, monerans, and some protists. (A10) The *cell wall* gives a cell its rigid shape.

chemical change A change in matter that results in one or more new substances with new properties. (C69) A *chemical change* occurs when wood burns and forms gases and ash.

chemical formula A group of symbols and numbers that shows the elements that make up a compound. (C40) The *chemical formula* for carbon dioxide is CO_2.

chemical properties Characteristics of matter that describe how it changes when it reacts with other matter. (C34) The ability to burn is a *chemical property* of paper.

chemical symbol One or two letters used to stand for the name of an element. (C36) Ca is the *chemical symbol* for calcium.

20
Ca
Calcium

chloroplast (klôr'ə plast) A tiny green organelle that contains chlorophyll and is found in plant cells and some protist cells. (A10) The chlorophyll inside a *chloroplast* enables a plant cell to capture solar energy.

chromosome (krō'mə sōm) A threadlike structure in the nucleus of a cell; it carries the genes that determine the traits an offspring inherits from its parent or parents. (A10, D22) Most cells in the human body contain 23 pairs of *chromosomes*.

cinder cone A kind of volcano, usually steep-sloped, that is formed from layers of cinders, which are sticky bits of volcanic material. (B86) *Cinder cones* result from explosive eruptions.

communicable disease (kə myo͞o'ni-kə bəl di zēz) A disease that can be passed from one individual to another. (A58) Bacteria, which are easily passed from organism to organism, are the cause of many *communicable diseases*.

competition (käm pə tish'ən) The struggle among organisms for available resources. (D77) *Competition* among members of a species is a factor in evolution.

composite cone (kəm päz′it kōn)
A kind of volcano formed when explosive eruptions of sticky lava alternate with quieter eruptions of volcanic rock bits. (B89) Mount Vesuvius is a *composite cone* in southern Italy.

compound (käm′pound) A substance made up of two or more elements that are chemically combined. (C34) Water is a *compound* made up of hydrogen and oxygen.

condensation (kän dən sā′shən) The change of state from a gas to a liquid. (C28) The *condensation* of water vapor can form droplets of water on the outside of a cold glass.

continental edge (kän tə nent′′l ej) The point at which the continental shelf, which surrounds each continent, begins to angle sharply downward. (E33) Beyond the *continental edge* the ocean increases rapidly in depth.

continental rise The lower portion of the continental slope, extending to the deep ocean floor. (E33) The *continental rise* slopes downward to the deepest part of the ocean.

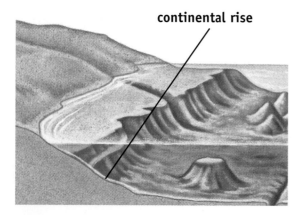
continental rise

continental shelf The gently sloping shelf of land extending from the shoreline to the continental edge. (E32) The *continental shelf* can extend hundreds of miles out into the ocean.

continental slope The steep clifflike drop from the continental edge to the deep ocean floor. (E33) The *continental slope* connects the continental shelf with the ocean bottom.

controlled experiment A test of a hypothesis in which the setups are identical in all ways except one. (S7) In the *controlled experiment*, one beaker of water contained salt.

convection (kən vek′shən) The process by which heat energy is transferred through liquids or gases. (B37) The air was heated by *convection*.

convection current The path along which energy is transferred during convection. (B37) Scientists think that *convection currents* in the mantle cause Earth's tectonic plates to move.

convergent boundary (kən vur′jənt boun′də rē) A place where the plates that make up Earth's crust and upper mantle collide or come together. (B38) Layers of rock may bend or break at a *convergent boundary*.

Coriolis effect (kôr ē ō′lis e fekt′) The tendency of a body or fluid moving across Earth's surface to have a curving motion due to Earth's rotation. (E54) The *Coriolis effect* causes air and water currents to move clockwise in the Northern Hemisphere.

crest The top of a wave. (E63) The *crest* of the wave seemed to tower over the surfer.

crust The thin outer layer of Earth. (B19) Earth's *crust* varies in thickness from 5 km to 48 km.

current Great rivers of water moving through the ocean. (E53) The strong *current* pulled the boat away from shore.

cytoplasm (sīt'ō plaz əm) The watery gel inside a cell. (A11) Various organelles, including vacuoles and mitochondria, are found inside the *cytoplasm* of a cell.

deceleration (dē sel ər ā'shən) A decrease in speed over time. (F23) Air resistance can cause the *deceleration* of objects.

density The amount of mass in a given volume of matter. (C13) Lead has a greater *density* than aluminum.

desalination (dē sal ə nā'shən) A process for obtaining fresh water from salt water by removing the salt. (E78) A few countries operate *desalination* plants, which obtain fresh water from ocean water.

diatom (dī'ə täm) A microscopic, one-celled algae with a glasslike cell wall. (A34) A single liter of sea water may contain millions of *diatoms* of various kinds.

diffusion (di fyōō'zhən) The movement of substances from an area of greater concentration to an area of lesser concentration. (A16) Oxygen can pass in and out of cells by *diffusion*.

divergent boundary (dī vʉr'jənt boun'də rē) A place where the plates that make up Earth's crust and upper mantle move away from one another. (B38) Most *divergent boundaries* are found on the floor of the ocean.

dome mountain A mountain formed when magma lifts Earth's surface, creating a broad dome, or bulge. (B45) Pikes Peak in Colorado is a *dome mountain*.

domesticated (dō mes'ti kāt əd) Tamed or bred to serve people's purposes. (D68) People breed *domesticated* animals such as horses for transportation and other uses.

dominant trait (däm'ə nənt trāt) A trait that will be expressed if it is inherited. (D43) Gregor Mendel found that tallness was a *dominant trait* in pea plants.

drag A force that resists forward motion through a fluid; it operates in the direction opposite to thrust. (F109) The air causes *drag* on an airplane.

E

earthquake A shaking or movement of Earth's surface, caused by the release of stored energy along a fault. (B56) Many *earthquakes* occur near the boundaries between tectonic plates.

electron (ē lek′trän) A negatively charged particle in an atom. (C71) The number of *electrons* in an atom usually equals the number of protons.

element (el′ə mənt) A substance that cannot be broken down into any other substance by ordinary chemical means. (C34) Oxygen, hydrogen, copper, iron, and carbon are *elements.*

endangered species A species of animal or plant whose number has become so small that the species is in danger of becoming extinct. (D25) The black-footed ferret is an *endangered species* that is found in North America.

epicenter (ep′i sent ər) The point on Earth's surface directly above an earthquake's point of origin, or focus. (B63) The *epicenter* of the earthquake was 2 km north of the city.

era (ir′a) One of the major divisions of geologic time. (D57) Many kinds of mammals developed during the Cenozoic *Era.*

ethanol (eth′ə nôl) A kind of alcohol used to make medicines, food products, and various other items. (A40) *Ethanol* is a flammable liquid that can be used as a fuel.

evaporation (ē vap ə rā′shən) The change of state from a liquid to a gas. (C27) Heat from the Sun caused the *evaporation* of the water.

evolution (ev ə lo͞o′shən) The development of new species from earlier species over time. (D56) According to the theory of *evolution*, the plants and animals alive today descended from organisms that lived millions of years ago.

extinct (ek stiŋkt′) No longer in existence; having no living descendant. (D25) Dinosaurs and mammoths are both *extinct.*

extinction (ek stiŋk′shən) The disappearance of species from Earth. (D60) Scientists do not agree about what caused the *extinction* of the dinosaurs.

F

fault A break in rock along which rock slabs have moved. (B63) The shifting of Earth's tectonic plates can produce a *fault*, along which earthquakes may occur.

fault-block mountain A mountain formed when masses of rock move up or down along a fault. (B45) Mountains in the Great Rift Valley of Africa are *fault-block mountains.*

fermentation (fŭr mən tā′shən) A chemical change in which an organism breaks down sugar to produce carbon dioxide and alcohol or lactic acid. (A19) The action of yeast caused *fermentation* in the sugary liquid.

fertilization (fŭr tə li zā′shən) The process by which a sperm and an egg unite to form a cell that will develop into a new individual. (D24) In humans, *fertilization* produces a cell containing 46 chromosomes, half from the female parent and half from the male parent.

fetch (fech) The distance the wind blows over open water. (E64) The longer the *fetch*, the bigger the waves become.

first law of motion The concept that objects at rest tend to remain at rest and objects in motion tend to remain in motion, traveling at a constant speed and in the same direction. (F59) According to the *first law of motion*, a stationary object will stay in place unless some force causes the object to move.

fission (fish′ən) A method of asexual reproduction in which a parent cell divides to form two identical new cells. (A32, D10) Many one-celled organisms, such as amoebas, reproduce by *fission.*

focus (fō′kəs) The point, or place, at which an earthquake begins. (B63) The *focus* of the earthquake was about 20 km beneath Earth's surface.

folded mountain A mountain formed when two tectonic plates collide. (B43) The Alps and the Himalayas are *folded mountains.*

force A push or a pull. (F33) The *force* of friction caused the rolling wagon to slow and then stop.

fossil (fäs′əl) The remains or traces of a living thing, usually preserved in rock. (D54) *Fossils* are usually found in sedimentary rock.

freezing The change of state from a liquid to a solid. (C28) The *freezing* of water occurs at 0°C.

friction (frik′shən) A force that resists motion between two surfaces that are in contact with each other. (F73) *Friction* keeps a car's tires from slipping off the road.

fungi (fun′jī) Organisms that feed on dead organisms or that are parasitic. (A41) Most *fungi* attach to and grow on organic matter.

G

gene (jēn) One of the units that make up a chromosome; genes determine the traits an offspring inherits from its parent or parents. (D33) Half of your *genes* come from your mother, and half come from your father.

gene splicing (jēn spli′siŋ) A process by which genes are manipulated to alter the function or nature of an organism, usually by being transferred from one organism to another. (D45) Through *gene splicing*, scientists have transferred a gene for making insulin from one organism to another.

genetic engineering (jə net′ik en jə nir′iŋ) The process by which genes are manipulated to bring about biological change in species. (D46) Using *genetic engineering* techniques, scientists have successfully combined DNA from different organisms.

gravity (grav′i tē) The force that pulls objects toward Earth; also, the attractive force exerted by a body or an object on other bodies or objects. (F33) *Gravity* causes a ball to fall to the ground after it is thrown into the air.

H

heat Energy that flows from warmer to cooler regions of matter. (C26) *Heat* can cause matter to change from one state to another.

hot spot A place deep within Earth's mantle that is extremely hot and contains a chamber of magma. (B100) Magma rising from a *hot spot* can break through Earth's crust to form a volcano.

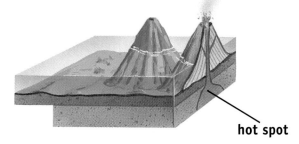

hot spot

hypothesis (hī päth′ə sis) An idea about or explanation of how or why something happens. (S6) The *hypothesis* about the expanding universe has been supported by evidence gathered by astronomers.

I

immune system (im myo͞on′ sis′təm) The body system that defends the body against diseases. (A56) The *immune system* produces antibodies to fight disease.

incomplete dominance (in kəm plēt′ däm′ə nəns) The expression of both genes (traits) in a pair, producing a blended effect. (D44) A plant with pink flowers, produced by crossing a plant having red flowers with a plant having white flowers, is an example of *incomplete dominance*.

indicator (in′di kāt ər) A substance that changes color when mixed with an acid or a base. (C81) Paper treated with an *indicator* is used to test whether a compound is an acid or a base.

inertia (in ur'shə) The tendency of an object to remain at rest if at rest, or if in motion, to remain in motion in the same direction. (F59) *Inertia* results in passengers in a car moving forward when the driver applies the brakes.

inherited trait (in her'it əd trāt) A trait that is passed on from parents to offspring through genes. (D32) Eye color is an *inherited trait.*

ion (ī'ən) An electrically charged atom. (C73) *Ions* form when atoms lose or gain electrons. Sodium chloride is made up of sodium *ions* and chlorine *ions.*

island arc A chain of volcanoes formed from magma that rises as a result of an oceanic plate sinking into the mantle. (B94) The Philippine Islands are part of an *island arc.*

kinetic energy (ki net'ik en'ər jē) Energy of motion. (C25) A ball rolling down a hill has *kinetic energy.*

lava (lä'və) Magma that flows out onto Earth's surface from a volcano. (B85) Flaming *lava* poured down the sides of the volcanic mountain.

law of conservation of momentum The principle that states that momentum can be transferred but cannot be lost. (F84) The *law of conservation of momentum* explains why the momentum resulting from the collision of two objects equals the total momentum of the objects before they collided.

learned trait A trait that is not passed on in DNA, but instead is acquired through learning or experience. (D34) The ability to speak Spanish is a *learned trait.*

lift The upward force, resulting from differences in air pressure above and below an airplane's wings, that causes the airplane to rise. (F109) Increasing the size of an airplane's wings increases *lift.*

lithosphere (lith'ō sfir) The solid, rocky layer of Earth, including the crust and top part of the mantle. (B36) The *lithosphere* is about 100 km in thickness.

magma (mag'mə) The hot, molten rock deep inside Earth. (B84) The *magma* rose from the underground chamber through the volcano.

magnetic field The space around a magnet within which the force of the magnet is exerted. (B26) The magnet attracted all the iron filings within its *magnetic field.*

magnetic reversal (mag net′ik ri-vur′səl) The switching or changing of Earth's magnetic poles such that the north magnetic pole becomes located at the south magnetic pole's position and vice versa. (B26) Scientists have found evidence of *magnetic reversals* in layers of rock along the ocean floor.

magnitude (mag′nə tōōd) The force or strength of an earthquake. (B57) *Magnitude* is a measure of the amount of energy released by an earthquake.

mantle The layer of Earth between the crust and the core. (B19) The *mantle* is made up of a thick layer of rock.

mass The amount of matter in an object. (C10, F32) A large rock has more *mass* than a pebble.

matter Anything that has mass and volume. (C10, F32) Rocks, water, and air are three kinds of *matter.*

meiosis (mī ō′sis) The process of cell division by which sex cells receive half the number of chromosomes as other body cells. (D22) Because of *meiosis*, a sex cell in a human has only 23 chromosomes instead of 46.

melt To change state from a solid to a liquid. (C27) The icicles began to *melt*.

metric system A system of measurement based on a few defined units and in which larger and smaller units are related by powers of 10. (F11) In the *metric system*, a centimeter is 10 times longer than a millimeter.

mid-ocean ridge A chain of mountains on the ocean floor. (B27, E34) New ocean floor forms at the *mid-ocean ridge.*

mitochondria (mīt ō kän′drē ə) Cell organelles in which energy is released from food. (A11) The more *mitochondria* a cell has, the more energy it can release from food.

mitosis (mī tō′sis) The process in which one cell divides to form two identical new cells. (A23) The new cells that are formed by *mitosis* have the same number of chromosomes as the parent cell.

mixture A combination of two or more substances that can be separated by physical means. (C34) This jar contains a *mixture* of colored beads.

model Something used or made to represent an object or to describe how a process takes place. (C71) The plastic *model* showed the structure of the heart.

mold fossil (mōld fäs′əl) A fossil consisting of a hollowed space in the shape of an organism or one of its parts. (D54) Footprints of animals left in mud that dried in the sun became a type of *mold fossil.*

molecule (mäl′i kyōōl) A particle made up of a group of atoms that are chemically bonded. (C39) A *molecule* of water contains two hydrogen atoms and one oxygen atom.

momentum (mō men'təm) A property of a moving object, calculated by multiplying the object's mass by its velocity. (F82) The train gathered *momentum* as its speed increased.

moneran (ma nir'ən) Any one-celled organism in which the cell does not have a nucleus. (A48) Bacteria are *monerans.*

multicellular (mul ti sel'yo͞o lər) Made up of more than one cell. (A32) Some protists are *multicellular.*

mutation (myo͞o tā'shən) A change in a gene's DNA that can result in a new characteristic, or trait. (D74) Certain *mutations* have helped species survive in their environment.

N

natural selection (nach'ər əl sə-lek'shən) The process by which those living things that have characteristics that allow them to adapt to their environment tend to live longest and produce the most offspring, passing on these favorable characteristics to their offspring. (D73) *Natural selection* helps explain why certain characteristics become common while others die out.

neap tide (nēp tīd) The tide occurring at the first and third quarters of the Moon, when the difference in level between high and low tide is smallest. (E69) *Neap tides* occur twice each month.

nekton (nek'tän) All the free-swimming animals that live in the ocean. (E25) The *nekton* group includes such active animals as fish, octopuses, and whales.

neutralization (no͞o trə lī zā'shən) The reaction between an acid and a base. (C83) *Neutralization* produces water and a salt.

neutron (no͞o'trän) A particle in the nucleus of an atom that has no electric charge. (C71) The mass of a *neutron* is about equal to the mass of a proton.

newton (no͞o'tən) A unit used to measure force in the metric system. (F67) A *newton* is the force needed to accelerate a one-kilogram object by one meter per second every second.

nuclear fission (no͞o'klē ər fish'ən) The splitting of the nucleus of an atom, releasing great amounts of energy. (C77) Bombarding a nucleus with neutrons can cause *nuclear fission.*

nuclear membrane The structure that surrounds the nucleus and controls what substances move into and out of the nucleus. (A11) The *nuclear membrane* appears to be solid, but it actually has tiny holes through which materials can pass.

nucleus (nōō′klē əs) 1. The control center of a cell. (A11) The *nucleus* contains the cell's genetic information. 2. The dense, central part of an atom. (C71) The *nucleus* is made up of protons and neutrons and contains nearly all of an atom's mass.

organ A part of a multicellular organism made up of a group of tissues that work together to perform a certain function. (A25) The heart, stomach, brain, and the lungs are *organs* of the human body.

organ system A group of organs that work together to perform one or more functions. (A26) The bones are part of the *organ system* that supports the body.

osmosis (äs mō′sis) The diffusion of water through a membrane. (A16) Water enters and leaves a cell through the process of *osmosis*.

paleontologist (pā lē ən täl′ə jist) A scientist who studies fossils. (D56) A team of *paleontologists* discovered the remains of a dinosaur.

Pangaea (pan jē′ə) A supercontinent that existed about 200 million years ago. (B9) *Pangaea* broke apart into several continents.

period 1. A division of geologic time that is a subdivision of an era. (D57) The Jurassic *Period* is part of the Mesozoic Era. 2. The time it takes for two successive waves to pass the same point. (E63) The *period* for the ocean waves was about ten seconds.

petrification (pe tri fi kā′shən) The changing of the hard parts of a dead organism to stone. (D55) Fossils of trees have been preserved by *petrification*.

photosynthesis (fōt ō sin′thə sis) The process by which green plants and other producers use light energy to make food. (A18, E24) In *photosynthesis*, plant cells use light energy to make sugar from carbon dioxide and water.

physical change A change in size, shape, or state of matter, with no new kind of matter being formed. (C68) The freezing of water into ice cubes is an example of a *physical change*.

physical properties Characteristics of matter that can be measured or detected by the senses. (C34) Color is a *physical property* of minerals.

phytoplankton (fīt ō plaŋk′tən) The group of usually microscopic plant-like protists that live near the surface of the ocean. (E10) *Phytoplankton* drifts with the ocean currents.

plankton (plaŋk'tən) The group of organisms, generally microscopic in size, that float or drift near the ocean surface. (A34, E10) *Plankton* is a source of food for fish.

plate boundary A place where the plates that make up Earth's crust and upper mantle either move together or apart or else move past one another. (B20) Earthquakes occur along *plate boundaries.*

pollution The contamination of the environment with waste materials or other unwanted substances. (E89) Dangerous chemicals dumped into the ocean are one source of *pollution.*

polymer (päl'ə mər) An organic compound consisting of large molecules formed from many smaller, linked molecules. (C90) Proteins are *polymers.*

protist (prōt'ist) Any of a large group of mostly single-celled, microscopic organisms that have traits of plants, animals, or both. (A32) Parameciums and algae are *protists.*

proton (prō'tän) A positively charged particle found in the nucleus of an atom. (C71) The atomic number of an atom equals the number of *protons* in the atom's nucleus.

protozoan (prō tō zō'ən) A protist that has animal-like traits. (A32) A paramecium is a *protozoan.*

— R —

radioactive element (rā dē ō ak'tiv el'ə mənt) An element made up of atoms whose nuclei break down, or decay, into nuclei of other atoms. (C76) As the nucleus of a *radioactive element* decays, energy and particles are released.

reaction force The force exerted in response to an action force. (F90) A *reaction force* is equal in strength to an action force but opposite in direction to the action force.

recessive trait (ri ses'iv trāt) A trait that will not be expressed if paired with a dominant trait. (D43) In his experiments with pea plants, Gregor Mendel learned that shortness was a *recessive trait.*

reproduction (rē prə duk' shən) The process by which organisms produce more of their own kind. (D10) *Reproduction* ensures the survival of the species.

Richter scale (rik'tər skāl) A scale of numbers by which the magnitude of earthquakes is measured. (B56) Each increase of 1.0 on the *Richter scale* represents an increase of about 30 times the energy released by an earthquake.

rifting (rift'iŋ) The process by which magma rises to fill the gap between two plates that are moving apart. (B106) *Rifting* in eastern Africa may split the continent into two parts.

salinity (sə lin′ə tē) The total amount of dissolved salts in ocean water. (E9) The *salinity* of the ocean varies in different parts of the world.

salt A compound that can be formed when an acid reacts with a base. (C83) When vinegar and baking soda interact, they produce a *salt* and water.

saprophyte (sap′rə fīt) An organism that lives on dead or decaying matter. (A42) Molds are *saprophytes*.

sea-floor spreading The process by which new ocean floor is continually being formed as magma rises to the surface and hardens into rock. (B28) *Sea-floor spreading* occurs as magma fills the space between separating plates.

seamount (sē′mount) An underwater mountain that formed from a volcano. (E34) Thousands of *seamounts* rise from the floor of the Pacific.

second law of motion The concept that an object that is at rest or in motion will not change its condition unless something causes the change. (F65) A gust of wind blowing an open umbrella out of your hands illustrates the *second law of motion*.

seismograph (sīz′mə graf) An instrument that records the intensity, duration, and nature of earthquake waves. (B72) Scientists use information from *seismographs* to determine the location of earthquakes.

seismometer (sīz mäm′ə tər) An instrument that detects and records Earth's movements. (B96) Data from the *seismometer* suggested that a volcanic eruption might soon occur.

selective breeding Breeding of living things to produce offspring with certain desired characteristics. (D68) People have used *selective breeding* to produce domesticated animals.

sex cell A female or male reproductive cell; an egg cell or sperm cell. (D22) Reproduction can occur when *sex cells* unite.

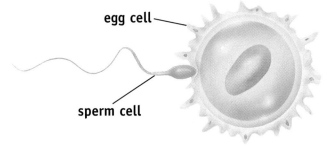

egg cell

sperm cell

sexual reproduction Reproduction that involves the joining of a male sex cell and a female sex cell. (D22) Most animals and plants produce offspring through *sexual reproduction*.

shield cone A kind of volcanic cone that is large and gently sloped and that is formed when lava flows quietly from a crack in the Earth's crust. (B87) Mauna Loa, a *shield cone* in Hawaii, is the largest volcano on Earth.

solute (säl′yōōt) The material present in the smaller amount in a solution; the substance dissolved in a solution. (C57) If you dissolve sugar in water, sugar is the *solute*.

solution A mixture in which the different particles are spread evenly throughout the mixture. (C57) Dissolving salt in water makes a *solution*.

solvent (säl'vənt) The material present in the greater amount in a solution; the substance in a solution, usually a liquid, that dissolves another substance. (C57) If you mix sugar and water, water is the *solvent*.

speed The distance traveled in a certain amount of time; rate of movement. (F16) The truck was moving at a *speed* of 40 mph.

spore A reproductive cell that can develop into a new organism. (A41) Ferns and mushrooms produce *spores*.

spring tide An extremely high tide or low tide occurring at or just after the new moon and full moon. (E69) At the time of a *spring tide*, both the Sun and the Moon are in line with Earth.

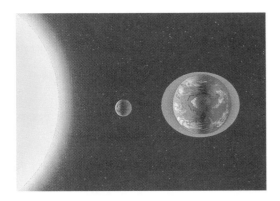

state of matter Any of the three forms that matter may take: solid, liquid, or gas. (C20) Water's *state of matter* depends on its temperature.

substance (sub'stəns) Matter that always has the same makeup and properties, wherever it may be found. (C34) Elements and compounds are *substances*.

tectonic plate (tek tän'ik plāt) One of the slabs that make up Earth's crust and upper mantle; also called *tectonic plate*. (B19) Some of Earth's *tectonic plates* carry continents.

temperature A measure of the average kinetic energy of the particles in matter. (C26) Water *temperature* rises as the motion of water molecules increases.

theory (thē' ə re) A hypothesis that is supported by a lot of evidence and is widely accepted by scientists. (S9) The Big Bang *Theory* offers an explanation for the origin of the universe.

theory of continental drift A theory that states that the continents formed a single landmass at one time in the past and have drifted over time to their present positions. (B10) The *theory of continental drift* was first suggested by Alfred Wegener.

theory of plate tectonics The theory that Earth's lithosphere is broken into enormous slabs, or plates, that are in motion. (B19) Scientists use the *theory of plate tectonics* to explain how Earth's continents drift.

H33

third law of motion The concept that for *every* action force there is an equal and opposite reaction force. (F90) When you watch someone's feet bouncing off a trampoline, you *see* the *third law of motion* at work.

thrust (thrust) The push or driving force that causes an airplane, rocket, or other object to move forward. (F108) *Thrust* can be produced by a spinning propeller or by a jet engine.

tide The daily rise and fall of the level of the ocean or other large body of water, caused by the gravitational attraction of the Moon and the Sun. (E68) As the *tide* came in, we moved our blanket back from the water's edge.

tiltmeter (tilt′mēt ər) An instrument that measures any change in the slope of an area. (B96) Scientists use *tiltmeters* to note any bulges that form in a mountain's slopes.

tissue A group of similar, specialized cells working together to carry out the same function. (A25) Muscle *tissue* contains cells that contract.

toxin (täks′in) A chemical poison that is harmful to the body. (A54) *Toxins* produced by bacteria can cause serious illness.

trade wind A planetary wind that blows from east to west toward the equator. (E54) South of the equator, the *trade wind* comes from the southeast.

transform-fault boundary (transfôrm fôlt boun′də rē) A place where the plates that make up Earth's crust and upper mantle move past one another. (B39) Movement occurring at a *transform-fault boundary* may cause cracks to form in Earth's rocks.

tsunami (tso͞o nä′mē) A huge, powerful ocean wave usually caused by an underwater earthquake. (B74) A *tsunami* can cause great destruction.

turbidity current (tʉr bid′i tē kʉr′ənt) A current of water carrying large amounts of sediment. (E59) *Turbidity currents* may cause sediment to build up in some places.

upwelling The rising of deep water to the surface that occurs when winds move surface water. (E58) *Upwelling* brings pieces of shells and dead organisms up from the ocean floor.

vaccine (vak sēn′) A preparation of dead or weakened bacteria or viruses that produces immunity to a disease. (A57) The *vaccine* for smallpox has eliminated that disease.

vacuole (vak′yo͞o ōl) A structure in the cytoplasm in which food and other substances are stored. (A11) A *vacuole* in a plant cell is often quite large.

variable (ver′ē ə bəl) The one difference in the setups of a controlled experiment; provides a comparison for testing a hypothesis. (S7) The *variable* in an experiment with plants was the amount of water given to each plant.

vegetative propagation (vej ə tāt′iv präp ə gā′shən) A form of asexual reproduction in which a new plant develops from a part of a parent plant. (D14) Using a cutting taken from a houseplant to grow a new plant is a method of *vegetative propagation*.

velocity (və läs′ə tē) The rate of motion in a particular direction. (F21) The *velocity* was northwest at 880 km/h.

virus (vī′rəs) A tiny disease-causing agent consisting of genetic material wrapped inside a capsule of protein. (A50) *Viruses* cause such diseases as AIDS, chickenpox, and rabies.

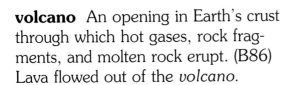

volcano An opening in Earth's crust through which hot gases, rock fragments, and molten rock erupt. (B86) Lava flowed out of the *volcano*.

volume (väl′yo̅o̅m) The amount of space that matter takes up. (C11) A large fuel tank holds a greater *volume* of gasoline than a small tank.

wave The up-and-down movement of the surface of water, caused by the wind. (E63) Ocean *waves* crashed against the shoreline.

wavelength The distance between two successive waves. (E63) At the height of the storm, the waves had a *wavelength* of 10 m.

weight A measure of the force of gravity on an object. (F33) The *weight* of this package is five pounds.

westerly (wes′tər lē) A prevailing wind that blows from west to east. (E54) Ships that sailed from North America to Europe were aided by the power of the *westerlies*.

zooplankton (zō ō plaŋk′tən) The group of tiny animal-like organisms that live near the surface of the ocean. (E11) *Zooplankton* float in the sea.

zygote (zī′gōt) A fertilized egg cell. (D24) A *zygote* develops into an embryo by means of cell division.

INDEX

* **Activity**

CREDITS

ILLUSTRATORS

Cover: Mike Quon.

Think Like a Scientist: 14: Laurie Hamilton. *Border:* Mike Quon.

Unit A 10–11: Teri McDermott. 13: Eldon Doty. 17: Michael Kress-Russick. 18–19: Ray Vella. *t.* Carlyn Iverson. 22–23: Keith Kasnot. 25: Walter Stuart. 26: *t.* Michael Kress-Russick; *m.* Briar Lee Mitchell; *b.* Michael Kress-Russick. 32: Virge Kask. 33: Kirk Moldoff. 37: Yvonne Walston. 41–42: David Flaherty. 48, 51: Barbara Cousins. 52–53: Eldon Doty. 59–60: Ken Tiessen. 61, 63: Barbara Cousins.

Unit B 7: Dolores Bego. 8–9: Eldon Doty. 10: Dale Glasgow & Assoc. 11: Claudia Karabaic Sargent. 12–15: Ray Smith. *maps:* Geo Systems. 17, 18: Eureka Cartography. 19: Warren Budd. 20: *l.* Warren Budd. 20–21: Eureka Cartography. 24–25: Greg Harris. 26: Bill Morris. 27: Greg Harris. 28: Delores Bego. 29: Warren Budd. 31: Eureka Cartography. 36, 37: Brad Gaber. 38: *m.r.* Brad Gaber. 38, 39: Julie Carpenter. 41: Eureka Cartography. 43, 45, 46: Bob Swanson. 47: *t.* Randy Verougstraete; *b.* Ben Perini. 49, 53: Eureka Cartography. 54–55: Eldon Doty. 57: Eureka Cartography. 58: Robert Schuster. 62: *t.* Bob Brugger. *b.* Robert Roper. 63, 65: Robert Roper. 73: Joe Spencer. 74–75: *border:* Julie Carpenter; *b.* Greg Harris; *t.r.* Dolores Bego. 76: Julie Carpenter. 77, 78: Patrick Gnan. 79: Robert Roper. 84: Bob Swanson. 85: Dolores Bego. 86, 87: John Youssi. 88: Eureka Cartography. 90: Laszlo Kubini. 91: Eldon Doty. 94: *t.* Laszlo Kubini. 94–95: Bob Swanson. 99: Eureka Cartography. 100: *t.l.* Eureka Cartography; *r.* Greg Harris. 100–101: Greg Harris. 103: Dale Glasgow & Assoc. 105: Stephen Bauer. 106–107: John Youssi. 107: *t.* Robert Roper. 108: *l.* Eureka Cartography; *r.* Susan Johnson Carlson. 109: Greg Harris. 111: Eldon Doty.

Unit C 3: Olivia McElroy. 10–11: Andrew Shiff. 12: *t.* Andrew Shiff; *b.* Scott Ross. 15: Terry Boles. 19–21: Scott Ross. 26–27: Robert Pasternack. 29: Patrick Gnan. 34: Bill Fox. 36–37: Paul Woods. 39–41: Nadine Sokol. 51: Bob Brugger. 56: Patrick Gnan. 57: Bob Radigan. 58: Adam Mathews. 61: Paul Woods. 69: Patrick Gnan. 70, 72–74: Nadine Sokol. 75: Eldon Doty. 76: *m.l.* George Hardebeck; *b.r.* Ken Rosenborg. 77: Ken Rosenborg. 82–83: Steven Mach. 88: Patrick Gnan. 90, 92: Robert Schuster.

Unit D 3: Olivia McElroy. 10–12: Karl Edwards. 14, 16–17: Wendy Smith-Griswold. 19, 21, 23: J.A.K. Graphics. 24: Kirk Moldoff. 32–34: Terri McDermott. 35: *border:* Terri McDermott, Terry Kovalcik. 36, 38: Barbara Cousins. 40: Linda Nye. 42–44: Marjorie Muns. 46: Terri McDermott. 54–55: David Uhl. 57: *b.l.* Andy Lendway; *t.r.* Raymond Smith. 58–59: Raymond Smith. 60: Richard Courtney. 64–65: Christine Schaar. 66–67: Drew Brook Cormack. 68: Rosemary Volpe. 72–74: Mona Conner. 75: Tina Fong. 77: Andy Lendway. 79: Patrick Gnan.

Unit E 8–11: Bob Radigan. 11: *t.* Robert Shuster. 17: *t.m.* Terry Boles. 24, 25: Jim Salvati. 32–33: Joe McDermott. 36–39: *t.* Steven Nau. 36: Jon Prud'Homme. 38: Stephan Wagner. 39: Jeff Seaver. 41: Barbara Hoopes Ambler. 42–43: Bob Radigan. 43: Eldon Doty. 47: Joe McDermott. 53, 54: Peter Spacek. 54: Jeffrey Hitch. 56–57: Adam Mathews. 57: *b.* Jeffrey Hitch. 58–59: Adam Mathews. 60–61: Steven Nau. 63: *t.* Catherine Leary. *b.* Greg Harris. 68, 69: Jon Prud'Homme. 71: Greg Harris. 78: Michael Sloan. 80–81: Eldon Doty. 82–83, 84: Gary Torrisi. 89: Dean St. Clair. 90–91: *b.* Bob Radigan; *t.* Dean St. Clair.

Unit F 3: Olivia McElroy. 8–10: Terry Boles. 14: A.J. Miller. 16–17: Jeffery Oh. 24: Art Cummings. 25: Linda Richards. 26: David Klug. 27: Terry Boles. 32–33, 35: Terry Boles. 38: Eldon Doty. 43: Rebecca Merriles. 46: Lois Leonard Stock. 47: Don Dixon. 48–49: Larry Jost. 55–57: Michael Sloan. 58–59: Scott Ross. 60–61: Jeffery Lynch. 65: Terry Boles. 73–79: Linda Richards. 82: Sergio Roffo. 91: Bob Novak. 93, 101: Larry Jost. 104–105: Terry Boles. 108–109: Patrick Gnan. 115: Terry Boles. 121–122: Peter Spacek. 123: *border:* Peter Spacek; *b.* Bob Novak. 124: Peter Spacek. 125, 127: Patrick Gnan.

Science and Math Toolbox: *Logos:* Nancy Tobin. 14–15: Andrew Shiff. *Borders:* Mike Quon.

Glossary 20: Terri McDermott. 21: *b.l.* Paul Woods;p *m.r.* John Youssi. 22: Joe McDermott. 23: John Youssi. 26: Greg Harris. 27: Nadine Sokol. 28: Patrick Gnan. 29: Barbara Cousins. 31: Terri McDermott. 32: Kirk Moldoff. 33: John Prud'Homme. 34: Jeffery Hitch. 35: Barbara Cousins.

PHOTOGRAPHS
All photographs by Houghton Mifflin Company (HMCo.) unless otherwise noted.

Front Cover: *t.* Robert Brons/BPS/Tony Stone Images; *m.l.* A. Witte/C. Mahaney/Tony Stone Images; *m.r.* Superstock; *b.l.* © Ken Eward/Bio Grafix-Science Source/Photo Researchers, Inc.; *b.r.* Alan Schein/The Stock Market.

Table of Contents: iii: *l.* © Don Fawcett/Photo Researchers, Inc.; *r.* © Biophoto Associates/Science Source/Photo Researchers, Inc. xi: Ken Lax for HMCo.

Think Like a Scientist: 3: *m.b.* Zig Leszczynski/Animals Animals/Earth Scenes; *b.* Fred Habegger/Grant Heilman Photography, Inc.

Runk/Schoenberger/Grant Heilman Photography, Inc.; *b.r.* Jim Strawser/Grant Heilman Photography, Inc. 17: *t.* Larry Lefever/Grant Heilman Photography, Inc.; *b.* Grant Heilman Photography, Inc. 22: © David M. Phillips/Photo Researchers, Inc. 25: The Granger Collection. 26: *t.* Ron Garrison/The Zoological Society of San Diego; *b.* Steve Kaufman/DRK Photo. 27: © M. Abbey/Photo Researchers, Inc. 28–29: *bkgd.* Dr. Jack Hearn/U.S. Department of Agricultural Research; *inset* Dr. Jack Hearn/U.S. Department of Agricultural Research. 31–33: Grant Huntington for HMCo. 34: *l.* Focus On Sports; *m.* Michael Ponzini/Focus On Sports; *r.* Sports Chrome. 37: Grant Huntington for HMCo. 39: Grant Huntington for HMCo. 42: Bill Horseman Photography/Stock Boston. 43: Austrian Cultural Institute. 44: Courtesy, Marcu Rhoades. 45: *l.* David M. Dennis/Tom Stack & Associates; *r.* David M. Dennis/Tom Stack & Associates. 48–49: *bkgd.* © Sinclair Stammers/Science Photo Library/Photo Researchers, Inc.; *inset* Courtesy, Jorge O. Calvo. 49: Courtesy, Jorge O. Calvo. 50: Ken Lax for HMCo. 51: *t.* Ken Lax for HMCo.; *m.* Breck Kent/Animals Animals/Earth Scenes; *r.* Breck Kent/Animals Animals/Earth Scenes. 52–53: Ken Lax for HMCo. 55: *l.* Wendell Metzen/Bruce Coleman; *r.* John Cancalosi/Peter Arnold, Inc. 56: *l.* Hinterleitner/Liaison International; *m.t.* Kenneth Garrett/© National Geographic Society; *m.b.* Kenneth Garrett/© National Geographic Society; *r.* Kenneth Garrett/© National Geographic Society. 61: *bkgd.* NASA; *inset* Peter Ward. 66: © Darwin Museum. 69: *l.* Sean Sprague/Impact Visuals; *r.* Larry Lefever/Grant Heilman Photography, Inc. 71: Ken Lax for HMCo. 75: E.R. Degginger/Color-Pic, Inc. 76: J.&C. Kroeger/Animals Animals/Earth Scenes.

Unit E 1–3: © 1997 Telegraph Colour Library/FPG International. 4–5: *bkgd.* Dave Fleetham/Pacific Stock; *inset* New Jersey News Photos. 8: *l.* © Francois Gohier/Photo Researchers, Inc.; *r.* William Johnson/Stock Boston. 9: *t.* William Johnson/Stock Boston; *b.* © Carl Purcell/Photo Researchers, Inc. 10: *t.* © Gregory Ochoki/Photo Researchers, Inc.; *b.* Ralph Oberlander/Stock Boston. 17: Michael Grecco/Stock Boston. 18–19: Thomas J. Abercrombie/© National Geographic Society. 20: *t.* Norbert Wu; *b.* Jack Stein Grove/PhotoEdit. 24: *t.* © Eric Grave/Science Source/Photo Researchers, Inc.; *b.* © D.P. Wilson/Science Source/Photo Researchers, Inc. 25: *t.* © Charles V. Angelo/Photo Researchers, Inc.; *b.* Larry Tackett/Tom Stack & Associates. 26: *l.* Frank Oberlander/Stock Boston; *r.* Dave Fleetham/Pacific Stock. 27: *l.* © Charles V. Angelo/Photo Researchers, Inc.; *r.* Frank Oberlander/Stock Boston. 28–29: *bkgd.* Greg Vauhgn/Tom Stack & Associates; *inset* Courtesy, Scientific Search Project. 34: Jim Watt/Pacific Stock. 35: *t.* Jeff Greenberg/The Picture Cube. 37: *t.* Superstock ; *b.l.* Peter Parks/Mo Yung Productions/Norbert Wu Wildlife Photographer; *b.r.* NOAA Photo Library, U.S. Dept. of Commerce. 43: *t.* Woods Hole Oceanographic Institution; *m.* Stephanie Compoint/Sygma Photo News; *b.* The Bettmann Archive. 44: *t.* Michael Holford; *b.* Michael Holford. 45: *t.* Michael Holford; *b.* Michael Holford. 46: Wildlife Conservation Society. 48–49: *bkgd.* AP/Wide World Photos; *inset* Ann Summa for HMCo. 53: NASA. 55: *l.* © 2000 Adam Woolfitt/Woodfin Camp and Associates; *r.* © 2000 Momatiuk/Eastcott/Woodfin Camp and Associates. 56: Superstock. 57: John Beatty/Oxford Scientific/Animals Animals/Earth Scenes. 58: *t.* © Francois Gohier/Photo Researchers, Inc.; *b.* E.R. Degginger/Color-Pic, Inc. 59: George Goodwin/Color-Pic, Inc. 60–61: Ken Karp for HMCo. 64: *t.* Erik Aeder/Pacific Stock. 65: The Bettmann Archive. 69: *t.* Groenendyk/Photo Researchers, Inc.; *r.* Bill Bachmann/Stock Boston. 72–73: *bkgd.* Jack Stein Grove/PhotoEdit; *inset* Courtesy, Natural Energy Laboratory of Hawaii Authority. 73: Courtesy, Natural Energy Laboratory of Hawaii Authority. 75: Ken Karp for HMCo. 77: border Richard Hutchings for HMCo.; *b.l.* Larry Brock/Tom Stack & Associates; *b.r.* Thomas D. Magelsen/Peter Arnold, Inc. 78: *l.* Greg Vaughn/Tom Stack & Associates; *r.* © Porterfield-Chickering/Photo Researchers, Inc. 79: *t.r.* Runk/Schoenberger/Grant Heilman Photography, Inc.; *b.l.* Runk/Schoenberger/Grant Heilman Photography, Inc. 81: *t.* J&L Weber/Peter Arnold, Inc.; *b.* © Andrew J. Martinez/Photo Researchers, Inc. 82: Greg Ryan & Sally Beyer/Positive Reflections. 85: *l.* Nancy Dudley/Stock Boston; *r.* Nancy Dudley/Stock Boston. 86–88: Ken Karp for HMCo. 89: *t.* Stacy Pick/Stock Boston; *b.* Steve Austin/Papilio/Corbis. 91: *t.* NASA; *b.* Robert Winslow/Tom Stack & Associates. 92: Exxon Co., U.S.A. 93: John Paul/FSP/Liaison International.

Unit F 1: Operation Migration Inc. 2–3: Operation Migration Inc. 4–5: *bkgd.* James L. Amos/Corbis; *inset* Kevin Jackson. 11: Imagery/Picture Perfect USA Inc. 15: Courtesy, Edwards Air Force Base. 21: Courtesy, Wet 'N Wild. 22: © NASA/Mark Marten/Science Source/Photo Researchers, Inc. 23: Co Rentmeester/The Image Bank. 28–29: *bkgd.* John Turner/Tony Stone Images; *l.* Carolyn Russo/National Air and Space Museum Smithsonian Institution; *r.* Budd Davison/Courtesy, Smithsonian Institution. 39: *l.* Al Tielemans/Duomo Photography; *r.* David Madison Photography. 40–41: Courtesy, Estes Industries. 45: E. Bordis/Leo de Wys. 46: NASA. 48: Tom Sanders/The Stock Market. 50: Corbis. 52–53: Express Newspapers/Archive Photos. 58: Superstock. 59: Jeff Foott/Bruce Coleman. 61: Romilly Lockyer/The Image Bank. 63: *b.* © H. Zwarc/Petit Format/Photo Researchers, Inc. 66: Leverett Bradley/Tony Stone Images. 66–67: Globus Brothers for HMCo. 69: Steven Pumphey/© National Geographic Society. 73: Richard T. Bryant/Aristock, Inc. 75: Reuters/Gary Cameron/Archive Photos. 78–79: *bkgd.* Nina Bermann/Sipa Press; *inset* Engineered Demolition. 82: Henry Groskinsky/Peter Arnold, Inc. 83: *t.* © Jerry Wachter/Photo Researchers, Inc.; *b.* Mitchell Layton/Duomo Photography. 84: Rick Rickman/Duomo Photography. 85: NASA/Corbis. 87: Globus Studios, Inc. 88: Grant Huntington for HMCo. 89: Focus On Sports. 96: Erich Lessing/Art Resource, NY. 97: *t.* Kingston Collection/Profiles West; *b.* © George Holton/Photo Researchers, Inc. 98: *t.* Kim Taylor/Bruce Coleman; *b.* Bruce Coleman. 99: David Madison Photography. 100: Stephen Frink/Southern Stock Photo Agency. 102–103: NASA. 107: North Wind Picture Archives. 111: Bruno de Hogues/Tony Stone Images. 116: *l.* Corbis; *m.* The Granger Collection; *r.* NASA. 117: Roger Ressmeyer/Corbis. 121: Paul Kenward/Tony Stone Images. 122: Richard Megna/Fundamental Photographs. 124: Adam Zetter/Leo de Wys.

Science and Math Toolbox 2: *r.* Grant Huntington for HMCo.

Glossary 24: Steve Kaufman/DRK Photo. 25: © Sidney Moulds/Photo Researchers, Inc. 30: Wendell Metzen/Bruce Coleman.